HOT SPOT

NORTH AMERICA and EUROPE

Joseph R. Rudolph Jr.

Hot Spot Histories

GREENWOOD PRESS
Westport, Connecticut • London

Library of Congress Cataloging-in-Publication Data
Rudolph, Joseph R. (Joseph Russell), 1942–
  Hot spot: North America and Europe / Joseph R. Rudolph, Jr.
    p. cm. — (Hot spot histories, ISSN 1934-631X)
  Includes bibliographical references and index.
  ISBN-13: 978-0-313-33621-8 (alk. paper)
  1. Hot spots (Political science)—Europe. 2. Hot spots (Political science)—Canada.
3. Hot spots (Political science)—United States. 4. Europe—Politics and government—
1945– 5. Canada—Politics and government—1980– 6. United States—Politics and
government—1989– I. Title.
  D1058.R84 2008
  355'.03301821—dc22   2008010077

British Library Cataloguing in Publication Data is available.

Library of Congress Catalog Card Number: 2008010077
ISBN-13: 978–0–313–33621–8

First published in 2008

Greenwood Press, 88 Post Road West, Westport, CT 06881
An imprint of Greenwood Publishing Group, Inc.
www.greenwood.com

Printed in the United States of America

The paper used in this book complies with the
Permanent Paper Standard issued by the National
Information Standards Organization (Z39.48–1984).

10 9 8 7 6 5 4 3 2 1

To my mentors of so long ago in Charlottesville:

Robert Kent Gooch
John V. Graham
Rouhollah K. Ramazani
George Washington Spicer

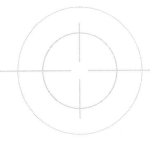

Contents

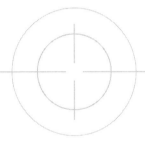

Preface

MOST BOSNIANS BELIEVE PEACEKEEPERS NO LONGER NECESSARY

A decade after the end of Bosnia's 1992–95 interethnic war, most Bosnians believe that the country would not disintegrate if the international community including a 7,000 strong peacekeeping force were to leave, an opinion poll showed Wednesday.

MRAKOVICA

Prime Minister of the Federation of Bosnia and Herzegovina, Ahmet Hadzipasic, confessed on Monday that the Governments of FBiH and Republika Srpska cannot even agree on the conditions of selling and distribution of mineral water at the level of the entire Bosnia and Herzegovina, not to mention to define political decisions of key importance for this country....

—Two stories appearing in the same edition of the Bosnia Daily, Sarajevo, August 18, 2005

This volume is part of a larger series on hot spots in the contemporary world. Although each volume covers a geographically and often politically distinct part of the globe, the books in this series share several common features. Each is internally organized on a geographical basis, exploring the regions or countries that constitute hot spots in their part of the world. To orient the reader, each volume contains a Timeline chronicling the development of its various hot spots and the significant events that have shaped their development. And each book provides suggestions for further research in an annotated bibliography and within the endnotes that accompany each chapter.

At the same time, each volume encompasses a broad segment of the world, and each of these segments has its own unique aspects. Consequently, examining the various slices of the globe often raises distinct analytical challenges, and the authors' treatment of their respective charges necessarily reflects the nature of the countries and the broad political forces at play in their assigned areas.

Coping with the Diverse Worlds of Europe and North America

The principal problem faced in structuring this volume on the United States and Canada in North America (Mexico and points south are properly left to the companion volume on hot spots in Latin America) and the nearly forty countries in Europe was the vast diversity to be found in these areas. To be sure, each of the world's major continents has its diversity, whether measured in the wealth of its various societies, the degree of ethnic and religious differences present, or form of government. Still, by so many criteria the distances separating the countries treated in this volume is striking, especially given the fact that all supposedly fall within the category of democratic or democratizing states. For example, both the oldest and nearly all of the newest states in the contemporary world lie within our study. England, Scotland, and Wales, for example, have been governed by a common monarch since 1607. Modern France was consolidated in its current borders a quarter century before the French Revolution of 1789, and the United States is still governed by a constitution written at the time of the French Revolution. At the other end of the spectrum lie the fallout states derived from the former Yugoslavia and the former Soviet Union, the oldest of which has been self-governing for less than two decades.

Defined in terms of mass affluence, Europe and North America also contain both the wealthiest states in the world, *and* countries with struggling, third world-type economies and remarkably low per-capita income by Northern Hemisphere standards.

Most significant for a study of contemporary global trouble spots, this slice of the globe contains the world's most established and durable states as well as some of the most fragile political processes on earth. Most introductory guides to the study of comparative politics depict the states in the contemporary world as lying along a developmental continuum with the long-established, consolidated democracies of Europe and North America lying at one end and the failing or failed states—mostly to be found in the third world—at the other. Excluding the infrequent exceptions, in most regions of the world the majority of countries are grouped at a common point on this spectrum. The states included in this volume, however, run the gamut from such long-established states as the United States, whose Civil War is now buried more than seven generations in its past, to post-Soviet entities such as Georgia, which has been confronting three separate civil wars since it gained its independence from the Soviet Union less than a generation ago.

The durability of so many of the political processes in North America and Europe posed a particularly difficult challenge to the construction of this study. To be true to its title, the volume needed to explore the troublesome issues, actors, and areas to be found within the advanced (consolidated) democracies of North America and Western Europe as well as political conflict in the newer states of post-communist Europe, virtually every one of which can be found on the watch lists of such global monitoring organizations as the International Crisis Group. The developed democracies, too, confront threats to their tranquility, sometimes experience low-intensity border disputes with their neighbors, and contain groups quite capable of undertaking acts of political violence. Yet they also have a capacity to cope with political shocks without exploding or imploding well beyond that of the newer self-governing areas of post-communist Europe. Between 1968 and 1974, for example, the United States withstood a racial unrest at home that resulted in the burning of urban ghettos in several of its major cities, a military failure in its foreign policy effort to prevent the fall of South Vietnam, a surge in unemployment and inflation as a result of the quadrupling of the price of imported oil during the 1973 energy crisis, and the resignation of almost an entire administration as a result of the Watergate scandal, which in 1974 forced President Richard Nixon to resign two years into his second term of office and resulted in jail sentences for several of his cabinet members and closest aides. Any one of these developments might have led to political turmoil in much of the world, but the United States' political process continued to tick along. Gerald Ford—himself vice president only because of the forced resignation of Nixon's running mate, Spiro Agnew—assumed the presidency, and two years later the country expressed a monumental, collective outpouring of patriotism in celebrating the 200th anniversary of its independence.

To permit at least some consideration of the more troublesome issues confronting the advanced democratic world and the semi-hot spots within it, in the name of inclusiveness this volume (1) parcels the broad geographical area of Europe and North America into three zones based on the normalcy of political violence in the political environment of each, and (2) utilizes a more flexible than usual definition of a "hot spot" in order to identify the danger points in each of these three zones. In only one of these zones—the one where the fall of communism has been followed by prolonged political disorder and, in some instances, led to civil warfare—does the traditional definition of a hot spot (as a point of political instability threatening to the tranquility of its region) hold. But there are issues that have either already disrupted the normal political order or are threatening to do so in both the advanced democratic world and the parts of post-communist Central Europe that have generally proceeded smoothly down the road to liberal democracy. By utilizing an abnormality of political violence test as our criterion for identifying present and future trouble spots in each of these three areas, it is possible to give the more stable areas of Europe and North America their proper coverage. (A more extensive explanation of this methodology is provided in the Introduction.)

Organization

Like the other volumes in this series, this book follows a strictly geographical layout. It begins with a consideration of those volatile elements affecting the largest geographical unit that it covers (that is, Europe *and* North America), and then moves downward to explore these two continents. In most instances, overviews are offered at this level for each of the geographically delineated regions in (first) Europe and (then) North America that contain identifiable hot spots. Finally, within each of these regions individual chapters are dedicated to those countries that *are* hot spots or contain them, and a concerted effort has been made throughout this volume to be consistent in the layout of each of these chapters. Each thus includes at least three elements, beginning with a background discussion of the evolution of the individual hot spot and of those factors contributing to its development. Second, each includes a descriptive analysis of the hot spot's current status and of the forces and issues driving the conflict there in today's world. Finally, each chapter concludes with a discussion of the degree to which conflict in the area is cooling down or heating up, and of the internal and external forces that may shape that hot spot's future.

Where more than one hot spot exists in a given country, these are organized in the case study chapters on a geographical/alphabetical basis, as in the case of France, where the increasingly explosive relationship between the native French and France's Muslim communities is localized in *continental* France whereas nationalist conflict and separatism are now found only on the isle of *Corsica*. Likewise, where more than one hot button issue or conflict lacking a geographical base exists in a given country, these topics, too, are alphabetically organized in the chapter devoted to that state. In fact, however, the need to organize the case study chapters internally into an alphabetized consideration of a series of problems is rare in this volume. Unlike the countries of Latin America or those of the

Middle East, there are few candidates in even post-communist Europe that are likely to become failed states or havens for global terrorist organizations. Nor is the broad public peace threatened by the operation of drug cartels or intra-societal warfare between rival religious sects. Indeed, most of the problems confronting the majority of states in Europe and North America are of a tractable nature and subject to accommodative politics. It is a rare event when appreciable political violence threatens the peace in most of our case studies, or that of their neighbors. Indeed, even where a convergence of factors intensifies conflict situations, the core of the conflict in hot spots is often only one thing: more often than not cultural or ethnic differences that have morphed into national conflict, separatist demands, or ongoing blood feuds. Thus, Albanian extremists in Kosovo have continued to kill and harass the relatively small number of Serbs still living in their province not because the Serbs have better jobs. It is because they are Serbs.

Facilitating Further Research

Because of the large number of hot spots covered in this volume, the many other areas hovering on the brink of becoming hot or hotter points of controversy, the diversity to be found in Europe and North America, the uneven amount of existing studies on the individual hot spots, and the uneven availability of objective Internet sources on some important topics pertaining to these areas, this volume departs in two other ways from its companion volumes.

First, in addition to an annotated bibliography at the end of this book there is also a chapter in the back matter devoted to the broad topic of conducting research on contemporary, ever-developing problem areas. It is hoped that the reader/researcher will find this helpful. Appropriate sources for background reading and valuable Internet sites for both background material and monitoring future developments are noted, and their value discussed briefly, in the endnotes accompanying each chapter.

Second, as a guide to additional, time-directed research, this study includes a substantially larger collection of timelines than its sister volumes. In addition to the general timeline found at the front of every volume in Greenwood's Hot Spot Histories series, also included here are more detailed timelines located at the end of each chapter devoted to the hot spots in the various regions of Europe. This author believes strongly in the multiple utility of timelines in orienting students to the broad historical panorama surrounding any specific problem area in our shrinking globe, and as tools for time-specific additional research. Hopefully you will find those provided here of value in both contexts.

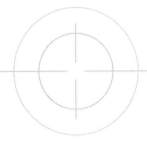

Timeline

Historical Background and Recent Developments Involving Hot Spots in the Western Democratic World and Post-Communist Europe

1600 BC	Six hundred years of Greek influence begins in Cyprus.
330 AD	Under Emperor Constantine Constantinople becomes capital of Byzantine Empire.
1290	Ottoman Empire begins under Osman's Sultanate; by 1361 Ottomans have crossed into Europe.
1330s	King of Baden establishes first recorded system of Romany enslavement in Europe.
1389	Ottoman Turks defeat Serbian empire at Battle of Kosovo and rule area until World War I; in interim, Kosovo becomes increasingly Albanian speaking and Muslim.
1453	Byzantine Empire ends as Constantinople falls to Ottoman Turks.
1689–91	Battle of Boyne and Treaty of Limerick bring all of Ireland under British control.
1759	Britain defeats "New France" in battle at Quebec City; France's Canadian empire soon vanishes.
1761	Maria Theresa, Empress of Hungary, makes first effort to assimilate Roma.
1768	Genoa cedes Corsica to France.
1774	Quebec Act formalizes British control of Quebec while preserving its distinctive French lifestyle.

1789	French Revolution ends old order in name of popular sovereignty.
1840–1914	The United States establishes itself as an immigrant country, receiving 44 million immigrants from abroad (mostly Europe); first large wave is composed of German and Irish immigrants between 1840 and 1850, the latter encouraged to emigrate as a result of Ireland's 1844 Potato Famine.
1856	Abolition of Romani Slavery.
1870–1914	First era of modern globalization results from the expansion of European empires over much of the world's surface and the subsequent emergence of transnational social and economic networks.
1875–78	Britain acquires Cyprus in return for promise to aid Ottoman Empire should Russia attack it.
1914	World War I begins after Serb assassinates Austrian Archduke Ferdinand in quest for a greater Serbia; Britain formally annexes Cyprus.
1916	Easter Uprising in Dublin during World War I: an independent Irish Republic is proclaimed, but the rebellion is quickly subdued and its young leaders executed.
1917	Communists seize control of Russia; Russian refugees arrive in Paris in large numbers; across the Atlantic, World War I raises issue of loyalty of German Americans and the United States ends open immigration.
1918	Anglo-Irish War for Ireland's independence begins as World War I ends, with the Ottoman and Austrian-Hungarian Empires on the losing side. In aftermath, Ottomans lose Middle East and European holdings and Yugoslavia and Czechoslovakia emerge out of Austrian-Hungarian empire.
1919	Mustafa Kemal (later Kemal Ataturk) launches struggle for an independent, secular Turkey. Ottoman Empire formally ends in 1922 when National Assembly abolishes Sultanate.
1922	Ireland's partition begins: Irish Free State created out of twenty-six of Ireland's thirty-two counties.
1930–37	Turkey's Kurds react to oppressive laws in a series of revolts, all harshly suppressed.
1931	California responds to Great Depression unemployment by deporting its Mexican workers.

1937	Roma Holocaust begins as Hitler orders extermination of Gypsies.
1939–45	World War II changes borders of European countries; Russian territorial holdings grow in West.
1945–50	An era of major change on multiple fronts: The build-up of non-European peoples in Western Europe begins as European countries rebuild after World War II. The Cold War begins with Soviet pressure on Greece and Turkey and creation of satellite states in Central Europe. Stalin also organizes lands acquired during war into new or reconfigured union republics in the Soviet Union, and Tito emerges to lead an independent, communist Yugoslavia. Finally, a second era of globalization is inaugurated by Western efforts to create a global economic order and to spur economic integration in Europe, and by the increasing activity of multinational corporations.
1950–60	Colonialism ends; former imperial powers and new states develop new patterns of interaction.
1954–64	Civil rights movement in the United States revives the Ku Klux Klan, and numerous violent acts against civil rights groups occur in the American South. U.S. civil rights activists inspire a civil rights movement in Ulster.
1959	ETA is founded to pursue independence of Spain's Basquelands and their union with Basque France.
1960	Cyprus achieves independence; Turkey, Greece, and Britain are to guarantee that independence.
1960s	Foreigner issue emerges in Western Europe as the number of immigrants and foreign workers grows.
1963–64	Communal violence occurs in Cyprus; UN authorizes a peacekeeping force to maintain order.
1968	René Lévesque forms the *Parti Québécois* for purpose of achieving Quebec's sovereign independence.
1969	British peacekeeping troops are deployed in (London) Derry and Belfast in Northern Ireland.
1970s	Birth of anti-immigrant parties and growth of anti-immigrant violence throughout Western Europe; emergence of radical antigovernment movements and hate groups in the United States.
1970	*Front de Libération du Québec* (FLQ) kidnaps and kills Quebec's minister of labor.

1971	Supreme Court in *Roe v. Wade* recognizes a woman's right to terminate an unwanted pregnancy in first trimester, launching an increasingly violent antiabortion movement in the United States.
1972	Bloody Sunday in Ulster: fourteen die when British troops fire on peaceful Catholic demonstrators; London subsequently assumes direct rule of Ulster.
1974	Government in Cyprus overthrown; Turkey invades island to protect Turkish Cypriots, resulting in massive population relocations and the de facto partition of the island along communal lines.
1975	Franco dies in Spain and King Juan Carlos succeeds him; the process of democratizing Spain begins.
1980	Tito dies in Yugoslavia; nationalism increases within all groups composing the Yugoslav state.
1980s	Global stagflation intensifies antiglobalization protests in the developing world even as it forces Western corporations to scale back their investments abroad.
1982	Ruby Ridge standoff with federal authorities encourages state militias to form in the United States; Army of God antiabortionist group emerges in the United States; Earth Liberation Front (ELF) founded in England.
1988–90	Liberalization in Soviet Union encourages its peripheral, non-Slavic union republics and communist Central European countries to become more self-assertive.
1989–92	Communism collapses in Soviet Union and Central Europe; overt discrimination against Romani spreads across Central Europe; non-Russian Soviet Union republics become independent and civil wars erupt in many, as well as in Russian federation when Chechnya secedes. Yugoslavia collapses into bloody civil war when four Yugoslav republics secede in winter of 1990–91.
1990–2000	Modern era of antiglobalization movements commences as globalization process begins to affect adversely some groups in the developed world.
1993	Waco standoff between U.S. federal authorities and religious cult ends in tragedy; in aftermath

militia movements spread across the United States. Meanwhile, U.S. states begin to deny social welfare benefits to illegal immigrants.

1995   NATO intervention ends civil war in Bosnia; subsequent diplomatic accord charges UN with overseeing Bosnia's democratization.

1998   "Good Friday Agreement" reached on conditions for new power-sharing government in Ulster; Republic of Ireland renounces constitutional claim to Northern Ireland.

1999   November antiglobalization protest at the WTO meeting in Seattle produces largest mass rally in the United States since the Vietnam war and results in considerable political violence.

        NATO intervenes to end ethnic conflict in Kosovo; UN is made responsible for Kosovo's future.

2001   Race riots occur in Britain during its general election campaign; al Qaeda's attack on the United States adds security concerns to immigrant debate everywhere.

2003   Despite their discrimination against Romani, Central European countries, except for former Yugoslavia states, are invited to join the European Union and many are invited to join NATO.

2004   Terrorist bombing of Madrid commuter trains produces crackdown on Spain's Muslim population.

2005   Terrorist attacks by Kurdish separatists and Islamic militants escalate in Turkey; fall rioting by Muslim youth in France spreads throughout Britain; scores die and nearly a thousand are injured when homegrown suicide bombers attack London's mass transit system.

2006   In Spain the ETA announces its abandonment of terrorism, but extremists announce they will continue struggle; in France, Muslim youth continue to riot throughout summer and into fall.

2007   Protestants agree to form government with Catholics and civilian government sworn in Ulster; UN proposal to give Kosovo independence destabilizes democratization process in Bosnia and raises fears of additional separatist activity in several of the states formally a part of the Soviet Union. Riots involving France's Muslim youth in late November again spread from Paris southward.

Delineating the Hot Spots in the Worlds of Europe and North America

Hot spots, hot potatoes, hot button issues, and hotheads—these terms are all a part of our daily vocabulary, and they are very much a part of the world in which we live. This book is about the hot spots you might encounter even in the political backyards of North America and Western Europe, not to mention in Europe's south and east. It is emphatically not intended as a guide to places you will necessarily want to visit. In some instances it is almost certainly about areas you will want to avoid, unless you are searching for adventure or the adrenalin rush of being someplace where something awful may happen or is already occurring. It is not about hot new clubs opening in the city, or new beach locales that have suddenly become the rage. It is about politically volatile locales, where hot button issues and hotheads make for a combustible political mix. In some instances, the fires are already burning or are ready to flare up at any moment.

Seeking Normalcy in the Twenty-first Century

It is a tenet of modern historians that most of us live in places where dreadful things once happened—where priests were martyred, gypsies hung, slaves imported, native Americans and Australian aborigines massacred or driven from their homes, and victims of mass murderers buried. These and other moments and scenes from the past we push from our sight and memories. The corollary is that most of us, even in the advanced democratic world, also live in—or are not too long a flight away from—places where very bad things are unfolding or waiting to unfold in the present. Of course, even across the economically developed countries of North America and Europe, the measure of what is "a very bad thing" can differ both culturally and experientially. We all view the world through our cultural prisms. Hence, different cultures will often weigh the same or similar actions differently—indeed, not all Americans viewed the destruction of the World Trade Center and the attack on the Pentagon on September 11, 2001, as an evil act. Even less did all members of the Muslim underclass in Britain and Spain respond with 100 percent repulsion to the terrorist acts carried out against commuters in Madrid in 2004 and London in 2005. In Yasar Arafat's most enduring image, one person's terrorist remains another's freedom fighter.

Additionally, societies as a whole become accustomed to different levels of disorder. A violent riot against Amtrak in Grand Central Station by Wall Street denizens angry over the delayed arrival of their evening ride to their comfortable homes well out of Manhattan would, at the very least, make the nightly news across the United States. A similar riot by travelers in the Indian state of Gujarat over the endless delay in the arrival of the next train to Bombay, unless accompanied by fatalities, might not even rate a mention on the evening news in New Delhi. In the same sense, politically motivated arson against Russian installations in Chechnya may no longer qualify as newsworthy or politically significant events in Moscow, given the now long duration of the fighting in that troubled region, but the deaths of soldiers and Chechen civilians as a result of fighting there almost certainly would. Whether publicized or not, however, danger and the disruption of life are cross-cultural concepts to be found in vocabularies throughout the world, and the presence of, or prospect for, violence or dislocations thus make convenient starting points for identifying politically troubled hot spots for our study. But they are only the starting points.

International Politics and the Traditional Definition of "Hot Spots"

References to "hot spots" and "trouble zones" likely to become hot spots are most often found in discussions of international politics and foreign policy. These are usually areas where conflicts within a state—whether emanating from ethnic turmoil, economic grievances, or the fragility of a corrupt and failing regime—are perceived to be so explosive or potentially explosive that they have the potential to affect the political stability of neighboring states, the region in which they occur, or even global security. Frequently, as in the case of the civil warfare in the former

Yugoslavia during the 1990s, such areas are even deemed candidates for international intervention because of the danger they pose to the broader international community.

Two points with respect to this conventional approach to delineating hot spots are particularly germane to our study. First, there is no shortage of international agencies, educational and governmental institutions, and human rights organizations identifying and monitoring critical areas, troubled zones, failing states, and existing hot spots in the contemporary world. Second, these observers are unanimous in identifying no such zones in North America and a diminishing few in Western Europe. Representative of these analyses is that of the well-respected International Crisis Group, whose Crisis Watch Report at the end of 2006 identified eighty troubled or deteriorating areas around the globe, with nineteen of these falling within the geographical reach of this study. Of these nineteen, none was located in North America, and only four (Basque Spain, Northern Ireland, Turkey, and Cyprus) lay within either western or southern Europe. The remainder were all to be found in post-communist Europe, most in either the states falling out of the former Yugoslavia or the former Soviet Union, including Russia itself (Chechnya).[1]

Designating hot spots on the basis of their international ramifications has obvious value in the search for global and regional stability through such organizations as the United Nations and NATO, and at least half of the entries in this volume can claim their hot spot status by that definition. At the same time, and despite the objective criteria that such organizations as the Fund for Peace use in identifying disaster-prone locales, such designations invariably involve a subjective element as well, if only in assessing the *intensity* level of existing conflicts or the impact of equal levels of intense conflict on the political structure of differing states. Moreover, David Dent, the author of the companion volume in this series on Latin America, is doubtless correct in noting the pervasiveness of (perceived) threat-based definitions in the U.S. government's discussion of hot spots around the world—most recently in identifying countries likely to support or be breeding grounds for terrorists with anti-American agendas. But the reverse is also likely: that areas preconceived to be friendly or stable are unlikely to be included in such inventories, even when they have become at the least momentarily volatile. The United States Department of State thus issued no travel advisory warning to U.S. citizens contemplating a visit to France during the nearly month-long and often violent demonstrations by members of its Muslim communities in the fall of 2005, despite the fact that the demonstrations, which began in Paris in October of that year, eventually spread to most parts of France and prompted the French government to declare a state of emergency in November before finally getting the rioting under control.

In a similar fashion, although no one expects Quebec to secede violently from Canada, the Quebec issue continues to hang over the future of the Canadian federation, and hence North American politics, sufficiently to qualify as at least a simmering issue. Certainly whenever Canada holds elections, the vote in Quebec province receives considerably more scrutiny than the vote elsewhere in Canada because the vote attained by its separatist party, the *Parti Quebecois*, is widely viewed as a gauge of the overall health of the Canadian federation. The United States, too, has its potential regional hot spot. When U.S. citizens discuss "the Border," they are not talking about the line separating North and South Carolina or even the international demarcation separating the United States from Canada, but the border region in their country's Southwest. There large numbers of illegal immigrants cross, drug trafficking thrives, and diplomatic clashes with Mexico over both issues ebb and flow. As in the case of Quebec, the border area with Mexico may not qualify under the domestic-conflict/regional threat definition of hot spots. But neither are these areas just another track of geography in the politics of their respective countries, any more than Europe's unassimilated and angry Muslim extremists are just another group of citizens in the European Union posing no more a threat to security on the continent than die-hard communist voters in France or Scot nationalists in Britain.

Other examples abound, but the point should be clear. There *are* more potentially dangerous or politically sensitive spots in the world—and even in the relatively serene world of North American and Western Europe—than would qualify for consideration under the conventional definition of hot spots. Accordingly, a less narrrow definition of hot spots is herein adopted for selecting the sometimes unconventional entries included in this volume.

The Propensity for Political Violence as a Criterion for Inclusion

The crux of our broad concern is not international conflict or even violence per se, but the potential for or existence of political violence in the political processes of North America and Europe—that is, the use of force to affect political processes and outcomes. Though somewhat crude, this concern is nonetheless relevant as a beginning point for locating political hot spots—and not just because those caught in areas ripe for or experiencing political violence may face danger. The jump to political violence is not a step lightly taken by those living in the political systems of the United States, Canada, and much of Europe, where for the most part citizens enjoy jobs, have a family life, and do not live under the daily fear that a tyrannical government will come knocking at their door to drag them arbitrarily to an uncertain fate. Such conditions do exist in large parts of the world, and there they occasionally give birth to revolutions and secessionist movements. With the obvious exception of some areas in the former Soviet Union and former Yugoslavia, however, they are not typically found in the economically developed states of North America and Europe. Thus, before citizens in these areas embark on a course of political violence—generally defined as "illegal physical attacks, or threats, on persons, property, institutions, and symbols in order to destroy, alter, and sustain systems or policies"[2]—it is highly likely that the political environment has already become unacceptable to some members of the political community. And hence at least potentially explosive.

On the other hand, the potential for, or even commission of, an act of political violence does not by itself a political hotspot make, especially where such potential triggers of violence as public protests and inflammatory speeches are not illegal and may even enjoy constitutional protection. The danger must necessarily be of a particular, durable character, especially given the context in which we live, where bombs can be easily assembled following instructions freely available on the Internet and international terrorist organizations use that same Web to recruit cells and plan acts around the world. Just as serial murderers of a Jack-the-Ripper hue may temporarily make London or Los Angeles an unattractive destination without rendering either a political hot spot, so a lone letter bomber conducting a private political war against pharmaceutical companies or the construction industry does not turn a country into a political hot spot. Nor, despite attendant political motivations, should the single violent act of one or two socially disconnected individuals—for example, the two men who bombed the Oklahoma City federal building on April 19, 1995[3]—catapult the locale of their action into anyone's roster of political trouble zones. Accordingly, in delineating our study the following criteria are added.

First, following in the footsteps of Fred R. von der Mehden's groundbreaking study of *Comparative Political Violence*, for an area to be included in this volume the prospects for political violence have to be of a sustained nature, either in the form of an intense level of conflict over a short period of time or a lower level of conflict over a longer period of time.[4] In practice, this means that not only must the violence be politically motivated but the threat must come from a dissatisfied and potentially dangerous group or organization, not from isolated individuals.

Second, the threat must be posed or at least executed by a *domestic* group, organization, or community, even if—in this age of Internet communication unknown when von der Mehden's work initially appeared—it is inspired, incited, or even abetted by outsiders. Thus, the attack carried out against the Pentagon and Twin Towers in the United States by foreign terrorists in 2001 does not qualify for inclusion in this book. Conversely, the attack on London commuters in July 2005 by homegrown members of Britain's Muslim population raises precisely the type of security issues that make Britain, at least for the immediate future, a potential political hot spot where radicals in a frustrated, culturally isolated minority underclass may pose a threat to domestic public safety either because of their personal grievances or their susceptibility to recruitment by agents of *al Qaeda* or other anti-Western, transnational terrorist organizations. And, in turn, terrorist acts by British Muslims may inspire similar action by alienated members of the Muslim communities in other Western European countries.

Third, the issues or objectives involved in any conflict must be political in nature in the sense of being directed at, posing a threat to, or otherwise involving the political process, as opposed to being the product of, for example, blood feuds or turf battles between contending gangs engaged in illicit activities.

Finally, the threat that a country or area will experience either political violence or turbulence must be plausible. Many groups engaged in political activity have grandiose objectives and make equally lofty threats, but few of these in developed democracies match their deeds to their rhetoric and fewer still find the following to engage in activities that achieve the notoriety required for a country or area to be included in the watch lists of organizations monitoring hot spots around the world. In terms of the likelihood of political violence occurring, considerable gaps separate the United States, Canada, and most of the established democracies in Western Europe from the remainder of the states to be found in the European theater.

The Three Worlds of Our Study

The likelihood that a member of a society will resort to the politics of violence is the product of both culture, which will influence a society's propensity toward violence, and circumstances, which affect the issues that lead citizens to disruptive behavior. Both political cultures and circumstances vary widely in the states encompassed in this study, but on the basis of these criteria the countries can be grouped into three broad categories: the established democracies; the successfully democratizing countries of post-communist Europe; and, the most volatile group, Russia, the Balkans, the Caucasus, and post-Soviet Eastern Europe.

The Advanced Liberal Democracies

By far the least prone to widespread political violence and disorder are the states normally categorized as "advanced liberal democracies," a designation referring to both their level of political development as mature democracies and to their level of socioeconomic development as advanced industrial or early postindustrial societies. Falling under this heading are the United States, Canada, and the "Old Europe" states of Western Europe. These are countries whose citizens enjoy a widespread material prosperity and have generally developed at least some effective identification with their political processes and participate in them, and whose governments can effectively enforce their decisions, respect the rule of law and individual rights, are constitutionally limited in terms of what they can do, and are held electorally accountable by their citizens.[5]

Within this category of states, political and social violence are scarcely unknown. Some states contain domestic separatist groups who employ terrorism or have done so until very recently (most notably in Basque Spain, Corsica, and Northern Ireland), and these are consequently treated in our study. Nevertheless, compared to other regions in the developed world, political violence is generally rare within the advanced liberal democracies. As Martin Shann phrased it in his recent introductory work on politics in the twenty-first century, the fact that "most people [in those countries] worry more about criminal than political violence is instructive. In most nondemocratic societies, political violence exceeds criminal violence."[6] Thus, hot spots in the liberal democracies are more likely to entail *the possibility of violence* in a situation or region than its probability, and even then the violence—outside of the recent spate of activity by the frustrated immigrant underclass in these states—is likely to be sporadic and often results as much from the actions of the affluent alienated as those of the economically or politically disempowered.

Democratizing Post-Communist Europe

The second category is composed of the successfully democratizing "New Europe" countries of post-communist Europe: the Baltic republics formerly a part of the Soviet Union, the major countries of Central Europe (Poland, the Czech and Slovak republics, Hungary, Romania, and Bulgaria), and Slovenia from the former Yugoslavia. Although some commentators already add several of these states to the list of advanced democracies—most notably those with some early twentieth-century experience with democracy or sustained economic development (e.g., Poland, Hungary, the Czech Republic, Lithuania, and Slovenia)—in general the political environment in post-communist Central Europe and the Baltic republics is less conducive to the peaceful settlement of political conflict than Western Europe's. The states are newer, the party systems are still consolidating, and many of the countries contain highly nationalistic parties not inclined toward accommodating their rivals. These societies are also less affluent than those of the advanced liberal democracies, and respect for the established rules of the game is less deeply rooted. Perhaps above all, given their rule by author-itarian and sometimes totalitarian regimes for at least two generations following World War II, the civic culture of peaceful participation and give-and-take, compromise-centered politics, which is often viewed as a pre-condition for durable democratic government, is less developed in these countries. Therefore, although the governments in these states have achieved efficient control over their territory and are beginning to acquire a widespread sense of political legitimacy, and although their citizens do widely participate in their political processes, divisive political issues— including the rights of minorities—can translate into a distinguishing *probability of political violence* and other disruptive conduct by the dis-satisfied and politically alienated even where the systems are genuinely open and democratic.

Russia, the Balkans, the Caucasus, and Post-Soviet Eastern Europe

Finally, there are those states of the former communist world that are still trying to establish control over separatist groups and disgruntled minorities within their borders and make the difficult transition from civil war to orderly civil society. Russia and many of the new states falling out of the former Soviet Union fit into this category, along with much of the former Yugoslavia and the countries in and around the Caucasus.[7]

Other factors also separate these states from their European brethren. In some instances, the democratization effort is conspicuously lagging. In fact, such fundamental rights associated with democracies as the freedom of the press and freedom of association often remain insecure and elec-tions in many of these countries are still often viewed as suspect by inter-national observers as well as the domestic losers. Old habits of arm-twisting and suppression of opposition thus seem to be lasting longer here than in other parts of post-communist Europe, and although the death squads and intense persecution of critics of the past are largely absent today, governments in many of the countries falling under this heading have engaged in enough anti-democratic behavior to be often labeled "illiberal democracies" (also known as faux democracies).[8]

In short, this is an area of Europe where post–civil war disorder, long memories of recent deep conflicts, the highly dislocating forces of social and economic change, or continuing, low-intensity conflict over the form of government and ways of life (for example, between liberals and old-line communists, and between centralizers and territorialized minorities) have created a more tenuous political environment in countries with little recent experience with democratic forms of government. Measured against the political standards of, and the political issues affecting, liberal democracies, the states in this category are not a part of the "Old Europe" or even the "New Europe." They are the "barely Europe," and the hot spots they contain can be defined in terms of *the presence of violence* within them rather than the potential for, or probability of, political developments taking a violent turn.

Notes

1. "CrisisWatch No. 39, 1 November 2006," available at the International Crisis Group Website at www.crisisgroup.org. For similar findings elsewhere, see, for example, the World Bank's listing of failed states and regions likely to support international terrorism, which includes only Kosovo in Europe, in Karen DeYoung, "World Bank Lists Failing Nations That Can Breed Global Terrorism," *The Washington Post* (September 15, 2006); the Fund for Peace's Failed State Index, which lists 146 states along a continuum, with the Sudan topping the list of most failed states and Sweden and Norway rounding out the listing as the most stable of the states surveyed, and which lists no European state among its most crisis-prone top 20 percent, and only six— Bosnia-Herzegovina (number 35), Belarus (50), Serbia (55), Moldova (58), Georgia (59), and Azerbaijan (60)—in its second tier, available online at www.fundforpeace.org; and Andrew Duncan and Michel Opatowski, *Trouble Spots: The World Atlas of Strategic Information* (Dollingdale, PA: Diane Publishing Company, 2000).

2. David C. Rapoport and Leonard Weinberg, in the Introduction to their edited volume, *The Democratic Experience and Political Violence* (London and Portland, OR: Frank Cass, 2001: 5).

3. Although the two men convicted for bombing the building, Timothy McVeigh and Terry Nichols, had prior contacts with militia and white supremacist groups, no evidence indicated the latter's complicity in their crime, which took the lives of more than 100 people, injured another 800, and constituted the worst terrorist attack in American history prior to the September 11, 2001, attack by *al Qaeda* on New York and Washington. Rather, at McVeigh's trial the federal government ascribed the crime to the accused's personal desire to avenge the deaths of the Branch Davidian Christian group who perished when the federal government stormed their compound in Waco, Texas, two years earlier.

4. Fred R. von der Mehden, *Comparative Political Violence* (Englewood Cliffs, NJ: Prentice Hall, 1973). See especially pp. 4–6.

5. For a succinct discussion of the concept of advanced liberal democracies and the process of political development, see Gregory S. Mahler, *Comparative Politics: An Institutional and Cross-National Approach* (Upper Saddle River, NJ: Prentice Hall, 2003: 41–51).

6. Martin Shann, Introduction to *Politics: Governments and Nations in the Twenty-First Century* (Zelienople, PA: Atomic Dog Publishing, 2004: 224).

7. Cyprus, which in 2004 was deemed European enough to be admitted to the European Union, might also fit into this category more easily than elsewhere given its continuing inability to govern itself under a single government. Similarly, the growing political violence in western and central Turkey is threatening to add that country to this grouping quite independently of the conflict involving the Kurdish minority in its east, which is more properly treated in this Greenwood series as a Middle East hot spot.

8. See Rapoport and Weinberg, *The Democratic Experience and Political Violence*, pp. 263–265.

CHAPTER 1

GLOBALIZATION AND ANTIGLOBALIZATION PROTESTS

When communism collapsed in the Soviet Union and its Central European empire between 1989 and 1992, the Cold War between the United States and the Soviet Union was pronounced over, and the world suddenly seemed a more tranquil place. In the midst of imploding, the Soviet Union had not vetoed United Nations resolutions authorizing the use of force to evict Iraq's occupying army from Kuwait, and when Iraq was speedily defeated and vanquished from Kuwait by United States-led international forces in the spring of 1991, the world seemed to be a more peace-loving place as well. The illusion was short-lived. By early 1992 the wars in the Balkans resulting from Yugoslavia's implosion were in high gear, adding "ethnic cleansing" and other image-evoking terms to our daily vocabulary of politics and vying for air time with other global hot spots on the around-the-clock broadcasts of an expanding number of global news networks. The post–Cold War world thus remained a troubled one, and conflicts and violence are still very much a part of daily life on every continent, including the most developed regions of North America and Europe.

The problems, issues, and forces that produce these conflicts are also to be found on most continents, and certainly among the advanced democratic—and democratizing—post-communist states of North America and Europe. The most visible of these are perhaps the threat or reality of terrorism, both domestic and transnational, and the force of nationalism, both benign and disruptive. Each has led to wars—for example, the United States assault on Afghanistan and the terrorist camps it harbored following al Qaeda's September 11, 2001, attack on New

York and Washington, as well as the major civil wars in the former Yugoslavia, in Russia between the Russians and Chechens, and in Rwanda between the Hutus and Tutsi. These conflicts, in turn, have produced refugees and internally displaced peoples whose presence has not infrequently triggered further tensions (Bosnian refugees in Germany) or warfare (Hutu and Tutsi refugees in Central Africa).

Refugees and asylum seekers from war-torn areas are not the only people in motion whose arrival has led to conflict. Yet another global issue is the movement of immigrants from one state to another country, often quite culturally remote. Principally, though not entirely, this movement has been from the less to the more economically developed worlds—more precisely, to the United States and the developed countries of Western Europe. Nor does the list of problems even begin to end there. Energy availability and cost, for example, have created fears and tensions throughout the developed, oil-importing world. Population trends—in particular, both excessive growth rates in the developing world and flat-lining in the economically advanced countries—have become significant concerns, especially when coupled with such issues as the declining terms of trade on the world market for the products from the developing world; the movement of large numbers of people, both legally and otherwise, to the economically and politically developed world; and the stress of simultaneously introducing marketplace economics and democratic political institutions in the post-communist world.[1]

Though many of these problems are shared by the United States, Canada, and most of the countries in Europe, not every problem or issue manifests itself in every state. Even where the same problem confronts governments in numerous countries, the intensity of that problem can vary widely, raising the specter of political violence in one state while scarcely causing a political ripple in another. Abortion, for example, is an issue that generates great emotions on both the pro-choice and pro-life sides; however, only in the United States has the anti-abortion movement taken a significantly violent turn, including the burning of clinics and the murder of doctors performing the procedure. Similarly, the issues related to the growing presence of legal and illegal immigrants and foreign workers that are so pervasive in the southwestern United States and throughout Western Europe are not concerns in the countries of post-communist Europe, which tend to be donor, rather than recipient states in the current global migration of workers from home countries to host societies.

Even nationalism and the struggle for home rule by regionalized, ethnically distinct communities in the developed world do not exist everywhere, and where they have emerged it has been with quite different propensities toward violence in different countries and differing political settings. Separatist rebellions justified in the name of national self-determination continue to rack parts of the former Soviet Union. Violent deeds done during the wars in the former Yugoslavia still give rise to war crime proceedings, both in the Hague and in those areas of Bosnia and Croatia where they were committed. Quebec nationalism, on the other hand—even allowing for the possibility that it may yet lead to the dismemberment of Canada—has outgrown its violent, Quebec Liberation Front days. And in many countries of the developed world the face of minority nationalism is entirely benign. The majority of the people of Wales, for example, still think of themselves as Welsh, not British, and anyone so naive or inebriated as to call a Welshman an Englishman in a Welsh pub may have cause to regret it, as well as have an occasion to check out the local branch of the British National Health Service. Yet after nearly 500 years of union with England, Welsh nationalists are hardly on the same playing field with Basque separatists, much less Chechen freedom fighters. Even if London were to revoke the right of the Welsh to teach their tongue in their school systems and hear it (often with subtitles) on the BBC regional programming allocated to Wales, a violent independence movement would be unlikely to materialize. However, some nasty public protests and demonstrations would almost certainly ensue for some time in Cardiff, Carmarthen, Llanelli, Caerphilly, Meirionnydd Nant Conwy, and other difficult-to-pronounce Welsh parliamentary districts.

In order to span the broad range of states and political environments of North America and Europe and have a real possibility of showing up throughout in a disruptive manner, an issue would have to be large, even global, in breadth. And just such an issue does exist—one that does potentially cover the globe, in fact. It is the issue of globalization itself, which provokes such great emotion among its detractors that the antiglobalization rallies that are regularly staged throughout the world still have the potential of turning violent at any point where there are meetings of government economic ministers or international bodies concerned with managing the economic transactions flowing between the developed and developing world.

Background: Development of the Globalization Issue

To students of international politics, globalization is customarily defined in a neutral manner. In the words of one popular college textbook, it is the increasingly rapid process through which a global community is forming across existing state boundaries as a result of "the growing pace and density of economic, political, social and cultural inter-action."[2] Manifestations of it are to be found in the development of transnational human rights groups (for example, Amnesty International) and women's rights groups; the expanding number of multinational corporations and international economic associations such as the North American Free Trade Association (NAFTA), European Union (EU), and World Trade Organization (WTO); and transnational environmental groups such as Greenpeace.

Proponents of this "shrinking globe" process stress its spontaneous nature and its economic dimensions—the increasing pace of trade, global financial transactions, and investment flow, all abetted by the fast pace of change in the technologies of transportation and communication. To those subscribing to a neoliberal philosophy, the marketplace is perceived as ultimately the best means of promoting the general welfare. Invest-ments will increasingly flow globally on the basis of comparative advantages in resources and such market conditions as labor cost and supply, resulting in the production of more goods at lower prices and hence a better global standard of living. Jobs will emerge in low-income countries, enabling them to develop a middle class and partake of the good life. In the long term, everyone (or nearly everyone) profits. To this argument some, but not all, globalization enthusiasts would add that as a result of these forces, sovereign states are becoming—or have already become—outdated obstructions in the way of global progress.[3]

Critics see matters differently. In the extreme case, globalism is viewed as a pernicious development that partners capitalist institutions and governments in the developed world in a global campaign to increase corporate wealth at the expense of (1) the environment, which is being damaged in the name of profits; (2) the poorer countries, whose resources are being plundered, and (3) the women and children of the Third World, whose labor is being exploited. Other casualties include (a) democracies in general and local governments in particular, whose authority is being usurped by global bodies at the cost of popular accountability; (b) the workers in high-labor-cost countries who are losing their jobs as corporations outsource tasks to low-labor-cost areas in the developing world; and (c) the poorer members of societies everywhere, because to date the consequences of globalization have not just included a widening of the gap between the richest and poorest countries of the world, but also—within the richer states—a widening of the gap between the richest members of society (the owners of the outsourcing corporations, for example) and the poorer members of society.

On one thing both the advocates and the opponents of globalization agree: the process has quickened significantly in the past decade and promises to increase in pace still further in the years ahead, unless governments are persuaded to oppose it. On the other hand, neither the process of globalization nor aggressive opposition to it is entirely new.

Empire and the Early Antiglobalization Movements

In a not too terribly tortured sense, the world's first significant antiglobalization demonstration was held in North America on December 16, 1773, when disgruntled colonialists in Boston rebelled against the collusion that they perceived to be occurring between the corporate conglomerate providing their tea and the government that incorporated the British East India Company—the government that exempted the company from the taxes everyone else had to pay, thereby giving it special privileges at the expense of colonial merchants in the sale and distribution of tea.

The American Revolution, which began two and a half years later, marked the end of the empire-building era in the New World launched by the principal European powers during the fifteenth, sixteenth, and seventeenth centuries, and the beginning of a series of independence movements that over the next century and a quarter would essentially free the British, French, and other European colonies in North America, South America, Australia, New Zealand, and South Africa from outside rule. But it did not mark the end of empire. Quite to the contrary, the principal era of European empire building was still a century away when the colonists in Boston donned their Native American disguises, turned Boston Harbor into a giant pot of iced tea, and set American caffeine addicts on the slippery slope that would eventually lead to a change in taste and send an increasingly affluent American society through the doors of coast-to-coast Starbucks stores for double mocha cappuccinos.

European outposts in the New World were essentially settler colonies, founded and settled by Europeans when colonization was necessary to hold the land against the weakly armed but numerous native peoples inhabiting it. Moreover, these early settlements were often limited to the coastal regions where ships from Europe could resupply the colonies and, if necessary, bring cannon to bear against native opposition. Most of the world remained off limits, its interior too far away from lines of supply and—in the case of large portions of Africa and Asia—too filled with diseases to be safe for conquest. All of this changed, however, in the relatively brief period between 1840 and the American Civil War as a result of "revolutions" in the areas of weaponry, medicine, transportation, and communication that made the interior of Africa and Asia fertile grounds for establishing empires at relatively little cost.

From the late seventeenth century—when Muslim Turk invaders armed primarily with bladed weapons were repelled by Europe's

Austrian defenders armed with cannon and firearms—until 1840, Europeans generally carried single-shot, muzzleloading guns into battle. The rifles were particularly hazardous; they could fire their projectiles greater distances than handguns, but soldiers had to stand erect to reload the barrels. A good soldier could fire an average of one round a minute, if he were not himself shot while reloading. Hence, most battles ended like those in the American Revolution, with the in-close fighting of armies that had initially engaged one another on battlefields flat enough to permit the dragging of small, but heavy cannon to the front, but concluded with sabers and the bayonets affixed to the ends of the rifles as the principal weapons.

Then, in 1840, the breechloading rifle made its appearance, and the art of war changed. Suddenly, a single soldier could fire seven rounds a minute, reloading while prone and behind cover. A generation later the machine gun was making its appearance on the American frontier, permitting a single soldier behind an armored shield to crank out more than a hundred rounds a minute. Meanwhile, the steam revolution had given birth to riverboats. Carrying these weapons, the new boats could open the interior of continents to exploration and conquests hitherto impossible, and the discovery of quinine to treat malaria made it a feasible undertaking. By the end of the century, steamships plowed the oceans between continents in days, whereas weeks or months had been needed before, depending on currents and the winds. Transoceanic cables and land-based telephone and telegraph lines permitted governments to be in direct contact with their settlers, administrators, and armies. President Lincoln, during the American Civil War, was the last head of government who had to go to the battlefield to communicate with his generals.[4]

Given these nineteenth-century marvels, European powers were able to extend their empires dramatically. Thus, by the eve of World War I, Europeans had come to dominate or control more than 84 percent of the surface of the earth.[5] In the process they inaugurated the first real era of globalization, between approximately 1870 until the advent of World War I in 1914. Trade and financial transactions became globalized as European countries traded with their far-flung colonies, as well as with one another in the developed world of the Northern Hemisphere.

Equally significant was the development of transnational networks during this era. The industrial revolution produced labor union movements in industrializing countries, and by the time of World War I, labor, too, had taken advantage of turn-of-the-century transformations in the fields of communication and transportation in order to establish international ties. Human rights groups in North America and Europe, concerned with such issues as the working conditions of women and children and women's suffrage, also formed international associations. Even environmental and animal rights groups began to emerge on a transnational basis during this period and some of them were as concerned with developments in the empire as with those in their own backyard. In the colonial world itself, on the other hand, home rule and anti-exploitation movements were still at least a generation away, awaiting in most instances a European-educated local elite to lead them. Consequently, global associations during this era were overwhelmingly limited to the states of the economically developed world of Europe and North America. To the extent that these states concerned themselves with conditions in their empires, it was usually either in the self-interest sense of urging that the areas of empire be economically developed for the benefit of the mother country, or in the paternalistic sense of caring for the less fortunate. Consequently, movements with an explicit antiglobalization focus were, on the whole, singularly absent.[6]

Globalization and Antiglobalization Movements in the Contemporary World

Two world wars, coupled with the political instability of inter-war Europe and the disruptive influence of the Great Depression in Europe and North America between the wars, deflected political attention away from peaceful global ties and even from the early stirring for independence in the colonial world. Simply put, the emphasis was squarely on national survival and national interests during the 1914–45 era.

With the conclusion of the Second World War, the inauguration of the Marshall Plan for rebuilding Europe, and the first steps toward economic integration on the continent, a second era of globalism began. From the outset it was earmarked by the emergence of a growing number of military, political, and economic international organizations and the spreading influence and operation of multinational corporations, both in the developed world and between the developed states and a developing world that was still largely under the political control of Europe as late as 1960. In the developing world, however, another transnational movement was simultaneously taking place to close out the earlier era of empire-based globalism. That movement was a steadily growing anticolonial opposition to rule by European states and—after independence, sometimes achieved only through bloody war with the colonial power—to neocolonial exploitation by the global businesses incorporated in the developed world. Thus, the current round of globalization, more intense than its predecessor and proceeding at a faster pace and in a wider arc than during the 1870–1914 era, can be generally dated from the post-World War II days. And, as in the case of the Boston Tea Party,

much of the initial opposition to it originated with an anticolonial focus
on the edge of empire—in this case, on the edge of Europe's empire in
what is today's developing world.

The process of decolonization began immediately after World War II.
In some instances, the transfer of power from ruler to the formerly ruled
was relatively peaceful, as in the case of the transfer of power from
Britain to its colonies in West Africa. In other instances—for example, in
French Indo-China and Algeria—wars were necessary to force out the
colonial power. In all instances, though, the loss of empire forced the
former colonial powers and colonies alike to create new trade relationships on an international basis, and the newly independent world had to
shop for new sources of funding for its economic development.
Meanwhile, the war-torn but economically developed states of Europe
and Japan needed funding to rebuild. Consequently, new international
agreements and institutions for managing trade and financial transactions
began to emerge, facilitating the heavy investment of American corporations in post-war Europe and the injection of United States Marshall Plan
funds for Europe's reconstruction. The most famous of these include the
International Bank for Reconstruction and Development (also known as
the World Bank) near the end of World War II, the General Agreement
on Tariffs and Trade (GATT) in 1947, the European Coal and Steel
Community (1954), and the European Economic Community (1957).

Throughout the 1960s and 1970s, the newly independent, economically developing world remained the heartland of opposition to the West-
centered, global economic order of the postwar world—the economic
order under which the rich countries and Western corporations continued economically to dominate the former colonies and control their
resources. The economic assistance crucial to their development was
otherwise available only from one of the Cold War superpowers—with
political strings attached—or from the international financial bodies
(principally the World Bank and International Monetary Fund) that
the developed states controlled—with economic strings attached.
Complaints and organized protests against this "inequitable" status quo
grew during the 1970s when the terms of trade continued to turn against
the developing states, as their raw material exports declined in value
compared to the services and finished products they were importing
from the developed world. These tensions between the rich and the poor
states further intensified during the global economic recession of the
1980s.

Ironically, that global recession and era of stagflation during the 1980s
was set in motion by a third-world international organization established
to give its members control over their own economic resources: the
Organization of Petroleum Exporting Countries (OPEC). By 1973,

OPEC had achieved that objective, and by decade's end it had used its power in a seller's market to increase the price of oil from less than $3 per barrel in 1973 to nearly $40 per barrel by the end of the decade. In the prolonged recession that followed, everyone eventually lost. The economic fallout led to loss of jobs and corporate profits in the developed world and, eventually, to a collapse in the price of oil on the world market, at OPEC's expense. The big losers, however, were the third-world countries, who lost economic aid from the developed states and investments from restructuring multinational corporations at the same time that soaring energy costs were forcing them to shelve their own development plans. Moreover, the 1980s witnessed a resurgence of neoliberal thinking in Washington and London, where the principal spokespersons for the Western world, President Ronald Reagan and Prime Minister Margaret Thatcher, championed private capital as the answer to poverty in the developing world, rather than the economic assistance or low-interest loans from Western lending institutions that developing states demanded. Their message to needy states was to pull themselves up by their own bootstraps to the point where companies would want to invest in them, rather than extending their hands for alms. To third-world ears, that message confirmed their worst fears: that western governments and financial institutions were aligned against them on the side of global corporatism.

Even the collapse of communism in the Soviet Union and its Central European Empire between 1989 and 1992 adversely affected the countries of the developing world, and it kept alive their opposition to the global economic order they perceived to be still exploiting their resources and insensitive to their needs. As the Western world recovered from the previous decade's recession and began to invest again in other areas of the globe, the democratizing and economically liberalizing states of Central Europe—with their developed economies, skilled labor, low wage structure, and likely future membership in an expanding European Union—began to receive investment capital that in the past would have gone, at least in part, to the developing world.

Backlash and Convergence: The Contemporary Antiglobal Movement Is Born

The final act in the birth of the current antiglobal movement also unfolded during the 1990s, when the process of globalization began to affect the economic way of life and the environmental and human rights sensitivities of the economically advanced countries, which are home to the overwhelming majority of the world's principal multinational corporations, financial institutions, and governments. By then, the continuing evolution of global means of communication and transportation had already been commandeered by social interest groups in these countries. Their goal was to link up with their counterparts in the developing world in order to pursue a much broader battle against social injustice than that fought by the transnational interest groups of the 1870–World War I era. Up to that point, however, average citizens in the developed democratic world had been largely spared the economic consequences of a growing number of profit-oriented multinational corporations organized and operating on a global basis.

The major reaction of these multinational organizations to the recession of the 1980s had been to pare back investments abroad and divest themselves of their unprofitable components. Divestiture sometimes meant the minor loss of jobs here and there, but no serious additions to the high unemployment rate that most developed countries ran during the 1980s. That changed in the mid-1990s, when business-friendly national leaders and their successors inaugurated new rounds of trade negotiations aimed at bringing down protectionist trade barriers in the *developed* world—for example, in North America, with the creation of the North American Free Trade Agreement (NAFTA). At the same time American corporations launched a new round of environmentally unfriendly economic activity at home, even as they were outsourcing well-paying assembly line jobs (for example, automobile construction) and less-well-paying service sector positions (such as telemarketing) to countries whose workers had lower wage structures, fewer expectations of fringe benefits, and no union affiliations. It was a prescription for bringing together "workers, farmers, and environmentalists in North America, Western Europe and East Asia," and it did—along with an assortment of transnational feminists and human rights organizations, ultranationalists, and others concerned with the direction that the world was taking. As the millennium ended, these diverse groups came together into an "unexpectedly resilient, far-reaching, and multi-faced coalition of resistance" to the growing pace and pervasiveness of the forces of globalization.[7]

The Issue Heats Up

The economic dimensions of globalization and the perceived environmental, economic, and social injustices resulting from it are the centerpiece of this antiglobalization network. So important are the network's individual components that many commentators argue that the antiglobalization movement is not a movement at all, but a coalition of diverse social movements, each with its individual agenda (anti-big business, anti-big government, pro-labor, anti-child labor, pro-environment, etc.), but for now marching together with a common aversion to what each perceives to be the status quo. Indisputably, the heat in the movement (or movements) comes from the emotional commitment of those composing it to their individual, albeit transnational causes. In this sense, the antiglobalization phenomenon is a classic case of protest politics achieving a high level of visibility and disruptiveness, sometimes with relatively small turnouts of highly committed protestors. And the protests have been disruptive, provocative, and headline-grabbing. On some occasions, demonstrators have successfully provoked authorities into over-reacting in order to advance their causes; on other occasions, individual protestors have been quite willing themselves to encourage or commit acts of political violence.

Antiglobalization Protests

The beginning of significant antiglobalization protests is usually dated from the November protest staged at the Seattle meeting of the World Trade Organization (WTO) in 1999. In the largest mass rally in the United States since the days of the Vietnam War, at least 50,000 protesters representing such organizations as the Washington, DC–based Mobilization for Global Justice confronted heavy-handed local authorities bent upon maintaining order and Seattle's positive image in the world. The resultant riots spilled across Seattle's main avenue to the extent that many of the 5,000 WTO delegates could not make it to their meeting, and U.S. Attorney General Janet Reno was moved to call upon Washington Governor Gary Locke to activate the state's National Guard in order to restore order. Meanwhile, President Clinton's planned address to the conference was canceled by his aides, citing safety concerns. The protests continued to escalate into two nights of rioting by protestors, on the one side, and police firing tear gas, pepper spray, and rubber bullets on the other. Protesters justified their disorderly conduct on the grounds that such activism was necessary, given the absence of public access to the antidemocratic (that is, nonelected) decision-making arrangements of the World Trade Organization. Law enforcement agencies caught on camera clubbing the senior citizens occupying the front line among demonstrators maintained a discrete silence, but that did not prevent the chaos from becoming a public relations disaster for the city of Seattle and a testimony to the purposefulness and willingness of the protesters to risk harm to get their messages across.

The seeds for the protests that bloomed and boomed in Seattle in 1999 were planted four years earlier when the GATT and its governing bodies were replaced as the world's principal entity in the field of trade by the WTO, and the latter was given significant enforcement powers over the

90 percent of international trade falling under its jurisdiction. Critics of the move saw it as a further shift of power from citizens and governments in democracies to global bureaucrats unaccountable to voters, as well as a further step toward a world run by the type of megacorporations that profit most from WTO decisions that favor free trade and dismantle the environmental regulations limiting it. To the extent that economic globalization is, as one commentator phrased it, "the focus of popular fears about the might of big business, the pace of economic change and a sense of powerlessness in the face of intangible global forces," the creation and empowerment of the WTO both elevated anxieties and gave antiglobalization groups a high-profile international target against which to demonstrate.[8] Also targeted, to a lesser extent, are the World Bank and the International Monetary Fund, which antiglobalization activists lump together with the WTO as the "unholy trinity" of the current global order.

Given their high visibility in the antiglobalization debate, virtually every meeting of the WTO, IMF, and World Bank—as well as the G-8 gatherings of representatives of the eight major industrial powers—provides an occasion for staging protests, clashes with local authorities, and even bombing incidents, and every locale hosting such a meeting becomes, in terms of our study, at least temporarily a potential political hot spot.[9] At least, so the record of such meetings to date would indicate. In fact, the evidence was already gathering before the WTO delegates boarded their planes for Seattle in 1999. In May 1997, for example, a self-congratulatory birthday party given in Geneva to commemorate the fiftieth anniversary of GATT's founding was marred by demonstrations that took a violent turn. Alienated young protestors, blocked by police barricades along the routes to the WTO buildings, overturned cars, smashed windows, and physically attacked local authorities. Likewise, on the eve of the Seattle talks, fears that the delegates in Seattle would treat forests and other natural resources as commercial commodities prompted demonstrations in Geneva, Paris, Lyon, Marseilles, and other locales in Europe, and in such developing world capitals as New Delhi. To be sure, the protests were not always large (only 3,000 gathered in Geneva, and 20,000 in Paris), but neither were they all entirely peaceful.

Following Seattle, the pace of protest quickened to match the growing pace of globalization, and cities chosen as WTO, G-8, or IMF meeting sites had to prepare for disruptive protests and even violent activity as part of the price of hosting such affairs (see Table 1.1). Moreover, as Table 1.1 indicates, unruly protests have by no means been limited to meeting spots in the developed states of North America and Europe. The WTO's 2003 meeting in Cancun drew protesters but passed without incident; however, its December, 2005 session in Hong Kong attracted a

Table 1.1 Significant Antiglobalization Protests, 2000–2007

Date	Locale and Activity
April 2000	Washington, D.C.: IMF and World Bank meeting draws first major protest since Seattle. An estimated 10,000 to 30,000 protesters gather but police – learning from the past – seal off routes to meetings, thereby making it impossible for protesters to shut down city, as occurred in Seattle.
Sept. 2000	Prague: World Bank and IMF summit results in central city standoff between 5,000 protestors throwing Molotov cocktails and cobblestones and erecting barricades on bridge to central city, and police using tear gas and water cannons. 100s detained and treated harshly enough to cause Amnesty International to demand a human rights investigation.
March 2001	Geneva: Protesters target World Trade Organization headquarters, arguing that the Services Agreement being negotiated will threaten global health, education, and water services in the third world.
	Genoa, Italy: Riots disrupt G-8 meeting; one protester is killed.
	Naples: 20,000 demonstrators protest Global Forum meeting; 6,000 police summoned to control stone throwing crowd with tear gas and rubber bullets; 100+ injured.
June 2001	Gothenburg, Sweden: 25,000 mostly "Black bloc" anti-EU and anti-capitalist protesters gather at EU summit; in resultant violence, 3 protesters are shot by police with live ammunition. Amid bomb scares, more than 500 demonstrators are arrested.
July 2001	Salzburg, Austria: Economic summit draws hundreds of protesters; clashes with police and arrests ensue.
Sept. 2001	Mexico City: Bomb goes off at Chevrolet dealership at time of WTO meeting.
Sept. 2002	Washington, DC: Small but noisy and potentially violent crowds greet IMF and World Bank meeting; suspects carrying explosives arrested near IMF; 600 in all arrested.
Sept. 2003	Cancun, Mexico: Protestors from Central America as well as Mexico demonstrate largely peacefully at WTO meeting focusing on farm policy.
June 2004	Brunswick, Georgia, USA: large police presence (20,000) plus National Guard contingent combines with small turnout of protestors at G-8 meeting in an intentionally less accessible areas to result in low profile demonstrations.

Table 1.1 *(Continued)*

Date	Locale and Activity
Aug. 2004	New York: Anti-Bush protests at Republican Party Convention draw wide assortment of groups; 1,400 arrested in Central Park; demonstrators numbering 400,000 block traffic, harassed delegates.
July 2005	Thousands gather to demonstrate prior to scheduled G-8 meeting in Scotland. Due to terrorist attack on London commuters on eve of conference, most protests are canceled.
Dec. 2005	Hong Kong: Demonstrators at the WTO meeting erect barricades around the convention center; a reported 1,000 protestors are arrested, many alleging police brutality.
May 2006	May Day protests in Turkey, Chile, Switzerland, and Sweden turn violent as hundreds of thousands around world protest globalization in general and its adverse effects in their individual backyards.
June 2007	Protests on eve of G-8 conference outside Rostock, Germany, are commandeered by 2,000 violent demonstrators; Molotov cocktails and pieces of pavement are hurled, injuring more than 150 police and scores of demonstrators.

large group of protestors and resulted in mild episodes of political violence and the arrest of approximately 1,000 demonstrators. Indeed, the events in Hong Kong were precisely the type of outcome that the WTO had sought to avoid by scheduling the meeting in an area deemed well controlled by the host government. Similarly, incident-avoidance logic has increasingly motivated the WTO and other targets of antiglobalization protesters to schedule their sessions in remote locales (for example, the 2004 G-8 meeting in Brunswick, Georgia, and the 2001 WTO summit in Doha, Qatar), where access is difficult and/or expensive and where the elements for crowd control are readily available. Meanwhile, emotions continue to run high.

An Ongoing Debate

In the scheduling of their meetings' locales and in their broader efforts to gain wider support, both the proponents and the opponents of the globalization process see the world increasingly in terms of a great gladiator contest. On the one side, in the eyes of globalization's advocates, lie the forces of power and progress—an advanced industrial world that can

Antiwar demonstrators, reinforced by a limited number of antiglobalization protestors, staged a largely peaceful rally in Seattle, Washington, in 2003, where disorder had been the rule four years previously. Courtesy of Rob LaPin.

profit from opening markets in the highly populated developing world even as it creates potential buyers for products there by outsourcing jobs formerly done by nationals in the countries of the developed world. The world's major multinational corporations, most with their homes rooted firmly in the developed democratic world, and such transnational manifestations of global capitalism as the International Monetary Fund and the World Bank still support this viewpoint. They are joined by the leading politicians of the world's major economic powers, whose G-8 meetings are agenda-heavy with items pertaining to free trade and advancing the economies of the economically rich countries, albeit also sprinkled with topics relating to the economic improvement of the less-developed world.

As to the matter of who is being thrown to the gladiators and lions, the opponents of globalism define the economically underdeveloped countries as the primary victims of the globalization process. Given the high cost associated with the production of their goods, it is argued that their products cannot compete in an era of free trade, and hence their governments must knuckle under to the demands of the large multinational corporations in order to gain the capital they need to become more competitive. Meanwhile, antiglobalization groups note that the distribution of benefits from globalization still goes primarily to those in the Northern Hemisphere, with the rich continuing to get richer from the process and the poor falling further behind. As evidence, globalization critics cite the continued impoverishment of not just individual countries, but virtually the whole continent of Africa, where the economic gap separating its 700 million people from the rest of humanity continues to widen.[10] Hence, wherever possible and always with the risk of attendant political violence, antiglobalization activists gather to protest at the regular meetings of those they hold responsible for the continued pillaging of the poor and powerless—now including workers in the developed world whose jobs can be outsourced to exploited labor in the developing world. It is somewhat ironic that antiglobalization groups use globalized communication and transportation systems to monitor (some would say "stalk") the activities of their adversaries, organize their own activities, coordinate their protests, and travel easily, if not cheaply, to the protest sites in ways that were impossible when communication was more primitive and borders more of an obstacle to travelers. Indeed, it is only through the effective use of modern communication and transportation technologies that it has become possible for antiglobalization protesters to gain the world's attention to their causes by staging newsworthy demonstrations.

To the outside world, the more notable (or infamous) of the antiglobalization protests—in particular, Seattle and Prague—have appeared chaotic. In fact, they have usually been well-choreographed events designed to culminate in confrontational politics, a newsworthy breakdown in the public order, and the overreaction of local authorities. This usually entails the presence of a computer-based coordinator assigning tasks prior to the demonstration, based on the level of militancy of the groups attending the protest. There is frequently at least one group willing to engage in militant, even illegal, activities, such as arson or street fighting with police. Others are likely not to go beyond civil disobedience— for example, lying down in the street or blocking off intersections. And still others will restrict themselves to peaceful protesting—carrying signs, chanting songs, and perhaps training themselves to render first aid should injury befall their more aggressive brethren. Protest planners have made optimal use of this mix, deploying the various participants like troops in battle to make the most effective impact on both the target of the protest and the television screen reporting the demonstrations. In Prague, for example, the protesters divided into distinct groups that approached the city from different points to tie up traffic as much as possible, in order to draw the local police away from the conference site and to thin out the forces restraining them. Much the same plan had been followed the previous year in Seattle, where geographically close-at-hand groups, such as the anarchists who journeyed north from Oregon, fleshed out the ranks of those traveling longer distances and added a larger component willing to engage in violent confrontations with authorities than has been present at subsequent antiglobalization protests.

Prospects for Future Violence

As in most areas of protest politics, antiglobalization politics and protests ebb and flow over time depending on a myriad of factors, including the activities of their designated adversaries, developments in the broader political world, the organizational cohesiveness of the carrier movements, and the mood of their members. Thus, antiglobalization protests in the early years of the twenty-first century abated somewhat, not only because WTO and G-8 members were unable to agree on agricultural policy, which slowed the pace of globalization, but also as a result of the growth of violent transnational terrorist organizations, whose successes dampened at least temporarily the enthusiasm of many antiglobalization groups for confrontations with local authorities. Certainly following the September 11, 2001, terrorist attack on New York and Washington, the antiglobalization movements based in the United States temporarily moderated their protests targeting the policies of the U.S. government. Similarly, protestors gathering for the summer, 2005 G-8 summit in Scotland essentially went home after the terrorist attacks on London's mass transit system on the eve of the conference.[11]

More broadly, neoliberal defenders of global capitalism argue that the antiglobalization movement suffers from inherent weaknesses that will eventually sap its vitality. In terms of organization, its diverse components make it a prototypical negative coalition—in this case, one composed, in Thomas Friedman's words, of disparate "backlash" groups: "protectionist labor unions, environmentalists, anti-sweatshop protestors, save-the-turtles activists, save-the-dolphin activists, anti-genetically altered food activists," and the like.[12] In some instances, their individual agendas clash. Thus, autoworkers are fundamentally concerned with wages and job security, even if achieving those goals means that their industries will have to continue using environmentally unfriendly energy sources in order to keep them on the assembly line. In the long term, these differences *are* likely to undercut the antiglobalization movement's intensity and cohesiveness; in the short term, they make it exceedingly unlikely that these coalitions will be able to develop a unifying ideological alternative to global capitalism that promises to simultaneously advance social justice and raise global standards of living.[13]

Moreover, it is reasonable to hope that even if antiglobalization protests remain a sustained, if geographically roving, source of violent activity, the future protests in the developed states of North America and

Europe will be less turbulent than the highly disorderly, rancorous, and often violent demonstrations of the past, if only because local authorities have the excesses of the past from which to learn. Thus, the response in Washington, DC, to the 2002 protests there was much more measured than the street anarchy that resulted from the overreaction of authorities in Seattle three years before. There are, however, no guarantees that this will occur. Politics is a dynamic, not static arena, and protestors can be expected to try to outflank preventive crowd control devices, as occurred on the eve of the G-8 meeting outside Rostock, Germany in June 2007. Then, 2,000 masked extremists commandeered the antiglobalization rally of tens of thousands of demonstrators and—throwing Molotov cocktails and pieces of the pavement—provoked many of the 14,000 police assembled in Rostock to control them into over-reacting. As a result, even before the conference had begun, dozens of the police and protesters had been injured, cars had burned, and teargas had enveloped the "Another World Is Possible" banners under which the protesters had gathered. Meanwhile, on the other side of the barricades, local cultures also affect learning curves; hence, despite the lessons of Seattle, some police in Prague apparently responded to those protesting against the 2000 World Bank and IMF meeting in their city by having the demonstrators arrested, stripped, and left to huddle in cold, unheated buildings while awaiting processing on charges of disrupting the public order. The Czech Republic is now (since 2004) a member of both NATO and the European Union, but neither there nor elsewhere in post-communist Europe are forty years of crowd-control training under communist regimes likely to disappear simply by virtue of a country's admittance to the pre-eminent organizations of the advanced democratic world.

Timeline

1773	Boston Tea Party. American colonialists protest British government-British East India Company collusion in discriminating against colonial merchants by dumping corporate tea into Boston Harbor.
1870–1914	First era of modern globalization results from the expansion of European empires over much of the world's surface. Transnational social and economic networks emerge, as do the first stirrings of antiglobalism protest in opposition to European exploitation of non-European lands and peoples.
1914–1939	Growth of global networks disrupted by World War I, inter-war instability in Europe, the Great

	Depression, and the world's drift into World War II.
1945–1950	Second era of globalization inaugurated by early postwar efforts in the West to create a global economic order and spur economic integration in Europe.
1950–1973	Spread of multinational corporations in developed and developing worlds creates new networks of economic relationships and interdependencies, spurring growth of opposition in the developing world to its neoimperialistic exploitation by Western corporations.
1950–1960	Colonial era basically ends, forcing former imperial powers and the new states to develop new structures for and patterns of interaction.
1970s	Antiglobalization protests become common in the developing world.
1980s	Global stagflation resulting from 1973 and 1979 oil crises intensifies antiglobalization protests in the developing world, even as it forces Western corporations to scale back their investments abroad.
1990–2000	Modern era of antiglobalization movements commences as globalization begins to affect adversely groups in the developed world. The antiglobalization banner becomes an umbrella for disenchanted and disempowered groups in the developed and developing world, who begin to link up.
1995	Antiglobalization protests begin to intensify as the World Trade Organization replaces GATT and presses aggressively for new rounds of trade negotiations.
1999	November protest against WTO meeting in Seattle produces the largest U. S. mass rally since the Vietnam War and results in considerable political violence.
2000–2007	WTO, World Bank, European Union, and G-8 summit meetings are frequently occasions for antiglobalization protests, often resulting in the destruction of property and injuries, even though the pace of globalization slows as the world's major economic powers are unable to agree on agricultural policy.

Notes

1. For an overview of these developments, see Andrew Duncan and Michel Opatowski, *Trouble Spots: The World Atlas of Strategic Information* (Sparkford, England: Sutton Publishing, 2000). For more detailed analyses of many of these topics, see infra for those in North America and Europe and the companion volumes in this series for hot issues and hot spots elsewhere in today's world.

2. Glenn P. Hastedt and Kay M. Knickrehm, *International Politics in a Changing World* (New York: Longman, 2003: 527–528).

3. For a brief synopsis of the current principal interpretations of globalism, see Vic George, "Globalization, Risk and Social Problems," in Vic George and Robert M. Page, eds. *Global Social Problems* (Malden, MA: Polity Press, 2004: 9–28). The major challenges to neoliberal thinking still come from those believing in the merits of pluralism, who consequently ascribe an important role to the state, as well as to the market, in improving the human condition. For more detailed discussions of globalization and antiglobalization politics, see especially Robin Broad, *Global Backlash: Citizen Initiatives for a Just World Economy* (Lanham, MD: Rowman & Littlefield, 2002); Bruce Podobnik and Thomas Ehrlich Reifer, eds. *Global Social Movements before and after 9-11*, Special Issue of the *Journal of World-Systems Research*, X.1 (Winter 2004); and Manfred B. Steger, ed. *Rethinking Globalism* (Lanham, MD: Rowman & Littlefield, 2003).

4. See Daniel R. Headrick's landmark study, *The Tools of Empire: Technology and European Imperialism in the Nineteenth Century* (New York: Oxford University Press, 1981).

5. Headrick, *Tools of Empire*, p. 3. In contrast, only approximately 35 percent of the world's surface was under European occupation or control in 1800.

6. See Bruce Podobnik and Thomas Ehrlich Reifer, "The Globalization Protest Movement in Comparative Perspective," Special Issue of the *Journal of World-Systems Research*, X.1 (Winter 2004: 3–9).

7. Podobnik and Reifer, "Globalization Protest Movement," pp. 6 and 3, respectively.

8. Philippe Legrain, *Open World: The Truth About Globalization* (Chicago: Ivan R. Dee, 2004: 17).

9. G-8 comprises representatives of the United States, Britain, France, Germany, Japan, Italy, Canada, and Russia.

10. A relatively recent report of the World Economic Forum, for example, found that average per capita income in all of Sub-Saharan Africa is now below $200—less than in 1975. In addition to very low levels of foreign investment, this downward slide was attributed to a high population growth outstripping productivity, resource-sapping military conflicts, governmental corruption, and poor infrastructures. See "Nearly Half the World's Poor Are African," *The Baltimore Sun* (June 3, 2004).

11. Reports indicate that only one demonstration was staged during the course of the conference and that only approximately 300 protestors showed up for it.

12. Thomas Friedman, "The Backlash," excerpts from Friedman's *The Lexus and the Olive Tree: Understanding Globalization* (New York: Farrar, Straus, Giroux, 1996), in Karen A. Mingst and Jack L. Snyder, eds. *Essential Readings in World Politics* (New York: W.W. Norton and Company, 2001: 440–46, 441).

13. Ibid.

PART I

Europe

CHAPTER 2

THE AEGEAN AND THE EASTERN MEDITERRANEAN

The area lying east of Italy has played a starring role in the world's recorded history and an important role in shaping the modern Western world. The Greek Empire laid the cornerstone for Western civilization, even if it required the Roman Empire to spread its contributions throughout Western Europe. One of Greece's leading thinkers and the father of modern political science, Aristotle, was anchored in both Turkey and Greece, teaching in the former before being summoned to Macedonia, in the latter, in approximately 345 BC. The area hosted numerous kingdoms in ancient times, and was the home of the Ottoman Empire that lasted for half a millennium and at its height stretched from Belgrade to Baghdad and beyond—the master of the Middle East and a good part of Central and Eastern Europe. In more recent times, it was the principal birthplace of the Cold War, when Soviet support of the communist insurgents in postwar Greece and pressure on Turkey to concede to it joint control over the Dardanelles prompted the United States to adopt the containment of expansionist Soviet communism as the guiding principle of its post–World War II foreign policy. Eventually Greece and Turkey would both join NATO, but their common alliance with the West against the Soviet threat never diluted the animosity that has colored the relationship between Greece and Turkey from ancient times, through the Ottoman Empire and Greece's occupation of post–World War I Turkey, to the present conflict between these two countries over the future of Cyprus—the third European actor lying in the sector of Europe stretching from the Aegean into the Eastern Mediterranean Sea.

Viewed from the vantage point of the Western world, Greece has now ceased to be regarded as a political hot spot. More than three decades have passed since the end of the dictatorial rule imposed on that country by the military that overthrew its elected government in April 1967. During that time Greece's commitment to democracy has never been doubted, and the country has fully integrated into the European Union. Even its long-standing conflict with Turkey over Cyprus has shown signs of healing in the early years of the millennium, as the following section on Cyprus indicates. The passage of time, however, has not removed either Turkey or Cyprus from the world's crisis watch lists; both continue to be troubled by potentially hazardous conflicts emanating from within and without, and each is explored in more depth here.

CYPRUS

Cyprus has been Europe's most established international hot spot beyond the communist and now noncommunist world for half a century. Unlike the other two widely recognized trouble spots in Western Europe—Northern Ireland and Basque Spain—Cyprus did not *raise* the specter of international conflict (Ulster involving the United Kingdom and the Republic of Ireland, the Basque problem involving Basque sanctuaries in France). The long-standing crisis involving Cyprus *was* substantially the product of international conflict between the two Mediterranean anchors—Greece and Turkey—of the North Atlantic Treaty Organization (NATO), which defended Western Europe during the Cold War years. The Cold War is now a thing of the past, but the conflict over Cyprus, and on the island of Cyprus between its approximately 80 percent Greek Cypriot majority and its 18 percent Turkish Cypriot minority is not.[1]

INTERNATIONAL RIVALRIES

Cyprus's status as a Mediterranean hot spot is the product of a convergence of elements, the most important of which are the political geography of the island, the ethnic and cultural differences separating its two dominant communities, and the political ambitions of Greece and Turkey, the mainland points of origin of Cyprus's two communities several centuries ago. Unlike Corsica, whose Italianate population is located nearer to Italy than to continental France but which is a recognized part of France, Cyprus lies closer to Turkey (50 miles to its north) than to

Greece (250 miles away), and its political status has remained a contentious one in which Greek Cypriot "unionists" on the island and political leaders in Athens have been willing to use violence in order to achieve its integration into Greece's political system (*enosis*). That plan has been frustrated historically by both the broader international community, which recognized the island as a British Crown colony from 1925 until its independence in the 1950s, and by its proximity to Turkey, which is far more powerful militarily than Greece and has not been hesitant to use that power to prevent Turkish Cypriots from falling under the control of Athens. Nor has the island's Turkish community been hesitant to accept that protection. Not only do they differ from the island's Greek Cypriots in ethnic origin, language, and religion (being Muslim rather than Greek Orthodox), but since the island's independence the government of Greece has maintained close political and military ties with the island's Greek Cypriot majority, including the long-term posting of Greek military personnel in Cyprus's security services.

Greek Cypriot and Turkish Cypriot Relations Prior to Independence

Located in the Mediterranean Sea in the pathway of the numerous empires that have lined its shores over the past three and a half millennia, Cyprus still retains the architectural footprints of many occupants. It was the Greeks, however, first arriving on its shore more than 3,500 hundred years ago, who gave it the ethnic and cultural heritage still shared by its majority, and who have continued to shape much of its recent history. In between, the island fell under Assyrian, Egyptian, and Persian control before becoming a part of the Roman Empire in 58 BC, and from there passing through Byzantine and Venetian hands before falling under the Ottoman Turks' influence in 1571.

Ottoman rule lasted for slightly more than 300 years (1571–1878) and bequeathed to Cyprus its first and only significant minority community: today's Turkish Cypriots. At the same time, rule from Constantinople did not significantly dislodge the hold of Greek culture on the isle's majority. Rather, the Ottomans' administrative system allowed non-Muslim people to be governed by their own religious institutions, thereby increasing the influence of the Greek Orthodox Church in Cyprus—even as the "us-versus-them" distinction inherent in outsider rule and the inevitable scars of being ruled by a foreign empire strengthened the Greek community's internal solidarity. So, too, did the subsequent four generations of rule by Cyprus's last outside "owner," Great Britain. The last days of British rule, however, were also marked as much by intercommunal conflict between Greek Cypriots and Turkish Cypriots as by the struggle of the former to end British control of the island.

Unofficially, Britain acquired jurisdiction over Cyprus's affairs during the late 1870s, when Turkey essentially gave London the island in return for Britain's pledge to assist the Ottomans if they were attacked by czarist Russia. That jurisdiction became open in 1914, when Britain formally annexed Cyprus at the start of World War I, and was firmed up in 1923 when Turkey, following its defeat in that war, renounced any further territorial claim to the island in the Treaty of Lausanne. Two years later, without Britain consulting either the Greek Cypriot or Turkish Cypriot communities, Cyprus became a British Crown colony.

There followed a thirty-five-year period during which relations between the island's native communities, none too good at the outset of British rule, further deteriorated as the Greek Cypriot community became noticeably better off economically than the Turkish Cypriots. In the 1950s, these intercommunal tensions exploded when Greece supported a Greek Cypriot terrorist organization, the EOKA (National Organization of Cypriot Fighters), seeking to drive Britain violently from the island. Its activists soon began to target Turkish Cypriots as well as British officials, and shortly thereafter Turkish Cypriot terrorist organizations formed and began their own activities directed against the EOKA's agents and, occasionally, innocent Greek Cypriot bystanders. By 1958 Cyprus had lapsed into political turmoil, casualties were becoming extensive in both island communities and among the British administrators singled out for assassination by the EOKA, and Turkey—which had not abandoned watching over the Turkish Cypriots—was demanding guarantees for the safety of Cyprus's Turkish minority.

From Independence to Turkey's Invasion: Communal Conflict, Confrontation, and Crisis-Driven Politics

When Cyprus became independent two years later in August 1960, it was within the framework of a complicated international oversight arrangement, detailed in the Treaty of Guarantee, that was intended to mollify all parties. Under the terms of that Treaty, Britain, Greece, and Turkey were charged with supporting the island's independence as a unitary, bicommunal democratic republic in which both its majority and minority communities were guaranteed basic rights. From the outset, though, the peace that was achieved under this arrangement was fragile, both on the island between the Greek and Turkish Cypriots, and between Greece and Turkey as competitively interested outside parties. The tenuousness was graphically obvious in the fact that Cyprus initially flew the flags of Britain, Turkey, and Greece—along with its own—over its seat of government.

For their part, both the Turkish Cypriots and Turkey favored partitioning the island, despite the often intermingled nature of its communities, or at least the adoption of a federal system of government in which the Turkish Cypriots would enjoy federal autonomy in that portion of the island where they constituted a majority. Meanwhile, not only Greece but a sizable portion of Cyprus's Greek community preferred having the island absorbed into Greece (*enosis*) at the end of British rule. Hence, while the pre-independence intercommunal violence largely ended at independence, the tension on the island did not, and between 1960 and 1963 the ethnically intermingled portions of the island began to erode into a pattern of ethnic enclave settlements as members of both communities relocated their places of residence.

The 1963 [Christmas] Crisis

The uneasy peace came to a temporary end in November 1963, when the island's president, Archbishop Makarios, attempted to rewrite the independence constitution in a manner prejudicial to the political interests of the country's Turkish minority. Greek Cypriot and Turkish Cypriot paramilitaries again went into action, this time joined in the violence by Cyprus's armed forces, and the revived EOKA alone was responsible for torching a hundred Turkish Cypriot villages, killing at least 500 Turkish Cypriots, and driving thousands from their homes. A month later, with the violence still mounting, Britain sent an interventional force to Cyprus to restore order. The following March the United Nations' oldest continuously operating peacekeeping force (UNFICYP, with a British contingent) was born, arriving on the island to relieve Britain's contingent at the request of all parties (Britain, Greece, and Turkey) guaranteeing the island's independence. Where possible, cease-fire lines—including one running through the island's capital of Nicosia—were quickly created to separate the warring factions, and when Makarios abandoned his proposed reforms, a fragile peace again settled over the island.

Turkey's Invasion and the de facto Partition of Cyprus

With the UN force in place on a long-term basis, that peace stretched out for more than a decade, and tensions on Cyprus very gradually subsided. Enclave formation slowed as well, and by the early 1970s the majority of Greek and Turkish Cypriots seemed to have eased into a pattern of mostly peaceful cohabitation on the island. In some quarters of the Greek community, however, the goal of *enosis* lingered, and in mid-July 1974 another effort was made to achieve it. At the direct instigation of the military junta then ruling Greece, and with the full participation of Greek officers stationed on Cyprus as security advisers to the island's National Guard, members of EOKA's successor organization (EOKA-B, under the leadership of Nikos Sampson) launched a bloody coup to depose Makarios and achieve that goal. This time the primary targets were other Greek Cypriots, and before a provisional government was created with Sampson as the island's acting president, EOKA-B killed hundreds of Makarios's Greek Cypriot supporters.

The coup immediately produced a barrage of diplomatic activity designed to return Makarios to power—he had fled the island for his safety—and prevent the obviously planned absorption of Cyprus by Greece. The colonels ruling in Athens had been tolerated, but they were never popular in NATO circles since they seized power by toppling Greece's democratically elected government in 1967. Moreover, the presence of Sampson—a self-confessed assassin of numerous British citizens in Cyprus during the 1950s—at the head of the provisional government was especially grating to the British guarantors of the island's independence. Nevertheless, despite the rumors that Makarios was dead, Britain initially rejected Turkey's request that it immediately intervene to restore order, as it had done in 1960. When the search for a diplomatic solution to the crisis stalled, Turkey—citing its right under the Treaty of Guarantee—acted unilaterally and militarily in response to the pleas of Turkish Cypriots for protection.

Turkey's military assaults came in two waves. First, invoking its right and duty under the 1960 agreement negotiated at the island's independence, and in spite of the danger of conflict with Greece, Turkish armed forces invaded Cyprus on July 20 (only five days after the coup), landing along the island's northern coastline and moving inland. Three days later the danger of a war between Greece and Turkey along the Mediterranean Sea's northern coastline eased considerably when the colonels' regime was itself overthrown in Athens. Removal of the colonels did not end the conflict on Cyprus, however, where Turkey's forces were establishing control over areas in northern Cyprus that contained sizable communities of Greek Cypriots. The matter then returned to the bargaining table for the next three weeks. During that period Sampson was removed from his rump presidency, Makarios returned to office in Nicosia, and Turkey's diplomats lobbied for reorganizing the island in the federal format that they and the Turkish Cypriot leaders had sought when Cyprus became independent. When the Greek Cypriot leadership vetoed that proposal, as they had fourteen years earlier, Turkey launched a second invasion of the island in mid-August, essentially ethnically cleansing large parts of Northern Cyprus of its Greek communities and establishing control over approximately 37 percent of the island.

The reshaping of Cyprus's demographics—and, consequently, its political face—did not end there. Paramilitaries in both communities resumed their killing ways, and by the time Turkey ended its military operations, thousands had died and tens of thousands in both communities were either forced to move or chose to relocate before being forced to do so. Indeed, when the post-conflict diplomatic negotiations designed to keep Cyprus's two communities cohabiting under a common government continued to fail and eventually died out, between 100,000 and 150,000 Greek Cypriots who had previously been intermingled with the Turkish Cypriots in the north evacuated to live in the predominantly Greek Cypriot south. Shortly thereafter, a second exodus occurred when approximately 40,000 to 50,000 Turkish Cypriots living in the south relocated to the Turkish-controlled north, where the Turkish Cypriots by then constituted practically the entire population. In both migrations it was usually only the eldest who stayed behind, and with mortality taking its toll, by the end of the twentieth century the total numbers of Greek Cypriots living north of the cease-fire line and Turkish Cypriots living to its south had become negligible.[2] Meanwhile, time passed and Makarios died (1977), but the political stalemate persisted, and gradually an estimated 120,000 additional Turks migrated from the mainland to settle in the island's northern sector and increase the Turkish presence on the island.

Very quickly the island's changing demographics spawned far-reaching political changes, and the emergence of a bizonal island with an internationally recognized government in the south (the Nicosia-centered Republic of Cyprus, which received independence in 1960 and still occupied Cyprus's seat in the United Nations) and a de facto Turkish Cypriot state in the north. The institutionalization of separatism began almost immediately, with units of Turkey's armed forces remaining in the north and regular Greek army contingents being deployed in the south. Greek Cypriot leaders immediately assumed full control of the island's official government in Nicosia, which still straddles the UN-patrolled, unofficial demarcation line between the island's two, now territorialized, communities. Matters further polarized in June 1975, when the Turkish Cypriots voted overwhelmingly in a referendum that was not recognized internationally to establish their own state in the island's north. Initially constituted as the Turkish Federated State of Cyprus—a title that held out the potential for its subsequent reintegration into a federally united Cyprus—the region formally seceded as the Turkish Republic of Northern Cyprus (the TRNC) on November 15, 1983. Its independence was instantly recognized by Turkey, but subsequently by no other country.

NATIONALISM

A quarter-century has passed since that time. The Turkish Republic of Northern Cyprus (TRNC), still recognized by only Turkey and economically propped up with annual Turkish subsidies, has remained only nominally independent. Meanwhile, relations between Turkey and Greece have sometimes been acrimonious—as late as during the highly confrontational period from 1996 to 1999—and have sometimes thawed into polite discourse, especially after the 1999 earthquakes that destroyed parts of Athens and Istanbul gave them something in common other than their battle over Cyprus. Likewise, the level of conflict has ebbed and flowed on the island as a function of both the position of Greece and Turkey on the Cyprus question and the personalities speaking respectively for the Greek Cypriot and Turkish Cypriot communities. The 2003 election of Tassos Papadopoulos as the island's official president, for example, revived an intransigent nationalism in the island's south at the same time that a shift in the TRNC's leadership (and outside pressure by UN Secretary-General Kofi Annan) was producing an increased willingness in the north to explore reunification options. Nevertheless, tension between Nicosia and the TRNC has been the norm throughout, and *the* central issue continues to be the need to find a way to reunite the island in a manner mutually acceptable to its two ethno-national communities. All other things—the presence of outside actors, the economic gap separating the communities, the role of the peacekeeping force, the issue of compensation for those displaced from their homes, and so on—find their import in that fundamental issue, sometimes complicating its resolution and sometimes easing the tension. On occasion, however, their importance has been significant.

The UN and the 2004 Referendum: Last Best Shot at Unification?

On the thirtieth anniversary of Turkey's invasion and the island's de facto partition, there was a major international effort to reunite Cyprus. Kofi Annan, Secretary-General of the United Nations, labored hard to find a diplomatic solution in negotiations with the governments of Greece and Turkey, as well as with TRNC leaders and Nicosia. The package that emerged was complex, but basically revolved around two elements: (1) a bi-zonal federal format designed to accommodate the autonomy desires of the Turkish Cypriots and to gain support in the Greek Cypriot community, and (2) restitution of property to half of those Greek Cypriots who formerly lived in northern Cyprus and were forced to flee their homes in 1974, and compensation to the other half for their losses.[3]

The vote on the proposal took place in separate referendums in the separate parts of the island, only two months before Cyprus was due to be admitted to the European Union (EU) in May 2004. The plan passed easily in the north, where nearly nine out of ten (87 to 88 percent) of those eligible to vote turned out, and nearly two out of three (64.9 percent) supported the plan. In the south, however, President Papadopoulos aggressively opposed the proposal on the grounds that it would legalize and institutionalize the boundary dividing Cyprus that had been established by violence. The outcome reflected his influence and a rising tide of Greek Cypriot nationalism stirred up by the debate preceding the vote. In the end, Greek Cypriots rejected the UN-crafted, EU-endorsed plan by more than a three-to-one majority (only 24.1 percent supported it) in a voting turnout similar to that achieved in the north.

Because the plan needed approval by both communities to take effect, reunification failed and the island remains politically divided. Moreover, two months later the European Union, as scheduled, admitted the Cyprus physically composed of those who opposed the unification scheme, and continued its economic sanctions against the TRNC, denying EU passports and other benefits of EU membership to those who had solidly supported the plan. In doing so, the EU effectively removed one of the major cards—EU membership—that the international community could play in its efforts to persuade the Greek government in Nicosia to compromise with the Turkish Cypriots on a federal reunification scheme.[4] By that time, though, the Cyprus question had already infected the EU.

The European Union

During the same period that Kofi Anan was laboring to find a formula to put before the voters in Cyprus, the European Union (EU), which had already offered Cyprus membership, was doing its part to bring the outside players together, most notably at the 2002 Copenhagen Summit. There, EU representatives lobbied Turkey and Greece to sign an agreement to settle the Cyprus issue before the island's planned 2004 accession to the EU. Turkey had long been under EU pressure to renounce its recognition of the TRNC as a precondition to beginning negotiations for its own entry into the EU. It was Greece, however, that most tenaciously rejected the EU's lobbying effort in Denmark, threatening to veto (as an existing EU member can) any further enlargement of the European Union until Cyprus too became a member. Greece's threat removed any possibility that the EU would reconsider Cyprus's scheduled admission whatever the outcome of the referendum on the island, and the admission of Turkey (which the EU officially views as illegally occupying a portion of an EU member state) to the European Union now faces a veto from two possible sources: Greece, an EU member since 1981, and Nicosia.

Despite the fact that admitting Cyprus reduced the EU's bargaining leverage with respect to the Greek portion of the island, the EU remains an important cog in any future settlement of the Cyprus conflict, given the considerable economic incentives it can offer as enticements to the north to dismantle the "independent" TRNC. On an island already poor by the standards of the EU's Western European members, the TRNC remains a conspicuous economic backwater with a per capita gross domestic product of a little over $7,000 in 2006, compared to approximately $23,000 in the south. Furthermore, although at the time Cyprus was admitted to the EU the unemployment situation was nearly uniform (approximately 5.5 percent) throughout the island, employment in the north is highly vulnerable to the continued imposition of EU sanctions on the TRNC. Tourism remains one of the principal sources of employment throughout Cyprus, but without an international airport or premier hotel facilities, the TRNC has been getting only a fourth to a third of all tourists visiting the island and has had to rely upon expanding government employment (with increased subsidies from Turkey) to keep its unemployment figures down. The EU thus has considerable leverage vis-à-vis both Turkey and Turkish Cypriots in pushing for a settlement of the Cyprus question, but that leverage is only likely to be useful in a compromise-laden format. Therein lies the EU's problem, insofar as it can offer far less to induce the Greek Cypriots to compromise than before Cyprus became one of its own.

NATO and the Cyprus Question

NATO's concern with the conflict in Cyprus has always been deep, but in a sense it has been tangential. For much of the Cold War, the fear was that the conflict in Cyprus might lead to a war between Greece and Turkey, two crucial anchors of NATO in the northern Mediterranean. That concern has not entirely disappeared, but the equation has changed since the collapse of the Soviet Union, which in the early days of the Cold War intervened in the affairs of both Greece (where it supported the communist guerrillas in a civil war) and Turkey (from which it demanded joint control of the Dardanelles area linking the Black Sea to the Mediterranean). With the end of the Cold War, Turkey's value to NATO has increased. Thus, whereas the internal politics of the EU now strengthen Greece's hand relative to Turkey's, the reverse has been true

A more peaceful Cyprus, 2007: a guard post, E16, no longer manned, along the Blue Line in Nicosia. Courtesy of Cynthia Cates.

in NATO, whose postwar missions have focused on the Balkans, the Eastern Mediterranean, and the Middle East. Moreover, what has been true of NATO has been even more the case with the United States, with its forces in Afghanistan and in Iraq in a U.S.-led "coalition of the willing" (which includes numerous NATO members) and with its growing concern with Iran. In all instances, access to Turkey's ports and military installations has become an important part of strategic planning and military operations.

The Conflict Today: Flashpoint Issues and Complicating Factors

The centerpiece of the Cyprus conflict thus remains the island itself, and a solution to the half-century of conflict between its majority and minority communities must begin and end there. Unfortunately for conflict resolution, the three decades that have passed since the island's partition have added new issues to the already existing tensions and mutual distrust between the two communities. Bereft of its Greek citizens, for example, the Turkish-controlled 38 percent of the island has undergone Turkification, with daily life geared to the customs and habits of its Turkish, Islamic population and its ancient Greek monuments and historical sites renamed in Turkish. Even if those Greek Cypriots who were displaced in 1974 were to return—a flashpoint issue in its own right—it would be to a different and less-environmentally-familiar north than the one they departed. Meanwhile, nationalists in both camps continue to rekindle the old grievances against Greek Cypriot leaders, who wanted to strip Cyprus's Turks of their political influence (if not merge Cyprus into Greece), and against Turkish Cypriots, who invited the army of Turkey in and drove Greek Cypriots out of the island's north. But other concerns also weigh heavily in overcoming those memories and bringing the island's communities together.

Greek-Turkish Relations

The most encouraging news in terms of finding a lasting peace on the island has been the diminished likelihood of a Greco-Turkish war over Cyprus, barring the extremely unlikely outbreak of a future civil war (versus isolated skirmishes) there. In the past the fear was that a blowback of conflict between Greek and Turkish Cypriots on the island would ignite a broader war, but the early twenty-first-century thaw in the formerly icy relations between Greece and Turkey— including Greece officially dropping its objection to Turkey joining the EU in mid-decade—has given birth to hope in European circles that these two states may now be able to persuade the leaders of Cyprus's rival communities to seek a political *modus vivendi* that will reunite the island. Boosting those prospects is the fact that Cyprus's entry into the EU has essentially eliminated any further talk of *enosis* as an obstacle to that reunion.

Peacekeeper Dependency: The Future of the UN's Peacekeeping Force

Reunited or not, talk of withdrawing the UN's peacekeeping force from Cyprus engenders considerable unease in both Cypriot communities and in wider diplomatic circles. The events of 1974 underscored the importance of the UN forces and also redefined the UN mission. It shifted from keeping the peace between two intermixed national communities to policing a buffer zone (the Green Line) between two suddenly territorialized communities that continues to exist more than 30 years after Turkey's invasion, and which still spans a 110-mile strip across the island. Normally from 4 to 12 miles in width, the buffer zone shrinks to less than a few blocks wide in Nicosia. Despite previous good will gestures—when Greek Cypriots in 2007 destroyed a portion of the wall previously erected to separate the communities in Nicosia and, earlier, when Greeks and Turks worked jointly to clear land mines from the island—it may still be dangerous to remove that small UN presence (less than 900 troops in 2005). At a minimum, having kept the peace on Cyprus for all but four years of the island's history since 1960, it provides both communities with a security blanket. Whatever the formula for reunification that might emerge, in the short term the implementation of any agreement is certain to raise rather than lower intercommunal tensions. Thus, however true it may be that the long-term presence of the UN force on Cyprus has allowed for such a normal way of life to develop that it removed some of the incentive for Greek and Turkish Cypriot leaders to settle their conflict, its presence is still necessary if unification is to occur. On this point, at least, the islanders agree. A February 2007 poll commissioned by the United Nations found majorities in both the Greek Cypriot and Turkish Cypriot communities expressing the view that the UN peace-keeping force still has an important role to play in Cyprus, *even though each community also felt that the UN is currently biased in favor of the other.*[5]

REFUGEE ISSUES

Whatever form it takes, the resolution of the refugee issue will also depend on the continuing presence of the UN's peacekeeping mission on Cyprus. Although Turkish Cypriot leaders gave their consent to the resettlement of Greek Cypriots in the north as part of the 2004 reunification proposal, the general consensus remains that a heightening of tension will inevitably accompany any effort to repatriate large numbers of them, because their return to the north will threaten the Turkish majority there. Moreover, their resettlement will again reshape the UN's mission in a more difficult direction from its current focus on separating the communities through a series of buffer zones. It will force the UN to augment its forces in order to provide assured protection for the returning refugee minorities in those areas of the north where communities would again be intermingled and around any minority enclaves they might establish. Such was the political geography of the UN's mission between 1963 and 1974, when relocation of the populations allowed it to redeploy to the current buffer zones, and *that* undertaking required considerably more personnel than the UN currently has in Cyprus.[6]

The Turkish Military Forces

In contrast to the calming presence of the UN force, the continuing presence of Turkey's military forces in the north, like the presence of Athens' less numerous military "advisers" in the south, remains a polarizing issue. At a minimum, the stationing of the Turkish force gives the government in Nicosia a daily excuse for not "giving in" to any federal compromise at the point of a Turkish gun, and thus constitutes a real obstacle to reuniting the island's population under a single government. In the north, though, the Turks' presence is viewed as essential to the security of a breakaway republic with no outside supporter other than Turkey, on an island where the Turkish Cypriots are outnumbered four to one by Greek Cypriots. Consequently, any dilution of their number under an international settlement agreement would depend on the continuing presence of the UN peacekeepers and the willingness of the Turkish Cypriots to entrust their security to those forces, despite their misgivings about the United Nations being biased in favor of the Greek Cypriots.

Looking Ahead: The Prospect for Settlement and the Danger of Future Violence

The decision of the government in Nicosia to bulldoze down a stretch of the 12-foot-high wall separating the Greek and Turkish communities in the old (tourist) part of Nicosia in March 2007 was widely heralded as another step toward the gradual resolution of the Cyprus drama from below—that is, via the gradual development of day-to-day interaction between the two societies as a step toward political reunification. Those hopes had begun four years earlier when the TRNC opened its border to residents of the south, and they acquired greater importance when the international effort to resolve the matter from above failed with the south's no vote in the 2004 referendum on reunification. To date, however, the reunification-through-increased-contact approach has moved slowly, to say the least. Not only was the 2007 action of the Papadopoulos government in Nicosia accompanied by the stipulation that no Greek Cypriots would be allowed to cross over until Turkey removes its troops from the north, but four years after the TRNC opened its border little sustained contact between Greek and Turkish Cypriots had resulted. As of 2007 only one in ten Greek Cypriots was crossing the border with any regularity (compared to approximately 45 percent of the Turkish Cypriots), and four out of ten had yet to cross over into the TRNC. Of the other 60 percent, most indicated that they only crossed one or two times after the border was reopened for the first time in nearly 30 years and—worse for the gradualist approach to reunification—that the "the experience had not enhanced their impression of their Turkish Cypriot neighbors."[7]

In the meantime, the tensions persist as life goes on, each community celebrating separate independence days (November 15, 1983, for those living in the TRNC; October 1, 1960, for the Greek Cypriots) on their separate soil, and that physical division of the island has now had more than a generation and a half in which to harden. Likewise, in the approximately half century since Cyprus gained its independence, the list of issues to be negotiated for a lasting peace has proliferated—from the original demands of the island's Turkish minority for an effective share of decision-making authority; to the continued presence of Turkish and Greek forces on the island; to the fate of the 1,613 Greek Cypriots who have been missing since Turkey's intervention ("invasion" in the minds and school textbooks of Greek Cypriots); to compensation for those in both communities driven from their homes by the fighting in 1974. Whether in an internationally negotiated package deal or as the result of a gradually developing *entente* between the Greek and Turkish Cypriots, working through those issues will keep Cyprus an international hot spot for the foreseeable future.

TURKEY

The Republic of Turkey may not currently qualify as a fully developed global hot spot, but it is close to becoming one on several counts, many of which are as much a product of political geography and its history of conflicts with neighboring areas as the result of the political choices that have been made by Turkey's leaders.

Geographically, today's Turkey—shorn of the possessions of the Ottoman Empire that preceded it—occupies the Anatolia Peninsula of Asia Minor, a land bridge that links Europe to the Middle East and beyond, and whose travelers have shaped European history for a thousand years. A millennium ago it carried the Crusaders to and from the Holy Land before becoming part of the famous Silk Road, along which spices and other riches from the Orient were imported into Europe. By the nineteenth and twentieth centuries those imports had become less elegant, but no less in demand in some quarters, as Turkey became the principal entrance point for the flow of opium and, later, heroin into Europe. Today the peninsula helps Europe meet its energy fix, as pipelines cross Turkey from the Caspian Sea with as much as 15 percent of the gas and oil that European Union states need to sustain Western civilization's contemporary, energy-intensive lifestyle.

As for its past, Anatolia's history is rich in significance and drama—like the Aegean and Eastern Mediterranean regions in general. In approximately 7000 BC, the world's first urban center emerged in what is today south-central Turkey, only to vanish completely twelve centuries later. The Trojan wars were fought there from 1275 to 1240 BC, and wealthy King Croesus ruled his kingdom in western Anatolia and produced the world's first coins between 560 BC and 540 BC, the year that the citizens of Xanthos chose mass suicide rather than accept slavery at the hands of their invading conquerors. Nearly 900 years later (330 AD) the Emperor Constantine established the capital of the Byzantine Empire in Constantinople, and there it remained until Constantinople's conquest by the Ottoman Turks in 1453 marked the end of the Byzantine Empire. In the intervening period, the first Crusaders had arrived in Constantinople in 1096, Frank and Venetian armies of the Fourth (and last) Crusade had sacked that Christian capital in 1204, and the Ottoman Empire, born in 1290 under the leadership of Osman I, had begun a series of wars and conquests that would stretch across more than six centuries and cost an almost inestimable number of lives in Europe, Western Asia, and the Middle East.

Treachery and ruthlessness were parts of the Ottoman Empire's history. In 1830, for example, 1,000 dissident Albanian leaders were invited to negotiate with an Ottoman general who promptly had half of them put to death as an object lesson to the other half. Those seeking freedom from Istanbul's rule were dealt with especially harshly. In 1894, for example, at least 6,000 autonomy-seeking Kurdistan Armenians were massacred, as were at least five times that number of Bulgarians in Macedonia in response to the 1903 uprising there. Meanwhile, on a happier note, the world's first merry-go-round made its appearance at a fair in Philippopolis in 1620, and the famed Orient Express made its first trans-European run from Paris to Istanbul in 1883.

The fact that so much of Turkey's history involves Asia and the Middle East, along with the fact that the overwhelming majority of its territory lies east of the Bosporus Strait, which officially separates Europe from Asia; the fact that it is thoroughly (more than 99 percent) Muslim in religion; and the fact that its capital lies deeply inside Asia have prompted those opposed to Turkey's entry into the European Union (EU) to argue that it is not a European country at all. On the other hand, in the distant past its capital ruled much of Central Europe, and in recent times Turkey has been formally associated with other European states as a member of the preeminent Western security organization, NATO, and it has been accepted as a candidate for EU membership. Even more importantly, the problems that it now confronts either frequently emanate from Europe or are the consequence of its relationship with

The Blue Mosque in Istanbul, Turkey, more formally known as the Sultan Ahmed Mosque. Completed in 1616 during the rule of Ahmed I, it is the national mosque of Turkey. Courtesy of Linda Bishi and Toni Marzotto.

European countries, and the degree to which it copes with them will have profound implications for Europe and the West.

ATATURK'S SECULAR ISLAMIC STATE

Along Massachusetts Avenue and its intersecting roadways in northwest Washington—the celebrated "Embassy Row" of the United States capital—the Turkish and Pakistani embassies stand less than 300 meters (one-fifth of a mile) from each other. Even the physical appearances of these buildings, however, reveal that in the world of Islam, these two countries are very far apart. As befits a state that was born when the Indian subcontinent was partitioned at the end of British rule along the boundary lines of the religious differences separating the vast majority of its Hindu and its Muslim peoples, the Embassy of the Islamic Republic of Pakistan is adorned with parapets and flies a flag dominated by Islam's crescent moon and star. That symbol also occupies a corner of Turkey's flag—but only a corner—signifying a past in which Anatolia controlled a large part of the Muslim world and a present in which its people remain Muslim.[8] Just as revealing, that flag flies over a dignified building whose national heritage is otherwise largely unmarked, as befits a country that for most of the twentieth century militantly chose to separate its people's faith from its political life. It was not always so, of course, but even at the height of the Ottoman Empire, when the acknowledged religious leader of the world of Islam (the Caliph) resided in Istanbul, the conquests that the Ottoman sultans undertook were at least as much about spreading the empire's power and achieving greater wealth as about spreading the Islamic faith.

The Ottoman Empire and Islam

Islam was born in the Mecca-Medina corridor of the Arabian peninsula during the seventh century and was rapidly spread northward by warriors of the nomadic tribes who were among its first converts. Within less than three decades after the death of Muhammad (570–632 AD), it had reached the Mediterranean Sea, and the first Sunni dynasty, the Umayyad, had been established under a religious leadership (the Caliphate) centered in Damascus. From there, the faith moved westward into Egypt and the North African region lying beyond. So swiftly and thoroughly did the warriors of Islam subdue the area that within approximately a century of Muhammad's death the region's peoples had not only adopted the faith of their conquerors but their language (Arabic) as well.

Thereafter, Islam journeyed back across North Africa and toward the east. In 750 the Umayyad dynasty gave way to the Abbasid Dynasty and the Caliphate was moved to Baghdad, where it would reside until 1258, when Baghdad was sacked by the Moguls and the Caliphate was stripped of its secular authority and relocated as a purely religious institution in Cairo. By then, Islam had spread into Central Asia, but the fervor of its initial evangelical warriors had waned. Thus, although Islam had been embraced by both the Persians and the Turks of Central Asia by the end of the first millennium, de facto political power in the Islamic world was by then already being exercised by local leaders who rarely deferred to the orders of the Caliph, whose all-embracing authority they purportedly acknowledged. Ultimately, the Persians would adopt the Shiite path in Islam to divorce themselves from the Sunni Caliphate in Baghdad, and the Turks of Central Asia who converted to Islam would themselves conquer Baghdad (in 1055), only to be halted in their westward march by the Byzantine army in eastern Anatolia sixteen years later.

For the next 200 years, during which the conflict between Islam and Christendom revolved around the great Crusades to free Jerusalem of Muslim control, power in the Anatolia peninsula see-sawed between the armies of the Turks and those of the Byzantine Empire centered in Constantinople—the former gaining in strength over time and the latter's power gradually weakening. The critical moment of tilt in favor of the Turkish forces is generally dated from 1281, when Osman I—the leader of one of the Turkish clans in Anatolia—came to power and began his campaign against the Byzantines. Nine years later, the birth of the Ottoman Empire was proclaimed under his sultanate, and by the time of his death in 1326 his armies had captured most of Anatolia and were poised on the edge of Europe. Nevertheless, it was more than another century and a quarter, during which the Ottoman Empire spread northward into the Balkans, before the Byzantine Empire officially ended when Constantinople fell to the Ottoman Turks and the Ottoman Empire's march into Europe's underbelly began.

Over the following centuries, as the regional timeline at the end of this chapter notes, the Ottoman victories were many and the lands they gained in adjacent areas of Europe—as well as in the Middle East—were considerable. They included the 1517 conquest of Cairo and the resultant relocation of the Caliphate to Istanbul (formerly Constantinople), where it survived under the obvious shadow of the Sultana and primarily functioned as a means of legitimizing the Sultan's temporal rule over the Islamic Middle East. In their conquests, the Ottomans spread Islam into Europe far more successfully than the Moors had managed to do in their invasion of Spain, and at the height of its power during the latter half of the sixteenth century, under the rule of Suleyman the First (also known as Suleyman the Magnificent), the Ottoman Empire was the largest empire on earth. Still, in spreading their empire the Turks were not so much warriors of Islam, pursuing a holy war against the Infidels in the latter's homeland, as they were Islamic soldiers concerned with conquering land and acquiring power. Where the local population embraced the faith, it tightened the Turks' control over the territory. Toward the same end, as when they won control of Kosovo from the Serbs, the Ottomans would sometimes encourage people previously converted in other areas to resettle in the newly claimed, non-Muslim lands. And claim European land the Ottomans did, although their advances were repeatedly—and eventually, *definitively*—checked by the Austrians and Hungarians, whose weaponry included gunpowder and projectiles fired from guns, which the Ottomans did not possess during the sixteenth and seventeenth centuries. Hence, outside of those parts of the Balkans that the Ottomans controlled until the end of the nineteenth century, Europe remained Christian. Moreover, following Greece's war for independence in the

1820s, the Ottoman Empire's losses in Europe gradually multiplied until finally, in the early decades of the twentieth century, it was utterly defeated by the forces of the West in World War I (1914–1918)—a secular defeat of the world's last Islamic Empire.[9]

Kemal Ataturk and the End of the Ottoman Empire

World War I set into motion forces that quickly culminated in both the end of the Ottoman Empire and a formal separation of Islam from the government of Turkey. The former occurred in practice during the postwar conference at Versailles, where implementation of the principle of national self-determination by the victors primarily involved giving the British and French control over the Empire's remaining Mediterranean and Middle Eastern possessions. The French gained control of what is now Syria and Lebanon, and the British eventually acquired Iraq and parts of contemporary Jordan, along with a mandate to prepare Palestine for self-rule. Yet for the Turks the matter did not end there. A year after the end of the war in 1918, foreign armies (including Greece's) still occupied parts of Anatolia, and much of it had also become protectorates of foreign powers. In response to their presence, and while the official government in Istanbul acquiesced to a series of foreign-imposed treaties—including one that would have given autonomy to Turkey's Kurdish southeastern region—Turks led by Mustafa Kemal (who later added the name Ataturk, an honorary title meaning "father of the Turks") established a rump capital and began a war for independence.

Kemal had previously acquired a following as one of Turkey's few successful World War I commanders for his defense of the Gallipoli peninsula during the war—a period already earmarked by the 1913 revolt of the military's Young Turks, who were angered by the concessions Turkey had made in the London peace talks after the first Balkan War. Like the initial revolt by Young Turks against the Sultan's growing despotism late in the nineteenth century, it was a rebellion against the direction of the regime, not a full-blown revolution against the form of the state (which would have been poorly timed, given the continuing atmosphere of war in Europe). In any event, the Second Balkan War resulted in Turkey gaining complete control over Bulgaria, and the revolt was over when World War I began in 1914. From the outset, Kemal challenged the nature of the postwar Ottoman state. In 1919 he established a base of operations in Angoro, a town in central Turkey that would soon be renamed the Republic of Turkey's capital of Ankara, and he issued a "National Pact" that promised to establish a secular republic in a Turkey that would be reduced to the borders of Anatolia, where the Turks constituted the vast majority of the population.

In June 1919, the Turkish National Congress founded by Kemal in Angora formally denounced the Treaty of Versailles and the postwar provisions that had allowed foreign governments to usurp parts of Anatolia and station their troops there. By then a national struggle for independence was under way, with the military and other Turks rallying to the cause. Turkey's 1919–22 war for independence was fought primarily between the Turks and the Greek forces, who were backed by the British units that formally occupied Istanbul in 1920, as well as the Italian, French, and even Russian forces that were deployed in Anatolia during and/or after World War I. The decisive battle ended September 9, 1922, when Turkish troops under the command of Mustafa Kemal occupied Smyrna, in Greece, and forced the Greeks and their allies to accept Turkey's independence as outlined in the National Pact. Shortly thereafter the National Assembly abolished the sultanate, formally ending the Ottoman Empire. The following year (1923) the Turkish National Assembly proclaimed the Republic of Turkey, with Ankara as its capital and Mustafa Kemal as its president.

The process of making Turkey a secular, democratic state along the lines of Western European countries began in earnest and proceeded quickly between 1924 and 1929. The caliphate was abolished in 1924, along with the mixing of religion and public life; Kurdish schools and publications were shut down; and the wearing of the tassel by men and the veil by women was outlawed in 1925, although the veil has continued to be tolerated outside of public buildings. Muslim law was replaced with civil codes in 1926, the Roman alphabet was adopted in 1928, and the consumption of alcohol was permitted. Capping the decade, Turkish women were encouraged to work, were given equal rights with men in matters of divorce and inheritance, and received the right to vote. Along the way, the reforms had created a backlash in some quarters of Turkey and produced a significant revolt in the country's Kurdish region (which was quickly quashed).

KEEPING THE REPUBLIC

One of the tales told most often about the writing of the United States Constitution has Benjamin Franklin emerging from Constitution Hall in Philadelphia following a debate on whether the United States would anoint George Washington as its king or have an elected head of state. "What will it be," Franklin is asked, "a Monarchy or a Republic?" and Franklin replies, "A Republic, sir, if you can keep it."

By 1930 Turkey could legitimately claim to be a secular, democratic republic, albeit one whose president enjoyed an unfettered authority conferred upon him by the elected National Assembly. Kemal's death in 1938 ushered in an era of competitive electoral politics, and eventually a shift of constitutional authority from the president to a parliamentary system and a prime minister elected by the country's legislature. Moreover, with the military's help and sometimes its direct (but short-term) intervention, Turkey has sustained that republic for more than three-quarters of a century. The struggle to do so has not always been easy or particularly peaceful, however, and so it is today when Turkey finds itself confronted by not just a number of potentially volatile issues, but by challenges so configured that what eases one can potentially aggravate another. The following issues are only the most challenging and/or violent, or potentially violence-laden, among them.

Maintaining Democracy: The Danger of Military Intervention
Defending the Republic

The selling of the secular, democratic Kemalist state in Turkey began with the long tenure of Kemal Ataturk and his political lieutenant-successor, Ismet Inonu (president, 1938–50), who collectively oversaw the Republic of Turkey's first thirty years. Its successful survival, however, has depended on the commitment of the country's military to Kemal's vision and its willingness to intervene when necessary to preserve both the Republic's democratic nature (in a state that previously had been governed by authoritarian regimes) and its secular status (in an overwhelmingly Muslim country).[10]

Inonu's last years in office were marked by a gradual willingness to accept the emergence of rival political parties (as opposed to the republic's previous era, in which only the Republican People's Party [RPP] was allowed to function). Ironically, in 1950 Inonu himself became a political casualty of his reluctant acceptance (mostly under Western pressure) of political opposition, when the first new party to organize—the Democratic Party—triumphed in Turkey's national elections that year and he choose to resign from the presidency in order to head the opposition in Parliament. Ten years later, the military that Kemal had kept out of Turkish domestic politics found it necessary to intervene in order to fulfill one of the two principal responsibilities that Kemal had assigned to it: to protect the reforming ideals of the secular, democratic republic.[11] Accordingly, citing the government's corruption and departure from the principles of Kemalism, in 1960 the Turkish army deposed the prime minister, ousted his party from office, and took control of the country's government. The following year it demonstrated *its* commitment to the principles of the republic by scheduling new elections and stepping aside. In the intervening period, though, the former prime minister was executed for his corrupt and despotic actions.

Another decade later, history repeated itself. A newly constituted party, with leaders less than democratically inspired in their corrupt administration of the state, was again misruling Turkey, and in 1971 the military responded to the mounting protests and violence by forcing the government's resignation and ordering new elections. Then, after yet another ten-year cycle, in 1980 the military directly intervened for the third and (to date) final time following another general decline of law and order throughout the country and an intensification of Kurdish separatist activity in the east. This time, as it departed, the military approved a new constitution for the country; it continues to serve as Turkey's basic document. It permits a multiparty system (although initially, pre-1980 parties were excluded from reorganizing on the grounds that they had collectively failed the ideals of Kemal Ataturk), and within that frame-work parties with Islamic roots began to form almost immediately after the military's withdrawal from power.

In 1995 one of these parties, the Islamic Welfare Party (Refah) for the first time gained more seats in the assembly than its rivals, and the military found itself confronted with a possible challenge to the state's secular nature. Although Necmettin Erbakan—Refah's leader, and hence the government's prime minister after those elections—repeatedly declared his adherence to the principles of the republic, in 1997 the army (which is designated as the guardian of the republic under the 1980 constitution) forced his resignation in favor of another civilian govern-ment by threatening more direct intervention. Subsequently, the military's leaders encouraged Turkey's state attorney to outlaw Refah on the basis of its alleged desire to impose Islamic law on the country. Erbakan himself—already in his seventies—was banned from further political activity for five years.

The Military, the EU, and Contemporary Turkish Politics

The military's ongoing role in Turkey's political process is constitu-tionally institutionalized in the country's National Security Council, which controls the agenda for important political issues, and whose ten seats are half filled by military commanders (the other five seats are held by the prime minister and four members of the cabinet). As part of its requirements for admitting Turkey, the EU wants the military's role there significantly reduced, regardless of how necessary Turkey's population may think the military is to preserving the secular nature of the state. And Turkey's military leaders are hardly the only Turks fearful of their government pushing the country in a less secular direction. Thus, when the prime minister sought to appoint a practicing Muslim to the country's presidency in the spring of 2007, tens of thousands of urbanized and well-educated Turks took to the streets in the capital, Istanbul, and elsewhere to protest his appointment. That created a tense situation, generating fear among Turkey's allies in the West that either the military would yet again intervene or that Turkey would, indeed, abandon its secular path.[12] The government itself defused the situation, however, by scheduling national elections earlier than required and giving the public the opportunity to approve or disapprove of the new president's appointment, in particular, and—more generally—the country's prior five years of governance by a party with Islamic ties but a secular agenda.

The prime minister's gamble was not a particularly wild one. From 1980 through 2007, despite the periodic outlawing of specific political organizations, parties with Islamic ties have remained at the heart of Turkey's elected political system. In 2007 the dominant one was the AKP—the Justice and Development Party—led by Recep Tayyip Erdogan, the former mayor of Istanbul and the country's prime minister following elections in 2002 and 2007. In 2007 his gamble on early elections paid off handsomely, with the election's outcome demonstrating that the Turks as a whole are as pragmatic as their Western counterparts when it comes to voting their pocketbooks. More specifically, in those early elections of the summer of 2007, Turkish voters focused on the five years of sustained economic growth (7.5 percent per year) under his party following the economic crisis that shook Turkey during the early years of the twenty-first century; the resultant doubling of per capita income; and the increase in foreign investment in Turkey that occurred under his, and his Islamic-connected party's, leadership.[13] When the final votes were counted, the governing party was returned to office with an impressive 46.7 percent of the vote and a sufficient majority in Parliament (341 of the 550 seats) to guarantee the election of its candidate for the presidency, Abdullah Gul, despite his status as a practicing Muslim. Nevertheless, Turkey's military continues to cast a large shadow over the daily workings of the republic's political process. Thus, even with the rousing electoral victory of Gul's party, which left the military no recourse but to accept his appointment to the country's presidency, the military was heavily represented at his swearing-in ceremony. Pointedly, the new president's wife and her controversial "urban chic" veil were not.

INTERNATIONAL POLITICS

The Cyprus Question Revisited

In today's Western world, Turkey is widely and justifiably well known in the region for its hospitality to foreigners, but its relationship with Cyprus strongly suggests that its hospitality must be a late-twentieth-century thing. Certainly there was little generosity shown to the Greek Cypriots after the Ottoman acquisition of Cyprus from Vienna in 1570. To the contrary, the Turks' first act upon arrival was the sacking of Nicosia, including its historic St. Sophia Cathedral, which the Ottomans converted to the Selimiye Mosque. It was an altogether rude introduction to Ottoman rule, which more recent Greek Cypriot experiences with the Republic of Turkey—including the 1974 occupation of northern Cyprus by Turkish forces—have done little to erase. To be sure, as the section on Cyprus notes, much has recently occurred to diminish the air of crisis involving that island; however, the Greek Cypriots have shown little enthusiasm for unification with the island's far poorer Turkish Cypriots, and Ankara's offer to open one of its airports and ports to traffic from the Republic of Cyprus in return for Nicosia doing the same for its Turkish minority has been routinely rejected by the island's (Greek Cypriot) government. Hence, Nicosia's political conflict with Ankara is apt to last as long as Turkish troops remain on Cyprus, and any conflict between Greek and Turkish Cypriots will continue to have an international dimension. Meanwhile, here too the EU has stirred the pot by making the withdrawal of those troops yet another condition for Turkey's admission to the European Union, even though the decision to withdraw those troops could have profoundly negative consequences inside Turkey for any government willing to do so. For the moment, concessions on Cyprus at the expense of the Turkish Cypriots remain a red flag for both Turkey's military and Turkish nationalists throughout the country.

Greco-Turkish Conflict and the Specter of Intra-NATO Warfare

Quite apart from their conflict over Cyprus, Greece and Turkey have had a long adversarial relationship. From 1469, when the Ottomans conquered southern Greece, until 1821, when the Greek war for independence began, the Ottomans fought the Venetians for control of Greece, won most of the time, seized Greek youth to be trained as the sultan's special forces, and enjoyed unchallenged control of the area during the last century of Ottoman rule. Then in the early twentieth century, the First Balkan War (1912–13) pitted Greece and its allies in the Balkan

League (Serbia, Bulgaria, and Montenegro) against the Ottomans and ended with—among other Ottoman losses—Greece gaining Macedonia from the Turks. Above all, as noted earlier, Turkey's 1919–22 war for independence was fought primarily against the Greek forces that had occupied Turkey after World War I.

More recently, these lines of animosity have been softened by acts of nature—and of human nature. The mutual devastation that both countries suffered as a result of earthquakes that struck the region in 1999 led to Athens and Ankara tendering assistance to one another. Likewise, their cooperative venture during the early years of twenty-first century in removing land mines previously sowed on Cyprus has been helpful in repairing previous political injuries, and the willingness of Greece to lift its objection to Turkey joining the EU (although it may be a meaningless gesture, given the number of other EU countries willing to delay or veto Turkey's admission) has made it significantly easier for Ankara to maintain friendly diplomatic relations with Greece only a decade after the ugly confrontation period that marked their relationship between 1996 and 1999. Similarly, Turkey's quick dispatch of a firefighting plane to combat the fires devastating Greece in the late summer of 2007, despite Turkey's continuing disagreements with Greece over the boundaries of their respective air spaces and the territorial waters in the Aegean Sea separating them, has made it easier for Athens to maintain cordial relations with Turkey. Cordiality, however, is a temporary state, and the building of a stronger foundation for good Greco-Turkish relations continues to await a lasting settlement of the Cyprus issue, which daily threatens that relationship. In the longer term, it may also await Turkey's admission to the European Union.

Joining Europe: EU Requirements as a Lose-Lose Conundrum

Objectively, the European Union needs Turkey and its large numbers of overwhelmingly secular and politically moderate Muslims as a counterweight to, and influence upon, the growing number of more radical Muslims in Western Europe's Islamic community.[14] Yet even though Turkey's entry into the EU is still perceived as a distant event, given an economic disparity between Turkey and other member states that is expected to require at least a decade to close, the numbers inside the EU opposed to Turkey's entry continue to mount. By mid-2007, countries in opposition included France, Germany, Austria, Denmark, the Netherlands, and Luxembourg, although several continued to pay lip service to Turkey's candidacy for EU membership. The opposition has been primarily mobilized in the form of (1) a general opposition to further EU enlargement and (2) a series of preconditions for Turkey to achieve membership, which have been far more strenuous than the EU has previously imposed on candidate countries and which will be politically difficult for the government in Ankara to implement. Nevertheless, the gist of the opposition consistently appears to be the fact that Turkey is an Islamic state, however secular it may be. If that is the principal reason, there is little that Turkey can do to make itself presentable to the EU, and the conditions remain onerous and potentially costly to any government trying to meet them. But there are other reasons for EU states to be wary of admitting Turkey, and there is continued skepticism toward its commitment to liberal democracy, even if that commitment has stretched across four generations since Kemal Ataturk's reforms.

Some of those other factors working against Turkey's EU candidacy are beyond Turkey's ability to control. Falling into this category, in particular, is the implication of foreign workers from Turkey in terrorist plots discovered inside EU states—for example, the planned attacks on the Frankfurt airport, the nearby United States air base, and popular tourist spots that were uncovered in Germany in September 2007. But Turkey itself continues to feed EU misgivings by such things as its unwillingness to acknowledge Ottoman responsibility for the massacre of perhaps a million Armenians between 1915 and 1923 (the Turks dispute the number and explain their deaths as wartime casualties) and its role in postponing a UN exhibit on the 1994 genocide in Rwanda because it contained a reference to the "murder" of Armenians in Turkey during World War I (the exhibit went on with the reference deleted). And Turkey continues to raise questions in European minds about its commitment to civil rights by such actions as (1) the decision of a Turkish court to block access to YouTube in Turkey because it contained clips that insulted Mustafa Kemal Ataturk; (2) the willingness of Prime Minister Erdogan in 2005 to sue a group of Turkish cartoonists who had criticized him in their work; (3) the threatened prosecution of one of the country's more acclaimed writers, Orhan Pamuk, for insulting the Turkish identity by referring in an interview for a Swiss newspaper to the taboo on talking about either the death of the Armenians in World War I or the Kurds who have died more recently in their struggle for autonomy; and (4) the prosecution of a Turkish author (Elif Sharfak), for "insulting Turkishness" in a novel that touched on the Armenia deaths (she was acquitted in 2005).

The other side of the coin is that Turkey needs to be in the European Union in order to anchor its secular nature and as a counterweight to the growth of radical, Middle East–focused Islam inside its borders. Turkey has been a member of virtually every other European and Western organization, including NATO and the Council of Europe, and it has participated in numerous Western peacekeeping operations, including Kosovo and Afghanistan. Yet the growing coolness among EU members to Turkey's eventual membership has produced a growing frustration and a stirring of anti-West nationalism inside Turkey that may eventually lead to a dangerous distancing of Ankara from Western Europe in general, and from the Brussels-headquartered European Union organization in particular. Those feelings have more recently combined with the anti-Western feelings generated in Turkey by the United States–led war in Iraq to give additional encouragement to Turkey's Islamic extremists in their violent campaign against the country's secular government.

RELIGIOUS EXTREMISM

Political Violence and Iraq's Kurdish Problem

In addition to southeastern Turkey, the Kurds are strung across a series of Middle Eastern countries, most importantly Iraq, Iran, and Syria. A thorough examination of their role in making those states perennial Middle East hot spots is properly left to the volume in this series treating the Middle East. At the same time, Turkey's Kurds—20 percent of the country's population—do not live only in the southeastern, Asian corner of the country. Rather, they are strung across Anatolia, with approximately half of its 16 to 18 million Kurds living outside of the predominantly Kurdish region of southeastern Turkey. Insofar as a militant portion of these broadly dispersed Kurds have been responsible for lethal terrorist attacks in Istanbul (western Turkey) and elsewhere well removed from their region of origin, they thus constitute a threat to the political order in Turkey quite apart from the secessionist movement centered in Turkey's Kurdish east and south.

The Kurds' story, in a nutshell, is one of being continually denied self-determination, both across Kurdistan and in the individual countries where Kurds reside. Yet despite those geographical divisions and the internal linguistic, tribal, and ideological cleavages within Kurdistan, the Kurds have possessed a well-developed sense of national identity since the latter part of the nineteenth century. That identity draws with pride on such major Kurdish historical figures as the great thirteenth-century Islamic warrior Saladin, and on such important historical moments as Sultan Abdulhamid II's decision in 1891 to create a separate Kurdish cavalry to protect the Ottoman Empire. Numbering more than 25 million in all, more than half of whom live inside Turkey, the Kurds constitute the oldest and at least one of the largest national communities in the contemporary world without a state of their own.

At the time of World War I, that state of affairs was not intended. Despite the fact that the Kurds fought bravely on the side of the Ottoman Empire, Point 12 of President Woodrow Wilson's 14 points was that minorities inside the Ottoman Empire were to be given the right of autonomous development. That commitment to Kurdish national self-determination progressed as far as the stillborn 1920 Treaty of Sevres, which was signed by the last sultan of the Ottoman Empire and provided for Kurdish autonomy in postwar Turkey. That commitment died with the Ottoman Empire following Turkey's successful 1920–22 war for independence (ironically with the Kurds supporting Kemal in his struggle against a sultanate propped up by outsiders), and the 1923 Treaty of Lausanne, which Kemal subsequently signed and which established Turkey's contemporary borders, and ignored Turkey's Kurds and the promises formerly made to them by World War I's victors.

Feeling betrayed, Turkey's Kurds began their rebellion against the Ankara government's control over their affairs almost immediately after the Treaty of Lausanne was signed, and for the most part, they have been rebelling for autonomy in one form or another ever since—invariably with the same outcome. Thus, prior to World War II Ankara faced, and crushed, three major rebellions: that of Sheikh Said, the leader of the dervish Islamic sect in Turkey, which began in 1925 and ended with Said's hanging; the 1930 uprising instigated by *Khoyboun* (Independence), a transnational Kurdish party founded in 1929 in Lebanon, which was completely crushed with Iranian assistance; and the 1936–38 rebellion led by Sheik Sayyid Rida, which ended with a similar, complete defeat of the Kurdish forces.[15]

For the next half century, discontent continued in Kurdistan, and Turkey was no exception; however, the center of the Kurdish struggle for a homeland shifted elsewhere. The initial front was Iran, the country with the second-largest number of Kurds in the Middle East. There, the short-lived Mahabad Republic of Kurdistan was proclaimed in 1946, only to be quickly erased and to have its leader hanged the following year by the government in Teheran. Thereafter, the epicenter of the Kurdish struggle shifted to Iraq, where the area's third-largest concentration of Kurds launched a war for autonomy against Iraq's government. Using Iran's neighboring Kurdish region as a sanctuary in which to regroup periodically, Iraq's Kurds were able to prolong the conflict until, in return for territorial concessions from Baghdad, the Iranian government sealed its border. Consequently, by the mid-1970s Baghdad was able to subdue the rebellion by its Kurds, albeit only temporarily. The movement for autonomy flared up again during Iraq's decade-long war with

Iran (1979–89), during which the government in Baghdad conducted a genocidal campaign against Iraqi Kurds, and again during the Gulf War (1990–91) following Iraq's invasion of Kuwait in the late summer of 1990. In both instances Baghdad ruthlessly repressed its Kurdish minority. In the aftermath of the Gulf War, however, the Iraqi Kurds acquired a significant amount of international protection for more than a decade and were able to achieve a degree of freedom from Baghdad's control—a de facto autonomy that substantially widened in the civil war–torn Iraq that followed the toppling of Saddam Hussein's regime by the United States–led coalition in 2003.

Kurdish Nationalism and Contemporary Political Violence in Turkey

In the meantime, the struggle for autonomy had flared up again in Kurdish Turkey and had evolved by the mid-1980s into a long-term insurgency against Turkey's government in Ankara. The struggle began in 1979 when Abdullah (Apo) Ocalan founded the Workers Party of Kurdistan (the *Partiya Karkaren Kurdistan,* or PKK), at that time a nominally legal movement to secure Kurdish rights. Following the military's 1980 coup against Turkey's elected government, however, the PKK was outlawed and considerably weakened as an organization by the arrest of more than a thousand of its members and the execution of many of its principal strategists—but not Ocalan. In 1983 he transformed the party into an underground organization dedicated to a guerrilla warfare campaign against the Turkish army in Turkish Kurdistan. Even the arrest of Ocalan in 1999 did not halt such activity by the PKK, whose campaign for Kurdish independence had by 2000 led to the destruction of thousands of Kurdish villages caught in the crossfire between Turkey's security forces and the PKK's guerillas, as well as the death of 40,000 or more people and the dislocation of as many as 2 million of the country's Kurds.[16]

The most recent development has been the spread of political violence into other parts of Turkey, including its European areas. The chosen means have featured suicide bombings and other clandestine terrorist tactics, and in this era of growing political violence the PKK has been joined by other, albeit smaller Kurdish separatist groups such as the Kurdistan Freedom Falcons (TAC), some of whom (mostly those composed of Kurdish Sunnis) are viewed as Kurdish wings of the Hezbollah organization that is partially funded by Iran. Consequently, in addition to a significant number of often violent skirmishes between Kurdish nationalists and Turkish authorities in southeastern Turkey and in the border areas between Kurdish Iraq and Kurdish Turkey, by mid-decade the Turkish government was having to cope with a number of terrorist events. Bombs killed dozens in Istanbul's tourist-laden old town in April 2006; gunmen invaded Turkey's highest court in Ankara, killing one judge and injuring four others in May 2006; and the TAC launched bombing attacks on Turkish resorts and again in Istanbul in August–September 2006. Subsequently, a May 2007 bomb attack in Ankara killed a half-dozen people and injured hundreds, an explosion rocked a Western fast-food chain in Istanbul the following month, and a percussion bomb was detonated in the parking lot of a local government building in Istanbul in July 2007.

At present, relations between Ankara and the country's Kurdish nationals are tense, and they are likely to remain so—or become even more precarious—because of two external variables complicating the picture: political developments in adjacent Iraq, and the EU's monitoring of how Turkey treats its Kurdish minority. Of the two, the first is the immediate concern of Ankara. The PKK and Iraqi Kurdish organizations have not always behaved as brothers—in fact, the PKK fought a brief war with one of them in northern Iraq because of the support that it was then giving Turkey in its war against the PKK. Since the United States occupation of Iraq, however, the PKK has again been able to establish a working sanctuary in the Kurdish portion of that country. Hence, four years after the fall of Saddam Hussein's regime in 2003, approximately 4,000 PKK guerrillas were reputedly operating from the mountainous areas in northern Iraq and crossing the border to lay roadside bombs, snipe at, and otherwise attack the nearly quarter-million Turkish troops deployed on Turkey's side of the border. In the resulting tension, Ankara has frequently refused to engage in diplomatic talks with the leaders of Iraqi Kurdish parties and has repeatedly urged Washington to eliminate the Turkish separatists' sanctuaries in Iraq. Otherwise, Ankara has made it clear, it will undertake the cross-border incursions necessary to eliminate those bases, even at the risk of having to fight the paramilitaries of those Kurdish Iraqi parties that the United States has backed since occupying Iraq.[17]

Nor is the sanctuary issue the only dimension of Turkey's Kurdish problem likely to ignite an international crisis. At some future point an independent or federally autonomous Kurdish state is expected to emerge in northern Iraq with control over the oil field located in that sector of the country. The specter of that Kurdish state's government using part of the revenue generated by that field to fund a war for independence in Kurdish Turkey, in the name of supporting the Kurds' long struggle for an independent Kurdistan, is a thing of nightmares to the Republic of Turkey's government in Ankara.

Meanwhile, Ankara also has to juggle its desire to fulfill Ataturk's dream of a secular, Western-oriented Turkey that is very much a part of democratic Europe by steering the country into the European Union with the rights-infringing security measures that it considers necessary to control Turkey's Kurdish separatists. Under EU pressure to respect its Kurds' civil liberties, Turkey's government has gradually expanded the rights of its Kurdish minority, including the right to educate its children in private Kurdish-language schools—although the capacity of free speech to incite rebellions has not been lost on Turkey's government. Consequently, the upsurge of terrorist activity throughout Turkey has resulted in the passage of anti-terrorist laws that are viewed with great suspicion by EU officials, who fear that they will be used to silence speech that legitimately airs the grievances of Turkish Kurds.

Religious Extremists, the Secular State, and the Growth of Political Violence

The trans-Turkish spread of political violence related to the Kurdish issue is not the only threat to public safety in contemporary Turkey. On the contrary, acts of politically motivated violence have occurred in several corridors during the early years of the twenty-first century.

To be sure, some of the most publicized of these acts can be dismissed as those of errant and perhaps unbalanced individuals, that is, the sort of political violence that can surface in even the most peaceful of societies. The bloody assassination of Swedish Prime Minister Olof Palme on the streets of central Stockholm in 1986 falls into this category, as does the 1981 attempt on President Ronald Reagan's life by a man apparently trying to gain the attention of the American movie star Jodie Foster, with whom he was obsessed. So, too, does the Turkish teenager's January 2007 assassination of the outspoken Armenian Turk who had urged Ankara to recognize Ottoman Turkey's genocide against Armenians. Less easily dismissed on this basis, however, is the emerging pattern of attacks on non-Muslim clerics in Turkey—the February 2006 murder of the Catholic priest suspected of paying Muslims to change their faith, for example. And after the execution by throat-cutting of three Bible-sellers in Turkey in April 2007, the government of Germany immediately attributed the crime to a climate of hostility toward Turkey's 1 percent Christian population, which Turkey's government has failed to dissipate.[18]

Most troubling of all has been the growth of suicide bombings in Istanbul and other popular tourist areas by anti-Western fundamentalists, some of whom have had ties with al Qaeda and who have constructed local logistical support networks among those who have recently moved to Turkey's urban centers from its more religiously devout countryside. Indeed, al Qaeda itself claimed credit for the November 13, 2003, suicide bombings near two Istanbul synagogues that killed 23 people and injured more than 300, and the nearly 70 people charged by the government of Turkey with conducting the attacks belonged to a Turkish cell of al Qaeda. The same group was also co-indicted eight days later for the suicide bombings in Istanbul of the British consulate and a major, British-based bank, with the loss of another 40 lives and injury to additional hundreds. Other blasts have followed in resort areas as well as in Ankara, and although most of these have been attributed to Kurdish groups, there remains little conviction among Turkish officials that all al Qaeda-affiliated cells in Turkey have been eliminated. Indeed, it is widely believed that others will inevitably arise as a result of the disenchantment in Turkey with the United States–led war in Iraq.

Timeline

1,600 BC	600 years of Greek influence begins in Cyprus.
700 BC	Cyprus becomes part of Mediterranean struggle for power; at various times during next 650 years falls under Assyrian, Egyptian, and Persian control.
129 BC	Anatolia becomes the Roman province of Asia.
58 BC	Cyprus becomes part of the Roman Empire and later the East Roman (Byzantine) Empire.
330 AD	Under Emperor Constantine, Constantinople becomes capital of Byzantine Empire.
600s	Kurds adopt Islamic faith.
1055	Turks from Central Asia conquer Baghdad; later defeated by Byzantine army in eastern Turkey.
1281	Osman I comes to power and begins campaign against Byzantines.
1290	Ottoman Empire begins under Osman's sultanate; by 1361 Ottomans have crossed into Europe.
1389	Ottoman Turks defeat Serbian Empire in Battle of Kosovo and expand rule in Balkans.
1453	Byzantine Empire ends as Constantinople falls to Ottoman Turks; three years later Islam's march into Christian Europe is slowed by Hungarians at Battle of Belgrade.
1517	Cairo conquered by Ottomans; caliphate taken to Istanbul (formerly Constantinople).
1570–71	Turks declare war on Venice for control of Cyprus, invade island, and sack Nicosia.
1820s	Greek war for independence frees Greece of Ottoman rule.

1878	Cyprus passes to Britain in return for Britain's promise to aid Turkey should Czarist Russia attack the Ottoman Empire.
1908	First Young Turk uprising by Ottoman army and navy officers revolting against despotic sultan.
1912	First Balkan War erases Ottoman holdings in Balkans, producing second Young Turk revolt in 1913.
1914	Britain formally annexes Cyprus; World War I begins, with Kurds supporting Ottomans.
1918	World War I ends with the Ottoman Empire on the losing side. In aftermath, Ottomans lose Middle East possessions, as well as holdings in Europe; foreign armies occupy Turkey.
1919	Mustafa Kemal (later Kemal Ataturk) launches struggle for an independent Turkey.
1919–22	Turkey wages war for independence, mainly against occupying Greek forces; after the war, Greeks are expelled from Turkey and Kurds are suppressed, even though they supported Kemal during the war.
1920	Treaty of Sevres, signed by sultan in Istanbul but rejected by Kemal's "government" in Ankara, promised Kurds autonomy.
1922	Ottoman Empire formally ends as National Assembly abolishes sultanate.
1923	Kemal selected by National Assembly as president; Republic of Turkey proclaimed, with Ankara the capital; Turkey renounces any future claim to Cyprus in Treaty of Lausanne.
1924–29	Modern, secular Turkish state (Kemalism) emerges in Turkey.
1925	Cyprus becomes British Crown colony; Turkey crushes Kurd rebellion.
1930–37	Turkey's Kurds react to oppressive laws in a series of revolts, all harshly suppressed.
1934	Turkey denies citizenship to its large gypsy community; a major Roma exodus follows.
1946–47	Cold War begins with Soviet support of Communists in Greek civil war and pressure on Turkey for control of Dardanelles; Turkey repays West for its support by sending troops to Korea.
1955	In response to looting and arson attacks conducted by Greek mobs in Istanbul, Turkey

	launches a pogrom that effectively eliminates the city's Greek community.
1960	May: Turkish military ousts the civilian government in Ankara, citing corruption and departure from principles of Kemalism. August: Cyprus achieves independence under terms of three treaties negotiated in 1959; Turkey, Greece, and Britain are made guarantors of its independence.
1963	November–December: President Makarios of Cyprus proposes a constitutional change that would effectively exclude Turkish Cypriots from political power; resultant communal unrest prompts Britain to intervene to restore order and preempt intervention by Turkey or Greece.
1964	March: UN Security Council creates UN Peacekeeping Force in Cyprus to maintain order.
1967	Colonels' dictatorial rule begins in Greece.
1971	Turkish military responds to mounting violence in Turkey by forcing resignation of existing government and ordering new elections.
1974	July: Colonels propose *enosis*, the annexation of Cyprus by Greece, as answer to ethnic conflict in Cyprus; July 15: Makarios government in Cyprus overthrown by pro-*enosis* regime; Turkey invades island to protect Turkish Cypriots; Colonels' regime falls in Greece.
1974–75	Turkey's invasion and military activity triggers massive, often forced migration of Greek Cypriots to the south, Turk Cypriots to island's north; de facto partition of Cyprus occurs.
1975	June 8: Turkish Cypriots vote to form separate federal state in north as step toward creating a biregional Federal Republic of Cyprus; remaining Greek Cypriots expelled from north of island.
1982	Turkey adopts current constitution with several provisions prejudicial to its Kurdish minority.
1983	November 15: Turkish Cypriot region declares itself independent Turkish Republic of Northern Cyprus (TRNC).
1984	Long-term Kurdish insurgency in Turkey led by Workers Party of Kurdistan (PKK) begins; Turkey diplomatically recognizes the TRNC's independence.

1989   Limited pullback of TRNC, Turkish, and Republic of Cyprus forces achieved.

1990   Cyprus peace talks collapse as result of Turkish demand for constitution recognizing minority's "right to self-determination."

1990s   Applications of Cyprus and Turkey for EU membership necessitate the settlement of ethnic conflict on Cyprus and offer encouragement it will be resolved.

1992   European Court of Justice prohibits export of many items from Turkish north to EU; Ankara launches major offensive against Kurds in northern Iraq.

1997   Under pressure from Turkish military, the government in Ankara resigns.

1999   Turkey captures the PKK's leader and sentences him to death; death sentence deferred when EU accepts Turkey as candidate for membership.

2001   European Court of Human Rights rules that Turkey violated Greek Cypriot rights in occupying Northern Cyprus in 1974; to make itself suitable for EU membership, Turkey abolishes death penalty and lifts ban on Kurdish education and broadcasting; additional reforms follow in 2003.

2003   Turkish Cypriots relax border restrictions; island's residents can cross boundary separating the two parts of the island for first time in nearly 30 years.

2004   In UN-sponsored peace initiative, citizens of the TRNC vote in favor of reunification, but plan fails when Greek Cypriots in south vote overwhelmingly against reunification; Greek Cyprus is nevertheless admitted to EU; bombings attributed to PKK rock Istanbul and eastern Turkey.

2005–06   Bombing attacks and other forms of political violence escalate in Turkey, and Islamic militants as well as PKK are now being blamed.

2007   In Nicosia, a portion of the wall separating the Greek and Turkish portions of the island's official capital is dismantled by the Cyprus government. Meanwhile, a political crisis in Turkey involving the secular nature of the state is averted by holding elections earlier than required.

Notes

1. The percentages are approximate and based on the island's population prior to Turkey's invasion of Cyprus in 1974, which was followed by the migration of a significant number of additional Turks to the island. What is definite is the fact that ethnicity, language, and religion reinforce one another in separating the island's two communities. The majority—77 percent of the CIA-estimated 900,000+ living on the island as of July 2007—are Greek ethnically and linguistically, and Greek Orthodox in religion; the minority is Turkish in language and ethnicity, Muslim in faith. For further reading on the politics on Cyprus and involving the island, see especially Joseph S. Joseph, *Cyprus: Ethnic Conflict and International Politics—From Independence to the Threshold of the European Union* (New York: St. Martin's Press, 1997), and a collection of multidisciplinary essays by Yiannis Papadakis, Nicos Peristianis, and Gisela Welzs, eds. *Modernity, History, and an Island in Conflict* (Bloomington: Indiana University Press, 2006). The CIA's data on Cyprus is available at the Central Intelligence Agency's "World Factbook" Website (www.cia.gov/library/publications/the-world-factbook/geos/cy.html).

2. Again, the numbers are estimates. In both instances, it has been in the interest of the respective communities to inflate the numbers of their people who were forced to relocate and to underestimate the numbers of the other community who fled their homes out of fear for their security. Some sources put the number of Greek Cypriots who were forced to leave the north as high as 200,000. Conversely, there is no disagreement as to the negligible numbers of minorities living north and south of the UN-patrolled cease-fire lines. By the 1990s, most commentators agree that there were fewer than 600 Greek Cypriots remaining in the Turkish-controlled north—where prior to 1974 the Greek Cypriots had constituted a slight majority of the population—and even fewer (under 100) Turkish Cypriots dwelling in the south.

3. Concerning the UN's efforts to resolve the conflict on the island prior to its entry into the European Union, see James Ker-Lindsay, *EU Accession and UN Peacekeeping in Cyprus* (New York: Palgrave-Macmillan, 2005), and Claire Palley, *An International Relations Debacle: The UN Secretary-General's Mission of Good Offices in Cyprus, 1999–2004* (Oxford, UK: Hart Publishing, 2005).

4. On the search for options since the south rejected the 2004 reunification plan, see International Crisis Group, "The Cyprus Stalemate: What Next?" (ICG Europe Report No. 171, March 8, 2006; www.crisisgroup.org).

5. The poll's results are reported in United Nations Peacekeeping Force in Cyprus, "The UN in Cyprus: An Inter-communal Survey of Public Opinion by UNIFCYP" (press release, April 24, 2007 (available at http://www.unficyp.org/Survey%202007/SurveyPressENG.doc).

6. On the continuing delicacy of the refugee issue, see Mustafa Aydin, "Crypto-Optimism in Turkish-Greek Relations: What Is Next?" *Journal of Southern Europe and the Balkans,* V.2 (August, 2003: 223–240).

7. "The UN in Cyprus: An Inter-communal Survey of Public Opinion by UNIFCYP" (press release, April 24, 2007), pp. 3–4.

8. Within Turkey's Muslim community, approximately 80 percent of the people are Sunni and the remainder are Shia, mostly concentrated in the country's 17 to 20 percent Kurdish minority.

9. On Turkey's modern history through the first three generations of the Republic of Turkey, see the recent translation by Dexter H. Mursaloglu of Sina Akcin, *Turkey From Empire to Revolutionary Republic: The Emergence of the Turkish Nation from 1789 to the Present* (Washington Square, NY: New York University Press, 2007). For an excellent analysis of more recent developments in Turkish society and politics, see especially M. Hakan Yavuz, ed. *The Emergence of a New Turkey: Democracy and the AK Party* (Salt Lake City: University of Utah Press, 2006).

10. The role of the Turkish military as the protector of the republic is well treated in Steven A. Cook, *Ruling But Not Governing: The Military and Political Development in Egypt, Algeria, and Turkey* (Baltimore: Johns Hopkins University Press, 2007).

11. The other major role that Kemal assigned to the military was to protect the country from outsiders.

12. As examples of the alarmism in Washington over the situation in Turkey, see Christopher Torchia, "Turkish Election a Struggle over Identity: Long Tradition of Secular Rule Seen in Jeopardy," *The Washington Post* (April 20, 2007), and the newspaper's editorial comment, "Turkey's Democracy Crisis: The 'Secular' Opposition and Military Try to Prevent the Free Election of a New President" (May 1, 2007).

13. See Hugh Pope, "Losing Turkey," *The Wall Street Journal* (August 20, 2007).

14. For an intensive analysis of Turkey's candidacy for EU membership and the obstacles to it, see International Crisis Group, "Turkey and Europe: The Way Ahead" (International Crisis Group Europe Report No. 184, August 17, 2007; www.crisisgroup.org). For a more extensive discussion of the same topic, see especially Burak Akcaper, *Turkey's New European Era: Foreign Policy on the Road to EU Membership* (Lanham, MD: Rowman & Littlefield Publishers, 2007), and Hacun Arikan, *Turkey and the EU: An Awkward Candidate for EU Membership?* (Aldershot, UK: Ashgate, 2006).

15. For an excellent, brief account of the Kurds' quest for autonomy in Turkey and neighboring states, see Michael M. Gunter, "The Middle East: The Kurds Struggle for 'Kurdistan'," in Joseph R. Rudolph Jr., ed. *Encyclopedia of Modern Ethnic Conflicts* (Westport, CT: Greenwood Press, 2003: 151–160).

16. Mir Zohair Husain, "Turkey Country Report" in *Islam and the Muslim World* (Dubuque, IA: McGraw-Hill Global Studies Series, 2006: 264–270, 268).

17. See, for example, the map-illustrated report by Ellen Knickmeyer, "Turkey to Warn Iraq on Rebel Sanctuaries: Cross-Border Attack on Separatists Appears Likely if Baghdad Fails to Act," *The Washington Post* (August 6, 2007).

18. One of the three murdered Bible distributors was a German national. For German Chancellor Angela Merkel's exact words, see Benjamin Harvey, "3 Bible-Sellers Slain in Turkey in Latest Attack on Christians," *The Washington Post* (April 19, 2007).

CHAPTER 3

THE BALKANS

It has often been said, both by diplomats assigned to the region and by historians studying it, that the Balkans has generated far too much history for its own good. Too many empires, old and more recent, have collided there. Too often yesterday's conqueror has become the newly conquered and oppressed. Its social landscape is an intermixture of numerous ethnic groups—Serbs, Croats, Montenegrins, Bosnian Muslims, Slovenes, Macedonians, Albanians, Turks, Hungarians, Romani, and others—each jealous of its own national heritage and resentful of the efforts of others to impose their cultures on them. Too often these and other old grievances have simmered until they exploded. In more remote periods, costly wars were spaced apart by generations and even centuries. In the twentieth century—the early years earmarked by the four Balkan wars that the Serbs fought between 1912 and 1918 and the end punctuated by the bloody civil wars that tore Yugoslavia apart—these conflicts became ever more frequent, closer in proximity, and ever-more severe in terms of the scars that they have left on the region.[1]

A Long History of Deep Divisions

National Identity and the Politics of State Making in the Balkans

The years and events that marked the last moments of Yugoslavia are far easier to chronicle than those that led to its emergence after World War I and shaped the history of the region even before that time. Nevertheless, three eras that span more than half a millennium stand out.

First, there was the fall of the ancient Serbian Empire at the hands of the Ottoman Turks in a series of decisive battles fought from near the end of the fourteenth until the middle of the fifteenth century. Collectively, the Ottoman victories opened the region's door to the spread of Islam and to the gradual entry of Albanians from the south. The Turks encouraged those Albanians to settle in the region in order to dilute the Serbian presence. As a consequence, by the time that the Kingdom of the Serbs, Croats, and Slovenes was formed after World War I, Serbia's Kosovo province—the birthplace of Serbian nationalism—already contained a large (but still a minority) Albanian community.[2] The results of those developments are still fueling Serbo-Albanian conflict in today's Kosovo.

For the remainder of the territory that would eventually become Yugoslavia, the more important period in the shaping of future events was the second era: the period of awakening modern nationalism within the Balkans' various ethnic communities during the mid- to late nineteenth century. Serbian nationalists, organizing against the region's continued rule by the Austro-Hungarian Empire, dreamed of recreating the ancient Serbian Empire in the form of a Greater Serbia. The Croatians and others also mobilized against their outside rulers, but they developed their own national identities and focused on achieving a self-rule of their own. Consequently, they were strenuously opposed to any future domination by the Serbs, with whom they shared a common history of outsider rule and—in the case of the Croats—a similar language.

Finally, there was the turbulent era surrounding World War I. Albania gained independence from Ottoman rule prior to the war, and the Kingdom of the Serbs, Croats, and Slovenes was born immediately afterward—on December 1, 1918. The reshaping process began shortly after Serbia and Montenegro gained independence from Ottoman rule in 1876, when Serbian nationalists started to agitate for the liberation of the other Serb-occupied lands under the rule of the Ottoman and Austro-Hungarian empires. Even before World War I, that quest had been partially fulfilled as a result of the intrigues and alliances enveloping the First Balkan War (October 1912 to May 1913)—which allied Serbia, Greece, and Bulgaria against Turkey and enabled Serbia to regain Kosovo and western Macedonia from the Ottomans—and the Second Balkan War (1913), in which Serbia and Montenegro joined forces with Greece and Turkey against Bulgaria, which had attacked its former allies in a dispute over the share of the Macedonian lands it was being offered.

Supercharged by Serbian gains in these wars, which nearly doubled the amount of land under Serbian control, Serbian nationalism next focused on Bosnia, which Austria had annexed in 1908. Caught up in the fervor,

Town square monument to the Serbian soldiers who fought in four wars between 1912 and 1918, in Kraljevo, Serbia.

a teenage Serbian nationalist in 1914 assassinated Austrian Archduke Franz Ferdinand in Sarajevo in the hope of ending Austria's control over that region. Instead, his act triggered the host of secret treaties of mutual assistance that produced World War I and—as a consequence of the defeat of the Austro-Hungarian and Ottoman Empires in that war—resulted in the end of outsider rule of the Balkans and the birth of the Kingdom of Serbs, Croats, and Slovenes.

The foundations for the new state were carved out during the war itself. Serb, Slovene, and Croat leaders agreed in July 1917 to create a democratic constitutional monarchy after World War I, and their agents abroad lobbied the allies to support that outcome. A National Council of Serbs, Slovenes, and Croats was duly formed to coordinate their efforts. When Austro-Hungarian rule over the Balkans collapsed in October 1918 and the war ended a month later, the Council became the region's de facto government, and efforts began to draft a constitution for the planned Kingdom. Before the issue of minority rights could be resolved, however, and despite the misgivings of the wartime victors who had blessed the union at Versailles, the process was hastily concluded. The catalytic factors were Italy—which had been promised large parts of Croatia in 1915 by the British, French, and Russians in return for its support in World War I—and its immediate postwar attack on Croatia's Dalmatia coast. On December 1, 1918, under the reign of Alexander Karadjordjevic (Alexander I of Yugoslavia), the union of the southern

Slavs declared its independence and began its short (1918–91) and trouble-filled life.

Inter-war Conflict, Wartime Duplicity, and the Escalation of Communal Tensions

The resultant state, united out of necessity, did not just lack a coherent identity. It was a statemaker's nightmare, containing nearly a score of different ethnic groups employing two different alphabets and five separate currencies, and linked together physically by a patchwork of four different-gauge railway systems.[3] What it did have was an over-all Serbian numerical majority, and during the 1920s the Croats' unease with their minority status quickly translated into political conflict with the Serbs over the shape of the state. The Croats favored creating a loose federation of states, each endowed with substantial autonomy under a constitutional monarchy. The Serbs preferred a highly centralized state under Belgrade's (and therefore Serbian) control. In 1929 the debate ended and tensions further escalated when King Alexander unilaterally ended the constitutional monarchy, abolished political parties, dismissed the legislative assembly, and essentially assumed dictatorial power over the state, which he renamed Yugoslavia ("Land of the Slavs"). That same year, not coincidentally, the Ustase, an extremist Croatian nationalist organization committed to Croatia's independence, was founded. Five years later, while he was vacationing out of country, King Alexander's reign ended violently at the hands of a Bulgarian assassin with Ustase ties. The state's subsequent search for stability in a federal framework ended a few years later, also violently, when Germany attacked Yugoslavia in June 1941 and subsequently occupied it.

Ironically, it was World War II that led the country created after World War I to its only period of political tranquility. Nevertheless, the gains came in a mixed package. On the one hand World War II significantly exacerbated Croatian-Serb and Serb-Albanian conflict, given the German strategy of granting aggrieved minorities a bogus autonomy in return for their support of the German occupiers. In the case of wartime Yugoslavia, the strategy was effectuated by creating puppet governments both in Croatia, with the Ustase's full cooperation, and in the province of Kosovo inside Serbia.[4] In turn, the anti-Serb collaborators in both areas frequently used the shield that Germany provided and the decision-making power that they were permitted to wield in order to settle old scores with the Serbs falling under their jurisdiction. Violence and score-settling affected Bosnia-Herzegovina as well, and by the time the war concluded an estimated one-tenth of Yugoslavia's pre–World War II population was dead (approximately 1.7 million people), half of whom died at the hands of their fellow Yugoslavs. But the war also produced a unifying hero who was able to give multinational Yugoslavia nearly two generations of postwar stability. He was Josip Broz, more popularly known by the code name, Tito, that he used while directing Yugoslavia's communist underground from Vienna in the early 1930s.

A Croat by birth, a blacksmith by training, and a rover in pre–World War I Europe, where among other things his wanderings led him to work as a test driver for Daimler in Austria, Tito found his calling in 1915 when he was sent to fight for the Austro-Hungarian Empire on the Russian front. It was there that he was captured, embraced communism, and joined the Russian Communist Party. Decades later, he was still serving Soviet Russia as one of the major leaders in Yugoslavia's outlawed Communist Party, albeit from Austria. When Germany attacked, occupied, and "dissolved" the post–World War I Yugoslav state, the Soviet Union named Tito the Secretary General of the Yugoslav Communist Party and commander of Yugoslavia's resistance forces fighting the German occupiers. Within three years, the extremely lethal Partisan forces under Tito's command had liberated the entire country, killing an estimated 800,000 German soldiers and another 200,000 to 350,000 collaborators, mostly Croatians, in the process. That accomplishment, coupled with his Croatian birth—which significantly neutralized the possibility of a backlash in Croatia over the casualty figures—made him a countrywide hero. By 1944 he was already fashioning a postwar communist regime for his country.

To Stalin's apparent surprise, it became evident after the war that Tito's vision of communist Yugoslavia did not involve subservient obedience to Moscow. On the other hand, when the break came and the independent communist state of Yugoslavia emerged in 1948, the ferocity of Tito's wartime campaign against the Germans must have weighed heavily in Moscow's decision to accept his move, even when he began to purge his pro-Soviet former associates from positions of influence. The Red Army, which consolidated its hold over Soviet-occupied Central Europe between 1945 and 1949 and which was still deployed in Vienna as late as 1955, was never poised to invade Yugoslavia.

Inside his country, Tito's answer to Yugoslavia's internal divisions was a federal system composed of six union republics (Serbia, Croatia, Slovenia, Bosnia-Herzegovina, Montenegro, and Macedonia). Except in multinational Bosnia-Herzegovina, one of the country's national communities constituted a majority in each of these republics, and hence had autonomous control over the wide area of governmental authority entrusted to the country's federal units (that is, the union republics). Holding the system together in the middle were (1) the monopolistic control of the Communist Party centered in Belgrade over government offices at all (local, state, and central) levels; (2) the fear of Soviet invasion should the country begin to disintegrate along the lines of its ethno-national divisions; and (3)—perhaps most important—the unifying presence of Tito. With Tito's death in 1980, that edifice began to erode as old tensions within the country resurfaced. Still, for another decade the country was held together by its communities' shared fear of Soviet intervention should it succumb to its internal centrifugal forces. But when communism itself began to liberalize and then collapse in the Soviet Union and Central Europe, the last of the glue holding the Federal Republic of Yugoslavia together began to give. Amid rising tensions between the Albanians and Serbs in Serbia's Kosovo province, and between the Serb-controlled central government in Belgrade and the increasingly independent and noncommunist governments in Slovenia and Croatia, in June 1991 Croatia and Slovenia declared their independence. In short order they were joined by the union republics of Macedonia and Bosnia-Herzegovina, with the latter soon lapsing into internal warfare among its Muslim, Serb, and Croatian communities as well as fighting a war for independence against Belgrade. Four years of often horrific communal civil war later, the Yugoslavia born of World War I was over—but not political conflict in the Balkans.

Civil Wars, Aftershocks, and the End of Yugoslavia

The Civil Wars in Slovenia, Croatia, and Bosnia

The 1991–1995 civil wars that destroyed the Yugoslav federation are largely explicable in both their duration and ferocity in terms of the percentage of Serbs dwelling in the respective seceding republics. The first and the shortest round of fighting occurred on the Slovenian front in northwestern Yugoslavia. Geographically remote from the heart of the ancient Serbian empire and with a population only 2.2 percent Serbian (approximately 42,000 Serbs), Slovenia hardly qualified as a part of Greater Serbia whose retention justified a long campaign. Once the Slovenian divisions in the Yugoslav army chose to support their homeland's independence, the fighting on the Slovenian front ended in a matter of weeks.[5]

The center of the conflict next shifted temporarily to Croatia. More than ten times as many Serbs resided there as in Slovenia (approximately 500,000 Serbs, slightly more than 11 percent of the Croat republic's population), and they had long demanded political autonomy for themselves in those areas of southern and eastern Croatia where they constituted a majority of the population. It was thus in Croatia that the Serb-dominated army of the government of the Federal Republic of Yugoslavia (FRY) in Belgrade launched its first major offensive, attacking and causing substantial damage to the ancient Roman town of

Dubrovnik along Croatia's Adriatic coastline during the winter of 1991–92. And it was in Croatia that the first real wartime atrocities were committed by the Belgrade-backed Serbian and Zagreb-backed Croatian paramilitary forces that quickly joined the fray. They continued to pursue their deadly activities of ethnic cleansing long after the warfare between the military units of the Yugoslav and Croatian governments essentially ended with the United Nations–imposed cease-fire in 1992. In fact, a decade after the wars in Bosnia and Croatia officially ended with the Dayton peace agreement in 1995, war criminals responsible for those acts were still being hunted and tried for their wartime activities.

Overall, however, the fiercest fighting, greatest atrocities, and highest fatalities occurred in Bosnia-Herzegovina, which was considered a part of Greater Serbia that was physically attached to Serbia's western border and possessed of an often ethnically intermingled population nearly one-third (32 percent) Serbian. The retention of Bosnia-Herzegovina was far more important to Belgrade than retaining Slovenia, Macedonia (which had peacefully separated at the same time Croatia, Slovenia, and Bosnia-Herzegovina declared their independence), or even Croatia. At the same time, as much as the Muslim and Croatian communities in Bosnia-Herzegovina held grievances against one another, they resented the treatment they had historically received at the hands of Belgrade even more. Consequently, once the war began in Bosnia following the February 1992 referendum on independence—in which an overall majority of Bosnian voters favored independence, despite the over-whelming vote against it by Bosnian Serbs—paramilitary units staging violent acts of ethnic cleansing, the use of rape as a tool of war, and other war crimes quickly multiplied on all sides.

By the time that the accumulated weight of these atrocities—including an attack by Serbian forces on three of the six "safe cities" that the UN had established as sanctuaries for the dispossessed—had become too heavy for the world to tolerate and NATO forces intervened to end the fighting there and lay the foundations for the settlement of the Yugoslav civil wars via the Dayton Peace Accord, approximately 200,000 had died in the fighting, another million had been displaced by the warfare, and each side had new and horrific grievances against the other that would take generations to fade.

Postwar Yugoslavia and the War in Kosovo

During the decade between Tito's death and the beginning of the civil wars in Slovenia, Croatia, and Bosnia, conflict also intensified between the government in Belgrade and the 90-percent Albanian Muslim popu-lation in Serbia's southern province of Kosovo. As in the case of the seceding republics, by the 1990s the lines of political conflict in Kosovo had been drawn in an essentially uncompromising manner between the Slobodan Milosevic government in Belgrade and the assorted clandestine Albanian organizations dedicated to Kosovo's independence. The latter had begun attacking Yugoslav police and security forces during the 1980s in an effort to liberate from Serbian rule the province that had been the birthplace of pan-Albanian nationalism during the nineteenth century. Their clashes escalated during the early 1990s while Belgrade was engaged in the struggle to retain Croatia and Bosnia, and it further intensified after Milosevic accepted Bosnia's independence by signing the Dayton Peace Accord.

Following the Dayton Accord, and no doubt inspired by NATO's eventual intervention on the side of Yugoslavia's seceding provinces, Kosovo's principal liberation organization, the Kosovo Liberation Army (KLA), basically adopted the strategy of intentionally provoking Belgrade into overreacting to its attacks on Serbian personnel in Kosovo, in the hope of attracting NATO support for its cause.[6] In 1999, the strategy paid off. With a growing number of Kosovo's ethnic Albanians pouring into neighboring Albania as refugees in order to avoid being caught in the crossfire between the KLA and the retaliatory activity of Serbian forces in Kosovo, and with rumors of Serbian atrocities in Kosovo circulating widely, Western diplomats demanded that Belgrade permit outside peacekeeping forces to enter the province to end the fighting and restructure Kosovo's status in Yugoslavia. When Milosevic refused, United States–led NATO units launched a seventy-eight-day air campaign against Yugoslav targets inside and outside of Kosovo in March 1999, forcing Belgrade to reconsider. That campaign, now referred to simply as "the war" by Kosovo Albanians, succeeded in achieving NATO's objective, but at the cost of further complicating the political situation and reducing the prospects for a peaceful resolution of the Albanian-Serbian conflict inside that troubled province.

Macedonia Is Infected: The Conflict Spreads

When Yugoslavia dissolved in 1991–92 with the secession of Slovenia, Croatia, and Bosnia-Herzegovina, its southernmost union republic, Macedonia, also declared itself independent. Unlike the other cases, however, its departure was entirely peaceful, largely for the same reason that explained the brevity of the warfare in Slovenia. Macedonia's Serbian population was minute (approximately 2 percent), and Belgrade had its hands full trying to prevent the secession of Croatia and Bosnia—both of which had substantial Serbian minorities, and parts of which clearly qualified as parts of the Greater Serbia that Serbian nationalism was committed to preserving.

With its sizable Albanian Muslim minority and its geographical location between Kosovo and Albania itself, Macedonia does, however, qualify as part of the Greater Albania that Albanian nationalists dreamt of when modern Albanian nationalism was born. Once rid of their Serbian controllers, it took the KLA little time to spread the gospel of pan-Albanian nationalism in Macedonia and stir up interethnic conflict in the semifertile soil of that adjacent, newly independent country.

The Balkans Today: Still Hot after All These Years

To summarize briefly, not only had four of Yugoslavia's six federal republics separated by the early twenty-first century to form independent countries with seats in the United Nations, but a fifth—Montenegro—was loosening its ties with Serbia to go in the same direction. It did so in mid-decade, when the Republic of Montenegro became the UN's 192nd member in late June 2006. In the meantime, neighboring areas as well were affected by Yugoslavia's various meltdowns—most dramatically Albania, the region's poorest country, which was already undergoing a turbulent transition from communism (sometimes by means of gangsterism) toward stable, noncommunist rule when flooded by Albanian refugees from the conflict in Kosovo.

Ironically, the war in Kosovo almost immediately resulted in Albanians being thrown a much-needed lifeline. Under communism, the Albanian government had done little to provide the country with much more than literacy, and the availability of state education ended when most children reached their low teens. A modern infrastructure of roadways and electrification facilities existed, but ox-drawn carts, standards of living based on meager earnings from agriculture, high unemployment (estimated at 40 percent in 1993), and family feuds and vendettas were the way of life for much of its 95-percent ethnic Albanian population. Even in the world of communism, moreover, Albania had become isolated in Europe because of its growing ties with China rather than Yugoslavia, whose government under Tito had helped Albania establish its own Communist system of government after World War II. Worse, political liberalization and the replacement of Albania's communist government by the Democratic Party under Dr. Sali Berisha in 1992 had led to financial turmoil by mid-decade. Then, despite the continuing flow of the limited foreign assistance upon which the economy was dependent, a pyramid-style economic policy caught up with the country. It not only left the government economically bankrupt, but also cost many of Albania's citizens their life savings and rendered the government politically bankrupt, as well. In fact, at the time of NATO's bombing campaign, substantial portions of Albanian territory had fallen under the de facto control of gangs, and law and order had become a major concern.

The arrival of large numbers of Kosovo Albanian refugees in 1999 helped Albania emerge from its economic crisis, as the large amounts (relative to Albania's economy) of Western funds that poured into the country in refugee relief efforts spilled over into the broader Albanian economy, providing jobs for Albanians in constructing the refugee camps and working for the internationals. More importantly, when the refugees left in mid-summer to return to Kosovo, Albania remained on Western radar screens. The United States and the European Union countries have subsequently continued to assist its economy, the latter with an eye to the very-long-term transition that will allow Albania to become an EU member. Thus, although the country remains small and poor (by 2006 CIA estimates, its approximately 3.6 million people had a per capita income of only $5,700, one of the lowest rates in Europe) and Albania remains on the crisis watch list of many international observers, it no longer seems likely to fail, become a haven for terrorists, or (and it never really did) foment or support an irredentist pan-Albanian movement.[7] Its economy has grown notably, as did its infrastructure in the early years of the twenty-first century. Its level of unemployment has been reduced to less than half its former rate, and in 2003 Albania had an orderly transfer of power from the governing party to an opposition party in an election that international monitors judged to be mostly free and fair. Even criminal activity has subsided, although Albania still functions in a diminished capacity in the region's notorious human trafficking trade, which is carried out along a route that runs northeastward from Albania through Kosovo, and into Bulgaria. In short, Albania remains a country that is very much in need of indirect but real help from the outside world to continue its orderly transition to stable democratic government; however, it is not a state where internal violence is likely to fall upon its citizens, or from which violence is likely to threaten the region around it.

Meanwhile, back in the former Yugoslavia, the settlement of the various conflicts has been slow and uneven across the region.[8] Slovenia remains the breakaway republic least affected by the wars, as well as the only one granted entry into the European Union thus far. It is also the most economically prosperous and politically stable republic, blessed by both its overwhelmingly (94 percent) Slovenian population and the postwar influx of tourists bearing hard currency. Consequently, despite the unfavorable publicity it has sometimes drawn to itself as a result of its hostility toward "darker skinned" immigrants (primarily the Romani) and its unwillingness to restore the rights of its Serb, Croatian, and Bosnian Muslim minorities that were lost in 1991 when Slovenia declared its independence and they were stripped of Slovenian citizenship, Slovenia also remains the component of the former Yugoslavia with the best post-conflict political and social history and brightest future outlook.[9] Indeed, given its geographical proximity to Western Europe and its remoteness from the center of the Balkans, as an independent state it is no longer included as even a part of the "Western Balkans" in many current maps of the region.

Croatia, too, has stabilized considerably since the death of its nationalist and authoritarian wartime leader, Franjo Tudman, in December 1999, four years after signing of the Dayton Accord officially ended the war in Bosnia and Croatia. On the other hand, like Bosnia and Kosovo, the Republic of Croatia has had to grapple not only with the problems associated with democratization (creating and permitting competitive political parties and combating political corruption, for example) and reconstituting its war-disrupted economy, but also with such divisive postwar issues as the trials of war criminals in all ethnic camps. That particular issue has periodically revived memories and inflamed passions throughout the region. In fact, the sluggishness of Croatia's government in arresting and prosecuting (or surrendering for prosecution in the International Criminal Court in the Hague) Croatian war criminals remained, nearly a decade after Tudman's death, one of the major stumbling blocks to Croatia's admission to the European Union.

Even Serbia, except for Kosovo, has become considerably more tranquil since protests in Belgrade led to the downfall of Milosevic's regime in Yugoslavia's 2000 federal elections and to the emergence of a more moderate government in Belgrade. At the same time, the transition to an orderly democracy has not been entirely smooth in the former Yugoslavia's most populous union republic (currently inhabited by approximately 10 million people). Neither Milosevic's surrender to stand trial for war crimes in 2001 nor his death by heart failure while on trial in The Hague ended the influence of ardent Serbian nationalists in Serbia's politics, and the transition to democracy was dealt a huge black eye when Serbia's moderate, post-Milosevic, pro-Western reformer, Prime Minister Zoran Djindjic, was assassinated by a sniper outside his government offices in March 2003.

In even mundane affairs, Serbia remains perhaps as much as a decade behind most of post-communist Europe in developing the behavior patterns expected of a liberal democracy. Five years after Milosevic's ouster, for example, it was still not unusual for Western guests in the Hotel Belgrade—the large hotel near the China Embassy, both of which were bombed during NATO's air war with Yugoslavia over access to Kosovo—to be awakened during the night by "repairmen" checking their room . . . and who is sleeping in their beds. On the other hand, there have been exceedingly few physical attacks against Americans and other Westerners in Serbia since that bombing campaign. Likewise, despite an economy still suffering from Milosevic's mismanagement; a UN-imposed embargo of Yugoslavia that ended only with Milosevic's departure from office; and the added economic burden of housing tens of thousands of Serbian refugees from Kosovo since 1999 (Serbia's unemployment rate was approximately 30 percent in 2006), the process of change to a marketplace economy has been proceeding recently in an orderly fashion. Politically, though, matters remain more problematic. Although Djindjic's assassination was immediately put to positive advantage by the post-Milosevic government, which used it to justify a major sweep-and-arrest operation against criminal elements and antidemocratic political dissidents accused of being involved in or providing assistance to those who were plotting to overturn the country's democratically elected government, the political trajectory has subsequently taken a decidedly nationalistic turn. In a country still mired in complex issues born of the loss of so much of the Yugoslav state in the 1990s, recent political developments have involved increasing support for its nationalist and ultra-nationalist parties, the electorate's approval of a new constitution that continues to treat Kosovo as an integral part of Serbia, and government leaders who have periodically given diplomatic support to threats by Bosnia's Serbs to secede from Bosnia-Herzegovina and merge with Serbia.[10] Moreover, Serbia has been criticized even more than Croatia for its lack of cooperation in apprehending wanted (Serbian) war criminals being sought for their actions in the wars in Bosnia and Kosovo, and—as in the case of Croatia—the war criminal issue has long held up discussions on bringing Serbia into the European Union.

Recovery has been slower still, as well as being laced with acrimony and periodic outbursts of violence, in Bosnia-Herzegovina and Kosovo, both of which were more deeply affected by wartime destruction and neither of which has a tourist industry to fall back on—unlike Croatia, which has cultivated tourism along its historic coastline, and Slovenia. Unemployment remains very high in both Bosnia and Kosovo, and the issue of resettling the refugees driven from their homes by the ethnic cleansing campaigns that accompanied the wars in Bosnia, Croatia, and Kosovo has been disruptive, especially in Kosovo. Macedonia, too, has continued to struggle since fallout from the war in Kosovo destabilized Macedonian-Albanian relations there. Thus, although Slovenia and Croatia have cooled off considerably since the wars ended there, and

Montenegro (32 percent Serbian)—despite the closeness of the vote in the referendum it held on the matter—appears to have made an utterly peaceful separation from Serbia since its citizens voted in favor of independence in 2006,[11] other areas are far less tranquil. Bosnia-Herzegovina, still under international tutelage; Macedonia, with its insecure border with Kosovo and internal communal conflict; and especially Kosovo remain hot spots in a Balkan region that has known little peace in the past century. Indeed, it remains not only restless, but also well armed, its recent conflicts having left distributed throughout the Balkans not only millions of buried antipersonnel mines, but also an above-ground arsenal estimated to include some 280,000 Kalashnikov rifles, 1 million antitank missiles, more than 3 million hand grenades, 24 million machine guns, and a billion rounds of ammunition.[12]

THE REPUBLIC OF BOSNIA-HERZEGOVINA

Bosnia-Herzegovina was the crossroads of the former Yugoslavia. It was the union republic where no ethno-national community constituted a majority, and where the Serbs to the east and south and the Croats to the west and north converged and mingled with the state's Muslim plurality (now known as Bosniaks), themselves mostly traceable to Croats and Serbs who embraced the Islamic faith during a much earlier era. It was also the republic whose people were most likely to identify themselves as "Yugoslavs," rather than as Croats, Serbs, Slovenes, and so on, and before the civil war there were large portions of its territory in which its national communities intermingled. Its capital, Sarajevo, was even toasted by the world as a symbol of multicultural harmony when it hosted the Winter Olympics during the 1980s. Then came the war; the relocation of Bosnia-Herzegovina's people as either refugees abroad or as separate national enclaves in the newly independent country; and the efforts of Sarajevo's by then overwhelmingly Muslim population to rebuild the republic's national library, to rebuild their city, and to rebuild their lives.

More than a decade after the 1995 Dayton Accord ended the war in Bosnia-Herzegovina and set that country on the road to independence, the country still remained under international supervision. Violence had receded, most refugees had returned, and Sarajevo itself had been largely rebuilt. The bridges no longer lay in the riverbed, the city's famous Muslim market was again filled with shoppers and tourists, and modern high-rise buildings had been newly erected. Yet, a melancholy left over from the war still remained in the city. Just as people sometimes never get over a great tragedy in their lives, Sarajevo seemed to argue that the same can be true for cities, as well. It was not just the shelled out and gutted buildings that continued to checkerboard the once-pristine capital of Bosnia-Herzegovina, but also a heavy mood of something lost. Sarajevo was once a city of theater and symphony orchestras, of international film festivals and other European events, and to an extent it has become that again. But it is no longer that poster child city of interethnic harmony that Sarajevo once showed to the world. That city disappeared sometime in 1992, and what remains of its population still seems to be in collective mourning for its loss. Certainly the bounce and life that are part of the soul of capitals around the world are missing to a degree, even in the midst of the gaiety surrounding Sarajevo's renewed, annual European film festival, and the likelihood that they will be revived remains at least an unborn generation away.

Melancholy for what once was, of course, does not a hot spot make, but neither does it make for the type of healing a country needs to put behind it, gradually but steadily, the memories of a bloody communal war in which Croats and Muslims and Serbs began to kill their neighbors because of the color of their eyes, while all of Bosnia plunged into a war so filled with massacres, use of rape as a tool of war, and ugly acts of ethnic cleansing that it led not only to the creation of a war crimes tribunal in the Hague to try the worst offenders in all communities, but also to the establishment of a permanent war crimes tribunal there as a deterrent to future ethnic cleansers. Meanwhile, back in Bosnia, the effort to construct a democratic, multinational government was launched in 1996 under international tutelage, with international officials controlling Bosnia's pace toward full self-government, even though it retained the United Nations seat that it was granted as a breakaway republic in 1992. Among the principal charges given to Bosnia's international overseers, none have been more important than (1) vouchsafing the rights of the minorities spread out in the regions of the country where its various national communities now constitute majorities, and (2) repatriating those who were driven from their homes as refugees into exile abroad, or those relocated as internally displaced people in other parts of the country during that conflict. The return of those refugees, however, continues to be a slow process and a hot-button issue in Bosnia-Herzegovina, as it is in the Balkans in general, and flashpoints continue to exist throughout the country. In communities that still stare at one another across bridges that are like international frontiers (Mostar), the refugees' return is reviving old memories and perhaps changing the mathematics of governmental power at the local level. Hence, Bosnia-Herzegovina remains very much a hot spot, with political conflict a given across its communal lines and the prospect of political violence a real possibility, especially after the departure of the last remnants of the international peacekeeping force deployed in the country to establish and maintain a peace pursuant to the Dayton Accord. On the other hand, as a result of international efforts Bosnia-Herzegovina it is both physically and emotionally far removed from the republic that existed when the war ended.

STATE AND PEACE BUILDING

Of all the small towns in what is now the Federal Republic of Bosnia-Herzegovina, none better illustrates the contentiousness and early passions of the Bosnian Civil War than Brzko. It is the first town you reach after entering Bosnia-Herzegovina from what is now Croatia, and—if you turn south toward the Croat and Muslim parts of Bosnia along the main roadway, which occupying NATO forces dubbed the Arizona Highway immediately after the war—it is the last town you leave in the Serb Republic's (SR) half of the federation. After crossing the bridge separating Bosnia from Croatia, which years after the war ended had a NATO tank stationed at its midpoint to guarantee the peace, you enter Brzko, and the captivating sight at the town's entrance is a large open space. Before the war, an historic Islamic mosque stood there, but scarcely had the war begun than its worshipers were driven from Brzko. The mosque was torn down and removed to the last stone as an insurance policy that the Muslims would not return. Two years after Dayton the town was again in the news when, attacked by rock-throwing Serbian nationalists embedded behind the aged men and women in the front lines of a local protest, the NATO forces withdrew and left exposed the unarmed International Police Task Force (IPTF) that was quartered in the region and charged with training a Bosnian constabulary. The protest turned into a riot, the riot torched more than thirty IPTF vehicles, and by the time the rioting was over it had not only proved to be a measure of the intensity of the hostile feelings still present among the Serbs left in the federation with a Croat and Muslim majority, but it had also left behind a torn relationship between NATO and the IPTF that never fully mended.

Today Muslims are living again, if perhaps uneasily, in Brzko's environs, one testimony to the qualified success of the international peace effort in creating an environment less saturated with fear in the Republic of Bosnia-Herzegovina (BiH). Other signs exist. In something of a quid pro quo for permitting Muslims to return safely to the Serbian parts of the Republic, Serbs have been allowed to return peacefully to now predominantly Muslim Sarajevo, which they vacated during the war when Serbian paramilitaries and regulars turned its main street into a sniper's alley and periodically shelled the city and its outlying areas.

The changing status of the military force that was deployed after the Dayton Accord, under NATO leadership, to prevent the war from flaring up again is another sign of the progress that has been made since the war ended. Initially constituted as an interventional, peace-enforcing contingent of more than 60,000 soldiers anchored by approximately 20,000 U.S. troops (IFOR), within two years the force had shifted its mission to peace-keeping and stabilization (SFOR), and its ranks began to diminish. In the early years of the twenty-first century it was reconstituted again into something of an SFOR-junior, with National Guard units replacing the regular army in the U.S. forces and their equivalent filling the ranks of the units sent by other members of NATO. Then, in 2005, NATO turned the mission over to the European Union (EU), which now maintains a small unit of peacekeepers that are primarily seen not in Humvees with machine guns mounted, as in the past, but in jeeps with EU flags. As often as not they can be seen parked in front of cafes, while their personnel from Italy, France, and other EU states sip espresso.

Elsewhere, at approximately the same time that NATO forces were being replaced by the EU contingent, the holding of elections was taken from the hands of international organizations and placed completely in the hands of Bosnia-Herzegovina's local election boards. A few years later, on the reasoning that they might represent a threat to the future of the republic because of their possible ties to international terrorist organizations and the alleged complicity of some in helping *al Qaeda* operatives obtain money, shelter, and false documents, the Muslim volunteers from outside states who came to BiH to fight alongside its Muslims were "invited" to leave the country in 2007.[13] Thus, while intercommunal tensions still exist, the prospect of a return to an all-out ethnic civil war has all but evaporated in the new republic.

In short, Bosnia-Herzegovina has become a more peaceful place, and in that sense it is something of an international success story, certainly so in respect to the failure of international efforts to create a durable, multiethnic peace in Kosovo following the 1999 war involving NATO peace-making in that contentious province of Serbia. But the country is not the political system that the international community envisioned emerging in Bosnia under the Dayton Accord, and at times the relationships between the country's major national communities still take dark and potentially dangerous turns.

The Dayton Accord and State Building in Bosnia-Herzegovina

The Dayton Accord was not just a peace settlement hammered out between the affected parties—Alija Izetbegovic, the acting Muslim president of the breakaway republic of Bosnia-Herzegovina: Franjo Tudman, the president of Croatia; and Slobodan Milosevic, representing Serbian interests in Bosnia in place of the Bosnian Serb leader who was under indictment for war crimes—who gathered under the guidance and pressure of American diplomats at Wright Patterson Air Force Base outside Dayton, Ohio, in November 1995. As subsequently ratified in Paris in the spring of the following year, it was an outline for the creation of a multinational democratic state in Bosnia-Herzegovina, the epicenter of the Yugoslav civil wars and the atrocities associated with it.[14]

A Settlement of Compromises

As a negotiated peace settlement the Dayton Accord contained the inevitable tradeoffs. The two most important ones involved the issue of refugee return and the future status of the *Republiika Srpska* (Serb Republic, or SR) located on Bosnia-Herzegovina's border with the residue of the Federal Republic of Yugoslavia, Serbia, and Montenegro. Given the emphasis in the Accord on establishing viable local governments as well as government at the regional level and in the center (Sarajevo), the repatriation of the hundreds of thousands of Serbs, Croats, and Bosniaks who had fled their homes during the war was a particularly thorny issue. As a result of their flight, large portions of the new state *had* been ethnically cleansed during the war and were essentially devoid of minority communities. Repatriation of the country's internally displaced persons and international refugees thus threatened the "inheritor" communities' control over local government, and hence was vigorously opposed at Dayton by both Tudman and Milosevic. In the final text, however, the right of Bosnia's displaced people to return was recognized without qualification, coupled with provisions recognizing as well the rights of minorities throughout the new republic.

The issue of the SR's future status was equally sensitive, and also forced those at Dayton to confront the still-bleeding wounds of the war in general, and the conflict between Bosnia's Serbian and Muslim communities in particular. Four months after the Federal Republic of Yugoslavia began to unravel in June 1991, with the secession of its Slovene- and Croatian-majority components, Bosnia's Serbian leaders unilaterally created a separate assembly for Bosnia-Herzegovina's Serbs and scheduled an end-of-the year referendum on whether they should separate from Bosnia and merge with Serbia and Montenegro. The proposal was overwhelmingly approved, and in January 1992, as Bosnia-Herzegovina's Muslim and Croat leaders were moving toward secession from the FRY, a rump Serb Assembly was convened in Banja Luka. That assembly's leader was Radovan Karadzic, a man who would subsequently become one of the former Yugoslavia's most hunted war criminals for his role in the murderous ethnic cleansing of Bosnia's Muslims from their homeland during the war.

After seceding from the FYI and gaining international recognition, one of the first acts of Bosnia-Herzegovina's leaders was to repudiate the Serbian referendum and declare the SR's secession invalid. Still, the SR functioned throughout the civil war in Bosnia, and although Milosevic was forced to deny its legitimacy as well as acknowledge the independence of Bosnia-Herzegovina in the Dayton Accord, its existence could not be denied if Bosnia-Herzegovina was to embark on the road to a lasting peace. Accordingly, as another part of the process of bestowing autonomy on various levels of government, the peacemakers at Dayton fashioned a two-unit federal system for the BiH, with significant degrees of federal autonomy to be bestowed on each of its federal entities: the SR and the remainder of the country, which was itself a federation of its territorialized Croat and Bosniak components. Even without the SR issue, however, it is doubtful that the BiH's postwar constitution would have embodied a unitary design. Croats and Bosnian Muslims had also fought one another and committed atrocities against one another during the war, and the country's Croatian leaders had little interest in a design that would have put the BiH's Croat provinces under the control of a strong, centralized government in Sarajevo. Such an arrangement would have given the country's approximately 40 percent Bosniak plurality (now nearly 48 percent) considerable leverage in policy making, and the country's 20-percent Croat community (now less than 15 percent) would have been even more in the minority than its Serbs.[15]

State-Building: Designing an Evolving Democracy

As a basis for state making, the federal design chosen at Dayton was only one piece of the elaborate machinery that was to be constructed in the republic to steer it toward complete independence, eventually, under a more centralized structure in which its communities would collaborate in policy making at the center. The key term, in the short term, was "supervised independence." The international recognition that Bosnia-Herzegovina had received during the war, which usually connotes an admission by the international community of a state's sovereignty, was suspended at Dayton in favor of a tutelage system, under which the new republic would be penetrated by several international actors and placed under their preeminent authority. The NATO military force that had been deployed to enforce the Dayton Accord was to remain for an indefinite period to keep the peace. It was to be augmented by a police force (the International Police Task Force, or IPTF) composed of police officers drawn from a number of Western countries, whose charge it would be to assist in the development of a professional, multinational domestic police force in BiH. Elections were to be held under the supervision of the Organization for Security and Cooperation in Europe (OSCE), with international monitors in every precinct until such time as domestic election boards could be trusted to hold free and fair elections. Most importantly, Bosnia-Herzegovina's fledgling political process was to be under the long-term control of a UN-appointed High Representative, whose responsibility it was to insure that political developments in the country would not rekindle ethnic conflict or detract from the building of a democratic political process. Toward those ends, the High Representative's powers included the authority to set aside the election of leaders likely to disrupt the building of a multinational democracy and the suspension of the licenses of radio stations airing inflammatory broadcasts.

Implementing the Dayton Accord

The unprecedented international effort to create democratic institutions and lay the foundation for a durable peace in Bosnia-Herzegovina encountered obstacles from the outset. The effort to create a multinational, domestic peace force, for example, met instant resistance from the Serb Republic. The efforts to return refugees met equally strong resistance, both where the refugees resided and were fearful of returning to their former homes, and in those areas from which they were driven. Likewise, at the local level the Communist Party bosses and ultranationalists who had often cemented their hold on power during the war by black market activities immediately dug in to resist any effort to replace them at the ballot box—even deploying their thuggish minions to intimidate voters who lined up in long queues before the polling booths even opened when the internationally supervised elections began to take place. Efforts to shut down hate-mongering radio stations and newspapers often provoked violent demonstrations against the international peacekeepers. And—perhaps most significant—all three communities in Bosnia-Herzegovina had a penchant for electing highly nationalist politicians whose campaign rhetoric often involved promises *not* to cooperate in policy making with the other communities. Consequently, the Office of the High Representative (OHR) was not infrequently confronted with a lose-lose choice: either accept the democratically expressed choices of voters and try to work with hostile political leaders, or abrogate election outcomes in the name of building a more durable democracy.

So intimidating was the initial political environment in the country that international administrators repeatedly delayed holding elections in Bosnia for nearly two years after Dayton. Moreover, when they finally were held it was largely because the United States forced the issue in the fall of 1997, despite the turmoil in Brzko, by rushing its approximately 500 monitors (about 25 percent of the OSCE contingent) into Bosnia-Herzegovina before its European partners in the OSCE could again reschedule the elections for a later date. A U.S. soldier aboard a NATO tank cradled his .50 caliber machine gun and waved at the first contingent of those monitors as their bus caravan from Zagreb rolled across the bridge separating Croatia from the SR. Local customs officials pointedly kept the buses standing there with their passengers on board for several hours before allowing them to proceed southward across the inter-entity boundary into the Croat-Bosniak Federation.

Gradually, as already noted, at least some parts of the situation began to improve. Refugees and internally displaced persons (IDPs) returned, if not in large numbers. The violent protests in the early years after the Dayton Accord gradually subsided, and it became possible first to reduce, and then to phase out NATO's presence, albeit only after NATO units had some-times been called upon to evict people illegally occupying the homes of the returnees. Sarajevo rebuilt gradually, profiting from the long-term presence of the OSCE and other international administrators who pumped money into its economy and hired its citizens. Other portions of the coun-try profited from the intensive international investment effort between 1996 and 2000 that was aimed at reconstructing infrastructure, easing the costs of adjusting to economic reforms, and abetting refugee returns. Other gains have been achieved elsewhere, largely as a result of the High Representative using the extensive powers of his office. These gains include the implementation of a common currency system, the establishment of a Central Bank, the adoption of national emblems (including a flag designed for the country by the OSCE, but not chosen by its citizens), the distribu-tion of common license plates, the levying of a value-added tax to increase revenue, and the beginning of reforms in the country's military services aimed at creating a single military out of the entities.[16] Nevertheless, Bosnia-Herzegovina remains far from the multicultural federal democratic republic that the peacemakers at Dayton envisioned. Its diverse communi-ties remain as unintegrated into a multicultural society as its capital city, Sarajevo, to which some of its Serbian inhabitants have gradually returned, but where they now live well apart from its Muslim majority. Moreover, the existing peace and democracy remain fragile, and they are prey to several troublesome issues that continue to plague those charged with implementing the Dayton Accord.

Although the political environment in Bosnia-Herzegovina no longer leans toward civil warfare, it contains a series of elements that sometimes produce conflict between the Serbian, Croat, and Bosniak communities on the one hand and the international authorities on the other, and they also have the daily potential of producing ugly, if usually isolated instances of intercommunal conflict between the members of the republic's national communities. In some instances these elements involve substantive issues that are still to be tackled; in other instances they pertain to the completion of tasks that have been undertaken but have stalled at sensitive moments; and in still other areas they encompass not so much substantive issues or problems as complicating factors that periodically make it more difficult to continue to implement the commitments and requirements of the Dayton Accord. Whatever their individual shape and importance to political conflict in contemporary Bosnia-Herzegovina, their mix is toxic.

CONSTITUTIONAL REFORM

The most basic and volatile issue facing the country and the one most important to its future direction—and perhaps its survival—involves the need for further progress toward the Dayton goal of establishing a democratic federal republic with an effective government at the center. Not only had little progress been made in effectuating that goal a decade after the signing of the Accord, but Serb, Croat, and Bosniak leaders have generally been able to use the "transitional" design adopted at Dayton in order to advance their individual, highly nationalistic agendas. In order to accommodate the mutual distrust that each ethno-national community had of the others, that transitional design created a very weak government at the center and emphasized the building of democratic institutions at the local, regional (in the Bosniak-Croat Federation), and entity (the SR, and the Bosniak-Croat Federation) levels. The result has been the emergence of an essentially bi-zonal federal state resting on its two entities, and the boundary between the SR and the remainder of the country is, despite some refugee returns, an institutionalized ethnopolitical divide in a state whose citizens were expected to develop a multicultural civic identity. For those living in the two entities, it is their respective governments, not the one in Sarajevo, that remain the more substantively important, as well as the more ethnically familiar. The institutions with which the people most frequently interact, including the police, remain those of the entity, not the central government.

Reversing this tide has become more difficult as time has passed. The highly nationalist leaders are now found in different parties from those that initially formed in the country's Croat, Serb, and Bosniak areas, but they are no less nationalistic or more inclined to compromise than their immediate postwar predecessors. Moreover, their individual agendas for the future of Bosnia remain at least as far apart as they were at Dayton. The Bosniaks, who are approaching a majority of the total population of Bosnia-Herzegovina, want to downgrade the powers of the lower levels of government and turn their multilayered state into a centralized republic. Some of their leaders would even altogether abolish the SR, which the country's newest Bosniak leader labeled a "genocidal creation" in successfully appealing to the communal emotions of the country's Muslim voters in the 2006 national elections. Meanwhile the Serbs, whose own nationalist leaders have not been above directly challenging the powers of the High Representative by daring him to remove them from office, want to create their own independent state or as weak a central government as possible in Bosnia-Herzegovina—or perhaps eventually unite with Serbia and distance themselves altogether from Sarajevo, where Serbs who have returned to live "do not feel at home." Finally, the Croat nationalists want to divide the Bosniak-Croat federal entity into two parts, so that they can have their own federal state inside the country.

Compromising on these differing objectives has been beyond the OHR and the international diplomats, who urged Bosnia's leaders in 2006 to scrap the country's highly peripheral federal system in favor of a more centralized system, and whose recommendations were almost immediately rejected by the BiH assembly in Sarajevo. Thus, in terms of its institutional structure, with a weak central government and a plural executive (composed of a member from each of the three national communities), Bosnia-Herzegovina remains a "fragile state comprised of two entities . . . with separate economic spaces [whose] . . . central government is . . . at the mercy of the entities . . . [and] with no real authority over the entities." In this sense, the country's fundamental problem remains the Dayton Constitution itself. It was meant to be an interim, transitional document, but it has become a "straitjacket" that prevents meaningful reforms, given the differing objectives of the major communities and the preference of each for the status quo over the preferences of the others. As one observer noted in late 2006, the Dayton Constitution has become a permanent arena for "war by other means" among the country's major communities, and in a country where a large NATO contingent no longer exists to put muscle behind the dictates of the OHR, any effort to restructure the country from above will be highly resisted.[17]

DISARMING THE PARAMILITARIES

Pouring additional fuel on the combustible issue of pushing additional constitutional reforms is the fact that NATO departed before the various paramilitary organizations that appeared during the civil war were fully disarmed. Most of the more notorious ones were stripped of their better firepower, but no one doubts that there are large caches of hidden weapons throughout the country's Croat, Serb, and Bosniak areas. Moreover, local politicians and entity police officers—many of whom were involved in those paramilitary organizations during the war—have little-to-no interest in continuing to ferret out those weapons.

THE ECONOMY

The nature of the country's economy is both an issue in the minds of each of the BiH's national communities *and* a factor that renders progress even more difficult in attacking the other issues confronting the state. Democracies thrive on thriving economies. Efforts to build democratic governments and persuade people to engage in give-and-take politics are undercut when few have much to give up in political compromises, and the economy of Bosnia-Herzegovina—Yugoslavia's second-poorest republic before the war—remains weak. In fact, a decade after Dayton, the United States Central Intelligence Agency still recorded its official unemployment rate at 45 percent (less in Sarajevo, but much higher in other parts of the republic). The CIA noted that even if the gray economy were included, 25 to 30 percent of the workforce was unemployed, and one out of four lived below the poverty level in a country whose average per capita income is only $5,600. Consequently, there is little appetite in any of the communities to undertake the additional privatization programs that the European Union has demanded of Bosnia-Herzegovina before discussing EU membership with the country's leaders.

EDUCATION REFORM

Education is a sensitive topic in any society, and an especially hot one in a country emerging from a civil war. *Whose* history is to be taught? *Whose* school system will students attend? In Bosnia-Herzegovina, the answers continue to be "the history and the school systems of the individual national communities," because education continues to be highly segregated along ethno-national lines within the country. Consequently, curricula and the process of socialization have remained in the hands of local schools under the jurisdiction of nationalistic Serbian, Croatian, and Bosniak leaders. Too often the stress has been on past injustices—not shared experiences, needs, and symbols—and international efforts to cajole or push the communities to integrate the school systems have been met by resistance throughout, even where two national communities cohabit in the same area. Nor is the outlook for the future much brighter. Given the importance attached to control over school curricula by all communities, any effort to force reforms might easily escalate into broad conflict between the communities and the OHR, if not between the communities themselves.

HUMAN RIGHTS

Meanwhile, the searing and divisive memories of the past continue to be rekindled in contemporary Bosnia-Herzegovina, fueling nationalism and inhibiting the international community's efforts to initiate or push further reforms in the substantive areas requiring action. Makeshift and more elaborate memorials to the war dead lace the country, as do hollowed-out buildings. Signs warn of the presence of antipersonnel mines, more than 5 million of which are believed to still lie buried in the country. Even the films shown at the revived annual International Film Festival in Saravejo continue to be absorbed with warfare in general, and Bosnia's civil war in particular.[18] Meanwhile, the anniversaries of atrocities are commemorated annually, most notably in the Muslim pilgrimages to Srebrenica. War criminals are still being ferreted out, with their trials reviving memories of the horrors of the war. Sometimes—as in the case of those tried in 2006 for the Srebrenica massacre—those trials are punctuated with video tapes taken by the aggressors of their victims. Such matters have particularly inhibited further efforts to guarantee human rights and protect cultural and religious minorities in the country's scarred zones. That task was begun, but it is far from finished, inasmuch as the minorities in one area were the majority who pursued brutal ethnic cleansing campaigns elsewhere.

POLICE REFORM

Among the common victims of ethnic civil wars are such devices of conflict resolution as the police and judiciary, and such arteries of community-building as the organs of mass communication, especially

U.S. Army personnel, attached to KFOR at Camp Demi, Bosnia-Herzegovina, in 1999, warn children of the dangers of antipersonnel mines during Kid's Day. Courtesy of the U.S. Army.

public broadcasting stations. Usually by the time communal warfare breaks out, they have already been tribalized and identified with one of the political communities. In the case of Bosnia-Herzegovina, the police became one of the primary instruments used by each community in its ethnic cleansing campaigns against the others; the Yugoslav judiciary disappeared during the war; and the radio stations that continued to broadcast were instruments of incitement as much as transmitters of (often well-doctored) news. Yet as the first decade of the new millennium wore on, reform lagged behind needs in each instance. Broadcasting channels, for example, have been supervised by the OHR, and their flagrant efforts to raise intercommunal tensions have resulted in temporary shutdowns and the firing of broadcasters. The Serbian stations broadcast from Serbia, however, and they hardly incur censorship at the entity level. Likewise, the country's unwillingness to undertake the reforms necessary to fight the corruption that is still a part of the judicial systems remains a major obstacle to BiH's entry into the European Union.

Nevertheless, the major areas requiring reform are the country's police and military services. In both areas the SR has opposed further efforts to integrate the police and army into single entities and has delayed compliance with the timetables established by the OHR for the efforts already undertaken. Thus, although there is officially only one Bosnia-Herzegovina army, the SR has in fact kept its units separate, and stationed inside the SR.

The picture remains even worse in the area of police reform, which is critical to establishing a Bosnia-Herzegovina system of law enforcement that transcends the national lines of identification.[19] As a result of the sectional breakup of the country during the war, there were three separate police forces in existence at the war's end, each tainted by its participation (in a major way) in ethnic cleansing operations. The design worked out by international administrators such as Donald Zoufal, who were sent to Bosnia-Herzegovina in 1996 to help create a professionalized, country-wide and ethnically integrated police force, remains unfulfilled. True, the Bosniak and Croatian units have been merged, but the SR, which continues to threaten to hold a referendum on whether to remain in Bosnia, has refused to integrate its police with the other units, and in the SR its police force continues to be an obstacle to refugee return and the arrest of Serbs wanted for war crimes. The Bosniak-Croat Federation police, however, also hinder the return of refugees, though less frequently and flagrantly than the Serbs. Furthermore, in many parts of the country the integration of Croats and Bosniaks into local units of the police force has been nominal, with Croats overwhelmingly represented in the "multinational force" in the Croat areas of the federation and the Bosniaks equally dominant in local police units in the Muslim parts of the state outside of Sarajevo.

Unfortunately, the ability of the OHR to push for an end to these ethnic imbalances and the unification of the Serb and Federation units necessary to create a true BiH institution has actually declined since 2002, when the EU assumed the International Police Task Force's responsibilities for creating a system-wide police service in Bosnia-Herzegovina. Unlike the IPTF, whose mandate gave it supervisory powers and the ability to recommend dismissal in the event of unprofessional conduct, the EU's police contingent is only charged with monitoring and mentoring the country's still-unintegrated police forces. Perhaps coincidently, crime began to rise in the country almost immediately after the IPTF's departure.

REFUGEES AND RETURNEES

Those driven from their homes during the war constitute another highly contentious issue. As already noted, the war massively redistributed the country's population. The prewar pattern, which had remained

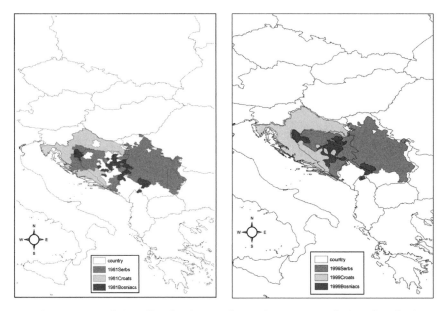

Bosnia, 1981 population distribution, and Bosnia, 1999 population distribution: population movements resulting from civil war in Bosnia. Created by Devon Rusk and used with her permission.

relatively stable throughout the twentieth century, included large areas of the country that did not contain a majority ethnic group. In the Bosnia-Herzegovina of today, by contrast, all three communities are now essentially territorially concentrated in areas in which they respectively constitute (usually very large) majorities. As a result, not only have many of those displaced by the war not returned to the country, but significant numbers of those who have returned have not returned to their home locales—and the likelihood of their return continues to diminish. Apart from the resistance from local authorities that their return in significant numbers might produce, their homes were often destroyed during the war. If still standing, those homes are often now occupied by members of the dominant national community, who themselves would have nowhere to go if deposed from these commandeered residences. Meanwhile, those who *have* returned often live in an uneasy state in areas where their ethnic group has been reduced in number and where they would face discrimination in finding good jobs, even if the economy were healthier. Often they find themselves under the jurisdiction of nationalist politicians elected by those who violently drove them from their residences.

KOSOVO

By any definition, Kosovo remains a hot spot in the Balkans—one not only likely to experience political violence within, but with the potential to spread its violence into neighboring areas. The Kosovo Liberation Army has already shown its willingness to foment conflict between the Macedonians and the Muslim Albanians in neighboring Macedonia. Those Albanians who are intermingled with the Serbs in southern Serbia and in Montenegro to the west of their border with Kosovo must also be regarded as tempting targets for mobilization efforts, whatever the long-term future of Kosovo itself. Above all, it is not a question of whether future political violence will erupt in Kosovo. At least at a low level, and often at a high pitch, political violence has been a part of the Kosovo political scene ever since NATO halted the bombing campaign it launched in order to protect Kosovo's Albanians from Serb persecution, and ever since Kosovo's Muslim Albanians returned from their refugee camps in Macedonia and Albania, sacking, torching, bulldozing, and often occupying Serbian houses and driving the province's Serbian, Romani, and other minorities into exile.

Kosovo, the Conflict: 600 Years in the Making

With Serbian-Albanian conflict in (and concerning) Kosovo still evolving, it is slightly presumptive to try to outline the conflict's origin and development in the space available here. Still, to appreciate the magnitude of the conflict management task in Kosovo that the international community assumed in 1999, some background information is in order.

1389: The End of Empire (and Beginning of the Muslim Hordes)

Whatever the ethnic origin of the peoples who originally inhabited the present-day province of Kosovo, by the fourteenth century it was more than just Serbian territory—it was the religious and cultural cradle of the ancient Serbian empire. In 1389, however, Serb rule ended abruptly when Serbian forces were decisively defeated by the Ottoman Turks at Kosovo Polje (the Battle of Kosovo), near Pristina. That defeat opened the door to migration into the region of Islamized Albanians from the south, who were encouraged by the Ottomans to settle there to dilute the Serbian influence in the region. Their numbers grew steadily thereafter, up to and throughout the twentieth century.

The Nineteenth Century and the Emergence of Dual Nationalisms

In the meantime, the second half of the nineteenth century witnessed the birth of modern Serbian nationalism, heavily interwoven with the symbolic importance of Kosovo and the landmarks of the ancient Serbian empire that survived there. Moreover, nineteenth-century Serbian nationalism was born in a Pan-Serbian framework, and as the first part of the greater Serbian nation to acquire its independence, Serbia's right to press for the attainment of a new Pan-Serbian state founded on the modern principle of national self-determination rested heavily on Serbia's control of Kosovo.

Unfortunately for the future tranquility of the area, the late nineteenth century also witnessed the birth of modern Albanian nationalism in Kosovo, approximately forty miles south and west of Pristina, in the city of Prizren. Thus, a generation before Serbia was able to cement its control over Kosovo amid the chaos that marked the end of the Ottoman Empire and the post–World War I birth of the Kingdom of Serbs, Croats, and Slovenes under a Serbian king, the same land was of symbolic importance to two different peoples and two colliding political movements.

For most of its interwar life, the history of that kingdom was dominated by Serbian-Croatian conflict, even as the numbers of Albanian Muslims in Kosovo continued to grow, and with them Serbian-Albanian tensions in the province. German occupation further worsened those relations when the Germans established a puppet Albanian government in Kosovo, paralleling the puppet Croatian government they created in Croatia. With German cover, Kosovo's Albanian leaders instituted their own reign of oppression over the province's Serbs, driving as many as 100,000 of them from the province and leaving Kosovo equally Serbian and Albanian by the war's end.

Still, it was the postwar policies of Yugoslavia's wartime hero and postwar leader, Marshall Tito (nee Josip Broz), that completed the Albanianization of Kosovo's population. Committed to creating a transcending "Yugoslav" identity out of the Serbian, Croat, Slovene, Albanian, and other ethnic communities that constituted the Federal Republic of Yugoslavia, Tito too saw a value in diluting the Serbian presence in Kosovo. Accordingly, he not only encouraged the migration of Albanian Muslims from the south into the province, but in 1974 he promulgated a new constitution that gave the province a measure of autonomy, as well as separate representation on the collective presidency that Tito fashioned to steer the country after his rule. That autonomy meant substantial Albanian self-government inside

The nineteenth-century home of the League of Prizren, in Prizren, Kosovo—the birthplace of modern Albanian nationalism.

Serbia by the time of Tito's death in 1980. By then the province's Albanian Muslim community was approximately 90 percent of Kosovo's population, and the Serbs were only 8 percent—although the Albanians continued to occupy a distinctly second-class status in the province's economy.

KOSOVO LIBERATION ARMY

Tito's death marked the end of Belgrade's failing effort to create a Yugoslav identity and the beginning of the struggle to succeed Tito within the country's communist party. For nearly a decade, that struggle—along with intercommunal tensions—was kept in check by the shared fear on the part of the country's principal ethnonational communities of outside interference from the Soviet Union if Yugoslavia should begin to fall apart from within. The collapse of the Soviet Union removed that glue, and by the late 1980s the communist party wings in the various union republics were already showing signs of rebelling against Belgrade's leadership and going their separate ways. They would eventually do so in 1991. By that time, however, the leader of Yugoslavia's communist party, Slobodan Milosevic, had heavily played the Serbian nationalist card in his own bid to rule Yugoslavia. He rescinded Kosovo's provincial autonomy at a time when its Albanian Muslims were calling for more control over their own affairs, and he celebrated the 600th anniversary of the Battle of Kosovo by making an inflammatory nationalist speech capped with the promise, "Kosovo will forever be Serbian." Two years later, amid riots by Albanians protesting Belgrade's actions, Milosevic declared a state of emergency and essentially emptied Kosovo's state institutions, including its police and state companies, of their Albanian employees.[20]

It is probable that Milosevic's emphasis on Serbian nationalism and a Greater Serbia accelerated the movement toward separatism in the country's union republics outside of Serbia and Montenegro. It clearly had an immediate and negative impact on the political terrain in Kosovo, whose Albanian majority within a year formed a government-in-exile in Albania under the leadership of Ibrahim Rugova and his fellow moderates in the Democratic League of Kosovo (DLK) party. At the same time, less-moderate Albanian Muslims in Kosovo were forming militant separatist groups and targeting Kosovo's Serbs and Romani, as well as Yugoslav security forces in the province. In fact, the mistaken belief in some European quarters that by 1991 Milosevic had his hands so full in Kosovo that he would be unable to act elsewhere led Germany and other EU states to encourage Croatia and Slovenia to secede, despite the warnings from Belgrade that such action would not go unanswered.

Matters further deteriorated in Kosovo in 1993 when, in the midst of the civil war in Bosnia, the Kosovo Liberation Army (KLA) was founded and inaugurated its guerrilla warfare campaign for an independent Kosovo. It did not spare those moderate Kosovo Albanian leaders who were still willing to settle for a restoration of Kosovo's provincial autonomy inside Serbia. That campaign escalated after NATO's intervention in the war in Bosnia in the summer of 1995 forced Milosevic to recognize the independence of its separatist republics in the Dayton Accord signed later that year. That intervention also encouraged the KLA to believe that if it provoked Belgrade into overreacting, NATO might well intervene on behalf of Kosovo, whose status had been ignored at Dayton. There were firm reasons for the KLA to draw that conclusion. First, there was substantial evidence that paramilitaries on all sides were guilty of committing atrocities during the warfare in Croatia and Bosnia. But more specifically, the massacre at Srebrenica—where Serbian forces slew thousands of unarmed Muslim men and boys before the helplessly under-armed European protective force assigned to that UN-designated "safe haven"—portrayed Serbs to the outside world as purveyors of genocidal warfare. Thus, even though reporters on the spot in Kosovo indicated that (1) Albanian extremists were at least as guilty as Belgrade for the outrages being committed against civilians in Kosovo; (2) that Albanian ethnic cleansing of Serbian areas (including attacks on Serbian churches and cemeteries and other acts of vandalism designed to erase the physical signs of Serbian cultural history) had been occurring in the area since the early 1980s; and (3) that most of Belgrade's action in Kosovo during 1996 and 1997 was in response to KLA attacks on Belgrade's forces, the mostly exaggerated rumors of Serbian massacres of civilians in Kosovo were often given instant credibility.

The conflict simmering in Kosovo moved into the terminal stages in 1998, when the KLA—by now well-armed with weapons looted from the arsenals of Albania, which was then in political chaos to its south—boldly attacked Serbian outposts and police stations in Kosovo. In March Belgrade aggressively responded to the KLA attacks on its security personnel with a brutal military campaign designed to eliminate KLA strongholds and intimidate the KLA's Albanian sympathizers into either flight or passive acceptance of Serbian rule. Excessive acts occurred, and although their number may have been multiplied by Albanian spokesmen, subsequent war trials at the Hague have documented the murder, rape, and arson that accompanied Belgrade's action. Nor is there any dispute that it resulted in at least 300,000 Albanian refugees fleeing Kosovo into neighboring areas.

A temporary cease-fire was attained by U.S. diplomats in October 1998 by threatening Belgrade with NATO air strikes, but the cease-fire became increasingly illusory as KLA operatives continued to assassinate Serb officials and Serbian forces ambushed alleged KLA agents along Kosovo's border with Serbia. The discovery in January 1999 of the murder of more than 40 Albanian civilians by Serb forces ended the patience of American diplomats, who had already essentially decided that Milosevic had to go, even as Milosevic was giving them additional reasons for seeking a military solution to the Kosovo conflict by expelling the 2,000-strong international contingent that had been permitted to enter Kosovo the previous year as "observers' of the conflict. There followed a hastily arranged, last minute diplomatic effort to resolve the Kosovo conflict at an international summit that convened in Rambouillet, France, in February 1999. There, Western diplomats explicitly demanded that Milosevic end his ethnic cleansing campaign of the KLA's strongholds in Kosovo, hold democratic elections in the province under the supervision of the Organization for Security and Cooperation in Europe (OSCE), and restore in a broadened form Kosovo's previously suspended provincial autonomy. Milosevic refused.

NATO INTERVENTION

The announced justification for NATO's prophylactic intervention (Operation Allied Force) on March 28, 1999, was threefold: (1) to halt any further war crimes allegedly occurring in Kosovo, (2) to minimize civilian casualties there, and (3) to stem the destabilizing flow of refugees into neighboring states. In fact, NATO's operation—which stretched across 78 days (75 more than were initially estimated to be necessary) and involved more than 10,000 attack sorties—produced results almost exactly the opposite of those intended. Within 48 hours of NATO initiating its bombing campaign, hundreds of thousands of additional Albanian refugees had flooded across Kosovo's borders into makeshift refugee camps in neighboring areas. Meanwhile, Serbian forces inside Kosovo took out their frustration against the Albanian civilians still there, who were left undefended throughout the 78 days because NATO at the outset had excluded the deployment of ground forces during the war. Indeed, several analysts have concluded that the Serbian ethnic cleansing operations actually increased during NATO's air campaign.

The matter did not end there. Rather, NATO's military action shortly thereafter morphed into an unfortunate example of conflict management, in which the device chosen to manage one problem—in Kosovo, the danger faced by its Albanian people—created another set of problems. When the war ended and the Albanian refugees returned from exile, the absence of NATO ground troops opened the door to Albanian-committed acts of revenge against Kosovo's vulnerable Serbian population, which—along with Kosovo's detested Romani community—was forced to flee to wherever they could find shelter elsewhere in Serbia, or in Montenegro. As a result, by the end of Operation Allied Force on July 10, when Milosevic at last acceded to the demands placed on him at Rambouillet, approximately 800,000 of Kosovo's 1.9 million people were refugees. Another 500,000 had become internally displaced persons in either Kosovo (chiefly Albanians), Montenegro (where two-thirds of Kosovo's Romani fled), or Serbia (which was soon hosting 90 percent of Kosovo's internally displaced Serbs).

The flight of the Serbian refugees, in turn, enormously complicated the task of peace-building in postwar Kosovo. In authorizing its operations there, the UN explicitly recognized the province as a part of Serbia—a stipulation that Kosovo's independence-minded Albanian community has rejected almost to a person. Kosovo Albanians have similarly opposed the return of Kosovo Serbs, lest their repatriation strengthen Belgrade's claim to the province. Thus, when NATO has sought to protect Kosovo Serbs and facilitate their return, its forces have been targeted by extremists in the Albanian community, and that community as a whole has shown an increasing inclination to elect former KLA leaders and other hard-line Albanian politicians to head Kosovo's provincial government. Caught between Belgrade's refusal to agree to Kosovo's independence and the unwillingness of Kosovo's postwar leaders to accept anything less, it is not surprising that UN negotiators were persistently unable to reach a consensual diplomatic solution to the Kosovo issue.

QUEST FOR CONFLICT RESOLUTION: UNMIK

Seeking a Strategy and Assigning Duties in a Compromised Environment

The same day that NATO's bombing campaign ended, the United Nations passed Resolution 1244, creating the broad structure for the rebuilding of a multiethnic Kosovo under the auspices of the United Nations Mission in Kosovo (UNMIK). Also authorized was the deployment of a Kosovo stabilization force (KFOR) to be composed of NATO military units and charged with maintaining the secure environment necessary for the erection of democratic institutions of provincial governance. Two days later KFOR was on the ground, its approximately 50,000 troops deployed on the basis of its various national units being assigned to individual zones throughout the province.[21] Shortly thereafter the European Union (EU) and the OSCE also became parts of the effort to reconstruct Kosovo physically, socially, and politically.

The reconstruction design was built extensively on international efforts at the time to rebuild and democratize multinational Bosnia-Herzegovina (BiH), which wove together global, trans-Atlantic, and European institutions in partnership missions. UNMIK was to preside over four broad task areas (dubbed "pillars" in the reconstruction process), but the individual tasks were organized under the daily charge of a specific international (governmental) organization, in each case with the assistance of the various nongovernmental organizations that soon arrived in Kosovo. These organizations offered their services in such humanitarian areas as caring for the refugees and providing temporary medical assistance to the province's displaced persons. The UN itself took charge of two of these areas: Civil Administration and Humanitarian Assistance. The latter's task was subsequently redirected from its initial focus on resettling refugees (after the bulk of Kosovo's Albanian refugees had returned) to an emphasis on police and justice, with the specific charge of eventually replacing KFOR's internal policing responsibility with an internationally trained, domestic Kosovo Police Service.

The third area, Democratization and Institution-Building, with its collateral concern to protect human rights, was placed in the hands of the OSCE, which established its Mission in Kosovo in July 1999. The European Union undertook the final task in the rebuilding of Kosovo: Reconstruction and Economic Development.

Pursuing a Strategy in a Compromised Environment

The Bosnia design fit the needs of Kosovo at the time (summer of 1999), but in at least three significant areas the operational environment in Kosovo was significantly different from, and far more challenging than the circumstances facing those involved in the state-building and refugee resettlement missions in the Republic of Bosnia and Herzegovina.

Mission Clarity

Those concerned with implementing the Dayton Accord in Bosnia were not given easy tasks, nor has the outcome of their work been entirely satisfactory, as noted in our examination of that hot spot. A factor in that outcome is the bi-zonal federation that has emerged as a result of the frequent control of one of its two federal entities, the Serbian Republic (SR), by hard-line Serbian nationalists who have been disinterested in enhancing the power of the center or collaborating with Bosnian Muslim and Croatian politicians in governing there. On the other hand, the goal of the post-Dayton mission was always clear: to create an independent, multinational democratic state. In contrast, the state-builders in Kosovo lacked a clear legal charge defined in terms of final outcome. Were they laboring to create a state that one day would be independent, or a province that was to have significant autonomy but remain a part of what was then left of the Yugoslav Federal Republic (that is, Serbia and Montenegro)? In authorizing UNMIK, UN Resolution 1244 left the matter cloudy. It simultaneously charged UNMIK with the vague goal of "facilitating a political process to determine Kosovo's future status," but it made that task exceedingly difficult by defining the institution- and society-building process as one in which in the people of Kosovo "can enjoy substantial autonomy within the Federal Republic of Yugoslavia." Belgrade interpreted that phrase as the UN's recognition of Kosovo as a part of Yugoslavia. Very quickly, mission murkiness compromised mission success in terms of sustaining the cooperation of either Belgrade or moderate Albanian politicians in efforts of the UN, OSCE, and NATO to calm and redesign Kosovo. Neither Belgrade nor Kosovo's nationalists could be sure of whether their labors would be lead to Kosovo remaining a part of Serbia or becoming an independent state.

The Shape of Society

This absence of mission clarity on the issue of final status especially handicapped the efforts of those involved in the resettlement of the province's refugees and internally displaced people. Not surprisingly, it was widely believed that the shape of Kosovo's society would heavily influence the determination of its final status. The more Serbs in Kosovo's population, Albanian nationalists reasoned, the better would be Belgrade's case for continued ownership of the province. This attitude led to the efforts of Kosovar Albanians to intimidate the remaining Serbs into leaving and their unwillingness to cooperate in resettling those minorities who had left the province as a result of the war. Indeed, because of the forced exodus of so many of Kosovo's minorities when the Albanian refugees returned to Kosovo, NATO's bombing campaign had made postwar Kosovo an even more overwhelmingly Albanian-Muslim province that was well positioned to argue its case for independence on the basis of the principle of national self-determination. To Albanian nationalists, doing nothing to restore the minorities to their abandoned homes in Kosovo and "encouraging" those few remaining there to leave made sense.

Compared to the situation in Kosovo, the constellation of international machinery thrust into Bosnia-Herzegovina to implement the Dayton Accord's vision of Bosnia as a future multinational state had far more bargaining room in securing the eventual resettlement of that former union republic's displaced people. To be sure, the war there disrupted the lives of hundreds of thousands who were forced into refugee status outside of Bosnia or became internally displaced within it, and the return process was extremely slow. When the war ended, however, the share of Bosnia's postwar population held by its Muslim, Croat, and Serb communities lay within essentially the same bounds as it had before the war. No community constituted more than 40 percent or less than 20 percent of the country's population, and thus, barring the SR's secession, its future as an ethnically and nationally mixed state was never in doubt. More importantly, each community had an interest in a return policy that would bolster its numbers at the local level, where it already controlled sub-state political bodies. Tradeoffs could thus be effected. Similarly, the Serbs had an interest in permitting Muslims to return to Brzko in the SR in limited numbers, in return for the Bosnian Muslims permitting a safe return of Serbs to Sarajevo, with its Muslim majority. To be sure, the returns did not immediately occur and were sometimes marred by violence, and the gathering of minorities into enclaves has normally been the pattern where repatriation has occurred. But ultimately it was possible to achieve a statistically meaningful return of Croats, Muslims, and Serbs to many of the areas they had inhabited before the war, because each community had an interest in accepting the return of the "other" ethnic fellow at the local level in its back yard. No such tradeoffs could be offered to Kosovo's Albanians by Kosovo's international administrators, however. The Albanians were already home.

Building Institutions for Multinational States

The small size of the minority communities in Kosovo has, in turn, made it impossible for the international community either to encourage the development of cross-communal parties or to structure multinational institutions there. The assembly in Pristina contains a permanent Albanian majority and—at best—the representation of a permanent small minority or sets of minorities. There is little incentive for the majority to make concessions to the minorities or to share power with them, and freed from the oversight of international administrators they are even less likely to do so. Thus, the political scene has been dominated by Albanian nationalist parties demanding independence on various timetables, not by parties offering different social and economic agendas.

The low number of minorities in Kosovo has likewise affected durable institution-building in such other areas as creating a regional multiethnic bureaucracy or an all-Kosovo police force that would operate on the basis of professional ethics rather than genetic heritage. The Kosovo Police Service has managed to achieve a 15 percent minority representation as a result of international efforts to attract minorities. That achievement has been facilitated by an economy where jobs are scarce for everyone, so that inducing qualified people to apply is not difficult. Serb recruits, however, have repeatedly expressed their anxiety over the tenuousness of their status if the international community were to leave.

The Problem with Kosovo: The Peacebuilding Process—Nation Building or Nation Threatening?

Early Progress: Repatriation, Reconstruction, and the Albanian Community

International efforts to accomplish the tasks assigned to UNMIK, NATO, the OSCE, and the EU were most successful in the early years following NATO's action. Parties were organized and certified, local and provincial governing institutions were created, and the OSCE was overseeing local elections within one year after the end of the military action, complete with out-of-province and out-of-country voting facilities for Kosovo's internally displaced persons (IDPs) and refugees (it had taken two years after the Dayton Accord to hold local elections in Bosnia-Herzegovina). The Albanian refugees returned immediately after the end of hostilities, and in some instances NATO helicopters provided safe escort to facilitate their return. Elsewhere, funds were found (if not always in the promised amount) for the reconstruction of housing for the returning refugees, schools, and other structures damaged during the fighting. In fact, the resettlement of the Albanian refugees went so quickly that the international nongovernmental agencies who arrived in 1999 to tender humanitarian assistance were within two years able to wind down their operations and/or turn them over to UNMIK, and depart. Even the decommissioning of KLA paramilitary units enjoyed some success, although not nearly enough—as evidenced by continued skirmishes in some of the border areas with Serbia and the presence of KLA "volunteers" in the Albanian-Macedonian fighting across the border in Macedonia at the century's end. Still, even the harshest critic of the community- and institution-building operations in Kosovo cannot indict the mission as a complete failure by any standard. The recent record, however, contains far fewer success stories.

Institution Building: Albanian Nationalism and the Absence of Consensus

Third-party intervention always constitutes meddling, and sooner or later the meddler is likely to encounter both resentment and resistance. In the case of Kosovo, where the intrusiveness has entailed a comprehensive international effort to build a system of constitutional government embodying a strong protection of minority rights and a qualified system of power sharing between the majority and minorities, that resistance was inevitable if for no other reason than the obvious one. Tolerance of the "other" community is going to be at a low ebb in an environment immediately following communal conflict. Even if refugee communities can be restored to their former dwelling areas, moving beyond the traumatic memories of violent ethnic conflict requires generations. So too does the development of the trust across communal lines that is necessary for durable constitutional government to exist. To date, there is little evidence to suggest that the peoples of Kosovo have as yet embarked on that path. In the zero-sum discourse over Kosovo's future, Belgrade refused to accept independence, and its Albanian majority was unwilling to settle for anything less. Meanwhile, the process of returning the displaced minorities is slow and still insecure.

In fairness to those who have tried to create democratic institutions in Kosovo, the ill health and subsequent death of President Rugova in January 2006 were serious setbacks. He was a well-loved spokesman for the Albanian community who had been willing to accept long-term political tutelage and international guarantees of minority rights in return for Kosovo's eventual independence. On the other hand, by the time of his demise, his party had already suffered from its (and Rugova's) moderation on the independence issue, having been outbid by the country's more militant Independence Now! parties and losing control of the province's assembly and premiership in 2004 to opponents philosophically nearer, and sometimes directly tied to the KLA.

The movement of the Albanian electorate toward more militant spokesmen was part of the more general tide of growing tension within the Albanian community. There was tension between its two leading parties, the Democratic Party of Kosovo and the more moderate Democratic League of Kosovo, headed by Rugova until his death. In addition, the Kosovo Albanians and UNMIK were at odds over UNMIK's unwillingness to decide Kosovo's final status because of continued unrest in the province and Kosovo's failure to meet established standards in areas of public safety. Tensions have also mounted between the Albanian community and UNMIK over the international community's failure to provide the funding necessary to resuscitate the province's economy, which suffered badly when the departing Serbs took their capital with them. Further aggravating the situation has been the difficulty of finding development funds elsewhere, because Kosovo's tenuous political status has made it extremely difficult for its provincial government to attract outside capital or international loans—both desperately needed in an area that has been experiencing unemployment rates in the 60- to 70-percent range. At times, the growing tensions exploded, severely challenging NATO's effort to maintain order and exposing its units to acts of violence. The most dramatic instance occurred during the upheaval in March 2004, when riots spread to more than thirty towns and "payback" attacks on unarmed minority Serbs left nearly a score of people dead and 1,000 injured. The damage also involved the widespread burning of Serb homes and churches, as well as dozens of UNMIK vehicles.[22]

Other Refugees and Internally Displaced Persons: Frustration and Failure

For their part, Kosovo Serbs have become increasingly frustrated with their continuing, unsettled status as displaced persons, as well as with the absence of a secure place to live in Kosovo and their lack of a significant voice in Kosovo politics. This frustration was most vividly dramatized by the highly effective Serbian boycott of the province's 2004 election.

Three years after the conflict ended in Kosovo, 231,000 non-Albanian IDPs from Kosovo (of the estimated 250,000 who initially fled the province) were still living in Serbia and Montenegro. In fact, the numbers of people continuing to leave the province were still exceeding the numbers returning through organized efforts. Of those who have returned, a significant number have been elderly, and the vast majority have settled in existing minority enclaves. Security is better there, but mobility is limited and job opportunities are few.[23] The situation *has* gradually improved, but despite the protocol on facilitating the return of the displaced that was signed in June 2006 by UN, Pristina, and Belgrade representatives, the United Nations High Commission for Refugees (UNHCR) reports that their inability to return safely to Kosovo and to be secure there remains the primary obstacle confronting those trying to assist Kosovo's displaced Romani and Serbs.[24] Indeed, many of those displaced Serbs who returned to Kosovo only to find themselves living in insecure circumstances have subsequently returned to Serbia. Those who have stayed have often become psychologically and physically dependent on KFOR's presence. Above all, the majority of Kosovo's displaced minorities have continued to remain in exile, and international officials predict that if Kosovo gains independence, its remaining minorities will vacate it within a decade, and probably much sooner.[25]

Concern with the safety and security of the returnees has not been the only factor inhibiting the return process. In addition to security, current international criteria for returning list self-sustainability—a criterion that international administrators have translated to mean requiring both a suitable dwelling in which to live and employment that allows the returnees to live without international assistance. Neither requirement is easily fulfilled. Serb and Romani living quarters were often demolished when their owners were forced to depart from Kosovo, so as to minimize the chance that they would return. Moreover, in cases where their domiciles continue to stand, establishing legal ownership is a time-consuming process—even when the original owners can document their claims. For this reason, too, the return of IDPs to Kosovo has gone neither smoothly nor according to design.[26] Yet even where housing has been available, jobs usually have not been, in part because of the high unemployment rates throughout Kosovo and partly because of the widespread discrimination against Kosovo's minorities as a result of hiring practices that international authorities have been unable to overcome.

Finally, there is the large problem of refugee mathematics and refugee politics that was noted earlier. Ethnic mathematics is an integral part of partisan politics throughout the world of multinational/multiethnic democracies. Where political power is related to a group's share of the population, even census taking can be highly contentious. Where those numbers can prejudice a final settlement based on the principle of national self-determination, the community pressing that argument has a powerful, vested interest in discouraging minority returns and encouraging its remaining minorities to leave. Violence is often a part of that "encouragement" process. For both communities, the refugee issue thus remains a potential detonator of violence and conflict in Kosovo.

The Problem of Peacekeeping and Continued Political Violence

As in Bosnia and Herzegovina, peacekeeping forces in general have become essential components of recent efforts to manage communal conflict. Only in the atmosphere of security that they provide can individual rights be secured and local and system-wide institutions of governance and justice be constructed. For the peacekeepers units to succeed, however, it is imperative that they be seen as neutrals enforcing the peace, not partisans with an interest in shaping the outcome. Yet, maintaining that aura of neutrality over time while enforcing international mandates is exceedingly difficult, especially in arenas of communal conflict where the legitimacy of any given status quo is an issue. And so it has been in Kosovo, where enforcing the established agreements meant facilitating the return of refugees whose repatriation strengthens Belgrade's claim on the territory that Kosovo's Muslim, Albanian population had come to regard as their own—a territory destined for independence. As a consequence, KFOR has frequently found itself in the crosshairs of Kosovo Albanian extremists. The March 2004 riots in Mitrovica and throughout Kosovo that forced NATO to bolster its force level temporarily underlined this development. Well before then, however, Albanian extremists had been firing on NATO forces and UN police force personnel were not infrequently involved in ugly altercations with Albanian crowds.

THE UN'S "SUPERVISED KOSOVO" PLAN

In June 2007, the UN finally began circulating a proposal pertaining to the final status of Kosovo. The plan called for a transitional period to a "supervised" independent Kosovo, with suitable protection for its minorities and their rights. In response, Serbia's parliament officially rejected the plan. Paramilitary units composed of Serbs who had fought in one or more of Yugoslavia's civil wars—units named after such Serb heroes as the valiant czar who was unable to stem the Ottoman tide at the Battle of Kosovo—were forming in Serbia and threatening to fight should the UN proposal be adopted. Serb citizens, who in an October 2006 referendum had just voted in favor of a new constitution that explicitly recognized Kosovo as still a part of Serbia, intermittently demonstrated against the UN's proposal on the streets of Belgrade and along Serbia's border with Kosovo. Also joining the chorus were militants in the Serb Republic in Bosnia, who declared their intent to pursue the SR's withdrawal from Bosnia in favor of reunification with Serbia if Kosovo were allowed to become independent. Meanwhile, inside Kosovo, the reaction to the proposal fell far short of jubilation. Only a few months earlier NATO had found a cache of antitank mines, artillery grenades, and other weapons of war being stored by two members of Kosovo's governing Albanian party (the Alliance for the Future of Kosovo). The Kosovo Assembly almost unanimously approved the proposal, but in the streets thousands carrying "Independence Now" banners protested that the proposal did not go far enough quickly enough. Elsewhere, KLA alumni—who were particularly upset over the inclusion in the UN proposal of provisions calling for the dismantling of the Kosovo Protection Corps (KPC), a somewhat watered-down reincarnation of the KLA—muttered dire threats about rekindling the conflict in Macedonia if they did not get their way in Kosovo. By the fall of 2007, even moderate Albanian nationalists (a very relative term) were threatening to declare the province's independence unilaterally if it were not granted by Kosovo's international overseers. Six months later, they did so—on February 17, 2008.

As for the international community, Russia (whose vote is essential for the UN plan to take effect) initially expressed solidarity with Serbia on the Kosovo (non) independence issue, and by mid-summer its threatened veto of the proposal had forced the UN to take the independence plan off the Security Council's agenda "temporarily." Soon, Croatia also counseled against an independent Kosovo, as did the Slovak Republic, which expressed its fear that an independent Kosovo would encourage Slovakia's territorialized Hungarian minority to agitate for either federal autonomy or reunification with Hungary. Even neutral outside observers, with little personally at stake in the outcome, generally expressed a fear that whatever direction the future of Kosovo took, there would be serious consequences for the mixed Serb and Albanian areas of adjacent southern Serbia. In an unofficial referendum held in 1992, 90 percent of their Albanians had voted in favor of unification with Kosovo.[27] It was springtime and then it was summer, fall, and winter 2007–08 in the Balkans, where Kosovo was still the hottest spot nearly a decade after NATO'S 1999 operation to end the conflict there, and where—more than ever—what happens in Kosovo does not necessarily stay in Kosovo.

MACEDONIA

Relations between the Macedonian people and the Macedonian government in Skopje, on the one hand, and Macedonia's Albanian minority, on the other, had been fragile for some time before the Kosovo Liberation Army (KLA) significantly changed the equation in the early twenty-first century by forming a liaison with the rebel Albanian National Liberation Army (NLA) across Kosovo's border, in order to advance the Albanian cause in Macedonia. By then, however, the Macedonian government—although still less than a decade old—was no stranger to international challenges to Macedonia's sovereignty.[28]

BORDER TENSIONS

Although spared involvement in the civil wars raging elsewhere in the former Yugoslavia during the 1990s, Macedonia—the poorest of all the former Yugoslav union republics—was almost immediately caught up in a series of other foreign disputes. As late as 2001, Macedonia was not only an oddity in its region—a self-proclaimed multiethnic state (under the Ohrid Agreement of that year) in a region surrounded by avowedly ethnic nation-states (Bulgaria, Greece, Serbia)—but it was also the target of reprobation and sometimes intrusive action by its neighbors. Serbia still denied the autonomy of its (Orthodox) church, and Bulgaria, which recognized Macedonia's existence as a sovereign state, refused to accept the existence of a distinct Macedonian language or nation. Still, the greatest initial challenge to its sovereignty came from Greece, which opposed the former Yugoslav union republic's desire to call its independent self the Republic of Macedonia.

Greece's problem with the new state was grounded in history and geography. The new country lay largely within, but did not entirely coincide with the ancient Kingdom of Macedonia, the birthplace of Alexander the Great (356–323 BC). The remainder of the territory, including Alexander's actual place of birth, is the province of Macedonia in northern Greece. Hence, at the outset the government in Athens objected to the new state calling itself Macedonia and wrapping itself in the symbols of that historical Hellenic region. The result was a diplomatic skirmish in which Greece imposed an embargo on trade across its border with Macedonia, which Greece did not lift until 1995. By then, the embargo had led to elevated tension between the two countries, incursions by smugglers, and occasional confrontations between Greeks and Macedonians across that border. Greece's response also involved a sustained effort by Athens to deny international recognition of the new state under any name other than "the Former Yugoslav Republic of Macedonia." The gambit succeeded for more than a decade, in terms of both the name under which Macedonia was seated at the United Nations in May 1992, and the support gained from all of Greece's allies in NATO, except Turkey. Then, in November 2004, the United States essentially rendered the ploy moot when it formally recognized the former Yugoslav republic as simply "Macedonia." That action angered Athens, and the name of Greece's northern neighbor still remains a diplomatic sore point there, with relations between Athens and Skopje further souring in mid-decade when Macedonia named the Skopje airport after Alexander the Great. Nevertheless, for all practical purposes the U.S. diplomatic action resolved, in Skopje's favor, the lingering and often very tense diplomatic standoff between Macedonia and Greece over the former's name, and the danger of that conflict turning violent along their border zone essentially disappeared in 2004.

Macedonian-Albanian Tension

In the meantime, relations within Macedonia between the country's nearly 65 percent Macedonian majority and approximately 25 percent Albanian minority had limped along in a tense, but generally nonviolent manner for nearly a decade between the country's secession from Yugoslavia in 1991 and the end of the millennium.[29] The secession itself was hardly a unilateral act by the Yugoslavia's Macedonian community. Rather, it had followed the route pursued by the other exiting republics. First, the union republic's communist government in Skopje held a referendum on the withdrawal matter in September 1991. Then, following the referendum's approval, the government declared Macedonia's independence and adopted an independence constitution two months later. On the other hand, throughout the 1990s the country's Albanian minority had reason to resent their inferior economic status and their scant political influence in a country that continued to be ruled by its Macedonian-dominated Communist Party until November, 1998, when that party was finally ousted by a coalition government led by its Macedonian parties but including the Democratic Party of Albanians. Even then, the grievances of the country's Albanian Muslim minority received little attention, and Macedonia remained a largely segregated country with little interaction between its two largest communities, even where they were geographically intermingled. Moreover, in terms of legitimacy there were few reasons for either the Macedonians or the country's Albanians to have any great confidence in their government's inclination to "do the right thing," whatever that might have meant to the two communities. The widely respected International Crisis Group summarized the situation in 2001, in the midst of violent Macedonian-Albanian fighting:

> The international community has contributed to an environment of mistrust and cynicism by reluctantly validating a series of elections dating from 1994 that were marred by deaths, violence, and widespread voting irregularities, including ballot stuffing, proxy voting and tampering with returns.[30]

Nevertheless, by the end of the 1990s the greatest threat to Macedonian-Albanian relations inside Macedonia had clearly become the deteriorating situation north of its border, in Kosovo. As the conflict intensified between the Kosovo Liberation Army and Serbian forces in that province of Serbia, the arrival of substantial numbers of Kosovo Albanian Muslim refugees in Macedonia placed an added strain on the country's economy and encouraged factions in Macedonia's Albanian community to contemplate their own armed struggle for economic and political rights. NATO's 1999 bombing campaign on behalf of Kosovo's Albanian minority produced yet another exodus of Kosovo refugees, and although most found their way to locations in Albania, such as the internationally sponsored Camp Hope, Macedonia's fragile economy sustained another blow when large numbers arrived there. There was also significant collateral damage. Albanian-Macedonian relations within Macedonia were often strained by the renewed attention being given to Albanian minority rights in the Balkans. The big blow to that relationship came, however, when the first rounds of internationally-monitored elections in Kosovo in 1999 and 2000 left the KLA's "independence now"-minded leaders in second place behind the leadership of the more moderate Kosovo Albanian parties, who favored working peacefully with the international community to secure Kosovo's regional autonomy first, and then its eventual independence.[31] Left out of power in their own province, disgruntled KLA factions looked for another means of advancing the cause of a Greater Albania and/or Albanian minorities in the Balkans. Macedonia, across Kosovo's southern, internationally patrolled border, beckoned.[32]

It is likely that the brewing tensions between Macedonia's Albanian and Macedonian communities would have eventually led to violence without outside prompting. Grievances still lingered in the Albanian community from the 1980s, when the state's communist government cooperated with Belgrade in its crackdown on Yugoslavia's Albanian communities. Likewise, Macedonia's government in Skopje was hardly reform-minded toward its Albanian minorities. The constitution adopted at independence was a particularly sore point among the country's Albanians because it defined the country essentially as a Macedonian ethnic state ("the nation-state of the Macedonian people"). Moreover, the economic disparity and political tensions between the country's two largest communities had grown following independence, as political leaders in both communities appealed to each community's more nationalistic elements. Nevertheless, the violent conflict that erupted in early 2001 in the heavily Muslim Albanian territories to the north and west of Skopje, along Macedonia's border with Kosovo, was largely instigated by KLA factions working in concert with Macedonia's own Albanian guerrilla forces.

Once the fighting began between the NLA and Macedonian security forces, it quickly gained a momentum of its own that was blunted only by the subsequent intervention of Western diplomats seeking to reconcile the conflicting parties. A cease-fire was reached on June 11, and at the formal request of the Macedonian government NATO forces arrived shortly thereafter to assist in the disarmament of the Albanian rebels. By then the warfare had already raged for several months, dislocating thousands of people. Reports of kidnappings and of Albanian guerillas and civilians torturing and executing captives and hostages were numerous, as were documented cases of abuses by Macedonian forces against Albanian civilians and outsiders caught in the conflict. Nor did these acts end with the August 2001 signing of the Ohrid Accord, which established a framework for resolving the conflict. Some of the heaviest and most violent fighting occurred shortly after the agreement's signing and continued until at least April 2002. Perhaps most notoriously, in March of that year Macedonia's Interior Minister allegedly choreographed the execution of seven Pakistani migrant workers to make it appear that al-Qaeda forces had entered Macedonia to join with Albanian rebels in a fight against the Macedonian people.

THE OHRID AGREEMENT

As an instrument of conflict resolution, the Ohrid Agreement—enacted by Macedonia's parliament two months after its negotiation—focused on three areas. First, local government was to be territorially reorganized at the local level in such way as to enhance the political power of the state's minorities in general, but principally that of its large Albanian community. Second, the status of the Albanian language was to be elevated throughout country, and an Albanian-language university—long opposed by the country's Macedonian leadership—was to be certified. Finally, the country's constitution was to be modified to redefine the country as a multiethnic "civil" state composed of the "citizens of the Republic of Macedonia," rather than as the nation-state of the Macedonians. In no instance has the implementation of these reforms fully resulted in the desired amelioration of Albanian-Macedonian tensions. In some instances, their implementation has exacerbated the conflict.

For their part, Macedonians continue to resent deeply the redefinition of their country as a "civil state" rather than as a Macedonian (ethnic) nation-state, especially given their location in the midst of a region of nation-states. They also resent the manner in which the Ohrid Agreement was reached—that is, under the double duress of the escalating violence being committed by Albanian paramilitaries and the international pressure placed on the government in Skopje to make concessions to Macedonia's Albanian minorities. As the International Crisis group put it, "Macedonians depend on the name 'Macedonia' as the designation of both their state and their people." The commitments that were made at Ohrid pertaining to the name of the state directly compromised that linkage.[33]

Meanwhile, the implementation of those provisions relating to the structure of the state via the Territorial Organization Act of August, 2004, has had mixed results. By amalgamating districts containing Macedonia's minorities, the Act increased the number of locales in which Albanians constitute at least 20 percent of the population, and accordingly the number of areas in which Albanian would become a second official language and Albanians would attain a greater representation in local governments. In doing so, however, the Territorial Organization Act also fostered fears still present among the Macedonians that by consolidating ethnic Albanian areas the plan would facilitate the division of their country and/or encourage Albanian separatism.[34] Albanian paramilitary units materializing on the outskirts of Skopje in early 2005 significantly increased the Macedonians' misgivings. Consequently, despite the Ohrid Agreement's commitment to make Macedonia a multiethnic civic state, the country's political parties remain rooted in their individual ethnic communities, and they continue to function, as International Crisis Group monitors phrased it, "more as mechanisms for distribution of patronage and running election campaigns than real engines of democratic inclusion."[35]

The threat of future violence does not end there. The political and judicial institutions charged with maintaining peace between the country's two largest communities—each separated from the other by reinforcing ethnic *and* religious cleavages (e.g., the Orthodox Macedonian Christians and the Muslim Albanians)—remain fragile and often tainted by a corruption so deeply embedded in the system that it will require a very long time to weed out. Indeed, it will take all the longer because it is often linked to an organized crime drugs-and-prostitution network in the country that, in turn, has tight links with Albanian separatist organizations.[36]

Conflict resolution is also complicated by the fact that, as elsewhere in the former Yugoslavia, unemployment remains high (running at 37.3 percent 15 years into the new state's life), despite the fact that economic growth between 2003 and 2005 was nearly double the growth rate over the previous three-year period.[37] Most importantly, violence has by no means disappeared from the country's political scene. Serious outbreaks of kidnapping and other acts of ethno-political violence were being felt long after the Ohrid Agreement. Indeed, two years after the agreement was signed, monitoring groups were reporting a general increase in lawlessness—including increases in shootings, kidnappings, bombings, and murder—even as most of its provisions were being implemented.[38]

In short, to cite another International Crisis Group (ICG) analyst, "Macedonia is not 'just another transition country' but an inherently weak state with external and internal challenges to its very existence."[39] It is a finding that the ICG shares with most other neutral observers, including Human Rights Watch, which noted in mid-decade that although by the end of 2004 all paper obligations of the Ohrid Agreement had been implemented, the government's failure to disarm the ethnic Albanian paramilitaries fully had led to a "worsening security situation in areas populated predominantly by Albanians" and "discrimination against national minorities, including in particular ethnic Albanians and Roma, and police violence continued to be problems in the country."[40]

Not all news coming out of Macedonia has been bad news; some has been mixed. In 2002, free and fair national elections were held under international supervision, with 800 international monitors observing the polling. The result was a new governing coalition that included the political party of the former Albanian rebel leader, Ali Ahmeti—a government with a greater sense of legitimacy in the eyes of the country's Albanian minority. Unfortunately, during much of the time since 2002, the inclusion of Ahmeti's party along with other Albanian parties in the governing coalition has also led to their jockeying for position against one another, and occasionally boycotting cabinet meetings. Sometimes they have even dropped out of the governing coalitions in order to improve their bargaining positions, at the cost of rendering the government incapable of functioning effectively. When they have done so they have blamed the Macedonian parties for slighting them in policy-making negotiations, at the cost of further aggravating Albanian-Macedonian relations in the country. Stated differently, in a country that needs a strong government to attack its economic problems, corruption, and crime, policy paralysis has sometimes been the price of political inclusiveness. Moreover, at least as far as the 2006 national vote is concerned, the elections giving birth to those parties in government continue to be tainted by allegations of attacks on campaign offices, vote buying, biased reporting on the state-operated broadcasting system, and isolated shooting incidents.

Meanwhile, on a more positive note, the threat of *international* conflict diminished in the early years of the twenty-first century. Diplomatic tensions over the country's name persist with neighboring Greece, but when Greece opened its border to trade with Macedonia, the danger of black market border incursions becoming flashpoints for a broader conflict faded. The border with Kosovo also quieted in mid-decade, as the KLA factions moderated their activities and concentrated on convincing the United Nations authorities overseeing Kosovo's political process that an independent Kosovo will live at peace with its neighbors.

Whether an independent, overwhelmingly Muslim Albanian Kosovo will be able to control its Pan-Albanian nationalists is an open and hot topic. But even if its government in the regional capital of Pristina is unable to do so fully, the threat of Macedonia being engulfed in a war dedicated to the unification of the Albanian people in the Balkans remains remote. As in the case of Kosovo's Albanians, the resentment of Macedonia's Albanian Muslims has focused on such local grievances as their status as an economic underclass and their need for local political autonomy and greater influence at the center—not on the attainment of a Greater Albania. These are goals subject to accommodation, and although the path to accommodating them will almost certainly be bumpy and mined with periodic, potentially violent political conflicts between the Albanians and Macedonians, it is not a road likely to produce a civil war in Macedonia. Civil war is not likely—at least, that is, without an outside spark, and neighboring Kosovo, frustrated in its desire for full, internationally recognized independence, *could* create a political firestorm.

Macedonian special forces keeping watch over the area to the northwest of Tetovo. © Kontos Yannis/Corbis Sygma.

TIMELINE

1389	Ottoman Turks defeat Serbian Empire at Battle of Kosovo and rule area until World War I dissolves Ottoman Empire; meanwhile, Kosovo becomes increasingly Albanian-speaking and Muslim.
1800s	Nineteenth-century Pan-Slavic movements arise, chiefly in Serbia.
1878	Serbia, including Montenegro, achieves independence from Ottoman rule.
1908	Austria-Hungary annexes Bosnia.
1912–13	Balkan Wars; Serbia gains northern and central Macedonia; Albania achieves independence from Ottomans.
1914	Serb assassinates Austrian Archduke Ferdinand, igniting World War I.
1918	Kingdom of the Serbs, Croats, and Slovenes formed following World War I.
1929	King Alexander I renames the country Yugoslavia, assumes authoritarian powers; the Ustase, an extremist Croatian nationalist organization, is founded.

1934	King Alexander I assassinated in France.
1941–45	World War II intensifies intercommunal animosity as Germany creates puppet Croatian and Albanian-Kosovar states, and the Croats and Albanians settle old grievances against Serbs.
1945–47	Federal Republic of Yugoslavia established; Kosovo a part of Serbia; Tito helps communists attain rule in postwar Albania.
1974	New constitution gives autonomy to Kosovo inside Serbia.
1980	Tito dies; nationalism increases within all groups composing Yugoslavia.
1989	Serbian nationalist Milosevic assumes power; Kosovo loses autonomy.
1990	Anticommunist revolutions sweep Central Europe; four Yugoslav republics elect noncommunist governments; Kosovo Albanians create separatist "government" in exile.
1991	Western countries encourage Croatia and Slovenia to secede; Albania begins to liberalize.
1991–92	Four republics secede; Macedonia exits peacefully, but civil wars follow secession of Slovenia, Croatia, and Bosnia-Herzegovina.
1992	UN creates peacekeeping forces for Croatia (Feb.), Bosnia (Sept.), and Macedonia (Dec.); Yugoslavia expelled from UN for aiding Serb aggressors in Bosnia.
1993	Kosovo Liberation Army (KLA) forms; UN authorizes creation of an international War Crimes Tribunal and six "safe havens" in Bosnia.
1994	Croatians and Bosnian Muslims agree to form joint federation in Bosnia.
1995	July: Serbs launch major offensive against safe areas. August: Croatia launches offensive against its rebellious Serb region; Serbs attack Sarajevo and NATO responds by attacking Serbian artillery. November: Spokesmen for Bosnia, Croatia, and Serbia reach an agreement to end war in Bosnia; resultant Dayton Accord provides for creating a democratic republic under international tutelage.
1997	Bosnia holds internationally supervised local elections; KLA attacks on Yugoslav units in Kosovo increase.

1997   Albania implodes, making weapons available to
              KLA.
1998   In Bosnia's elections its nationalist parties do well;
              ethnic cleansing begins in Kosovo, producing
              nearly 300,000 Kosovar refugees.
1999   January 28: NATO tells Milosevic it is prepared
              to use military force to end ethnic cleansing in
              Kosovo;
              March 24: NATO begins 78-day air offensive;
              number of refugees soars; June: hostilities end;
              UN authorizes creating Kosovo Stabilization
              Force (KFOR) and UN Administration Mission
              in Kosovo.
2000   October: In Kosovo municipal elections, voters
              support moderates; KLA begins to agitate across
              the border in Macedonia's Albanian community;
              violence continues even after international peace-
              keeping forces arrive and conclusion of the Ohrid
              Agreement—designed to settle conflict in Mace-
              donia—in August.
2000–01   Safety of Kosovo's Serbs becomes an issue.
2002   Nationalists do well again in Bosnian elections;
              UN's International Police Task Force turns
              mentoring of nascent Bosnian police force over to
              European Union.
2003   Federal Republic of Yugoslavia dissolved in favor
              of looser Montenegro-Serbia relationship; inter-
              national peacekeeping forces remain deployed in
              Bosnia, Kosovo, and Macedonia.
2004   March: Riots in Kosovo force NATO to increase
              size of its peacekeeping forces.
              December: NATO leaves Bosnia to be replaced
              by a small EU contingent (EUFOR).
2006   Discussions on final status of Kosovo begin;
              United States and UN urge Bosnia to draft a new
              constitution that puts more emphasis on its cen-
              tral government and intercommunal collaboration
              in decision making.
2007   April–May: UN recommends independence as
              final status for Kosovo; Russia indicates it will
              block that decision in the Security Council, if nec-
              essary; Serbs in Bosnia-Herzegovina threaten to
              hold referendum on reintegration with Serbia if

Kosovo gets independence; Bosnia revokes citizenship of foreign Muslims who came to Bosnia to fight for its independence, citing need to collaborate in international effort to counteract threats of terrorism.

July: Russian ambassador on the UN Security Council informs his colleagues that the chances of passing the proposal to set Kosovo on the road to full independence "are zero," effectively tabling the proposal for the immediate future; Kosovo Albanians threaten to declare independence unilaterally.

August: Kosovo Albanians again threaten to announce independence unilaterally if not given independence by UN.

November: Kosovo voters give plurality to party of former KLA leader who in campaigning pledged to declare Kosovo's independence within one month of becoming prime minister.

2008   February 17. Kosovo's provisional government unilaterally declares Kosovo independent. The United States alone quickly recognizes that independence. In response, protesting Serbs attack U.S. embassy in Belgrade on February 21.

Notes

1. For general reading on the origins and turbulent history of Yugoslavia see Sabrina P. Ramet, *Nationalism and Federalism in Yugoslavia, 1962–1991* (Bloomington: Indiana University Press, 1992) and *The Disintegration of Yugoslavia: From the Death of Tito to Ethnic War* (Boulder, CO: Westview Press/ Harper Collins, 1996); Tim Judah, *The Serbs: History, Myth, and the Destruction of Yugoslavia* (New Haven: Yale University Press, 1997); and Laura Silber and Alan Little, *Yugoslavia, Death of A Nation* (New York: Penguin Books, 1995).

2. The most important of these battles occurred in 1389 at Kosovo Polje (the Battle of Kosovo), although some observers prefer to date the end of the ancient Serbian Empire from its final stand at the Battle of Varna in 1444. On the Albanianization of Kosovo, see especially Alexei G. Arbetov, "The Kosovo Crisis: The End of the Post-Cold War Era" (Washington, DC: Atlantic Council Occasional Paper, 2002: 7–8).

3. Fred Singleton, *A Short History of the Yugoslav Peoples* (Cambridge, UK: Cambridge University Press, 1985: 13).

4. A similar strategy was also pursued in Belgium, where Germany exploited anti-French sentiment in Belgium's Flemish-speaking north, and even more

notoriously, in occupied Czechoslovakia, where anti-Czech sentiments in Slovakia were encouraged and the "First Slovak Republic," a German puppet, was created by the country's German conquerors.

5. The figure is pre-civil war, based on the last official census (1981) conducted in the former Yugoslavia, as reported in Glenn E. Curtis, ed. *Yugoslavia: A Country Study* (Washington, DC: Library of Congress, 1992: 70, 293). The same census found less than 5 percent of the country's population identifying themselves as Yugoslavs, as opposed to Serbs (33+%), Croats (19.7%), Muslim Slavs or Bosniaks (8.9%), Slovenes (7.8%), Albanians (7.7%), Macedonians (6.0%), Montenegrins (2.6%), and assorted others (1.9%).

6. See, for example, "Kosovo Albanian Leader Demands Independence," *The Baltimore Sun* (March 12, 1998); "Kosovo Rebels Insist on Independence Amid New Violence," *The Baltimore Sun* (December 5, 1998); and Peter Finn, "Squeezing Out Kosovo's Serbs," *The Washington Post* (January 4, 1999).

7. See International Crisis Group, "Pan-Albanianism: How Big a Threat to Balkan Stability?" (International Crisis Group Europe Report No. 153, February 25, 2004: www.crisisgroup.org). The report notes that, if anything, Albania has been courting the West since 1999 (clamping down on corruptions at home, for example, and supplying troops for Western military operations in Afghanistan) as a solution to its pressing economic needs, and has not embraced the cause of Pan-Albanianism in any form.

8. For an exhaustive analysis of the Balkans in the early days of the twenty-first century, see especially International Crisis Group, "After Milosevic: A Practical Agenda for Lasting Balkans Peace" (International Crisis Group Europe Report No. 108, April 1, 2001; www.crisisgroup.org).

9. In a national referendum held in early April, 2004, Slovenes overwhelmingly voted against (95 percent to 5 percent) restoring the rights of citizenship to the country's remaining Bosnian, Croat, and Serb minorities (locally known as "the Erased"). See Associated Press, "Slovenian Vote Denies Rights to Minorities," *The Baltimore Sun* (April, 5, 2005).

10. See International Crisis Group, "Serbia's New Government: Turning from Europe" (ICG Europe Briefing No. 46, May 31, 2007; www.crisisgroup.org).

11. On Montenegro's peaceful departure from the Serbia-Montenegro federation which continued to call itself Yugoslavia long after the rest of the country disintegrated, see Tom Hundley, "Montenegro Votes to Secede: 55.4% Back Independence from Serbia; Final Result Expected Today," *The Baltimore Sun* (May 23, 2006) and Associated Press, "Montenegro Declares Independence: Balkan Nation Severs Union with Serbia," *The Baltimore Sun* (June 6, 2006). For a background discussion of the political issues that eventually led to Montenegro's decision to separate from Serbia, see International Crisis Group, "A Marriage of Inconvenience: Montenegro, 2003" (ICG Europe Report No. 142, April 15, 2003; www.crisisgroup.org). A more detailed discussion of the vote and its significance can also be found in "Montenegro's Referendum" European Briefing No. 42, May 30, 2006; www.crisisgroup.org).

12. ICG, "The Macedonian Question: Reform or Rebellion" (Europe Report No. 109, April 5, 2001; www.crisisgroup.org). Statistics are taken from the Report's "Summary," p. 2.

13. See Jonathan Finer, "In Bosnia, Former Fighters Face Expulsion: Many Foreign-Born Muslims Who Came During 1992–95 War Now Losing Citizenship," *The Washington Post* (September 4, 2007).

14. On the Dayton Peace Accord and the subsequent international peace-keeping and state-building operations in Bosnia, see especially: Wolfgang Biermann and Martin Vadset, eds. *UN Peacekeeping in Trouble: Lessons Learned from the Former Yugoslavia* (Brookfield, VT: Ashgate, 1998); Sumantra Bose, *Bosnia after Dayton: Nationalist Partition and International Intervention* (New York: Oxford University Press, 2002); Derek H. Chollet, *The Road to the Dayton Accords: A Study of American Statecraft* (New York: Palgrave-Macmillan, 2005); and Michael A. Innes, ed. *Bosnian Security after Dayton: New Perspectives* (New York: Routledge, 2006).

15. For purposes of allocating those positions based on the proportionality principle, the 1991 census figures, which predate the civil war, have continued to be used as a means of minimizing minority fears. Since the war, the Bosniak share of the population has continued to grow and the Croat share has shrunk. That situation is either a result of the unwillingness of Croats driven from their land during the ethnic cleansing operations to return to Bosnia or a result of the migration of Bosnia's Croats to Croatia.

16. See International Crisis Group, "Ensuring Bosnia's Future: A New International Engagement Strategy" (International Crisis Group Europe Report No. 180, February 15, 2007: 3; www.crisisgroup.org).

17. The direct citations are from ICG, "Ensuring Bosnia's Future," pp. 2, 10.

18. See, for example, the account of the 2007 festival in Jonathan Fines, "War Casts Large Shadow on Sarajevo Film Screens," *Washington Post* (August 24, 2007): A8.

19. See especially International Crisis Group, "Bosnia's Stalled Police Reform: No Progress, No EU" (International Crisis Group Europe Report No. 164, September 6, 2005; www.crisisgroup.org).

20. See International Crisis Group, "The Challenge of Transition" (ICG Europe Report No, 170, February 17, 2006; www.crisisgroup.org).

21. A contingent of Russian troops was also initially present in Kosovo, having landed and secured the airport in Pristina before the arrival of the NATO forces. Citing improved conditions, Russia withdrew those forces in 2003, exactly four years after their arrival.

22. See Michael J. Jordan, "Even in Eager Kosovo, Nation-Building Stalls," *Christian Science Monitor* (September 22, 2004); International Crisis Group, "After Haradinaj" (ICG Europe Report No. 163, May 26, 2005), published one year after the violent rioting in 2004 and shortly after the province's prime minister had to resign after being indicted for war crimes by an international tribunal.

23. ICG, "Return to Uncertainty: Kosovo's Internally Displaced and the Return Process" (Pristina, Kosovo: International Crisis Group Balkan Report

No. 139, 2002: 6). The report notes that the Romani, in particular, fit into this "enclavization" of minorities pattern in Kosovo. The Romani, however, have traditionally sought living arrangements apart from their host populations throughout Central Europe

24. See UNHCR, "UNHCR Condemns Violence Targeting Kosovo Serb Returnees" (Briefing Notes, September 22, 2006), with specific reference to the Klina Kilne municipality to which 552 Serbs and Roma had returned since 2000. See also the UNHCR report, "Kosovo Minorities Still Need International Protection, Says UNHCR" (August 24, 2004) Both are available at www.unhcr.org/news.

25. See Nidzara Ahmetasevic, "Bosnian Returnees Quietly Quit Regained Homes," Institute for War and Peace Reporting, August 31, 2006; www.iwpr.net); Christopher Deliso, "Botched Kosovo Intervention Dims Hopes for Peace," *The Baltimore Sun* (May 10, 2006).

26. Three years after NATO's bombing campaign, for example, more than 15,000 Kosovo IDP's had filed applications for the return of their homes, but only 138 of these had actually repossessed their property. See United Nations Office for the Coordination of Humanitarian Affairs (OCHA), "Humanitarian Situation, Protection and Assistance: Internally Displaced Persons in Serbia and Montenegro (Belgrade: OCHA, Humanitarian Risk Analysis No. 18, 2002: 20).

27. See International Crisis Group, "Southern Serbia: In Kosovo's Shadow" (ICG European Briefings No. 43, June 27, 2006) and "Southern Serbia's Fragile Peace" (ICG Europe Report No. 152, December 9, 2003). Both are available online (www.crisisgroup.org).

28. For a background exploration of Macedonian politics on the eve of its 2000 mini-civil war, see Loring M. Danforth, *The Macedonian Conflict: Ethnic Nationalism in a Transnational World* (Princeton, NJ: Princeton University Press, 1998).

29. According to Central Intelligence Agency estimates, Macedonia's total population was slightly more than 2 million (2,050,554) in 2006. Within the population, the breakdown along ethnic lines continues to use the figures recorded in the country's census report of five years earlier, which listed Macedonians at 64.2 percent of the population and Albanians at 25.2 percent The remainder of the population was distributed among the country's Turkish people (3.9%), Roma (2.7%), Serbs (1.8%) and "others," a category that included people of Greek origin (2.2%). See the "CIA Factbook" (https://www.cia.gov/cia/publications/factbook/geos/mk.html, accessed October 5, 2006). Albanian nationalists reject these figures and argue that Albanians actually represent between 35 percent and 45 percent of the country's population.

30. International Crisis Group/Executive Summary and Recommendations, "The Macedonian Question: Reform or Rebellion" (International Crisis Group Europe Report No. 109, Recommendation 5, April 5, 2001; www.crisisgroup.org).

31. See International Crisis Group, "Macedonia: Towards Destabilization? The Kosovo Crisis Takes Its Toll on Macedonia" (ICG Europe Report No. 67, May 21, 1999; www.crisisgroup.org). The report noted in particular that given

the cost of hosting the approximately 200,000 Kosovar Albanians entering Macedonia during NATO's bombing campaign, there was "hardly any money left for unemployment benefits, pensions, and health care provisions."

32. On the spread of the conflict to Macedonia, see International Crisis Group, "Macedonia: Towards Destabilization?" op. cit.; International Crisis Group, "Macedonia: Make or Break" (ICG Europe Briefing No. 33, August 2, 2004); International Crisis Group, "Pan-Albanianism: How Big a Threat to Balkan Instability" (ICG Europe Report No. 153, February 25, 2004). All are available online (www.crisisgroup.org).

33. International Crisis Group, "Macedonia's Name: Why the Dispute Matters and How to Resolve It: Executive Summary and Recommendations" (ICS European Report No. 122, 10 December 10, 2001). Available on line (www.crisisgroup.org).

34. Ibid.

35. International Crisis Group, "Macedonia: Make or Break," op. cit.

36. See International Crisis Group, "Macedonia's Public Secret: How Government Corruption Drags The Country Down" (ICG Europe Report No. 113, August 14, 2002; www.crisisgroup.org); Toby Westerman, "Albanian Separatists Reportedly Getting Rich off Drugs, Prostitution" (WorldNet Daily report, May 7, 2001, retrieved on line May 20, 2001).

37. The growth rates for the 2003–05 period ranged from 3.4 percent to 4.1 percent. See the CIA Factbook, Macedonia entry (https://www.cia.gov/library/publications/the-world-factbook/geos/mk.html).

38. See International Crisis Group, "Macedonia: No Time for Complacency" (ICG Europe Report No. 149, October 23, 2003; www.crisisgroup.org).

39. The ICG report noted that the international efforts to curtain corruption in the country have erroneously emphasized process and "capacity building" rather than cracking down on an existing corruption that prevents prosecutors from pursuing sensitive cases and discourages international businesses from trusting Macedonia's banking system. International Crisis Group, "Macedonia's Public Secret: How Government Corruption Drags The Country Down: Executive Summary and Recommendations," op. cit.

40. Human Rights Watch, "Macedonia" (http://hrw.org/english/docs/2005/01/13/macedo9875.htm, accessed April 28, 2005).

CHAPTER 4

CENTRAL EUROPE

When the communist regimes of Central Europe collapsed—one after another and overwhelmingly peacefully—between 1988 and 1991, the leaders of the European Union began to contemplate what had once seemed so remote: a united Europe stretching, as French President Charles de Gaulle once phrased it, "from the Atlantic to the Urals." It was clear, of course, that none of the newly liberated states was immediately ready for admission to the European Union—then a Western European organization dominated by countries with established democratic regimes and competitive economies. Consequently, the countries of post-communist Central Europe began to democratize and reshape their economies around the principles of economic liberalism, and to think longingly of admission to NATO and the European Union (EU). At the same time, Western European leaders began to group them based on the anticipated time that each would require before being admitted to a European Union already committed to the principle of a unified Europe with a common currency and without controls on the borders separating its member states.

Those states with already (relatively) high per capita incomes deemed able to adjust more easily to a capitalist economy, with at least some prior experience with democracy, and with generally ethnically homogenous populations were placed on the "fast track." Composing this category were Hungary, Poland, the Czech Republic half of the former Czechoslovakia (which chose to peacefully separate into the Czech and Slovak Republics on January 1, 1993), Slovenia (which seceded from the former Yugoslavia in 1991), and at least one of the Baltic Republics (Lithuania, Latvia, and Estonia) that had formerly been a part of the Soviet Union. Next came several post-communist countries on a slower track—countries such as the Slovak Republic, whose immediate post-communist history suggested that it would require more time than the fast-track states in making the adjustment to a capitalist economy and/or a functioning democracy that respected such basic rights as freedom of the press. Third, there were those states—principally Romania and Bulgaria—that were placed on a "back track" schedule that seemed to require a longer time still before they would be ready for admission to the EU. Finally, there were the "off track" areas of the former Yugoslavia and the underbelly of the former Soviet Union, regions troubled by civil wars or the scars of recent civil warfare that were perceived to need the most time of all before being ready for admission to an economically integrated Europe.

The fast-track states spent much of the 1990s waiting for the EU to call and preparing themselves as well as possible for the pangs of entry, accelerating the pace of economic liberalization and making the necessary adjustments in their environmental laws to gain EU acceptance. Some, most notably Hungary, even erected "Welcome" banners and separate visa aisles at their airports for EU citizens. In the end, their courtship went largely for naught. Internal disagreements among existing EU member states complicated the EU's enlargement process, and when the long-awaited expansion occurred, both fast-track and slower-track states were admitted in May 2004. In the intervening period, even the back-track states had sufficient time to nearly catch up with their better prepared post-communist cousins, and in early 2007 both Romania and Bulgaria acceded to the EU as well. That left only the off-track areas such as Bosnia-Herzegovina (still under international tutelage), Serbia, and Georgia still waiting for a likely membership date.

The accession of most post-communist states in less than a decade and a half reflects the tremendous progress each made in stabilizing its economy, shunning old authoritarian habits, accommodating their internal minorities' demands for inclusion, and establishing democratic constitutional systems. There was one exception. Despite the fact that both NATO and the EU demanded an end to discrimination against the Romani as a precondition for membership, violence against this much-detested minority continued throughout the 1990s and did not dissuade either organization from opening its doors to the countries engaging in such practices. Nor did a state's entry into NATO and the EU end the discrimination and not-infrequent violence against its Romani minority. On the contrary, such persecutions often increased, but in the early years of the twenty-first century the Romani have begun to fight back, and the violence between the Romani and Central Europeans has become a two-way street.

THE ROMANI

A Legacy of Expulsion, Enslavement, and Extermination

The Romani first arrived in Europe approximately 700 years ago. They were greeted in some parts with enslavement, which lasted until nearly the time of the American Civil War. Elsewhere, over the course of the centuries, they were used as game in the nineteenth-century Gypsy hunts in Germany; subjected to forced assimilation on two occasions; targeted for instant hanging in earlier times and forced sterilization in more recent eras; and banished from countries shortly after arrival on almost innumerable occasions. During World War II, they were earmarked for mass extermination (the Romani Holocaust). They have never been welcomed and have never integrated—in part by their own choice—into the societies hosting them or through which they have passed. Unlike Europe's Jews, who prospered as money lenders in the Middle Ages and were the Austrian Empire's administrators and part of Europe's nineteenth- and early twentieth-century intellectual elite—the Romani have never enjoyed a moment of collective prestige or honor. What they have managed to do is survive as the most detested, poorest, and least-educated community in the region that remains their home. Like Western Europe's unassimilated Muslim underclass, the Romani are increasingly frustrated with their status, to the point of constituting the one shared threat to the public order in the states of post-communist Central Europe.

Migration to Oppression and Forced Nomadism

There are nearly as many stories chronicling the arrival of the Romani (or Roma) in Europe as there are names by which they have variously been known in the lands into which they migrated and through which they have traveled. They are known as Gitanos, Sinti, Romanichal, "Egyptians," the travelers, and—most commonly—simply as Gypsies. One legend has them in Europe at the time of Alexander the Great (356–323 BC); others relate their presence in the early days of the Byzantine Empire (circa 345 AD). Likewise, as the names attached to them indicate, their point of origin was long debated as well. Based on modern methods of linguistic mapping, however, the general consensus today is that the Romani departed from northwestern India ahead of the Muslim conquerors approximately a thousand years ago, and began arriving in the southern and central parts of Europe in significant numbers between the late ninth and early fourteenth centuries. What has never been in doubt was the nature of the reception they received upon arrival, and as the time line notes, the rejection that they encountered was not limited to Central Europe. The principal variable over time and space was only the degree of hostility that they soon encountered.

The worst reception in the early years was in Walachia, a region partly encompassing contemporary Romania, where the Romani were enslaved from the fourteenth century until 1863. Still, nowhere did they find a welcome mat. Rather, a pattern of hostility developed virtually everywhere they roamed. Even where they were initially accepted for the amusement (primarily music and fortune-telling) and crafts that they brought, their arrival on the outskirts of towns was almost immediately followed by laws forbidding their presence. Over the centuries those laws came to cover greater areas. The pope banned the Romani from the domain of the Catholic Church in 1568, and later they were banned from all of Spain (1619) and from all of Louis XIV's France (1666). During the same period, the crimes of which they were accused, fed by rumors, escalated from petty theft to baby stealing to cannibalism, and the penalties for noncompliance with the exile laws that targeted them increased from forced exile to branding, and eventually death.[1] Ironically, the efforts in Western Europe to be rid of them not only resulted in their gradual concentration in those areas of Central Europe where their capture did not result in enslavement, but also brought them to the Americas during the age of New World colonialism. Portugal, for example, banned the Roma language and deported its Romani to Brazil in 1685, and Britain dispatched large numbers of its unwanted Romani to North America prior to the American Revolutionary War (1776–83). In turn, the newly independent countries of the New World enacted their own anti-Romani statutes. Argentina and the United States both barred Romani from entering their countries during the 1880s, the same decade in which Chancellor Bismarck was advocating the deportation of any non-German-born Romani from the recently unified Imperial Germany.

Forced Assimilation, Round I

Prior to the 1950s, there had been only one sustained departure in Western and Central Europe from the general pattern of ridding one's land of Romani tribes. In 1761, Hapsburg Empress Maria Theresa abandoned the policy of banning the Romani in favor of a sustained policy of assimilating them. Their caravan-like, nomadic ways were to end, they were to abandon their traditional means of earning their livelihoods, their children were taken from them to be raised in foster homes, and—to accelerate the assimilation process—they were forbidden to speak their own language and marry other Romani. The policy died with its author, but from the beginning it was a failure that primarily resulted in the illegal migration of the Romani from the core of the Austro-Hungarian Empire into its rural backwaters and adjacent countries—including a Germany where, in the 1800s, Gypsy hunts became a popular sport. Indeed, that sport continued even after the formal abolition of Romani slavery in the last areas of Europe still condoning the institution (Moldavia and Romania) in 1855 and 1856 (and the end of its practice over the following decade). Then came the twentieth century, and matters worsened for the Romani, both in Germany and throughout Central Europe.

The Romani Holocaust

After World War I, the victors' application of the principle of national self-determination in Central Europe in the course of breaking up the Austro-Hungarian empire brought little relief to the region's Romani communities. Old policies continued, especially in newly created Czechoslovakia. There, Romani men were tried for cannibalism in the eastern region of Slovakia during the mid-1920s, and the national government in Prague followed Maria Theresa's lead by forbidding Romani nomadism and authorizing the taking of Gypsy children from their parents as a means of controlling the Romani population. The forced sterilization of Romani women also became a common practice in Central Europe during this period, as well as in such "enlightened" European countries as Sweden. As in the past, their outsider status, clannish ways, unique language and culture, and unwillingness to associate with the local communities (whom the Romani viewed as "unclean") conspired repeatedly to make them stand out wherever they settled, and to make them the target of both public laws and social discrimination.

In short, even before Hitler came to power in Germany and designated the Romani—along with Jews, gays, and other "undesirables"—for extermination, they had become an unwelcome, often despised outer class. Living apart from the societies around them, whose tongues they often did not speak or spoke only in such a primitive fashion as to emphasize their outsider nature, made them easy prey for governments bent on attacking them. Consequently, Hitler had little difficulty finding local support for executing his plan, even in the Central European countries occupied by Germany during World War II.[2] Indeed, one year after Czechoslovakia was occupied, Czech authorities executed 200 Romani at the country's Lety "re-education" camp without any explicit orders from Berlin to do so.[3] In the end at least 500,000 of Europe's Roma were exterminated, with the numbers particularly high in densely populated, urbanized areas such as the Czech lands, where an estimated 95 percent of the region's prewar Romani population were killed. The death toll was much lower in Central Europe's more remote and lightly populated rural areas such as eastern Slovakia, where contact with the Romani had been less frequent and anti-Romani sentiments were less hardened. In some of these areas the number of Romani even increased during the war, as Romani fled into them from more urbanized neighboring states.

Forced Assimilation, Round II: The Romani under Communist Rule

Under orders from Moscow, the advent of communist rule in postwar Central Europe ushered in a second effort to change the Romani's ways and assimilate them into the host populations. This time the effort was defined in terms of the solidarity of an international proletariat class, which, by definition, recognized no internal cleavages based on national or ethnocultural criteria. The consequences of that policy are still being felt among both the Romani and the host communities.

Designed as a multilayered attack on the status of the Romani in post–World War II Central Europe, the assimilation program had three major parts. First, as in the earlier assimilationist effort, the Romani's traditional nomadic ways were curtailed; in this instance by closing Central Europe's western borders and, to a certain extent, by closing off the countries' borders with one another. As a consequence, the Romani population throughout Central Europe was transformed into a permanent part of each country's population, and it remains so today—steadily growing at a faster rate than that of the native populations. Second, many of the traditional means by which the Roma earned a livelihood—including such formerly legal if disreputable activities as selling used clothing, providing music in restaurants and wine bars, and fortune telling—were once again forbidden. Some Roma continued to practice these activities illegally; others turned to such illicit activities as currency dealing and trading in the black markets, which gradually were tolerated throughout the region as the command nature of Central European economies resulted in persistent shortages of consumer goods. Finally, and supposedly to prevent the Romani from drifting into forbidden practices, there was a major effort to resettle the Romani from their rural, backward locales into Central European cities, where they were to be provided with better schools for their children, apartments in which to live, and jobs in the workforce. The "brotherhood of the proletariat" expectation here was that the Romani and the indigenous workers, now forced to interact, would peacefully coexist as assimilation of the one into the other occurred.

Unfortunately, most of the Central European countries lacked the resources to undertake such an ambitious plan as it existed on paper.

Hence, in practice, the reality was more often that the Romani were given housing in urban slums; their children were put into segregated, special-education programs because they lacked fluency in the national languages; the jobs they received were sometimes at the expense of the existing workers; and in the name of assimilation Romani women were disproportionately singled out for forced sterilization. To be sure, some positive results did ensue. Literacy increased, along with the living standards of those with marketable skills, and the web of discrimination that had prevented Romani from previously achieving such employment developed some holes. On balance, however, the multilayered program produced ill will on both sides, especially where its implementation remained in the hands of local officials with little love for either the Romani or the Moscow-inspired idea of integrating them into their respective countries' society, and where the perception was strong that the Romani were being favored by the affirmative action features of that policy in assigning jobs and housing.[4]

Post-Communism: Score Settling and International Oversight in Turn-of-the-Millennium Central Europe

Given the combination of (1) an outsider state (the Soviet Union) freezing the border to curtail the Romani's nomadic ways and pressuring the Central European communist governments to improve their status, and (2) the insider perception that the Romani were receiving preferential treatment under communism coupled with the general disdain for the Romani within the native population, the collapse of communism was particularly hard on Central Europe's Romani communities. Indeed, because of the local perception that the Romani were doing better than the general population because of their illicit activities during the harsh adjustment to marketplace economies in the early 1990s, the backlash against them was extremely harsh. In isolated incidents pickpockets had their thumbs broken by local authorities, and in one infamous case in Slovakia, Romani thieves were taken to a remote locale and executed by the police. More broadly, in part because of their diaspora and lack of a homeland, the Romani were perceived throughout the region as untrustworthy and often criminal elements in the population, and were treated accordingly.[5] The timeline at the end of the chapter lightly captures the fact that discrimination against the Romani was extensive across post-communist Europe. Walls were erected to keep them out, employers ignored their applications, Romani tenants were evicted from their housing, and in some instances—most notably in Romania, where the collapse of communism led to a short-term breakdown of the criminal justice system—the Romani were spontaneously targeted for ethnic cleansing campaigns.

Likewise, within the more orderly post-communist environments—and even allowing for the fact that Romani commit a disproportionately large share of the petty crime (pick-pocketing, for example) in Central European cities—the Romani have been disproportionately charged with criminal activity everywhere, and crimes against the Romani were normally treated lightly by the judicial systems. Meanwhile, outside of the formal criminal justice system, Romani children have continued to be given remedial education in segregated schools. Where civil wars have occurred—as in Kosovo—the Romani have invariably been among the first to be driven out and the last to be resettled, and they are the internally displaced persons and international refugees treated the worst in areas giving them temporary sanctuary.[6] Moreover, the picture has been the same on virtually all fronts. Job discrimination has kept Romani unemployment in the 70-percent-and-above range throughout most of Central Europe (100 percent in some areas), housing remains substandard, and incidences of disease are far higher than those in the population as a whole. Thus, statistics throughout the region continue to tell much of the story of the Romani's status in contemporary Central Europe. With rare exceptions—most notably in Hungary, where there is a small Romani middle class—the Romani remain the poorest community in the countries where they live, and throughout the European Union as well. In some instances, their per capita income is only a tenth of the majority community's, and 80 percent of them live on less than $4 a day. Fewer than 1 percent have the equivalent of a secondary education, and only one in ten has some secondary schooling. On the average, Romani life expectation is ten to fifteen years shorter than that of the Czechs, Slovaks, Poles, Romanians, and other Central Europeans surrounding them.[7]

For outsiders, the most troubling issue since the fall of communism has been continued instances of violence committed against the Romani and the insensitivity of local governments to their distressed conditions. This issue persists in spite of the repeated admonitions of international watch groups, including both nongovernmental organizations such as Amnesty International and governmental bodies such as the United States Congress, the United Nations, NATO, the World Bank, and the European Union, which required its Central European members to adopt antidiscrimination laws before admitting them to the EU. Yet the official discrimination and sporadic violence have continued, now with three new twists in the early years of the new millennium that threaten to make the Romani an increasingly explosive issue in Central Europe's future.

First, there are the changing demographics of the Romani question. As before, the numbers of Romani in Central European countries remain significant and will likely continue to increase, insofar as Romani birth rates are consistently higher than those in non-Romani communities across the region. Current estimates suggest that 7 to 8 million Romani live in Europe, and at least 70 percent of them— perhaps as many as 80 percent—live in Central Europe. The numbers are always estimates, in part because the Romani move about, but also because they have learned that those who might pass as non-Romani but officially declare themselves to be Romani have been on the receiving end of bad things over the ages. Indisputably, they constitute significant numbers among the peoples of the Central European states—especially in Slovakia (with its 500,000+ Romani), Bulgaria (approximately 700,000), Romania (1.8–2.5 million), and Macedonia (200,000)—where they constitute between 9 and 11 percent of the population.[8] The difference in contemporary Europe is the age distribution. Fully 40 percent of the Romani population is now under twenty-five, and much like the Muslim underclasses in Western Europe, many are growing increasingly restless as they find their treatment at the hands of the majority communities unacceptable. This is a prescription for Romani-committed violence in Central Europe's future, either in the form of spontaneous uprisings along the line of the mass protests that gripped France in the fall of 2005, or in direct retaliation to the violence they perceive to be directed against them.

Second, there is already evidence that violence involving the Romani has become a two-way street, both inside and outside of Central Europe. The lethal clash between the Romani and the Muslim underclass in the south of France is discussed in Chapter 7, *infra*. Similar, if nondeadly, collisions between Romani and unemployed Central European youth are now being recorded in areas such as the Czech Republic, where years of intimidation directed at them have prompted the Romani to establish their own neighborhood patrols to "keep the peace." Mass demonstrations by Romani have also become increasingly common. In a region where government-sponsored sterilization of young Romani women is not only still practiced but also became the basis of cases argued before the Constitutional Courts in both Slovakia and the Czech Republic in mid-decade, issues are not hard to find for those seeking to stage Romani protests against contemporary injustices.

Finally, the condition of the Romani has become a European problem, not just a problem in the Central European countries where the largest numbers live. Despite its willingness to look the other way and admit states with tainted records regarding respect for Romani rights, in

Refugee camp in Podgorica, Montenegro, of the Romani driven from Kosovo in 1999 and still awaiting relocation well into the next decade.

enlarging to the east the European Union absorbed as member states the countries with the largest Romani concentrations in Europe. The addition of Bulgaria and Romania alone in 2007 brought another 3 million into an EU now largely without restraints on internal travel among its member states, and the continuing ill treatment of the Romani is now an EU problem—and an embarrassment. Plans to improve the Romani's situation continue to be launched. Among them is the "Decade of Progress" commitment—made by representatives from Bulgaria, Hungary, the Czech Republic, Croatia, Macedonia, Romania, Slovakia, Serbia, and Montenegro at a 2003 conference in Belgrade—to increase the inclusion level of the Romani in Central European societies. With that decade ticking away, however, the commitment remains mostly verbal, the disparities in living standards separating the Romani from other Central Europeans remain wide, and the unwillingness of the Romani to accept their fate continues to grow with an ever-expanding capacity to erupt into violence. It did erupt in Slovakia in February 2004, when the government's plan to cut back welfare benefits to rural Romani prompted thousands of unemployed Romani to go on a looting and rioting binge that took days and more than 2,000 soldiers and police to quell.

Timeline

12th century	First recorded arrival of Romani in Central Europe (in Slovakia and along Croatia's coastline).
14th century	Romani's arrival now chronicled in Serbia, Bulgaria, Greece, Romania, and Hungary.
1330s	King of Baden establishes first recorded system of Romani enslavement in Europe.
1416	Romani expelled from Meissen region of Germany.
1471	Anti-Gypsy laws passed in Lucern; 17,000 Romani deported to Moldavia as slave labor.
1504	Louis XII prohibits Romani from living in France.
1540	Gypsies allowed to live under their own laws in Scotland.
1541	First anti-Gypsy laws passed in Scotland.
1549	First anti-Gypsy law passed in Bohemia (Czech lands).
1568	Pope expels Romani from domain of Catholic Church.
1589	Denmark condemns to death all Romani not leaving the country.
1637	First anti-Gypsy laws passed in Sweden; expulsion ordered under penalty of death.
1710	Prague orders hanging of adult Romani men without trial; women and boys are to be mutilated.
1721	Austro-Hungarian empire orders extermination of Romani throughout its domain.
1733	Russia forbids Romani from settling on the land as serfs.
1761	Maria Theresa, Empress of Hungary, makes first effort to assimilate Romani, ordering removal of Romani children from parents for assignment to foster homes.
1776	Prince of Moldavia prohibits marriages to Romani.
1782	200 Romani charged with cannibalism in Hungary.
1800s	Gypsy hunts become popular sport in Germany.
1803	Napoleon prohibits Romani from residing in France.
1856	Abolition of Romani slavery (the *Slobuzenia*).
1924	Romani tried for cannibalism in Slovakia.
1926–27	Czechoslovakia permits taking Romani children from parents.

1933	Hitler orders arrest and sterilization of Romani; by 1937, sterilization orders are replaced by extermination orders, and Romani Holocaust begins.
1938	June roundup of Romani in Germany and Austria.
1941	Concentration camps opened in Poland, Croatia, Ukraine, and Serbia.
1945–47	World War II ends; Central European communist regimes consolidate and begin policies of assimilating Romani.
1972	Czechoslovakia initiates sterilization program for Romani and bans Romani associations.
1976	Indira Gandhi recognizes Romani as a national minority of Indian origin.
1989–92	Communism collapses in Soviet Union and Central Europe; overt discrimination against Romani spreads across Central Europe.
1992	Skinhead attack in June on Romani family during eviction proceedings in Brno sparks riots; 200 armed Romani protest in town square of Czech Republic's second-largest city.
1993	January: Czech Republic immediately passes a citizenship law based on parental heritage; Romani lacking documents or with criminal records are ineligible. Eviction of Romani from illegally held apartments commences in northern Bohemia.
	July: Slovak village of Spisske Podhradie imposes curfew on Romani and "other suspicious persons;" Romani homes torched in ethnic cleansing campaign in Romania.
1994	January: Romani leaders in Kosice, Slovakia's second-largest city, criticize ethnic Hungarian parties for intentionally increasing tension between Romani and Slovak Hungarians.
1995	Brutal murder of Romani construction worker by four bat-wielding youths in front of his family.
1996	National poll in Czech Republic finds that 69 percent of respondents harbor ill feelings toward Gypsies.
1996–98	Anti-Romani violence escalates in Czech Republic. June 1998: depressed industrial town of Ústí nad Labem erects a wall separating its Czech citizens from Romani tenements.

1997	Slovak Deputy Premier Jozef Kalman blames Romani for not doing enough to improve their position in Slovakia.
1999	In a case involving the death of a Romani woman, a Czech court reduces the charge to hooliganism and the sentence to 15 months.
2000	Skinhead violence against foreigners and Romani continues to grow in Czech Republic.
2001	January: the number of racial beatings again increasing in Slovakia.
2002	Czech Romani establish neighborhood patrols to protect themselves from skinhead attacks. School texts in Hungary discovered that refer to Romani as criminals and uncivilized; Slovak police officer involved in gang attack on Romani in Kosice. Slovakia's government refuses to discuss a draft law to prohibit discrimination based on race, age, religion, and sexual or political orientation, though encouraged to pass it by EU officials. September 25th: announcement that Slovakia will be invited to join NATO; October: Czech Republic and Slovakia invited to join enlarged European Union.
2003	Despite continuing discrimination against Romani, Central European countries outside of the former Yugoslavia states are invited to join the European Union and many are invited to join NATO. May: two high ranking officers in Slovak army are fined 125 Euros each (approximately $150 at the time) for arguing that 97 percent of the country's Romani "are unable to adapt and should be shot."
2004	January–February: Slovakia joins EU; begins drafting required antidiscrimination law, even as it deploys 2,000 police and soldiers to Eastern Slovakia to quell rioting by Romani protesting welfare cuts.
2005	Muslim-Romani clashes in southern France leave two dead and many injured.

Notes

1. For additional reading on this topic, see David M. Crowe, *A History of the Gypsies of Eastern Europe and Russia* (New York: Saint Martin's Press, 1995).

2. For a discussion of the Romani in Nazi-occupied Europe, see Donald Kenrick's translation of Karola Fings, Herbert Heuss, and Frank Sparing, *The*

Gypsies During the Second World War (Hatfield, Hertfordshire, England: Gypsy Research Center, University of Hertfordshire Press, 1997).

3. Following the war, "Czech postwar authorities added insult to injury by pardoning the camp commandant and the guards, because they considered the Romani low-class citizens and thieves." David Short, "Group Strives to Keep Lety Memory Alive," *The Prague Post* (May 7, 1997). Today, Lety is a pig farm and the locale's wartime history is unmarked.

4. See, for example, David J. Kostelancik, "The Gypsies of Czechoslovakia: Political and Ideological Considerations in the Development of Policy," *Studies in Comparative Communism*, XXII.4 (1989: 307–321).

5. See the Project on Ethnic Relations report (May, 1993), "Countering Anti-Romany Violence in Eastern Europe: The Snagov Conference and Related Efforts" (http://www.per-usa.org/snagov.htm).

6. See, for example, the Social Rights Bulgaria Group report (April 9, 2007), "Human Rights Problems Facing Romani Women in Serbia" (http://socialniprava.info/article1791.html).

7. James D. Wolfensohn and George Soros, "Roma People in an Expanding Europe," a World Bank news release available on the organization's Website (http://web.worldbank.org).

8. Other countries with significant numbers of Roma include Hungary (with perhaps as many as 800,000 Roma, or approximately 7 percent of its population), Serbia (400,000 to 600,000, perhaps 5 percent of its population), and the Czech Republic (slightly more than 200,000, or 2.5 percent of the Czech population). See Arno Tanner, "The Roma of Eastern Europe: Still Searching for Inclusion" (Migration Information Source report of May, 2005, available on line at the MIS Website, www.migrationinformation.org).

CHAPTER 5

EASTERN EUROPE

The collapse of the Soviet Union was economically hard on its satellites in Central Europe for a variety of reasons, not the least of which was the fact that many of their manufactured goods depended on the captive markets of the Soviet Union and Soviet Union-controlled Central Europe, and that their individual economies had been developed based on their inclusion in that Soviet Union–centered system. The adjustment period has been even more difficult for the newly independent states that fell out of the Soviet Union itself. Their leaders have faced all of the problems confronted by the leadership of the countries of post-communist Central Europe, and more. What Arnold Isaacs, a noted journalist and author with global reporting experience stretching back to the Vietnam War, observed with respect to the former Soviet Socialist Republic of Georgia more than a dozen years after the fall of communism can be said of most of the former components of the former Union of Soviet Socialist Republics.

> Russians and citizens of the other former Soviet republics remember dark times too, but they also remember an orderly and safe society, factories that worked, secure jobs, enough money, freedom from economic worry. And many who know about the oppressive side of Soviet history do not feel it touched their own lives. In the Communist era "there were no clouds in my sky," a Russian friend said to me. But no one has escaped the economic, social, political, and moral crises of the post-Communist experience.[1]

Isaacs goes on to put the matter into a broader context, noting that, "while the decline and fall of the Soviet Union may seem in the western mind like relatively recent history, the post-communist crisis has been going on for more than 15 years. That's a half of a generation, a very long time for those having to live through it."[2]

The psychological fear of losing one's job, and hence the real possibility of losing one's domicile as well for lack of income was not a fear that previously haunted the region. Moreover, the need to allay these fears is layered atop the same basic challenges as those that have confronted the post-communist countries of Central Europe: the everything-at-once syndrome in terms of democratization (or expectations thereof); market-based economic liberalization, and managing the end of communism's comprehensive welfare state; the problem of finding experienced political leaders outside of the Communist Party; and the need to establish democratic institutions, organize parties, hold honest elections, write constitutions, establish rule-of-law systems, and create an independent judiciary and media in areas where both were long-time extensions of the government. Finally, and to a far greater extent than in post-communist Central Europe, the new states in Eastern Europe (and especially the post-communist states of southern Europe and the Caucasus) have also faced a variety of other, sometimes interrelated problems that were either kept within manageable bounds or suppressed under Soviet communism, only to burst into the open in the aftermath of the Soviet Union's collapse. Unfortunately for the future of these new countries, the list here includes energy-sapping border conflicts and investment-discouraging corruption at levels more common to third world countries than to Europe; pernicious criminal activities; and internal ethnic strife that often infects electoral outcomes in the same manner as in today's Balkans. And yet, these hot-button issues have not resulted in the emergence of political hot spots throughout Eastern Europe.

Geographically, Eastern Europe covers the eastern border area of the former Soviet Union from the Baltic Sea to the Black Sea. From north to south, that span now encompasses the independent, former Baltic union republics of Estonia, Latvia, and Lithuania (the latter two of which lie between Russia proper and a detached, western segment of Russia sandwiched between Lithuania and Poland (Kaliningrad Oblast), Belarus, the Ukraine, and—nonadjacent to Russia—Moldova, along the border of southwestern Ukraine. Except for the Baltic Republics, all of these states share in the hitherto mentioned, highly toxic combination of corruption, economic decline, and ethno-nationalist and territorial conflicts.

CORRUPTION AND CRIMINAL ACTIVITY

The level of government corruption in all three of the Baltic Republics is at approximately the same, generally low level of malfeasance as is found in such countries of Central Europe as the Czech Republic and—for that matter—in most of the advanced Western democracies. Elsewhere, a substantial degree of corruption is a basic part of political and economic life in the European and Asian states formerly composing the Soviet Union. "In Belarus," for example, in the words of one respected observer, "corrupt practices have infected almost every sphere of life: government, customs, the judicial system, hospitals, administration of every kind and [the] education system."[3] Ironically, in terms of the degree of corruption involving economic and financial affairs, Belarus has consistently been ranked as one of the better (that is, less corrupt) states to have fallen out of the former Soviet Union. Consequently, most analysts paint these Eastern European, Eurasian, and Asian republics with a broad and dark brush, identifying corruption as "the greatest obstacle to the integration of Eastern Europe into the European Union." It is also seen as one of the most serious barriers to achieving "sustainable economic growth" in the region as a whole, in part because governments have used privatization to distribute rewards to their cronies, and in part because the bribery costs essential to get the licenses to invest in and operate businesses in these countries discourage outside investment.[4]

In turn, the absence of economic opportunity in the region is seen as widely responsible for the fact that Eastern Europe in general, and the Ukraine and Moldova in particular are major donor areas to postcommunist Europe's infamous "Natasha" trade. In fact, in some surveys the Ukraine alone has been identified as the point of origin for between a third and 40 percent of the women who have been moved into prostitution either consciously or through duplicity (with promises of marriage, domestic employment, or other jobs of a nonsexual nature).[5] Once at their destination—commonly such countries as Italy and Israel—their passports are normally confiscated by those paying for their transport, and slave sexual labor essentially marks the end of the trail.

ECONOMIC DECLINE AND AUSTERITY

Quite apart from its role in contributing to the growth of crime, the economic decline of the states once composing the Soviet Union since its breakup significantly complicates the task of democratization. Mature democracies have invariably benefited from their ability to fashion distribution networks that spread the economic benefits of modern life to a solid majority in their respective populations. In much of the former Soviet Union, however, the states and their peoples remain less well off than they were under communist rule nearly two decades after separating from the Soviet Union (compared to the decade that it took for Central European states to return to the economic levels they enjoyed when their communist regimes fell). In fact, sustained economic growth and the distribution of the fruits of that growth to the wider society is not just one of those factors that have been regularly identified as conducive to the development of stable democratic government. It is often viewed as a test of the level of *political*, as well as economic development in a country.

In a variety of ways, a declining economy also makes it difficult for governments, even when they are interested in doing so, to launch an effective attack on the corruption and criminal activity occurring within their borders. Usually they cannot pay well enough or hire enough law enforcement agents to devalue even petty bribes, prevent criminal activity, or catch those taking bribes or engaging in lucrative criminal activity. Yet the widespread presence of corruption in the public and private sectors not only inhibits the process of democratization by eroding public confidence in public institutions, but, as noted earlier, it deters outsiders from investing in these countries. This climate that perpetuates corruption thus makes it difficult for the new states to attract the loans and other outside capital necessary to stimulate their economies and improve the standard of living of the often dangerously high percentage of their populations living below the poverty level—thereby making petty corruption and crime less attractive.

"IMPERIAL REMNANTS"

Russian minorities, known as "imperial remnants" throughout Central Europe and the former union republics of the once Soviet Union, are the residue populations of the former rulers that continue to threaten the public order in the post-communist world of these areas. In Central Europe, especially Slovakia, the focus has been on the resident Hungarian minority. In the independent states that once composed the former Soviet Union, it is the Russian community whose presence or numbers are issues to the majority communities. Even more sensitive are the concerns of Russian minorities who desire to retain their own culture in those parts of the countries where they remain majorities. In these areas Russians have frequently clashed with the majority population's efforts to require non-Russian instruction in at least some subjects in the new public schools after a certain grade level. Sensitivities are still being aroused as well by the majority population's efforts to remove the symbols (for example, statues and historical markers) of their former rule by Moscow—also known as "Soviet occupation" from the perspective of the majorities in the Baltic states. The problems posed by the Russian minorities in the former USSR are particularly acute in border areas where the majority's language in the new states virtually disappears and only Russian is still heard on the streets,

Table 5.1 The Independent European States Created from the Former Soviet Union

Country	Dominant Nationality		Percentage of Russians		Population (July, 2007)
	c. 1991	c. 2004	c. 1991	c. 2004	
Armenia	Armenians	93%	97.9%	Negligible		2,971,650
Azerbaijan	Azerbaijani	90%	90.6%	Negligible		8,120,247
Belarus	Belarusian	79%	81.2%	13%	11.4%	9,724,723
Estonia	Estonian	62%	67.9%	30%	25.6%	1,315,912
Georgia	Georgian	70%	83.8%	6%	1.5%	4,646,003
Latvia	Latvian	52%	57.7%	34%	29.6%	2,259,810
Lithuania	Lithuanian	80%	83.4%	9%	6.3%	3,575,839
Moldova	Moldovan/ Romanian	65%	78.2%	13%	5.8%	4,320,490
Russian Federation	Russian	82%	79.8%	82%	79.8%	141,377,752
Ukraine	Ukrainian	74%	77.8%	22%	17.8%	46,299,862

and where governmental efforts to broaden the teaching and use of the majority tongue are seen as highly threatening, even where Russian is constitutionally recognized as an official language. Nor is the problem limited to the smaller states such as Estonia. Of the five geographically distinct regions in the Ukraine—Eastern Ukraine, Southern Ukraine, the Crimea (an autonomous republic), Central Ukraine, and Western Ukraine—the Ukrainians (three-fourths to four-fifths of the country's overall population) constitute a majority in only the latter two.

It is possible that in the next decade the hot-button nature of the Russian minority issue may lessen considerably throughout Eastern Europe, and in the post-Soviet republics as a whole. As Table 5.1 indicates, the percentage of Russians constituting these new states shrank considerably between the time of the Soviet Union's 1991 breakup and 2004.[6] That decline was a result of both the natural desire of expatriate Russians to leave uncomfortable locales and the intense efforts of Russia to bolster the numbers of its Russian majority by encouraging Russians living abroad to return to their homeland. On the other hand, the fears of the transplanted Russians can also be expected to intensify as their numbers thin, and hence the potential disruptiveness of those issues involving Russian minorities is just as likely to increase in the immediate future of the former union republics.

INTERNATIONAL TERRITORIAL DISPUTES

Even greater threats to the peace in post-Soviet Europe are those international disputes involving territorial disagreements. Some of these— such as the dispute between Russia and the Ukraine over Black Sea rights—are unlikely to lead to open conflict. Others, however, already involve open conflict and/or the presence of foreign armies occupying territories currently within the official boundaries of other states. The most serious of these conflicts in the former Soviet Union involve separatist movements such as those facing Russia in Chechnya and other parts of the Russian Caucasus, Georgia, and Azerbaijan, and—in Eastern Europe—in Moldova's breakaway Transnistria region.

Identifying Hot Spots in Post-Communist Eastern Europe

The economic, social, and political problems posed by the transition from Soviet rule since 1991 have not been evenly distributed in kind or intensity among the former Soviet Union's breakaway republics. The Baltic Republics of Estonia, Latvia, and Lithuania have not been entirely spared these problems, but they have generally faced them only in a much-diminished form. The other states have not been so fortunate.

With their advanced position on the frontier with Western Europe and their experience with self-government between World War I and their forced annexation into the Soviet Union after World War II, the Baltic Republics have meshed the most easily into the West, joining the European Union as of May 1, 2004, one month after having been admitted to NATO—much to Russia's displeasure. To be sure they have not been trouble-free. Latvia and Estonia, in particular, still contain large Russian minorities left over from the days when Russia colonized them in order to control the Baltic area better. In fact, the civil services of some of these states once contained Russian majorities, and nationalist conflict involving the majorities in these states and their Russian minorities still surfaces today—ever less often, perhaps, but always acrimoniously. In spring, 2007, for example, the Estonian government's decision to remove a statue of a World War II Red Army infantryman and disinter the bones of Russian soldiers from a prominent square in the country's capital in order to relocate them to a military cemetery led to massive protests. In fact, as the action became a symbol to Estonia's ethnic Russians of a widespread attack on their culture, the protests not only spread throughout much of Estonia—where the police had to employ tear gas and blank explosive charges to disperse thousands of protesters in the capital—but they quickly took on an international dimension in Moscow. There, allegedly government-backed youth besieged the Estonian ambassador to the point where her bodyguards had to use chemical spray to repel them, and the European Union was moved to condemn Russia for not affording Estonia's embassy in Moscow the same protection and respect that Russia was demanding for its Russian-speaking minority in Estonia.[7]

Elsewhere, however, the Baltic Republics have faced few of the difficulties that have confronted their sister states in Eastern Europe. Their political processes have lacked the political drama (and trauma) of those in Belarus, Ukraine, and Moldova. They have ranked well on most indices of corruption, and no part of their territory is occupied by a neighboring state. Nor are their armies occupying disputed areas. Above all, in terms of smoothing their passage into the European Union, at independence their economies were the most advanced of the Soviet Union's union republics, with per capita income estimated by 2006 to range from $16,000 (in Latvia) to more than $20,000 (in Estonia)—more than twice that of the citizens of Belarus and the Ukraine, and eight-to-ten times greater than the $2,000 per capita annual income in Moldova.[8] More broadly, the Baltic Republics are never found on any monitoring group's crisis watch list, and often they are not even included on the list of Eastern European countries that were once a part of the Union of

Soviet Socialist Republics. In short, they are not hot spots in today's world, nor are they likely to be tomorrow. The same, however, cannot be said so unequivocally for Belarus or Ukraine and certainly not for the region's present hot spot, Moldova.

LUKASHENKO'S REGIME IN BELARUS

Isolated, dictatorial, and corrupt are the terms that Western commentators most frequently use to describe Alexander Lukashenko's regime in Belarus. Ironically, Lukashenko rose to public prominence on an anticorruption platform, and his 1993 work as chairman of the Belarus parliament's anticorruption committee—attacking the corruption and self-granted privileges of the Belarus Communist Party's *nomenklatura* (the Party's highest-placed members in Soviet bloc countries)—essentially alienated him from the party with which he had long been associated.

A former member of the Soviet army and state administrator, Lukashenko was elected in 1990 to the Belarus union republic's legislature, where he championed the idea of reforming the Soviet Union along democratic lines, but with a continued commitment to the economic principles of Marxism. When the Soviet Union dissolved in 1991 and Belarus became independent, he claims to have been the only member of that assembly who voted against the resolution that dissolved Belarus's membership in the Soviet Union in favor of a looser association between Belarus and Russia in the Commonwealth of Independent States (CIS). After being elected president at the age of forty in 1994 on pledges to continue his work in ridding the country of its "mafia" and to maintain close economic ties with Russia, Lukashenko subsequently used his anti-corruption drive to rid the government of his principal political opponents (who may or may not have been deeply involved in using state funds for personal purposes, as he charged). He then moved on to propose a new constitution that was approved in a November 1996 referendum and extended his term in office, confirmed the president's ability to dissolve the parliament by executive decree, and generally widened the president's power relative to parliament's.

By the time of the 1996 referendum, Western observers were already concerned with the direction Belarus was taking under Lukashenko's leadership, both in terms of his continued ties with Russia and his intolerance toward those opposed to his rule. Nevertheless, that vote was the first time that the United States and the European Union had officially challenged the legitimacy of a Belarus election. Subsequently, charges of election fraud, intimidation of political opponents, and the widespread use of other practices designed to ensure Lukashenko's regular reelection by 80 percent margins have become common, even as these practices have become increasingly brazen. Matters peaked in the country's 2006 presidential election. Lukashenko's principal challenger was beaten and arrested before the vote for allegedly planning an armed coup, and the Organization for Security and Cooperation in Europe (OSCE) monitors witnessing the voting indicted it for failing to meet the standards of a democratic election. Afterward, when a rally gathered to protest Lukashenko's reelection, the security police beat and arrested some 200 demonstrators. The rally's organizer was also arrested for holding an unsanctioned rally and was quickly convicted and sentenced to five and a half years in prison for his crime.[9]

The Western world's response to these developments went beyond just condemning the election as rigged. In addition, the European Union banned Lukashenko from travel into the EU zone and froze his assets in Europe. Also banned from EU countries were more than thirty other senior officials of the Belarus government and their families, further isolating Lukashenko's regime from the Western world. Meanwhile, Belarus also found itself at odds with Russia, whose CIS observers had found the 2006 election to be legitimate, on the energy front. Much of Belarus's economic success has been built on revenue derived from purchasing natural gas from Russia and then transhipping it through the gas pipelines running across Belarus into the EU, for sale to Europe at a higher price. In January 2007, however, Moscow demanded higher prices for its natural gas, as well as a controlling share in Belarus's pipelines. Belarus and Russia eventually reached a compromise that averted disruption of the flow of that gas, but that controversy—and a second one seven months later over Belarus duties on Russian oil and the money Belarus owed for previous gas deliveries—underscored the continuing tension between Belarus and its Russian former backer.

The Western press and outside monitors of political developments in Belarus, like Western governments, have in the early years of the twenty-first century been consistently critical of political events there. Newspapers have editorialized these developments with captions such as "The Rape of Belarus" and "A Dictator's Elections,"[10] and a respected international institution monitoring government practices added Belarus to its list of the ten most corrupt countries in the world in 2006 because of the events surrounding Lukashenko's reelection.[11] At the same time, other forms of corruption have been scarcely lacking, even if there may be less financial fraud in Belarus than in most of the Soviet Union's former republics. Bribes are required for most students to gain admission to the country's more prestigious universities and such faculties as medicine, law, and international affairs, whereas students of politically connected parents are assured of entry.[12] Economic authority and political authority are closely connected, and the country's legal system remains "tailored to suit the interest of *nomenklatura*."[13] And in terms of human rights, Belarus is often ranked among the countries least supportive of freedom of speech, with foreign journalists finding themselves unwelcome and local journalists critical of the regime not infrequently being set upon by "skinheads." Likewise, police attacks on political opposition are not limited to election time, fair trials remain the exception to the rule, and the state continues to dominate the electronic media, which constitute the principal access to news for most Belarus people.[14]

As much as they have been opposed to the nature of Lukashenko's regime, the Western governments that have actively condemned Lukashenko and have hoped for his ouster have been perplexed by the breadth of his popularity and the likelihood that "Europe's last dictator"—who was born only in 1953—is likely to be around for years to come. To be sure, what passes for his popularity at times can be traced to his firm hold on office and the hard-nosed calculation on the part of many that it would be costly to openly oppose him—and not just because of the way protesters are treated in the Belarusian legal system. Lukashenko has consolidated power in his hands, complete with the authority to appoint all members of the country's parliament, which selects Belarus's prime minister, and the power to review the jobs of all state employees annually. Consequently, there are no immediate heirs to office who are near enough to him and have their own independent power base to threaten a palace coup. When any have threatened to rise to that position, he has shown an adroit ability to strike preemptively against them.[15] But Lukashenko's hold on office appears to rest as well on his personal popularity inside Belarus, and there are substantive reasons for that popularity.

Topping the list is the fact that Belarus's still largely centrally planned economy, which journalists have described as "Soviet lite," has made the country able to avoid much of the economic decline that has beset most other former union republics, and which the Belarus people fear might befall them if Lukashenko were to be replaced by more market-minded reformers.[16] Belarus was one of most economically advanced of the former Soviet Union republics at the time of its independence, and it has remained comparatively healthy as a result of its planned economy, its sustained welfare system, and subsidies to its inefficient agricultural sector. Belarus has kept its official unemployment figure low (under 5 percent for the 2000–05 period) for several reasons, despite the fact that its close contact with Russia and its highly regulated economy have discouraged outside investment. Its underground economy has been estimated to account for as much as 30 percent of its economic productivity, and it derives significant revenue from the oil and gas that cross it into the European Union. It has also periodically experienced impressive annual economic growth rates near the 10-percent range that have enabled it to maintain an outward appearance of prosperity. Its capital, Minsk, where nearly a fifth of the country's 10 million people live, is a modern, comfortable city with a well-developed public transportation system. Outside the city, the country has retained its well-developed industrial base from pre-independence days, and 15 years after independence it still enjoyed one of the highest standards of living of any of the Soviet Union's former union republics.[17] As a result, the population as a whole has remained relatively content with the governance that Lukashenko has offered, in spite of its antidemocratic drawbacks, and support for the regime has been particularly high in three areas: (1) among those who have profited from the post-independence redistribution of income during Lukashenko's rule, (2) among the elderly, who grew up under the economic security of the Soviet regime, and (3) among the rural dwellers who continue to receive state subsidies at levels that permit them to remain on the land that they love.[18]

Finally, and, again, unlike most of the Soviet Union's former union republics, Belarus has managed to avoid internal ethnic conflict between its multiethnic communities, as well as international conflict with its neighbors. Known as "White Russians" even before Belarus was absorbed into the Soviet Union, the Belarus have always been ethnically close to the Russians who long ruled them from Moscow and who constitute slightly more than a tenth of Belarus's current population. In addition, the Belarus have recognized their debt to Moscow for having rebuilt their devastated economy after World War II. There was, therefore, little of the acrimony between the Belarus and the Russians that in other areas accompanied the breakup of the Soviet Union. *That* came later, and in a much more limited dose, as a result of Russia's economic dispute with Lukashenko over oil and gas, and Lukashenko's retaliation against Russia's media outlets in Belarus and his success in selling his version of the dispute to his people. In general, Lukashenko has maintained close relations with Russia. Belarus's Soviet-era flag was restored to use when Lukashenko came to power, and a large statue of Lenin, often adorned with carnations, continues to occupy a prominent place in Minsk.

Meanwhile, the conflict that has taken place in Belarus involving the Russian culture has been largely confined to the division between the more Russianized elements of the Belarusian population and the non-Russianized communities. The former is led by Lukashenko and composed of pre-independence communists and political centrists. It has generally prevailed in its efforts to continue the Russianization program that the Soviet Union launched after World War II, which by the time of

Belarus's independence had been so successful that a quarter of the Belarus people no longer used Belarusian as their daily tongue.[19] More recently, and to the dissatisfaction of those who have wanted Belarus to be the sole official language, Russian has increasingly become the sole language of the media in the country.

The language dispute, though it evokes considerable emotion, has nevertheless been just a small part of the fabric of politics in Lukashenko's Belarus. The bottom line is that despite the country's increasing tensions with Russia over energy matters and its alienation from the West because of Lukashenko's undemocratic style of leadership, the Belarus people as a whole remain satisfied with their government. Belarus does not now constitute, nor is it likely to explode into, a regional hot spot as long as Lukashenko continues his currently successful policies.

UKRAINE'S DEMOCRACY

The political situation in Ukraine is more fragile, complex, and democratic than that in Belarus. Whereas in the immediate future the political stability of Belarus may depend on Lukashenko continuing his hold on power in his not particularly democratic regime, Ukraine's ability to avoid becoming a European hot spot is directly tied to the further development of its participatory institutions of government.

The Birth of Ukrainian Democracy

Competitive, free, and fair elections basically came to the Ukraine 13 years after the fall of Soviet communism, albeit earlier than in Belarus, which is still awaiting its democratic awakening.

Ukraine became independent on August 24, 1991, in the aftermath of the failed military effort to oust Mikhail Gorbachev from power in the Soviet Union. It spent its first years of independence under the executive leadership of Leonid Kravchuk, who was elected its president on December 1, 1991, the same day that the Ukraine, in a referendum, chose full independence rather than remaining a part of the Soviet Union. Later that month, Kravchuk played a leading role in the formal abolition of the Soviet Union and in the formation of the replacement confederacy: the Commonwealth of Independent States. Initially, the country's chosen path of political democratization, mixed with a continuing close association with Russia, seemed to work, but gradually the new state lapsed into a system characterized by political disorder, widespread corruption, and economic decline.

Matters took a turn for the worse in 1994 when Leonid Kuchma replaced Kravchuk in the presidency. Despite the fact that two years later a new constitution, which had been in the works for years, was adopted with guaranteed individual rights for all, the charges of corruption multiplied. The November 2000 abduction of a journalist critical of the regime and the implication of Kuchma in his murder seemed to confirm the suspicions of the majority of Ukrainians that their rights were being regularly infringed. Kuchma nevertheless served the full two terms, during which disillusionment steadily grew among a public that felt that it lacked any true influence over public officials who were largely in politics for their personal gain.

The turning point came during the country's 2004 presidential election. Kuchma was constitutionally limited to two terms in office, but his prime minister and heir apparent, Viktor Yanukovych, seemed ready to continue the policies of his administration, including a continuance of close relations with Russia rather than with Western Europe. The election process quickly turned ugly when Yanukovych's principal rival, Viktor Yushchenko, was poisoned during his campaign. Recovered, he continued his quest for the presidency in an election that the outside world did more than watch at a distance. In the run-up to the November vote, Moscow openly backed the candidacy of the pro-Russian candidate, Yanukovych. For its part, the United States, in the name of helping Ukraine develop a competitive democratic system, steered outside funds into the campaigns of the parties contesting the election, with Yanukovych's pro-Western opponents being the prime beneficiaries. East and West likewise maintained different positions after the vote, in what one commentator described as "a proxy geopolitical contest between Russia and the West."[20] The outside monitors from the OSCE concluded that the vote was marred by numerous elements incompatible with that organization's definition of free and fair elections (including voter intimidation and direct fraud in tabulating votes), whereas the observers from the Commonwealth of Independent States found no fault in the proceedings, which culminated in Yanukovych's election.[21]

As soon as the outcome was officially announced, Ukrainians assumed the lead by ushering a more open and democratic system into their country. Yanukovych's supporters, many clad in the orange colors of his party, took to the streets in the capital city of Kiev and elsewhere, and as the protests continued the cabinet convened to pass a no confidence vote in the prime minister/president-elect. Facing the probability of governmental paralysis, the country's Supreme Court went to step two. They intervened and ordered a new election because of the irregularities characterizing the previous vote. Ukraine thus voted again, this time in an election widely deemed to be open and fair, and the country's democratic

Voting in rural Ukraine in the 2004 election that preceded the Orange Revolution. Despite such safeguards as the transparent ballot box, OSCE monitors found widespread fraud in the announced results. Photograph by Fred Osgood, courtesy of Mitchell Polman.

uprising—now known as the Orange Revolution—culminated in Yushchenko's clear victory with 52 percent of the vote to Yanukovych's 44 percent. On January 23, 2005, Yushchenko became Ukraine's third president, but his inauguration ended neither the charges of government corruption nor the political turbulence in the country.

Two years later, in March 2006, the country held its first parliamentary elections since the Orange Revolution. This time there was considerably less international involvement, although protests largely carried out by Yanukovych's backers forced the United States to cancel its prescheduled war games in Ukraine. OSCE monitors described the vote itself as the freest and fairest election in Ukraine history. Afterward, however, quarrels between the two parties that had united to unseat Yanukovych in 2004—President Yushchenko's party and that of Yulia Tymoshenko, who became prime minister after Yushchenko's victory—cost them control of the parliament and allowed Yanukovych to return as the country's prime minister in August 2006.

After a brief, turbulent period Yushchenko scheduled new parliamentary elections. He faced a parliament increasingly backing Yanukovych, who organized his own street protests in opposition to the Yushchenko's decision to dissolve the parliament and hold new elections in May 2007. As in the case of the 2006 vote, the 2007 election reflected a political landscape that continued to be fragmented—but was by no means disintegrating. Yushchenko's party (Our Ukraine) fell to third place with only 72 parliamentary seats, largely as a result of Yushchenko's fading popularity because of the political problems that had confronted the country since he won the presidency. The Party of the Regions of Yanukovych, who had moderated his *apparatchik* image since the 2004 election, finished first with 175 seats in the 450-seat parliament. Tymoshenko's party, Bloc Tymoshenko, finished second with 156.[22] That outcome means that whatever alliances may be struck in parliament between or among these parties, Ukraine will face its immediate future with marriages of political convenience between its three leading figures, rather than with a strong, unified front against a series of problems that continue to be serious.

Corruption and Criminal Activity

Given the still-fragile nature of Ukraine's evolving political system, the problems confronting it are particularly taxing. Not only does the government possess less political capital to spend on tackling such problems as corruption, economic sluggishness, and ethno-national conflict than a regime with the type of legitimacy and aura of permanence that only comes with time, but each of these issues has a direct bearing on the government's ability to establish that sense of legitimacy. And nowhere is the link between the development of durable democracy in Ukraine and the government's success in dealing with the problems confronting it more clear than with respect to the corruption and criminal activity that have been associated with its economic and political life since Ukrainian independence.

In seeking the presidency in the aftermath of the Ukraine's Orange Revolution, Viktor Yushchenko pledged that if elected in December 2004 he would root out corruption and restore "the letter and spirit of the law," and most international watch groups agree that the level of corruption in the Ukraine has declined since that time.[23] Nevertheless, some of the most vital areas of the government's economic activity—such as its natural gas business based on imports from Russia—remain largely invis-ible, and overall the Ukraine is still ranked below Belarus on most corruption indices. Yushchenko's own government was rocked less than a year after he took office by the resignations resulting from allega-tions of corruption inside his administration, and financial scandals involving high members of the administration forced the scheduling of new parliamentary elections in 2007.

Such developments would seriously undermine the credibility of a government in most Western societies, but they fall especially hard on Ukraine's governmental efforts to create a sense of self-legitimacy. Corruption was hardly unknown under communism, but scarcely at the levels of economic corruption and profiteering that it achieved after the fall of Soviet communism. As the 2006 report on Ukraine by the United States Agency for International Development summarized it,

> Corruption in the Ukraine still remains one of the top problems threaten-ing economic growth and democratic development. Administrative corruption is widespread and visible in the everyday lives of citizens and businesspeople, and grand corruption is also widespread, though not as visible, in the higher levels of government where large sums of money and political influence are at stake. . . . Top political and business figures col-lude behind a facade of political competition and colonize both the state apparatus and sections of the economy.

Rooting corruption out of the system will take a very long time, even with the willingness of the government to strip the legislators of their immunity from prosecution and to enforce less selectively the existing anti-corruption laws. It also depends on a judicial willingness that has hitherto been lacking to impose stiff sentences on those convicted of economic crimes.[24] Convincing the public that corruption is being addressed may take even longer, given their current attitudes and experiences. A poll taken only a year before the Orange Revolution revealed not only that 78 percent of all respondents believed that government officials were on the take, but also that 44 percent indicated that they had paid bribes or made gifts in some form or other at least once during the past year, and 23 percent felt that it was tolerable—if not exactly acceptable—to have to make payments beyond the assigned cost in order to get government service.[25]

Economic Disorder

Despite the turbulence that has continued to be a part of Ukraine's political scene since its pro-democracy Orange Revolution, its economic conditions have recently improved. Moreover, the country now has a substantially better chance of attracting the outside investment needed to sustain its economic progress. That is partly the result of increased consumer-credit spending, and partly a result of the economic reforms— which provoked a fistfight in the Ukraine parliament while they were being debated—that were adopted in 2006 under World Trade Organization pressure as a pre-requisite to WTO membership. Nevertheless, Ukraine remains one of the poorer former Soviet Union republics. Its per capita income is only a little over half that of Russia, and the economic situation affecting its nearly 47 million people remains blighted by three daunting factors.

First, the economy still has much ground to cover to escape the decade-long shambles into which it fell after the collapse of the Soviet Union. Unemployment soared from zero percent under communism to double digits; industrial output dropped to 40 percent of its 1990 level; inflation soared into the hyper-inflationary sphere; and the standard of living throughout the country plummeted. Unemployment subsequently dropped to single-digit levels—2.7 percent in 2006, according to the government, and 6.7 percent according to outside evaluators—but inflation was still running higher than 10 percent in mid-decade, and economic consumption remains sharply skewed.[26]

Inflation remains a problem because of the second factor casting a shadow over Ukraine's economic life: its continuing dependence on Russian oil and gas for approximately 75 percent of its energy needs and Russia's decision in 2006 to nearly double the price of those exports to Ukraine. As a consequence, inflation has rippled from the energy field through the country's industrial and mechanized agricultural sectors, dampening economic growth and further squeezing consumer purchasing power.

Finally, there is the relationship—noted earlier—between Ukraine's post-Soviet economic disorder and the rise and continuance of Ukraine as a European center for the trafficking of women. The crime remains a major problem because demand has remained high in the most common destination points for Ukrainian women forced into prostitution (Germany, Holland, Turkey, the Balkans, and Israel), and because profits still fall within the range of $1,000 (in the Balkans) to $25,000 (in Israel) per person.[27] To enable the trade, those involved in this trafficking often pay substantial bribes to get government officials to look the other way, which in turn contributes to the continuance of Ukraine's corruption malaise.

Ethnic and National Conflict

Ukraine is a multinational state whose minorities include the Tatars in its Crimea region. Stalin deported the Tatars en masse from their homeland to Central Asia in 1944, and they were not allowed to return until the Gorbachev era during the 1980s, some 20 years after Khrushchev had transferred the Crimea to Ukraine in 1954 because its economy was congruent with the Ukraine's. Still, the most important source of ethnic cleavage continues to be the division between the country's 78 percent Ukrainian majority and its approximately 17 percent Russian minority, which is territorially concentrated in the country's center and east.

Eastern and central Ukraine fell under Russian rule in 1654 under the terms of a treaty between Poland and the Czar that Ukrainians at the time interpreted as guaranteeing the area's autonomy. A century and a quarter later (1775), the last vestiges of that autonomy were gone when serfdom was imposed in the Ukraine. Tight control followed, imposed by a government that denied the Ukrainians separate existence as a nation (they were called Little Russians in the same fashion that the Belarus were the White Russians, as distinct from the Russians themselves, who were the Great Russians). When the mid-nineteenth century witnessed the development of modern Ukrainian ethnic consciousness, the Czar's answer was to repress the Ukrainian culture and prohibit the publication of books in the Ukrainian language.

The situation further worsened under Soviet rule of the region. Following the revolutions that toppled the Czar and brought the communists to power in 1917, a short-lived Ukrainian People's Republic was proclaimed in Kiev. By 1919 it was gone, however, and the region was again under Moscow's rule—as the Ukrainian Soviet Socialist Republic. Ukraine was one of the union republics hardest hit by the famines resulting from the collectivization of agriculture schemes implemented by Moscow, with a total of 8 million Ukrainians dying from starvation during the famines of 1921–22 and 1932–33. Then, in 1939 much of the western Ukraine, which had been under Austro-Hungarian control until 1919 and then under Polish rule, became a part of the Soviet Union under the terms of the 1930 German-Soviet treaty that dismembered Poland. During World War II another 7 to 8 million Ukrainians died as a result of the warfare in the Ukraine between the German and Soviet armies. After the war, the rest of the western Ukraine—that is, those parts previously held by Czechoslovakia and Romania—fell under Soviet control as well, although it took a strong effort by the Soviet army in 1946 to quell the guerrilla resistance to Soviet rule that Ukrainian nationalists launched after the war.

Despite this history, the conflict between the Ukrainian and Russian ethnic regions in the independent Ukraine has remained overwhelmingly peaceful, in part because the ethnic cleavage does not perfectly coincide with the linguistic one (88 percent routinely identify Ukrainian as their native language), but largely as result of the way Soviet rule ended there. The beginning of the end came in 1989, two generations after the last of the Ukraine had been brought under Moscow's rule, when mass protests against Soviet rule coincided with a shakeup in the leadership of the Ukrainian communist party that brought Leonid Kravchuk to power. Kravchuk quickly cemented his hold on office by making a series of concessions to the Ukrainian nationalists, including the declaration that Ukrainian was the country's only official language. As a result, when the Soviet Union collapsed soon thereafter, Kravchuk was well positioned throughout the country to become its first president, and the independent country of Ukraine was born with the thorny and potentially volatile issue of official language already resolved.

Peaceful as the division between the country's Ukrainians and Russians has been, it *has* nevertheless remained, and it has permeated much of the country's recent political history. Since the fall of communism, nationalist parties have organized on both sides of the divide, although their rhetoric has remained mostly moderate and they all function in the sea of more than a hundred different political parties that still contest elections in the country. Issues such as border disputes between Russia and Ukraine have often been viewed differently in the heavily Russian portions of the country, and the most egregious vote rigging in the country's disputed 2004 election occurred in the heavily Russian east, in favor of the Soviet Union-supported candidacy of Viktor Yanukovych. International politics have also reflected the divide, with Ukrainian leaders overwhelmingly favoring closer contacts with the West, membership in the European Union, and withdrawal from the Commonwealth of Independent States (CIS). The leading politicians in the eastern Ukraine, on the other hand, favor closer ties to Russia and more involvement in the CIS. Still, only in the Crimea, where the two-thirds Russian majority—mostly descendants of the Russians Stalin sent there in the 1930s—continues to harbor the idea of reunification with Russia, does even the threat of a secessionist movement exist. Until that threat materializes, there is little on the nationalist front likely to make the Ukraine a hot spot in the troubled post-communist world.

In Eastern Europe *that* distinction (hot spot status) belongs only to Moldova, whose territorial dispute with its breakaway region of Transnistria is commonly regarded as the most explosive issue in post-communist Europe, outside of Kosovo.

MOLDOVA

Moldova's situation is similar to Ukraine's in three respects. First, Moldova did not emerge with its contemporary borders until after World War II. Second, the country did not achieve independence until the failed effort of the Soviet military to seize power in the summer of 1991 provided Moldova's leaders with the opportunity to declare their independence in August of that year, and to gain Moscow's assent to it that December. Third, like Ukraine, Moldova has suffered from economic decline, from conflict embodying an ethno-national element, and from rampant corruption and crime since its independence. Unlike Ukraine, however, by the time Moldova established its independence it had to contend with a breakaway region, Transnistria.[28] Also known variously as the Transdniestria, the Trans-Dniester Republic, and the Dniestrian Moldovan Republic (DMR), this separatist zone has continued to run a parallel political and economic process for nearly two decades, and its presence has persistently exacerbated the other problems facing this former union republic of the Soviet Union, Moldova.[29]

TRANSNISTRIA

Creating Moldova: The Origin of the Problem

Moldova was formerly known as Moldavia while a member of the Union of Soviet Socialist Republics. After World War II, Stalin created it in its present boundaries by fusing two previously separate and quite distinct areas, and by transferring territory from one of them to the Ukraine union republic. The fusion process involved the Bessarabia region of eastern Romania, annexed by Stalin in 1940 and initially merged with the Russian-occupied area of the Soviet Union lying between the eastern border (right bank) of the Dniester River and today's Ukraine. In 1941, Russia lost the entire area to the Romanian and German armies, but in 1944 it retook it and merged the Russian sector and Bessarabia into a single autonomous republic within the Soviet Union: Moldavia. At the same time, the southernmost part of Bessarabia, which opened onto the Black Sea, was transferred to the Ukraine, leaving Moldavia—and today's Moldova—landlocked.

Both before and after the Transnistria area's integration with Bessarabia, multiple elements have separated these two areas. A trickling of Moldovans lived in Transnistria even before it was united with Bessarabia, but the region was heavily Slavic, having been colonized by Russians and Ukrainians at the end of the eighteenth century, after its transfer from the Ottomans to the Tsar. After union with Bessarabia, Transnistria quickly became even more Slavic in nature. Approximately 300,000 Russians then relocated there, and the region was subjected to an intense Russianization process between 1945 and 1959—even as large numbers of its ethnic Romanians were deported to Siberia and Kazakhstan and not allowed to return until the era of de-Stalinization after Stalin's death in 1953.

Furthermore, during the ensuing years of Bessarabia's union with Transnistria more Moldovans moved across the Dniester River and established their lives there, but the differences between that region and the rest of the country continued to widen, as Transnistria became the recipient of an intense industrialization program. As a result, by the time the Soviet Union collapsed, the small segment of Moldova's population living in Transnistria accounted for approximately 40 percent of Moldova's gross domestic product, and 90 percent of its electrical production. The same period also saw Moldova become the target of an educational campaign "in which Soviet linguists and historians attempted to prove that the Moldovan language and nation were different from those of Romania." In the meantime, Moldova's governmental process was dominated by a combination of rule from Moscow and, inside Moldova, by Russians drawn from both the Russian federation and Moldova's [trustworthy] Russified communities.[30]

Independence and Separatism

As the Soviet Union began to crumble, and even before the failed coup led Moldova to declare its independence on August 27, 1991 (and be officially recognized by Moscow on Christmas Day of that year), the approximately 60,000 Russians and Ukrainians on the east side of the Dniester River were fearful that the Moldovans, if independent, would reunite with Romania. As their concerns mounted, they too began to lobby for their own independence and the right to reunite with the Russian Ukraine.[31] Their concerns intensified in August 1989 when the Moldovan-dominated Moldavia Supreme Soviet (the union republic's legislature) declared Moldovan (a tongue closely related to Romanian) to be the country's official language, to the disadvantage of the Russian-only speakers. The month after Moldova declared its independence, the Transnistrian regional assembly consequently declared its independence from Moldova. Two months later, in December 1991, the assembly held its own referendum on independence, adopted a separatist constitution, and elected its own executive leadership. Since then it has tightened its grip on political power and the media in the region, enabling its leader, Igor Smirnov, to continue to rule (he won his fourth five-year term in 2006), despite the various sanctions that Moldova has tried to impose on Transnistria.

Meanwhile, having achieved independence, the Moldovan-dominated government in Chisinau, where ethnic Moldovans held nearly 90 percent of the leadership posts, exacerbated matters by Romanizing the country's formerly Cyrillic alphabet and adopting as the country's symbol a flag with same colors as Romania's. In response, opposition to Moldovan rule continued to mount—not just in Transnistria, but also in the industrial city of Bender on the Moldovan side of the Dniester River, where a large concentration of Russian-speaking laborers lived. Concurrently, the predominantly Slavic, Moldovan officers of the Soviet 14th Army stationed in Transnistria responded to the political developments in the country's capital by refusing to acknowledge Chisinau's control over Transnistria and declaring their loyalty to the region's Slavic leadership, which was inclined toward separatism.

In early 1992 the Transnistrian Slavs announced their withdrawal from Moldova and their intent to unite with the Russian Republic. In doing so, they profited openly from the assistance of the Transnistria-garrisoned Russian 14th army, which by early 1992 had become largely independent from Russia's control. The pivotal moment in the short, but sometimes fierce civil war that followed came when Moldova's army tried unsuccessfully to seize control of Bender from the Transnistrian forces on June 19 of that same year. Amid the bloody fighting that reportedly left between 700 and 1,500 people dead in largely urban warfare, the 14th Army intervened to secure a cease-fire and prevent Moldovan forces from marching on the breakaway province's capital of Tiraspol. The resulting end of military activity left Bender's fate in the balance, but it essentially "secured Transnistria's de facto independence."[32]

Concerned with his own image as a peace-maker, Russian President Boris Yeltsin intervened diplomatically in mid-1992. A Russo-Moldovan agreement was concluded on the basis of a peace plan in which Moldova agreed to accord its Transnistrian separatists considerable provincial autonomy, in return for an end to the insurrection. To enforce the plan, Yeltsin appointed Aleksandr Lebed as the 14th Army's new commander, but over the next two years it became clear that Lebed's agenda was less concerned with fostering peace than with encouraging the region's Slavic Russians and Ukrainians to continue pursuing independence from Moldovan rule and reunification with Russians elsewhere. Tensions thus continued to run high, even as the breakaway republic consolidated its hold on the Transnistrian region.

In August 1994 Moscow recalled Lebed and concluded a second agreement with Chisinau, this time agreeing to a phased withdrawal of Soviet troops over the following years, during which it was hoped that the Moldovan government and the leaders of the ersatz Transnistria Republic could satisfactorily settle their dispute under Moscow's diplomatic guidance. Subsequently, the number of Russian troops in Transnistria was reduced—from 7,000 in 1995 to approximately 2,000 a decade later. The plan to remove them completely essentially died in March 1995, however, when—in a referendum on their presence—more than 90 percent of Transnistria's voters elected to retain a Russian "peace-keeping" presence

The people of Transnistria cast their votes to decide whether the independence-seeking region would continue the pursuit, with the hopes of one day joining Russia, or if it would reunite with Moldova. ©Denisov Vadim/ITAR-TASS/Corbis.

on their soil. The Moldovan government quickly repudiated the vote as illegal, but Russia's troops remain there as an assurance to the region's Russians and Ukrainians that they have not been forgotten by Moscow. Nearly two years later, in December 1996, Moldova elected a new president—one much more concerned with focusing internally on Moldova's free-market economic liberalization program than continuing to expend political energy on a separatist region which, after all, accounted for less than 100,000 of Moldova's more than 4 million people.

Transnistria: A "Frozen" Hot Spot?

Political tension has subsequently ebbed and flowed between Chrisinau and Moldova's separatists in Transnistria as a result of (1) the behavior of those in authority in Transnistria, (2) the agenda of those governing Moldova, and (3) the role played by the outsiders involved in or affected by Transnistria's breakaway regime. Moldova's leaders have been aggressive in defending the territorial integrity of their country at times, usually when provoked by such actions of the Transnistrian government as the creation of customs posts on its border with adjacent states, refusal to surrender its weapons to Moldovan authorities, and (in 2004) closure of some schools catering to its Moldovan population on the grounds that they were still using the Latin alphabet. On other occasions, there have been efforts to revive the peace process by offering autonomy (and frequently more) to the region in return for its reintegration into Moldova. In May 1997, for example, Moldova's leaders agreed to a short-lived plan that would have allowed Transnistria to play a role in Moldova's foreign policy-making process and maintain its own international contacts. And on still other occasions the relationships between Chisinau, Moscow, and such outside actors as the OSCE have significantly shaped the Transnistria issue. Thus, when Moldova elected a former communist as its leader in 2001, relations with Moscow warmed temporarily and Moldova's leaders began yet again to pursue a diplomatic solution to the Transnistria problem. Then, in 2003, frustrated with the absence of progress and active assistance from Russia in resolving its separatist problem, Moldova shifted its emphasis to closer relations with the West. In response, Russia took a harder line in its support of Transnistria's Slavic separatists and retaliated against Chisinau by disrupting Moldova's energy imports.

Moldovan-Russian relations reached a particularly ugly low in 2005 when Russian election monitors heading to Moldova to observe its scheduled parliamentary election were stopped at the border, and Moscow responded by placing its troops in Moldova on alert. More recently Moldova's leaders have again embraced less-confrontational diplomatic avenues designed to isolate and put maximum pressure on the breakaway Transnistria Republic. These efforts have benefited from the assistance of both the European Union and the OSCE, which have lent their support in an effort to resolve the Transnistria issue, and Ukraine, which in 2006–07 agreed to try to shut down the illegal shipment of goods into Ukraine from Moldova.[33]

As for Russia, despite its agreement in 1999 to a phased withdrawal of all of its forces from Transnistria, its troops have subsequently remained there, albeit in much smaller numbers. Even in their diminished number, however, their presence continues to offer considerable support to the Slavic population of the self-proclaimed Trans-Dniester Republic. In fact, given the cover provided by the continuing and now OSCE-sanctioned presence of the protective Russian forces in Transnistria, the government of Transnistria has had little incentive to negotiate its reentry into Moldova. Indeed, at times the Republic's leaders have been quite brazen in flaunting their unwillingness to pursue a diplomatic solution via the five-way talk arrangement worked out by the OSCE in 2006 that involves Russia, Moldova, Transnistria, the United States, and the OSCE. On several occasions in 2007, for example, the breakaway region's border guards, without bothering to give any explanation, refused to allow U.S. representatives into the country for scheduled talks. More generally,

Transnistrian authorities seem generally content to wield the power they have, even if they lack international recognition. On the other hand, they have not been invited to join the adjacent, Russian-populated region of the Ukraine, and hence the cease-fire achieved in 1992 has stretched well into the early years of the twenty-first century. In the parlance of post-Soviet politics, the Transnistria issue has ceased to be a burning hot spot in the post-Soviet world and has become "frozen" instead.

Moscow also has powerful economic weapons capable of limiting Chisinau's designs on bringing Transnistria back into Moldova. In particular, Moscow's ability to squeeze Moldova economically, given its dependence on Russian oil and gas imports, was starkly demonstrated in 2004 when the Russian-owned electrical plant in Transnistria cut off deliveries to Moldova at the same time that Russia cut its natural gas exports to the country—ostensibly because of a dispute over pricing. Moldova's economy has also been hurt by Russia's boycott of further imports of Moldovan wine, one of the products upon which its agriculture-based economy depends.

Economic Deprivation and the Transnistria "Problem"

In 2007 Moldova remained the poorest country in Europe. Despite steady economic growth between 2001 and 2006, its per capita income (approximately $2,000) at mid-decade remained less than a third that of Russia's, and 29.5 percent of its population continued to live below the poverty level (and a substantial portion of those were living on not much more than a dollar a day). A principal source of its income was derived from the money repatriated to the country by the 25 percent of Moldova's working-age population who are employed abroad.[34]

Moldova is hardly a good candidate for EU admission or a country whose government would, under the best of circumstances, be able to use economic enticements to lure Transnistria into reconsidering its separatism. Its natural resources are limited, and Moldova is landlocked and dependent on Russia for energy, with 40 percent of its population still in agriculture. Unfortunately, circumstances are far from being optimal on at least three counts. First, tension with Russia and the latter's decision to double the cost of its gas exports to Moldova in 2006—at the same time that Russia was banning Moldova's wine and agricultural exports to Russia—have made it hard for the country to continue to expand its economy, even with the steady flow of remittances being sent home by its citizens working abroad. Second, corruption, especially in Transnistria, and the continuing existence of a breakaway republic in part of its official territory make it difficult for Moldova's government to attract the foreign investment needed to improve its economy. Finally, at present the inhabitants of the breakaway province are economically *better off* than the citizens of Moldova proper.

General poverty has led Russians and Ukrainians in Transnistria to relocate from that region in large numbers, although combined, they still constitute more than 60 percent of Transnistria's population. At the same time, the better-than-average economic conditions in Transnistria have encouraged large numbers of Moldovans to remain there in separatist limbo, rather than cross to the Dniester's west bank to live among their ethnic brethren. The international monitoring agencies that usually have been barred from observing referendum votes in the Transnistria have expressed doubts about the magnitude of its voters' support for independence. There is no dispute, however, that a substantial portion of the Moldovans there prefer to see Transnistria remain in its frozen, separatist condition rather than risk the economic setbacks it (and they) would likely suffer if reintegrated into Moldova. Their agreement with the region's Slavs on that point has been important in preventing the Moldova-Transnistria conflict from lapsing into a volatile, predominantly ethno-national conflict, and that is good news in terms of the susceptibility of the conflict to management in the long term. The bad news is that there is little reason to believe that the conflict will, for economic reasons, become more tractable in the near future. As long as Moldova continues to court the EU, the reacquisition of control over Transnistria will have to be accompanied by a sustained effort to stamp out the illegal economic activity that has developed there—activity that, at least in part, explains why Transnistria's economy compares favorably to that of the rest of Moldova. Resistance to such moves by the breakaway region's government and population is a given.

Profiteering from Crime: Transnistria's Contraband Economy Business

If Moldova relies on the funds being sent home by its citizens working abroad to facilitate its economic growth, Transnistria relies heavily on Russia's economic assistance. Nearly two decades after it declared its independence, its economy continues to be subsidized by Russia, both directly and indirectly. The indirect subsidy is in the form of a rate for the country's energy imports that is substantially less than what Russia charges others, and also absorbing nearly half of the products produced in Transnistria. Next to these subsidies, however, the republic's principal source of income is its legal and illegal trade business, especially the smuggling operations that pass through it in the form of re-export schemes (typically, when contraband is taxed both entering and leaving the country). These activities benefit the Russian, Ukrainian, and even Moldovan business interests that have learned to exploit Transnistria's corrupt economy for their own gain.[35]

Material objects are not the only contraband, however. Given the poverty in the country as a whole, Moldova is not only a major supplier of "Natasha" exports in its own right (as well as being a leading source of human organ sellers at the turn of the century),[36] but the secessionary republic is the principal route by which women are trafficked to Russia or, through the Ukrainian port city of Odessa, to Arabia. Bribery of republic officials in the region's "capital" of Tiraspol thus remains a business expense for those engaged in human trafficking. Finally, because international law enforcement bodies are banned from the republic's soil and nongovernmental organizations are harassed when they try to function in Transnistria, the area quickly became a haven for criminals who are wanted elsewhere shortly after it broke free from Moldova. Add to all of this the fact that the republic's officials have been able to insinuate themselves into the area's legitimate industrial enterprises (for example, the Moldovan Metallurgical Plant and the KVINT Brandy Factory), and it is not surprising that many outside observers have concluded that illicit activities now operate in Transnistria on a scale that constitutes "a threat to the security of the wider region."[37]

Transnistria, Kosovo, and the Future

Ironically, the element most likely to produce an undesirable thaw in the frozen nature of the Transnistria conflict lies west of Moldova and its separatist sliver of land on the east bank of its Dniester River. It is in Central Europe, where the Kosovo conflict continues to cast a long shadow over politics in post-communist Europe. If the Western World in general were to bypass Russia's veto of Kosovo independence in the UN Security Council by choosing to recognize its independence *without* UN authorization, Russia could retaliate by recognizing Transnistria as an independent state. Were Russia to do so, it would confront Moldova and its supporters in the European Union, who have shared a border with Moldova since Romania's admission to the EU, with a fait accompli. It would also confront the world with a real trouble spot, with only Russia's policing of the new entity standing between Transnistria and the spread of its illicit activities widely into adjacent areas. But even if Russia does not recognize Transnistria as a sovereign entity, Kosovo's independence—with or without UN approval—will create an awkward situation in Transnistria, where it will embolden the separatists once again to push the issue of independence and merger with Russian areas. And *that* development, in turn, would almost certainly lead the Moldovans in Transnistria to reconsider their support of the status quo. Such a train of events would sharpen the Transnistria issue into an ethnoterritorial conflict by removing an important buffer—the support that Transnistria's Moldovan population now gives the breakaway status of the republic in which they live.

Even without the Kosovo element, however, the Transnistria problem remains a potential hot-button issue on the edge of the European Union. It is capable of affecting the politics of both the EU and Russia whenever a nationalist gains office in Chisinau on the pledge to pursue the reunification issue aggressively, or when a future Slav nationalist gains power in Transnistria by mobilizing support for a merger with the Slavs living in the Ukraine.

Timeline

1945–46	World War II ends with the Soviet Union annexing Estonia, Latvia, and Lithuania, as well as other territories; Ukraine and Moldavia acquire their current borders in Moscow's manipulation of its prewar boundaries and wartime territorial acquisitions.
1945–57	Transnistria region of Soviet Union's Moldavia republic subjected to extensive Russianization program and receives large influx of ethnic Russians.
1988–90	Liberalization in Soviet Union encourages its peripheral, non-Slavic union republics and communist Central Europe to become more self-assertive; in some instances, their territorialized Slavic minorities threaten secession.
1991	Effort of Soviet military to oust Gorbachev fails; in the aftermath (primarily August), the Baltic republics, Moldovia, and Ukraine declare their independence. Soviet Union formally dissolved in December, with Ukraine and Belarus taking the lead in forming the Commonwealth of Independent States (CIS) as a means of maintaining close relations between Moscow and its former union republics.
1992	Transnistria secedes from Moldova, producing a brief civil war before Russian forces impose a cease-fire that leaves the region's final official status undecided.

1994	Alexander Lukashenko is elected president in Belarus; Leonid Kuchma becomes president in the Ukraine and charges of corruption increase; Moscow concludes the first of many short-lived agreements intended to end the political stalemate involving Transnistria.
2001	Moldova becomes the first former union republic to elect a former communist as its president.
2003	Frustrated with absence of progress in resolving Transnistria issue, Moldova begins to court the West; Russia retaliates by increasing the cost of its energy imports to Moldova and ceasing to import Moldovan agricultural products.
2004	April–May: Estonia, Latvia, and Lithuania join the European Union and NATO; November–December: Orange Revolution occurs in Ukraine when massive protests follow the tainted victory of Viktor Yanukovych in presidential election, and the new vote that is ordered brings democratic reformers to power.
2006	Lukashenko wins fourth term in Belarus in election widely condemned as undemocratic; EU responds by denying him and his entourage access to EU; EU, OSCE, and Ukraine begin to collaborate with Moldova in isolating Transnistria region to force it to accept a diplomatic solution to its separatist status; squabbles between architects of Orange Revolution allow Yanukovych to return to influence as Ukraine's prime minister.

Notes

1. Arnold R. Isaacs, "Post Soviet Blues: Georgian Sketches" (Dart Center for Journalism and Trauma Special Report, 2005; www.dartcenter.org).

2. Ibid.

3. Olia Yatskevich, "Corruption in Education in Belarus" (www.10iacc.org).

4. Liz Barrett, "Corruption in Eastern Europe" (Centre for European Reform Bulletin No. 10, February, 2000; www.cer.org.uk/articles/n_10_2.html).

5. See Taras Kuzio, "Ukraine's 'Natasha trade': Modern-day Slavery and Organized Crime" (Radio Free Europe's RL Newsline report, 2002; www.ukrweekly.com/Archive/2002/490227.shtml). Kuzio notes that in 2001 alone, some 140,000 Ukrainian women were the victims of trafficking—many from Odessa, which was also then the "AIDS capital of Europe."

6. Sizable Russian minorities are also to be found in Kazakhstan and Kyrgyzstan in post-Soviet Asia. There too the numbers have been declining— from 37 percent to 30 percent in Kazakhstan between 1991 and 2007, and from 18 percent to 12.5 percent in Kyrgyzstan

7. See Peter Finn, "Protesters in Moscow Harass Estonian Envoy over Statue," *The Washington Post* (May 9, 2007).

8. All figures are taken from the CIA's on-line *Factbook* (http://www.cia.gov). Estimating per capita income in the post-communist world continues to be a competitive arena, with some sources (such as the CIA) factoring in government subsidies and social welfare programs as well as income in estimating average per capita income. Others (such as the United States Institute of Peace) focus essentially on only take-home pay, which remains extremely low in many of the former union republics. The spread can be significant—for example, although all agree that Moldova is the poorest of the former union republics and poorer than any other country in Europe, the CIA's figure is nearly five times greater than the $400 per year reported by the United States Institute of Peace for 2002. The latter's data were taken from the United States Institute of Peace's "U.S. Online Training Course for OSCE, Module 4. Eastern Europe" (revised April 2004).

9. See, for example, Peter Finn, "Challenger to Belarus President Beaten, Arrested Ahead of Vote: Security Service Says Opposition Was Planning Armed Coup," *The Washington Post* (March 3, 2006); Kim Murphy, "Protesters Beaten in Belarus: Riot Police Break Up Nonviolent Rally, Clubbing and Arresting Dozens," *The Baltimore Sun* (March 26, 2006); Erika Niedowski, "Opposition Leader Jailed: Milinkevich to Serve 15 Days for Denouncing President at Rally," *The Baltimore Sun* (April 28, 2006); and the unattributed new report, "Defeated Candidate Convicted in Belarus," *The Baltimore Sun* (July 14, 2006), on the five-and-a-half-year jail term given to Alexander Kozulin for his role in the protest rally.

10. *The Washington Post* (October 19, 2004 and March 6, 2006, respectively).

11. The group was Transparency International, which defines corruption as the use of public office for private gain. Belarus was ranked in a five-way tie for ninth place. The listing is available at www.transparency.org.

12. Yatskevich, op. cit.

13. "State of Corruption in the Republic of Belarus" (Liberty monitoring organization, March 17, 2006; www.liberty-belarus.info/content).

14. See the 2005 Country Report on Belarus compiled by Freedom House (www.freedomhouse.org).

15. On Lukashenko's political adroitness, see especially Vitali Silitski, "Still Soviet? Why Dictatorship Persists in Belarus," *Harvard International Review* XXVIII.1 (Spring, 2006: 46–53).

16. See, for example, Ilana Ozerneoy, "The Revolution is on Hold, OK?" *U.S. News and World Report* (May 16, 2005: 30–32).

17. United States Department of State, "Belarus" (January, 2007; www.state.gov).

18. On Lukashenko's continuing popularity, see especially Freedom House, "Belarus (2005): Executive Summary" p. 4 (www.freedomhouse.org).

19. United States Institute of Peace, op. cit., pp. 8–9.

20. Paul Abelsky, "The Real Divide within Ukraine," *The Baltimore Sun* (December 10, 2004).

21. For an excellent discussion of the background to and impact of the Orange Revolution, see Anders Aslund and Michael McFaul, *Revolution in Orange: The Origins of Ukraine's Democratic Breakthrough* (Washington, DC: Carnegie Endowment for International Peace, 2006).

22. For a report of the 2007 election's results with helpful background analysis, see Clifford J. Levy, "Orange Revolution Parties Will Share Power in Ukraine," *New York Times* (October 16, 2007).

23. Cited in Peter Finn and Daniel Williams, "Yushchenko Vows to Prosecute Political Crimes if Elected: Opposition Leader Puts Priority on Ukraine's Admittance to E.U.," *The Washington Post* (December 9, 2004).

24. Bertram I. Spector, Svetlana Winbourne, Jerry O'Brien, and Eric Rudenshiold, "Corruption Assessment: Ukraine, Final Report, February 10, 2006" (Washington, DC: USAID Management, 2006: Executive Summary, iv). Studies indicate that, prior to the Orange Revolution, the courts imposed sentences below the minimum prescribed penalties in almost half of the cases. See Alexander G. Kalman, "Organized Economic Crime and Corruption in Ukraine" (http://www.ojp.usdoj.gov/nij/international/programs/OrganizedEconomicCrime.PDF).

25. Roman Woronowycz, "Nationwide Survey Reveals Culture of Corruption in Ukraine," *The Ukrainian Weekly* (January 26, 2003; www.ukrweekly.com/Archive/2003/040302.shtml).

26. All figures are taken from the CIA's *World Factbook* section on "Ukraine" (www.cia.gov/library/publications/the-world-factbook/up.html).

27. For a turn-of-the-century account of the trade and the European Union's efforts to curtail the recruitment and forcing of Ukrainian women into prostitution, see Todd Prince, "Stanching the Slavic Sex Trade: EU Project Aims to End Trafficking of Women," *The Russian Journal,* VII. 7 (2001). For a mid-decade update, see Craig S. Smith, "Turkey's Sex Trade Traps Slavic Women: Many Are Hired by False Promise of Jobs," *International Herald Tribune* (June 26, 2005; www.iht.com/articles/2003/06/27/news/turkey.php).

28. Moldova has received relatively little treatment in the literature on post-communist states, perhaps for several reasons: its poverty, small size (4.5 million people), and relatively inaccessible geographical location away from the main European tourist spots, as well as the blasé nature of its political problem with its small breakaway region, when compared to the Yugoslav civil war and Russia's struggles with its Chechen separatists. For that matter, Moldova received little attention while a part of the Soviet Union, compared to the attention given to its history during World War II when, under German occupation, a significant amount of the Roma (Gypsy) Holocaust occurred on its soil. For a general, easily available snapshot account of post-Soviet Moldova, as well as an extensive discussion of its Transnistria problem, see the International Crisis Group, "Moldova: No Quick Fix" (ICG Europe Report No. 147, August 12, 2003), and the Group's follow-up report, "Moldova: Regional Tensions over Transdniestria" (ICG Europe Report No. 157, June 17, 2004; both available at www.crisisgroup.org).

29. Given the unrecognized status of the breakaway region and the two tongues (Moldovan and Russian) involved, referring to the conflict between Moldova and Transnistria has become a delicate matter, especially for outsiders seeking to report on and/or resolve the conflict. The Moldovans prefer to use the term Transnistria. The leaders of the Transdniestria Republic prefer the DMR designation. Neutral parties seem inclined to use either Transdniestria or the Trans-Dniester Republic, in the hope of only minimally offending either side. In common parlance outside of the area, they have become essentially interchangeable.

30. ICG, "Moldova: No Quick Fix," op. cit., pp. 2–3. The quotation is on page 2.

31. The fear that Moldova would reunite with Romania also generated calls for autonomy and talk of secession within Moldova's small, largely territorialized Bulgarian minority (1.9 percent of the country's population in 2006) and Gagauz minority (a Christian group with a language related to Turkish and accounting for approximately 4.4 percent of the country's people in the early years of the twenty-first century). These concerns nearly led to violent confrontations between Gagauz demonstrators and Moldovans in the fall of 1990. Once Moldova embarked on an independence course instead of reunification with Romania, however, the protests of these groups subsided and their concerns for the protection of their minority rights became treatable within the Moldovan political process. The population figures are taken from the Central Intelligence Agency's *Factbook* entry on "Moldova" (www.cia.gov/library/publications/the-world-factbook).

32. Ibid., p. 4.

33. On the importance of outside developments in regard to the Transnistria conflict, see especially International Crisis Group, "Moldova's Uncertain Future" (ICG Europe Report No. 175, August 17, 2007; http://www.crisisgroup.org).

34. Despite the absence of a quarter of its work force, Moldova's in-country unemployment rate was still 7.3 percent in 2006. All figures are taken from the Central Intelligence Agency's *Factbook* on "Moldova," op. cit.

35. ICG, "Moldova's Uncertain Future," op. cit., pp. 4–6.

36. See Peter Baker, "In Struggling Moldova, Desperation Drives Decisions," *The Washington Post* (November 7, 2002).

37. ICG, "Moldova: No Quick Fix," op. cit., p. 1.

CHAPTER 6

RUSSIA AND THE CAUCASUS

The breakup of the Soviet Union was hard on all of its constituent parts, and Russia itself was no exception. That being said, it remains equally true that no part of the former Union of Soviet Socialist Republics has been more turbulent, or spawned more separatist movements and global hot spots than the Caucasus. Not a single state (Russia, Georgia, Armenia, or Azerbaijan) has been spared territorial disputes and separatist politics in this pivotal southern Eurasian slice of the former USSR that is located strategically north and west of the oil- and gas-rich Caspian Sea.[1] Indeed, nowhere in Europe does the term "Third World Europe"—often used to refer to Europe's less democratic and economically less developed regions—have a greater claim to validity than in the Caucasus.

The chapters following this one are devoted to those countries in our study that lie at the opposite end of the developmental spectrum. Often referred to as the advanced democratic world or the consolidated democracies, the countries of Western Europe, the United States, and Canada are not just economically richer and older as stable democracies than the new states of post-communist Europe and the troubled areas of the eastern Mediterranean. As noted in the introductory chapter to this volume, they have—overwhelmingly as a group—successfully traversed a series of developmental hurdles to attain that stature. *They* have successfully established and generally secured their borders (thereby overcoming the challenge of state-making). They have developed, at the least, an overarching sense of shared community that bonds together the vast majority of their people (the challenge of community-building), to the point that even in multinational states, the national communities such as those in Scotland see themselves as both Scottish and British. They have found ways of integrating their citizens into their democratic political processes in such a way that their participation enhances the state's stability by giving voters a share in the ownership of their government (the challenge of participation). They have further enhanced their citizens' support for the state by developing economic distribution systems that have created societies where mass poverty is unknown and a good life, backed by a social welfare network, is available to the masses (the challenge of distribution). As a consequence, they have not only developed administrative and law enforcement networks that enable them to enforce their laws throughout their territory (the challenge of penetration), but their governments have also achieved the widely recognized sense of legitimacy that allows them to provide that enforcement authoritatively, with the widespread support of the governed.

Even now, a half-century or more since their independence, few countries in what is popularly described as the Third World (or developing world) can lay claim to having accomplished more than one or two of these developmental tasks. Likewise, more than anywhere else in Europe, the governments of Russia, Georgia, Armenia, and Azerbaijan can be described as still struggling to cope with several of these challenges simultaneously, and the issues that make them hot spots reflect that fact.

Border Unrest

In the aftermath of the era of decolonization, which generally stretched from the liquidation of the British empire in India in 1947 to the withdrawal of the European powers from their colonies in Africa in 1960, the widely respected historian Harrison Salisbury characterized the Soviet Union as the world's only surviving, nineteenth-century-style empire. There, the borders that the Czars had imposed on neighboring territories by conquest and their successors in the Kremlin had retained after the fall of Czarist Russia in 1917 (and in some instances expanded and rearranged by Stalin's fiat during and immediately after World War II) remained intact.

When the Soviet Union broke apart during the winter of 1991–92, these borders that had been established by the Czars and Commissars became the borders of the resultant independent states. But because they had been internal boundaries more like the borders separating Arkansas, Missouri, and Oklahoma than the boundary between Arizona and Mexico (unlike the borders of Western Europe's colonies), they were insecure or only very lightly patrolled in the immediate aftermath of independence. This fact has invited border disputes between neighboring countries, most conspicuously the war between Azerbaijan and Armenia in the early 1990s that was based on the Kremlin's decision decades earlier to transfer a predominantly Armenian-speaking slice of eastern Armenia to western Azerbaijan.

Corruption and Crime

The porous nature of their newly international boundaries has also encouraged various types of criminal activity, from the trafficking of drugs from the Middle East into Europe to the trafficking of people. Organized crime has thus flourished throughout the region. Moreover, in such areas as auto theft, black market activities involving stolen property, and the "Natasha" trade in predominantly Slavic women for purposes of prostitution, Russia itself has functioned as both an importer and exporter of illegal contraband. In fact, by the twenty-first century the abduction of young women on the public transit system of St. Petersburg had become so common in some quarters that it was raising little alarm among their fellow passengers. And as elsewhere in the former Soviet Union, this criminal activity has not only been facilitated by the bribery of border guards and public officials, but its persistence has signaled the inability of the new governments to protect their citizens and enforce their laws throughout their territory. That undercuts their claim to legitimacy, even where their political processes have been retooled in democratic directions.

Failed State Scenarios

Their failure to develop this sense of legitimacy has left Georgia, and arguably its neighbors in the Caucasus, as comparatively fragile political entities, often made more fragile when their governments have opened the door widely to popular participation, only to find their ability to function routinely challenged by massive public protests. These protests are often staged by ethno-national parties demanding the dismantling of the state or by ultranationalist groups urging the state to expand its borders by annexing the territory of neighboring countries containing their ethnic compatriots. All of this has made it difficult for some of these areas to work out their form of government, and it has gradually led some to follow Belarus's example and opt for stability via strong executive leadership rather than highly participatory, representative forms of democracy.

The fragility of these new states has also been a function of their collective inability to improve significantly their citizens' quality of life. Soviet rule did much to alter the lives of its citizens for the better. It repressed ethnic and religious conflict, produced a population with universal literacy, created more modern infrastructures, diversified the economies of its union republics, and—until the centralized planning model began to fail in the 1960s—generally (outside of the Baltic republics) produced a better standard of living for its diverse peoples than they had enjoyed under Czarist rule. But it did nothing to prepare any of its union republics to go it alone, either economically or politically. Thus, issues of public safety aside, the new states have struggled in terms of general economic performance, fostering the self-respect that comes from employment, and providing welfare services comparable to those enjoyed during the communist era. However imperfectly the Soviet economy may have been performing when the Soviet Union imploded, it was predicated on an integrated economic system in which geographical units contributed to the whole on the basis of something like comparative advantage. When it broke apart, the Ukraine breadbasket went in one direction, industrialized peripheral states in another, and energy-producing Russia yet another way. To use the United States analogy again, it was as if the United States retained its energy-producing Southwest but lost its Midwestern wheat belt, its outlets on the Pacific Ocean, and its cattle-raising heartland. Add to that destabilizing situation the problem that many of the departing states were initially in possession of Soviet nuclear warheads (think Colorado seceding with its Strategic Air Command missile silos), and you have a general picture of the challenges confronting the policy makers in Moscow and the former union republics as of January 1992.

It is thus not surprising that much of the period since the collapse of the Soviet Union has been economically harsh and turbulent for Russia and the other fallout states. In Russia, for example, the overall quality of life for the majority has fallen since the Soviet Union's collapse, and despite a relatively healthy recent economic picture, as of 2008 less than 20 percent of the Russian population was middle class. Moreover, the gap between the rich minority at the top of the social pyramid and those below has continued to widen, with the top 10 percent earning 15 times more than the lowest 10 percent (versus 13 times more a few years earlier).[2] Yet as Table 6.1 indicates, in terms of economics Russia is the economic strongman in this region.

Even compared to Belarus, Moldova, and the Ukraine, the percentage of the population living under the poverty level in Georgia, Azerbaijan, and Armenia is extremely high—shockingly so in Azerbaijan, considering that this small state maintains a lively oil-exporting industry at a time when oil prices on the international petroleum market have been very high.

Also prominent in this table are the relatively low life expectancies of males in this part of the former Soviet Union. Life expectancy for Russian males nosedived after the fall of communism, from a high average of approximately 67 years in 1985 to nearly 10 years less before bouncing back to the average of 59 years recorded in 2006. At that level, the average Russian male's life expectancy is 15 to 17 years shorter than that of his counterpart in such Western countries as the United States,

Table 6.1 Russia and Selected Former Union Republics in a Comparative Context

Country	Population	Per capita income	Percent below poverty level	Workforce unemployed	Male Life expectancy
Canada	33,391,141	$35,700	15.9%	6.4%	76.98 years
Cyprus	788,457	Greek: $23k Turkish: $7.2k	not available	5.5% both sectors	75.6 years
France	63,713,926	$31,200	6.2%	8.7%	77.35 years
Spain	40,448,191	$27,400	19.8%	8.1%	76.46 years
United Kingdom	60,776,238	$31,800	17.0%	2.9%	76.23 years
United States	301,139,947	$49,800	12.0%	4.8%	75.15 years
Czech Republic	10,288,744	$22,000	not available	8.4%	73.41 years
Estonia	1,324,912	$22,300	5.0%	4.5%	66.87 years
Hungary	9,956,108	$17,500	8.6%	7.4%	68.73 years
Belarus	9,734,723	$8,100	27.1%	1.6%	64.31 years
Moldova	4,320,940	$2,000	29.5%	7.3%	66.51 years
Ukraine	46,299,302	$7,800	37.72%	not available	62.16 years
Bosnia	4,552,198	$ 5,600	25.0%	45.5%	74.57 years
Serbia	10,150,265	$4,400	30.0%	31.6%	72.49 years
Russia	141,377,752	$12,200	17.89%	6.6%	59.12 years
Armenia	2,971,650	$5,700	34.6%	7.4%	68.52 years
Azerbaijan	8,120,247	$7,500	49.0%	1.2%	61.36 years
Georgia	4,646,003	$3,900	54.5%	12.6%	73.00 years

Source: Central Intelligence Agency *World Factbook*, accessed November 2007; most data current as of July 2007.

Germany, and France. Multiple factors have contributed to this decrease, but the principal ones, according to most experts, remain "alcohol abuse, psychological stress caused by economic uncertainty, widespread smoking, poor personal safety practices, and unhealthy diet and a general lack of exercise." With the exception of the latter, all of these variables have resulted from, or been intensified by the general economic uncertainty that has gripped Russia since the fall of communism.[3]

None of this means that Russia, Georgia, or any of the other former union republics have failed in the sense of breaking down completely, being overrun by criminal cartels, or being commandeered as safe-haven training grounds by international terrorist organizations. Nevertheless, their fragile economies and sliding social conditions, combined with the porous nature of their borders and the inability of their central governments to gain full control over their respective territories, are enough to keep Russia and its southern Eurasian neighbors on most international watch lists. Still, the element most likely to define any one of them as a "failed state" lies elsewhere: in the troubling number of separatist movements affecting politics in Russia and the Caucasus. These movements have at times led not only to prolonged periods of violence, but also to the central governments of Russia, Georgia, and Azerbaijan losing control over portions of their territory and their claim to legitimacy in the regions affected by those separatist movements. These are two significant indicators of failing states in the contemporary world.[4]

Nationalism and Separatism

The Soviet Union's attempt to build a transcending sense of community (the new "Soviet" Man) out of its diverse, large and small national communities was a dismal failure. It spent seventy years of effort to inculcate that identity in the children through youth groups and educational institutions, and in the adults through control over all aspects of the entertainment industry and all outlets of mass communication—from the factory newspaper to the all-Soviet state and party news agencies. But when the moment of accounting came in 1991, there was no new Soviet Man to save the Soviet Union. There were only Russians, Ukrainians, Armenians, Chechens, Georgians, Belarus, and so on. Thus, when the military's effort to oust Gorbachev failed, the Soviet Union never recovered. Instead, it broke up along the lines of its constituent union republics, each of which was dominated by its own ethno-national community. Table 6.2 indicates, however, that with respect to Russia and the Caucasus, each of these union republics also continued to retain minority elements who often had as little in common with the new majority population controlling their state as they had with the Russians

Table 6.2 National Composition of Russia and the Former Union
Republics in the Caucasus

Country	Majority (% Population)	Principal Minorities (%)
Armenia	Armenian (97.9%)	Yezidi [Kurd] (1.3%) Russian (0.5%)
Azerbaijan	Azeri (90.3%)	Dagestani (2.2%) Russian (1.8%) Armenian (1.5%)
Georgia	Georgian (83.8%)	Azeri (6.5%) Armenian (5.7%) Russian (1.5%)
Russia	Russian (79.8%)	Tatar (3.8%) Ukrainian (2.0%) Bashkir (1.2%) Chuvash (1.1%)

Source: Central Intelligence Agency *World Factbook*, accessed November 2007; most
data current as of July 2007.

who had formerly governed them. Each of these newly coined, multinational states has thus faced its own community-building challenge. That
task has been particularly taxing in the ethnically and religiously diverse
polyglot that is the Caucasus, home to more than forty different recognized languages spread across three linguistic families (Caucasian, Altaic,
and Indo-European), and in some instances that task has not been going
well—or even progressing at all.

The conflicts themselves have taken several forms. Armenia's desire to
fuse a heavily Armenian segment of western Azerbaijan onto itself would
qualify as irredentism, were it not for the fact that those Azerbaijan
Armenians once desired to separate and join Armenia. By contrast, the
nationalist movements in Chechnya, Ossetia, and neighboring areas in
the Northern Caucasus (which remains under Moscow's control) and the
nationalist movements in Georgia that have produced two secessionist
regions can be much more easily defined as instances of national
separatism, especially given the fact that the Ossetian speakers in the
Southern Caucasus in Georgia have expressed no interest in being joined
with the Osseti people to their north. The numbers involved in these
conflicts also differ widely. Georgia's Osseti, for example, number only
approximately 70,000, less than 2 percent of Georgia's population,
whereas more than a million Chechens confronted Moscow in Russia's
rebellious Chechnya region, although they accounted for only three-
quarters of one percent of Russia's population at the time of the civil wars
in Chechnya. In each instance, however, these conflicts have led to

warfare, occupation, or threatened occupation of separatist areas by outside armies, as well as prolonged periods of political unrest that for nearly two decades have kept the Russian Caucasus, the Nagorno-Karabakh area contested by Armenia and Azerbaijan, and a Georgia that has had to confront multiple rebellious regions on the list of hot spots in postcommunist Europe.

Terrorism

Finally, largely because of the separatist movements that are active within their borders, many of the central governments of the states in this region have also faced terrorist threats to their public's safety in areas far removed from the rebellious regions. Political figures have been assassinated, schools and apartment complexes have been attacked, trains have been derailed, and in Russia and Georgia the hand of outside terrorist organizations has been detected alongside that of the homegrown terrorists. Thus, even where the civil wars have ended in the successful repression of the separatist movements, or in a "freezing" of a hot conflict for a prolonged period (similar to what has occurred in Moldova's Transnistria region), the conflicts have continued as a less conventional, but nonetheless deadly form of warfare.

ARMENIA AND AZERBAIJAN

NAGORNO-KARABAKH CONFLICT

The breakup of the Soviet Union led to a series of rebellions in the minority regions of the resultant states, the relocation of citizens who were suddenly unwanted and/or unprotected in their new countries, the de facto emergence of secessionist regimes, and a not-inconsequential number of civil wars. In this troubled context, the conflict involving the heavily Armenian, officially Azerbaijani territory of Nagorno-Karabakh stands out on three counts. First, as Stuart Kaufman has noted, the conflict between Azerbaijan and Armenia over this mountainous region in western Azerbaijan *preceded* the breakup of the Soviet Union, dramatized the inability of Moscow to control nationalism-inspired conflict between and within its union republics, and thereby "helped open the door to other strident nationalist demands that literally tore the country apart." Second, it led to the only international war between the former union republics that has occurred since the disintegration of the Soviet

Union. Elsewhere in the former union republics, the ethno-national factor has resulted in "only" internal civil wars and insurrections. Finally, although the war between Armenia and Azerbaijan over Nagorno-Karabakh ended quickly, with Armenia in control of the region, the conflict involving the resultant de facto, Armenia-supported, native Armenian government in that region has continued to simmer. Unlike the other "frozen" conflicts in the realm of the former Soviet Union, it simmers without the dampening effect of an international peacekeeping force.[5]

International Conflict

Although the conflict is preeminently a conflict involving nationalism and separatism, combined with—at different moments in time—a deadly mixture of irredentism, dreams of national unification, and commitments to territorial integrity and sovereignty, the Nagorno-Karabakh conflict from the beginning has been complicated by its international dimension.

At its heart, of course, the conflict has been between Azerbaijan and Armenia. On the only two occasions during the twentieth century when they were independent (1918–20 and 1991–94), they immediately fought wars against one another over the Nagorno-Karabakh region Even when restricted to the international relations between these two states, however, the conflict has had a wider international context that has significantly affected its evolution since the collapse of the Soviet Union. Neither contemporary Azerbaijan, with its capital at Baku on the Caspian Sea, nor Armenia, with its capital in Yerevan, rests entirely within the zones historically associated with these entities.

The heartland of the ancient Armenian empire lies south of the current borders of Armenia, in what is now a portion of Turkey. The area was almost entirely cleansed of its Armenian peoples as a result of Ottoman action against its "disloyal" Armenian citizens in the 1890s, and during World War I. Meanwhile, contemporary Azerbaijan's border with Iran divides the ancient Azeri lands, the northern half of which passed to Russia in the early nineteenth century and which now constitutes independent Azerbaijan. The southern half of that ancient Azeri territory remained a part of Persia, and hence now lies in present-day Iran. The practical outcome of this history, in terms of modern-day tensions over Nagorno-Karabakh, is that Turkey has supported Azerbaijan in its current conflict with Armenia. It has done so because a Greater Armenia on its border might threaten to expand into the historic Armenian lands of Turkey. Meanwhile, Iran supports Armenia on the geopolitical logic that as long as Baku is focused on regaining control over the Nagorno-Karabakh region, Azerbaijan has limited means with which to stir up trouble in the heavily Azeri-populated areas of Iran. To be sure, the assistance provided to Armenia and Azerbaijan respectively by these neighboring states has been limited to diplomatic support and occasional economic favors. Neither Iran nor Turkey has militarily bound itself in mutual assistance treaties, and what fighting has been done has been limited to battles involving the Armenian and Azerbaijan armies and Nagorno-Karabakh's evolving military units. On the other hand, given the support that they have received from their powerful regional neighbors, Armenia and Azerbaijan have perhaps been better able to sustain their hardline positions on the Nagorno-Karabakh conflict than might have been possible otherwise.

Regional political considerations also explain Georgia's diplomatic support of Armenia during much of the conflict. Without that support, particularly trade access to Georgia during the period when Turkey and Azerbaijan were collectively closing Armenia's normal trade outlets, Armenia might have succumbed to Russian pressure to admit a peace-keeping force into the area of Azerbaijan it has controlled since the 1994 cease-fire that ended the war between Armenia and Azerbaijan. Minimizing Russia's influence elsewhere around its borders has become an important goal of Georgian foreign policy, given its conflict with Russia over the ethnic conflicts in Georgia's South Ossetia and Abkhazia regions. Seeing Armenia succumb to the introduction of a Russian-led peacekeeping force, in addition to those forces already present in the military base Russia has retained in Armenia, was not in Georgia's interest.

Finally, although the United States has intentionally refrained from taking sides in the conflict, two American foreign policy decisions may well contribute to the Nagorno-Karabakh conflict taking a more violent term in the near future. First, the U.S. quest for global partners in its war against terrorism has led to a closer link between Washington and Baku than existed at the end of the last century. As a Muslim country willing to assist the United States in ferreting out extremist Islamic cells in the area, Azerbaijan's help was much appreciated, and the U.S. has responded by enhancing Baku's military capabilities—in particular, its air power. Secondly, and quite indirectly, the United States intervention in Iraq also contributed to the considerable recent enhancement of Baku's military capability. At the time of the U.S.-led invasion, the fear Iraq might add as many as 2 million additional barrels of oil per day to the world market if freed from UN sanctions was one of the factors that encouraged OPEC states to keep prices moderate throughout the 1990s. Once the occupation and the armed resistance to it began, and Iraqi production capacity fell to the point that Iraq itself had to import oil, that restraint on OPEC pricing disappeared, even as China's and India's increased demand was turning the international petroleum trade into a seller's market. As a result, within four years after Saddam Hussein's government fell, the price of OPEC oil had tripled to more than $90 a barrel. As an oil exporter, Azerbaijan reaped a profit harvest that has enabled it to steadily increase the size of its military budget and the capacity of its military to inflict major casualties in the event of another war over Nagorno-Karabakh.

Nationalism and the Nagorno-Karabakh Conflict
Development of the Conflict

As with most protracted ethno-national conflicts, it is difficult to decide where to begin in describing the events that have shaped the Armenia-Azerbaijan conflict over Nagorno-Karabakh. Moments in the far and not so distant past have clearly played a role. Religion, for example, was injected into the conflict more than eight centuries ago when Armenia became the first country in the world to adopt Christianity as its national religion, in the early days of the fourth century (301–314 AD). The Azeri converts to Islam established their intermingled presence in the region during the early twelfth century. Those religious differences became particularly important when modern Azeri and Armenian nationalism emerged in the mid-nineteenth century, because religion played an important role in each country's self-definition as a distinct nation entitled to self-determination. Shortly thereafter, the Ottoman massacre of Armenians in 1894–96 in response to an Armenian nationalist uprising against Ottoman rule hardened the division between the Armenians and the Azeris because of the latter's ethnic Turkic origins and the favored position of the Azeris under Ottoman control, compared to that of their Armenian counterparts. Most searing and divisive was the 1915 ethnic cleansing campaign launched against Turkey's Armenians by the Ottomans. It resulted in an estimated 1 to 1.5 million deaths and the almost complete expulsion of Armenians from their historic homeland. That event still lives in the collective consciousness of all Armenians, and nearly a hundred years later it led to a diplomatic battle between the government in Ankara and an Armenia bent upon getting the Ottoman action recognized as genocide by the outside world. The Turkish government continues to define the action as a lamentable by-product of a war in which Ottoman Armenians constituted a disloyal, potentially dangerous internal element, at a time when the Ottoman Empire was struggling to survive.

To these larger moments can be added dozens of lesser ones, such as the 1905–06 Armenian-Tartar wars that gave Azeris and Armenians an opportunity to kill one another in the areas of Armenia and Azerbaijan that were then controlled by Russia (in particular, the 1905 communal clashes in Baku). There were countless lesser clashes—still ugly and violent—that took place between them earlier in the framework of the Ottoman empire. All weigh heavily and cumulatively as obstacles to resolving the contemporary dispute over Nagorno-Karabakh, given the Armenian tendency to blur the line between the Azeris, who ethnically belong to the Turkic family, and the Turks themselves. As a consequence, neither the Armenians in Armenia nor those now controlling the Nagorno-Karabakh area have been willing to accept any diplomatic proposal that requires Armenians to trust Azeris to abide voluntarily by a peace agreement. Nevertheless, in terms of those moments shaping the *territorial framework* and *complexity* of the current struggle over Nagorno-Karabakh, three pivotal eras stand out.

First came the 1813 to 1828 period, when Czarist Russia acquired the Armenian lands north of modern-day Turkey from the Ottomans in the 1813 Treaty of Gulistan, and then gained the northern Azerbaijani land from Persia via the 1828 Treaty of Turkmenchai, which also established the official boundary between imperial Russia and what is today Iran. Both treaties were the result of Russian military success, and in that process the Azerbaijanis had more reason to regret the outcome than the Armenians. Resistance to Russian rule in Baku had resulted in that ancient city being leveled, and the Baku of today can point to few standing remnants of its former self. In any event, those two annexations brought into the Russian empire the territory that would, in the Soviet era, become the union republics of Armenia and Azerbaijan. In addition, the second treaty launched a century-long migration of Azeris from their former home in the Armenian lands (where in the early nineteenth century they still constituted a majority) to the predominantly Azerbaijani lands to the east, at the same time that Russia was encouraging the Armenians who still lived in the Ottoman territory to the south to migrate northward to Czarist Armenia. Consequently, by the time of World War I, the Armenians had become the majority in their own territory (thus setting the stage for the creation of the Soviet Socialist Republic of Armenia after the communists took control of Russia), and the Azeris had become a preponderant majority in the much more populous Azerbaijan territory that Russia had annexed in 1828.

The second era, from 1917 to 1922, built on these population changes. When the Czarist regime collapsed in 1917 and turmoil engulfed a Russia technically at war with the Ottomans and Germany, Armenia and Azerbaijan declared their independence and almost immediately went to war against one another over ownership of the disputed Nagorno-Karabakh region. The war lasted two years (1918–20) and ended inconclusively when the communists, who had gained control of Russia, reestablished Moscow's authority in what had been the periphery of the Russian empire. They quashed the nationalist regimes in Armenia and Azerbaijan and re-annexed those two territories as union republics in 1920. In July 1921 Stalin temporarily "settled" the Nagorno-Karabakh ownership issue by assigning the region to Azerbaijan, and two years later it was given status as an autonomous *Oblast* within Soviet Azerbaijan, entitling it to its own legislative assembly.

Stalin's fiat was never accepted by the Armenians in either Armenia or the Karabakh region, but for 60 years Moscow was able to forcefully repress both that issue and the serious outbreaks of communal violence between Azeri and Armenian citizens within the two union republics. Nevertheless, nationalist sentiment continued to run high in both camps, fueling the continuing slow migration of Armenian Azeris to Azerbaijan and Azerbaijan Armenians to Armenia.

Then came the third noteworthy era, which began in approximately 1986 when the freedom of discussion permitted under Soviet Premier Mikhail Gorbachev's *glasnost* policy led to renewed demands by the Armenians in Nagorno-Karabakh to be transferred to Armenia. That era continued through the collapse of the Soviet Union and the emergence of independent Armenia and Azerbaijan, and it concluded with a steadily deteriorating communal situation inside both Armenia and Azerbaijan and the outbreak of full-scale warfare between those two countries in 1992.

The Road to War

The drift toward open warfare began in Nagorno-Karabakh in 1986–87, when petitions were circulated within the region's Armenian community requesting that Moscow reconsider Stalin's decision and transfer their region to the Soviet Socialist Republic of Armenia. Moscow's rejection of those petitions in February 1988 led to a second round of efforts to achieve that outcome, this time taking the form of formal requests by the local councils and legislative assembly of Nagorno-Karabakh. When Moscow again rejected the request, protests moved to the street, and not just in the Nagorno-Karabakh district. Within a few days, Armenian nationalists "linking the Karabakh issue to other Armenian nationalist symbols, especially the [1915] genocide" were able to mobilize a million protestors to attend a February 26 rally. At last Gorbachev agreed to consider the issue, but by then the conflict over Nagorno-Karabakh had moved beyond easy accommodation. Responding to the rumors circulated by Azeri chauvinists that Armenians had just committed atrocities against Azeris, Azeri mobs in the Azerbaijan city of Samgait just north of Baku attacked the Armenians living there, reportedly killing dozens and raping and beating more while the local (Azeri) police did nothing. In the aftermath, Moscow dispatched troops to maintain order in the city, but by then Samgait was largely empty of Armenians.

The conflict over Nagorno-Karabakh continued to gain momentum throughout 1989. The legislature of the Armenian union republic voted to annex the region, while the legislature in Baku accused Armenia of trying to dismember Azerbaijan. Altercations between Armenians and Azeris in Nagorno-Karabakh and throughout Armenia and Azerbaijan escalated. At least 150,000 Azeris fled from Armenian cities and areas around Nagorno-Karabakh, and equal numbers of Armenians left Azerbaijan.[6]

Matters worsened in 1990, and within two years climaxed with Armenia and Azerbaijan going to war. There were belated Soviet attempts to accommodate the nationalist desires of the Karabakh Armenians with promises of economic assistance and cultural guarantees. Moscow also made efforts to control violence on both sides, including the dispatch of troops to Baku following the widespread rioting there in January 1990, which effectively cleansed Azerbaijan's capital of Armenian citizens. Nevertheless, fighting between Armenians and Azerbaijanis continued to escalate throughout 1990 and into 1991 along the Armenian-Azerbaijan border and in the Nagorno-Karabakh area. By then, an autonomous Karabakh Armenian army had emerged in the region and was shouldering most of the formal fighting on the Armenian side. Azerbaijan was still largely relying on the Soviet army to quell what at the time was still considered an uprising inside a union republic of the Soviet Union or a low-grade civil war inside the Soviet Union between two of its union republics.

Baku's strategy of relying on Soviet support exploded in the summer of 1991, when the Soviet military failed in its bid to seize power in Moscow and the Soviet Union began its rapid slide towards disintegration. In the aftermath of the abortive coup, Moscow withdrew its forces from Armenia and Azerbaijan. The two republics then declared their independence within three weeks of one another in late August and September of 1991, and two months after Azerbaijan declared its independence from the Soviet Union (on August 20, 1991) Baku revoked Nagorno-Karabakh's autonomy. Nevertheless, the end of the year found the Armenians there pursuing a largely peaceful approach in their quest to separate from Azerbaijan, although by then their goal had shifted to a push for independence. It was a goal that Nagorno-Karabakh's Armenians overwhelmingly approved in a referendum on December 10. For their part, the region's Azeris boycotted the vote, and Baku immediately disavowed it as illegal.

From War to Frozen Status: Tabling the Conflict

The withdrawal of Soviet forces from the region had two important effects on the conduct and ultimate outcome of the war. First, the departing Soviet army left behind heavier weapons than either of the already fighting sides had previously possessed, intensifying both the nature of the fighting and the widespread population flight—which was already under way—of Armenians and Azeris from their previous residences in Armenia and Azerbaijan, as well as from the war zone. This time the principal migrants were the Azeris, especially following Armenia's brutal assault on Khojaly, an Azeri village in which hundreds of civilians were killed as the Armenians effectively cleansed the area of its Azerbaijani population. By the time the migration ended, at least 600,000 Azeris from the Nagorno-Karabakh region and Armenia had become displaced persons living in other parts of Azerbaijan.

The second effect of Soviet withdrawal was that the early 1992 military successes enjoyed by the Armenians, combined with the Khojaly incident, forced the resignation of Azerbaijan's president and ushered in a short, but costly, period of political instability in Baku. By the time that a new government was again in control, Azerbaijan had irretrievably lost both time and territory. The combined and better-organized forces of Armenia and the Karabakh Armenians had not only taken most of Nagorno-Karabakh, including the militarily significant high ground, but also several districts that had been predominantly Azeri circling the Nagorno-Karabakh region and part of the section of Azerbaijan lying between Nagorno-Karabakh and the Armenian border. Briefly, in the summer of 1992, it appeared that a regrouped Azerbaijani military under the command of Colonel Surat Husseinov might be able to reverse the Armenian gains, but an internal political struggle between Husseinov and Azerbaijani President Abulfez Elchibei quickly got in the way of military strategy. When Husseinov retaliated against Elchibei's attempt to fire him by withdrawing his forces in early 1993, Armenian forces were able to counterattack. In short order they reversed their losses and expanded their gains to the point where they controlled all Azerbaijani land between Karabakh and the Armenian border.

The war continued for another year before a Soviet-arranged cease-fire was established in May 1994, but the lines of battle and areas of control shifted very little during that period. The war thus ended with a substantial, de facto Armenian military victory that was shared by the Armenian Karabakh provisional army and the forces of Armenia itself. Their combined successes had resulted in Azerbaijan losing 13.4 percent of its territory, including 92.3 percent of the former Nagorno-Karabakh

Autonomous Oblast and twice as much land (more than 7,400 square kilometers) outside of that area.

As for human costs, the conflict resulted in the loss of approximately 30,000 lives, and an estimated 413,000 Armenians left Azerbaijan and the border areas of Armenia adjoining it. Nearly 725,000 Azeris and very limited numbers of Kurds were displaced from Armenia, Nagorno-Karabakh, and its surrounding area—a number that gives Azerbaijan, as a percentage of its overall population, the distinction of hosting the largest IDP community in the world.[7] Moreover, because Azerbaijan thereafter used the plight of its internally displaced people as a public relations tool to indict Armenia for its aggression, it did little until recently to improve the economic and social conditions under which these IDPs have lived. For all practical purposes, neither the Armenian nor the Azeri victims of war have been offered either compensation for their personal and property losses or the option of returning securely to the homes they abandoned since the Armenian-Azerbaijan war over the ownership and status of Nagorno-Karabakh was "frozen" by the Soviet-sponsored cease-fire in 1994.

POLITICS AND OIL

Armenia, Azerbaijan, and the Frozen Years

As in the case of most of the former union republics, the early years of independence were politically turbulent ones for both Armenia and Azerbaijan—perhaps even more challenging than in most of the other post-Soviet states. In addition to having to face the economic dislocations resulting from their exodus from the integrated Soviet economic system, both also faced dislocations caused by the war and the economically crippling closure of their borders with one another and neighboring states caused by the war and postwar diplomatic maneuvering. Also straining their resources was the need to absorb and/or support the large numbers of refugees and internally displaced persons resulting from the prewar clashes between Armenians and Azeris in both countries, as well as the wartime fighting. That fighting had concluded by essentially turning each of the formerly multinational countries into ethnically homogeneous states, each of whose dominant populations share a common language, religion, and ethnic origin significantly different from those of the other.[8]

The continuing conflict over Nagorno-Karabakh was also a major cause of political turmoil in both Armenia and Azerbaijan during the 1990s. Occasionally bowing to international pressure during that time, the leaders of both countries agreed to compromises that resulted in their fall from power. In 1998, for example, the previously popular Armenian nationalist president Levon Ter-Petrosian was forced to resign in the backlash resulting from the concessions he had made in the previous year's negotiations with Azerbaijan president Heidar Aliev. Ter-Petrosian had agreed to a phased withdrawal of Armenian forces outside of Nagorno-Karabakh in return for economically advantageous concessions from Azerbaijan. By the time the dust settled, he had been replaced as Armenia's president by the acting premier of Nagorno-Karabakh, Robert Kocharian.

Given this turmoil, the governments of both emerging republics remained relatively weak during their first decade of existence, and it is not surprising that high levels of crime and the corruption of public officials soon became associated with the workings of both regimes, to their detriment. Frustration with the perceived widespread corruption in the system, for example, has been widely viewed as the reason behind the October 1999 attack by gunmen on the Armenian parliament, which resulted in the death of the country's prime minister, the leader of its second most important party, and seven other officials.

For its part, Azerbaijan has been consistently ranked by international monitoring groups as one of the most corrupt of the former Soviet Union republics.[9] Among cited transgressions, Azerbaijani officials have reportedly continued to profit from the war in their own way by demanding bribes from displaced Azeris for the documents they need in order to seek employment. Nor has Nagorno-Karabakh itself been spared this problem. There, profiteers have taken full advantage of the region's general economic isolation to maximize their gains, and the abandoned homes of the Azeris who fled the region have been routinely plundered for items of value to be sold on the black market. It came as no shock to international monitors that when recently queried, nearly half (48 percent) of the citizens of Nagorno-Karabakh indicated their belief that corruption has prevented their court system from functioning fairly. A similar number (47 percent) indicated a lack of confidence in the police to protect public safety and rights, for the same reason.[10]

Elsewhere, graft and corruption have been at least partly to blame for the Azerbaijan government's slowness to implement the reforms necessary to make the country attractive for investment outside of the oil industry. On the political front, Azerbaijan's 2005 elections were widely faulted by international observers who found that fraud—including ballot stuffing and improper tabulations—were still a nationwide problem in a country that has long been victimized by fraudulent elections.[11] Armenia's elections since 1994 have likewise been described as "marred by some degree of ballot stuffing, vote rigging, and similar irregularities."[12] Finally, as in the Ukraine, the modern slave industry involving Europeans has found a home in the region—with one twist in Armenia. There, women are not only the preferred gender being trafficked, but the primary traffickers running the enterprise as well.

To date, the governments of both Armenia and Azerbaijan have been able at critical moments to use the threat of a renewed conflict to divert their respective citizenry's attention away from such issues as government sluggishness in combating corruption and addressing the economic needs of their refugee and internally displaced communities. Armenians in Armenia and Azeris in Azerbaijan (as well as Armenians in Nagorno-Karabakh), for example, are regularly reminded by their governments of the past injustices that the "other" has committed, including massacres, ethnic cleansing operations, and wartime atrocities. The media in Azerbaijan, in particular, have been singled out by human rights groups for their role in keeping the conflict alive. For example, as late as 2007 one Azerbaijan television station still began its daily news reports by saying "Armenia's aggression toward Azerbaijan continues," and another consistently referred to the 1992–94 conflict as the "first Karabakh war," implying that a second, rectifying war will someday follow.[13] As a result of these "selective interpretations of history, myths, symbols and religious imagery, both states have developed complex claims to Nagorno-Karabakh that exclude the others' historical presence and rights." Consequently, "primordial nationalism" has continued to grow, along with security concerns, and mutual distrust has hardened in the affected communities, leaving less room all the time for compromises by governmental spokesmen.[14]

In Nagorno-Karabakh itself, the de facto government in control of that territory has consolidated its position, with significant assistance from Armenia. Nearly 20 years away from the region's original desire to merge with Armenia, the leaders of the self-proclaimed "Nagorno-Karabakh Republic," which represents the Armenians living in Nagorno-Karabakh and those adjacent areas considered essential to retaining its security, have redefined their goal as independence.[15] Their "republic" has not been recognized by any country, including Armenia, but operates on the basis of a constitution approved by referendum at the end of 2006, under which they continue to establish the Nagorno-Karabakh Republic's own administrative, security, and education and welfare systems. All are run from the capital of the former Autonomous Oblast, Stepankert.

Given the internationally unrecognized status of this republic, the factors surrounding its birth, and the fact that Azerbaijan still claims ownership of it, much of the budget goes to sustaining the entity's armed forces. In fact, international observer groups regard the NK Republic as "the world's most militarized society," eclipsing even Israel in the percentage of its population either actively serving in its army or on standby as reservists. Demurrers note that the actual number of Nagorno-Karabakh residents serving at any given time is probably no more than 65 percent of its claimed number in uniform, and that the others are actually members of Armenia's army assigned to serve in Nagorno-Karabakh and wearing the NK uniforms.[16]

The new republic's economy also depends heavily on subsidy. It is able to generate only slightly more than a quarter of its budget locally. Most of the extra funding comes from the Armenian community living abroad, whose repatriated funds play a major role not only in the budget of the Nagorno-Karabakh Republic, but also in the national budget of Armenia itself. It was on the basis of funds provided by this diaspora, for example, that the modern roadway connecting Armenia with Nagorno-Karabakh was constructed, and this money forms an important part of the Nagorno-Karabakh Migration and Refugee Department's annual budget of $600,000, which is used to build houses and to subsidize the land and cattle purchases of those moving there.

In short, nowhere have the years since the end of hostilities worked in favor of the resolution of the Nagorno-Karabakh conflict. That contested region's de facto government has repeatedly declared its current goal to be outright independence, rather than its original goal of incorporation into Armenia, although given the continuing economic, political, and military connections between Yerevan and the breakaway state of Nagorno-Karabakh, the goal of independence is probably negotiable. On the other hand, the Nagorno-Karabakh government has certainly done its part in rejecting compromise and sabotaging the peace plans (at least three) that have failed since 1994. Moreover, Azerbaijan's position clearly remains far less negotiable than either Armenia's or Nagorno-Karabakh's. To Baku, Nagorno-Karabakh is a nonnegotiable part of Azerbaijan, albeit one that might be given considerable autonomy and self rule if Armenia were to withdraw its forces from Azerbaijani territory and cease supporting the separatist faction that now, in practice, governs most of the Nagorno-Karabakh territory and its surrounding, formerly Azeri districts.

Arms Races and the Prospect for Future Violence

In her study of the relationship between the international oil industry and international politics, Jill Shankleman focuses extensively on what she calls the "curse of oil"—the fact that some of the richest oil exporting countries are also, on a per capita basis, among the poorest countries in the world. Frequently, this trend has resulted from a disproportionate share of the profits from oil sales being siphoned off into military budgets. In turn, regional tensions have often heightened as those bene-fiting from higher oil prices have expanded their political ambitions and/or have sought to reverse former foreign policy embarrassments. Significantly, Azerbaijan, one of the world's oldest oil producing areas, is one of Shankleman's principal case studies.[17]

Three years after the cease-fire tabled Azerbaijan's conflict with Armenia over Nagorno-Karabakh, its petroleum exports were still less than 200,000 barrels a day and the price of oil was hovering between $20 and $30 a barrel, netting the country approximately $1.6 billion a year in revenue. Ten years later, Azerbaijan's oil industry was producing nearly a million barrels a day, oil was selling at more than $90 a barrel, and the country's treasury was being augmented by nearly $2.5 billion *a month.* This enhanced revenue has not only enabled Azerbaijan to increase its military budget annually (up 51 percent for 2004–05 and an additional 82 percent in 2006), but also to add new and highly destructive capabil-ity to its military apparatus—including 12 Smerch multi-launch rocket systems, 72 100-mm anti-tank guns, more than a hundred T-72 tanks, 6 SU-25 fighter-bombers, and 14 MiG-19 fighters between 2004 and 2006.[18] Collectively, the new money that Azerbaijan has been receiving from its oil exports, and the self-confidence that this money and the resultant military buildup have produced, has encouraged Azerbaijan "to postpone any peace deal until the military balance has shifted decisively in its favor."[19] Azerbaijan, however, does not unilaterally control the timing of any future conflict, and the Nagorno-Karabakh Republic's government has frequently indicated that before it will permit Baku to acquire the military capability to threaten its region's security, *it* will ini-tiate a preventive war (i.e., one fought on a smaller scale before a larger war is likely and against an enemy that threatens to acquire military superiority first). Nor does the threat of another war end there.

Arms buildups are frequently destabilizing and usually not one-sided. Azerbaijan's has spawned both an increase in tensions—reflected in the increase of violent incidents along the border between Azerbaijan and Armenia—*and* a mini-arms race with neighboring Armenia. Although it lacks the capital to match Azerbaijan's acquisitions, Armenia has taken advantage of its own economic growth, which was in the double digits for five consecutive years between 2001 and 2006, to upgrade its military establishment. Most notably, Armenia purchased ten SU-25 aircraft from Slovakia in 2005, thereby guaranteeing that any new war over Nagorno-Karabakh will include an air component as well as ground warfare. Moreover, Armenia and the ethnic Armenian government of Nagorno-Karabakh have two military assets beyond hardware to equalize Azerbaijan's military advantages on paper. In the advent of war,

Nagorno-Karabakh will adopt a defensive, frontline strategy that will begin with its control over the strategic high ground in the area. That will give Nagorno-Karabakh and Armenia a considerable advantage over advancing ground forces if Armenia's air force can neutralize Azerbaijan's ability to control the sky.[20] Second, the continued presence of a Russian base inside Armenia is likely to discourage Azerbaijan from carrying the war to Armenia itself, lest it prompt Russia to abandon its official stance of neutrality in the dispute. Ultimately, however, Armenia and the NK Republic's best hope of prevailing lies on the diplomatic-political front, not the military front. Both governments appear convinced that time is on their side—that is, that the longer the NK Republic exists and the larger its Armenian population becomes, the more likely that its independence will become a political fait accompli. That is especially likely if a large part of the international community chooses to recognize the independence of an Albanian-majority Kosovo, over which Serbia has a more legitimate historical and territorial claim than Azerbaijan can assert over the predominantly ethnic Armenian region of Nagorno-Karabakh. Accordingly, it is not in Azerbaijan's interest to allow too much more time to elapse without readdressing the Nagorno-Karabakh issue in some fashion.

The clock may also be ticking in terms of internal politics in both Armenia and Azerbaijan. Armenia's long delay in aggressively attacking poverty—in a country where only a few years ago more than half of the population still lived under the poverty level—produced a series of protests by opposition parties during April 2004. They raised yet-unanswered questions concerning the long-term stability of its political process.[21] Provoking another confrontation with Azerbaijan may have more appeal to Armenia's government than returning to the conference table, in terms of diverting the public's attention away from their living conditions. Similarly, outside analysts have cautioned that time may be running out in Azerbaijan, both in terms of the willingness of its public to continue to tolerate their situation, and in terms of its ability to sustain its arms buildup and the cost of a new war over Nagorno-Karabakh. Azerbaijan's oil production and exports are expected to peak in 2012, and thereafter the revenue derived from petroleum exports will begin to fall, even if the price of oil remains stable on the world market.

GEORGIA

The Caucasus has long been one of the most ethnically diverse areas on earth, and it is perhaps the most linguistically and ethnically diverse area outside of Sub-Saharan Africa and Asia proper. In a sense, Georgia is the epicenter of the Caucasus. Its capital, Tbilisi, sits on the edge of two Georgian provinces whose people have more in common with the Armenians and Azeris to their south than with the Georgian people who now constitute more than four-fifths of the country's population. The Georgians, however, are themselves internally divided by religion: the ethnic Georgian Muslims concentrated in Georgia's south-central and southwestern areas continue to assert a religion-based claim to political autonomy. Georgia's Armenians, in the southeast, claim political autonomy on the basis of their ethnicity. And these groups have thus far raised the fewest challenges in terms of Tbilisi's territorial management problems. To the northeast and in north-central Georgia lie the Georgian regions of Abkhazia and South Ossetia, both of which are homes to separatist movements and conflicts that have been "frozen" for more than a decade, but still threaten to dismember the state. Yet these various regional conflicts are not the only elements that make Georgia a political hot spot in post-Soviet Europe.[22]

A Failed State?

The conventional definition of a state in the contemporary world is that it is an internally sovereign political entity with three characteristics: it has a government, it controls an identifiable territory, and it effectively rules the people living in that territory. By this definition, it is hard to argue that Georgia is not a failed enterprise, or at least a state that has been teetering on the brink of failure for nearly two decades. For most of that time, laws passed in Tbilisi have had little to no effect in Abkhazia, South Ossetia, and Ajara (the Muslim Georgian region). Moreover, the separatist movements in two of these have been managed only by the presence of foreign (Russian) peacekeeping forces, whose deployment on Georgian soil has been a persistent source of tension between Tbilisi and Georgia's powerful northern neighbor. Similarly, when rumors that the Panski Gorge—yet another part of Georgia beyond the control of Tbilisi and long a center of criminal activity and suspected links between local criminal barons and Georgian officials—had become a staging ground for al Qaeda operatives involved in the conflict in Russia's rebellious Chechnya region to its north, Tbilisi had to turn to the United States for assistance in dealing with that threat to its security.

Controlling one's territory also means being able to control borders and collect revenue, but so many of the country's external borders lie in rebellious provinces. As a result, Georgia's government in Tbilisi has found it difficult to prevent smuggling operations, even though they have been a drain on its economy since the country's birth in April 1991, months before the late-summer coup in Moscow opened the door to independence to the Soviet Union's other union republics. Likewise, the government's inability to collect taxes from its citizens, who have been generally opposed to paying them even in those parts of the country controlled by Tbilisi, has chronically undermined Georgia's fiscal integrity. Recent efforts to step up enforcement in collecting internal revenue have improved the situation, but even in Tbilisi it is estimated that collections still amount to only the 60 percent of the taxes owed.[23]

There are, to be sure, areas where Georgia's government has not fared notably worse than some of the former Soviet Union's other union republics, but in such matters as combating corruption and avoiding general political turmoil its performance has been closer to that of a third-world country than what is normally expected of a European democracy. For much of the time since independence, corruption in Georgia has been epidemic—so much so that in 2003 it brought down the presidency of the country's most famous politician, former Soviet Union Foreign Minister Eduard Shevardnadze. His successor has been more aggressive in attacking the problem, beginning with having his interior minister dismiss 12,000 police officers during his first year in office. The 2007 report of Transparency International (which ranked Georgia 79th out of 180 countries) moved Georgia up from the category of states mired in rampant corruption to the next tier, which is composed of governments beginning to make progress. Still, Transparency International noted that Georgia has a long way to go in ridding itself of corruption.[24] The same sentiment was echoed loudly in October 2007 when NATO's Secretary General, Jaap de Hoop Scheffer, visited Tbilisi and took the opportunity to urge the country's judiciary to assert a greater independence from political control and Georgia's politicians to make its governmental operations more visible.[25] Meanwhile, on the economic front, more than half of Georgia's population continues to live below the poverty line, and its economy has continued to languish. This situation has developed in part because of the quasi-dismembered nature of the state and in part because nearly 40 percent of its people remain in agriculture. The market for agricultural products has declined, sometimes because Tbilisi's diplomatic confrontations with Moscow have resulted in Russian boycotts of Georgia's products.

Finally, add to this short list of the country's ills the occasional presence of political violence and turmoil involving the highest levels of government, and the overall picture that emerges is a bleak one of a country still struggling to upright itself politically and economically, nearly a generation after breaking away from Soviet rule. As a consequence, the United States and Western Europe continue to worry about not just the future of democracy in Georgia, but about the future of Georgia itself if the reforming presidency of Mikhail Saakashvili fails to make headway in resolving the myriad problems facing his country.

ABKHAZIA, SOUTH OSSETIA, AND AJARA

The problem of managing contending nationalisms and their separatist manifestations that still confronts Tbilisi has its origin both in the multi-ethnic nature of the land Georgia occupies and in the country's history under Russian and (later) Soviet rule.

Following centuries of invasions and rule by Persians and Ottoman Turks, Georgia's tenure under Russian rule began on July 24, 1783, when Czarist Russia acquired the territory. For a short while Georgia was a Russian protectorate whose autonomy the Czars had pledged to protect, but by the first quarter of the nineteenth century Russia's rulers had abandoned that initial commitment in favor of a system of direct rule under the Czar's agents. Those agents quickly settled in Tbilisi as their administrative center, and when the Russian revolutions of 1917 enabled Georgia to temporarily declare its independence, Tbilisi became its capital.

There were three years of independence from 1918 to 1921—a short period of self-governance, but not so brief that it did not increase existing tensions between the country's Georgian majority and its regionalized Abkhaz and Osseti minorities. Neither accepted Tbilisi's rule, and the government in Tbilisi was forced to deploy troops in Abkhazia in order to subdue the Abkhaz rebellion that erupted there almost immediately.

By 1921 the Bolsheviks were in control in Moscow and the process of re-enfolding the former Czarist empire into a Union of Soviet Socialist Republics was under way. By February 1921 the Red Army had retaken Georgia, and shortly thereafter it occupied much of the southern Caucasus. Most of these territories were initially reincorporated into the Soviet Union as the federal Transcaucasian Soviet Federated Republic— an entity that gave Abkhazia a separate administrative existence equal to that of its three other constituent units (Georgia, which violently resisted Soviet rule until 1924, Armenia, and Azerbaijan). In 1931, however, Moscow forcibly merged Abkhazia into Georgia. Five years later the Transcaucasian Republic was dissolved, and its remaining three components were given separate union republic status within the Soviet Union's federal system.

For the Abkhaz, the losses did not end there. The same year that the Transcaucasian federation was dissolved (1936) also marked the beginning of Stalin's effort to repress the Abkhaz ethnic identity by revoking the area's autonomy inside Georgia and abolishing education in the

Abkhaz language within the Abkhaz region. These policies did not end until Stalin's death in 1953, more than a quarter-century later. In the interim, anti-Georgian feelings further hardened in the region. The fact that Stalin was himself a Georgian by birth enabled Abkhaz nationalists to define Moscow's efforts to repress Abkhazia's culture as an effort to "Georgianize" them, and they viewed the government of the Georgian union republic in Tbilisi as guilty by association, at the very least.

The heavy hand that Russia exercised over politics in Georgia began to ease only in 1972, when Eduard Shevardnadze assumed the leadership post in Georgia's Communist Party. He not only responded to the protests of Georgian nationalists by persuading Moscow to abandon its efforts to make Russian a second official language in the union republic (1978), but he also responded to the protests of Abkhaz nationalists by promoting more Abkhazians to state positions and permitting television programming in the Abkhaz language. Unfortunately, there was a backlash among Georgian nationalists, who viewed those concessions as a way of rewarding the violent protests of a disloyal community.

Whatever the merits of his years in office, in 1985 Shevardnadze was summoned to Moscow to become Mikhail Gorbachev's foreign minister. Shortly thereafter, Gorbachev's encouragement of liberal dialogue opened the door to nationalist demands throughout the Soviet Union, as well as colliding assertions of nationalism by the Georgian, Osseti and Abkhaz communities in Georgia.

Nationalism and Separatism in South Ossetia

Although Abkhaz nationalists had been the most aggressive in protesting their status under Moscow and Tbilisi's rule prior to Gorbachev's years in office, the first violent challenge to the unity of Georgia arose in Georgia's northwestern province of South Ossetia, whose people speak a language akin to Farsi that is linguistically remote from the language of Georgia's majority. There, encouraged by Russian leaders and motivated by the ultranationalism being expressed by the political leaders of an independence-minded Georgia, in November 1989 the legislature (Soviet) of the autonomous Soviet Socialist region of South Ossetia declared itself sovereign and free of Tbilisi's rule. At the same time, South Ossetia's assembly also stated their region's intent to secede from Georgia in order to unite with the neighboring North Ossetian Autonomous Republic of the Russian Federation. When South Ossetia followed these pronouncements the following September with an announcement that it was now separate from Georgia, Georgia's governing assembly in Tbilisi declared South Ossetia's declarations null and void, revoked the region's autonomy within the union republic of

Georgia (December 1990), declared that a state of emergency existed in South Ossetia, and ordered Georgian police into the region to end the rebellion and restore order there. Violent clashes between Georgia's military units and South Ossetian paramilitaries occurred immediately, and the Tbilisi-South Ossetia war had begun. Thereafter, paramilitaries on both sides of the conflict did most of the fighting—and committed most of the atrocities that occurred during the war.

The first cease-fire was reached in May 1992, following talks in which both North and South Ossetia participated, along with Tbilisi. That truce, however, collapsed almost immediately, and it was the cease-fire negotiated in late June under Russian auspices at Sochi, a resort town on the Black Sea, that finally brought the fighting to an end. The same agreement also provided for a peacekeeping force whose composition is unique for such units, in that it is composed of Russian forces and a limited number of troops drawn from the protagonists (Georgia and South Ossetia). By the time of the cease-fire, more than 1,000 had died in the fighting, numerous war crimes had been committed, and approximately 100,000 refugees had fled a region whose pre-war population was estimated at only a little over 160,000 into either other parts of Georgia or to North Ossetia in the Russian Caucasus.

The conflict subsequently remained "frozen" along the 1992 cease-fire lines for more than a dozen years. The peacekeeping force there was bolstered in March 1994 by the arrival of Organization for Security and Cooperation in Europe (OSCE) observers, who were sent there as much to monitor the peacekeepers as to help them control the situation.[26] Indeed, for most of that time the South Ossetia conflict remained far more frozen than the more deadly conflict involving Abkhazia separatists. Unfortunately, little was done during those twelve years to resettle the war refugees—approximately 40,000 of whom continue to live in Georgia—or to compensate them for their losses.[27] Consequently, when the conflict revived in 2004 there was no lack of pent-up anger or potential new recruits for the paramilitaries that remained on both sides.

The trigger for the revival of the South Ossetia conflict was Mikhail Saakashvili's pledge to reunite his country when he assumed Georgia's presidency in early 2004. By August of that year, gunfire was again heard along South Ossetia's border with Georgia, and within a week a dozen Georgian servicemen involved in the peacekeeping operation along the cease-fire zone had been wounded or killed. The situation has remained tense since that time, despite a peace initiative put forth by Saakashvili in 2005, and Georgia has grown increasingly frustrated with Russia's failure to put enough pressure on South Ossetia to force its government to accept a diplomatic solution to the conflict. In addition, rival administrations have emerged in South Ossetia—one in Tskhinvali under the region's de facto president, Eduard Koloidy, who has long been backed by Russia, and a new one in a small, predominantly Georgian zone near the border. Koloidy held a referendum in November 2006, in which 99.88 percent of those voting were said to have reaffirmed South Ossetia's desire for independence. Finally, Saakashvili's 2004 strategy of trying to isolate Koloidy from the South Ossetia people by clamping down on the region's illegal smuggling operation has proven to be counterproductive, because it adversely affected the many average South Ossetia citizens who depend on that illegal trade and who have subsequently regrouped in support of Koloidy.[28] Consequently, whatever may occur with respect to Georgia's other nationalist conflicts, the volatility of the South Ossetia conflict guarantees that Georgia will remain a hot spot in southeastern Europe for at least the near future.[29]

Nationalism and Separatism in Abkhazia

The people of Abkhazia participated in the general nineteenth-century awakening of modern nationalism in Central and Eastern Europe and were among those in the Czar's empire who first sounded the call for self-determination. In the case of the Abkhaz, it came in the form of an 1878 uprising that resulted in Imperial Russia deporting approximately 100,000 Abkhaz citizens (half of the Abkhaz population) to Turkey and in opening their region to settlement by Georgians and other neighboring peoples, who were able to establish homes in the territorial vacuum that resulted from the deportations. Resentment of their treatment built quickly thereafter among the remaining Abkhaz, and the modern origin of the anti-Georgian feelings in the region today can be traced to this period.

Tensions between the Georgians and the Abkhaz heightened during Georgia's brief interval of independence after World War I, and intensified when Stalin reintegrated Abkhazia into Georgia. Then, with the assistance of his fellow Georgian, Lavrenty Beria, Stalin inaugurated policies that forced all of Georgia's minorities to learn Georgian and encouraged Georgians to migrate to still sparsely populated Abkhazia. Not surprisingly, Stalin's policies awakened fears there that the indigenous Abkhaz culture would not just become marginalized by these "Georgianization" policies, but would be made extinct. Those fears continued to linger until the Soviet Union itself began to erode in the 1980s, even though Abkhazia had gradually won a series of economic and cultural concessions from Moscow in the interim. Despite those policies, on the eve of Georgia's independence the Abkhaz community still constituted less than 20 percent of the population of its native region.[30]

As in South Ossetia, Gorbachev's policy of liberalization opened the door to national conflict in much of the former Soviet Union. The current conflict between Georgia and Abkhazia is generally dated from the spring of 1989, when fighting erupted between rival Abkhaz and Georgian nationalist groups, who were then still intermingled in Akbhazia. The first clashes were reported in Gagra in April, but the large-scale fighting occurred later in the region's capital of Sukhumi. A July attempt by Tbilisi to open a branch of the Tbilisi State University in Sukhumi was seen as a threat to the continued existence of the Abkhaz State University there. The fighting quickly escalated as armed nationalists from other parts of Georgia arrived in Abkhazia to aid the Georgians living in the province, and it was not until the Soviet army intervened that order was temporarily restored.

A volatile year followed. The Abkhaz assembly in the region declared that Abkhazia was a Soviet union republic separate from Georgia, but the legislature in Tbilisi nullified its action. Georgia declared itself independent of Soviet rule, and—at the end—a war erupted between Georgia and South Ossetia. Then, in August 1991, Georgia's President Zviad Gamsakhurdia negotiated a tentative political truce with his counterpart in Abkhazia by agreeing to organize the next round of elections in that region on the basis of ethnic quotas. The truce lasted less than a year. In July 1992, Abkhazia adopted as its basic law the constitution that it had adopted in 1925 (that is, when it was politically separate from Georgia), and the following month a Georgian military column responded to the region's assertion of independence by entering Abkhazia and capturing its capital city, while its political leadership sought asylum at a Russian military base in the region.

Georgia's August 1992 military operation inaugurated a thirteen-month-long war between Georgia's forces and those of the breakaway region. During that time the fighting claimed between 6,000 and 10,000 lives and destroyed Abkhaz and Georgian cultural treasures in the province. Both sides committed numerous atrocities before Abkhazia emerged as yet another de facto, though internationally unrecognized, state in former Soviet Union territory. Like South Ossetia, Abkhazia achieved its independence as the result of timely Russian assistance, even though the war also left Georgia's leader in Moscow's debt. Abkhaz forces were bolstered by Chechens and other volunteers from the northern (Russian) Caucasus, as well as by some Russian Cossacks. Receiving air support from a Russian military that was officially neutral in the conflict, they counterattacked Tbilisi's units (and those of the various Georgian paramilitaries operating in Abkhazia) in July 1993. After penetrating Georgia's defensive lines, Abkhaz forces quickly retook Sukhumi and all of Abkhazia by the end of August, thereby

forcing almost the entire Georgian population in the region (approximately a quarter of a million people) to flee their homes. In the process,
Abkhaz troops almost captured Shevardnadze as well. He was in
Abkhazia when its capital fell back into Abkhaz hands, but the Russians
evacuated him safely back to Tbilisi-controlled territory. As payoff, in
the same year (1993) that Abkhazia formally declared its independence,
Georgia chose to join Russia belatedly as a partner in the post-Soviet
Commonwealth of Independent States (CIS). In return, Russia diplomatically backed Shevardnadze against the Abkhaz rebels, forcing the
rebels to accept a cease-fire line in December 1993.

Shortly after the cease-fire lines were accepted, a contingent of 2,500
Russian peacekeepers, operating within the framework of a CIS mission
and backed by a United Nations observer group, arrived to enforce the
truce. Initially deployed with a mandate due to expire in 1996, they
continue to patrol a demilitarized strip (originally 15 miles wide) along
the border between Abkhazia and Georgia. The Abkhazia matter thus
remains unresolved, despite off-and-on talks since that time between
Georgia's president (beginning with Shevardnadze in July 1996) and
Abkhaz leadership. Furthermore, in spite of the conflict's frozen nature,
occasional fighting still occurs between Abkhaz forces and Georgian
paramilitaries inside and around the Russian-patrolled buffer zone. The
most notable of these conflicts were (1) in 1998, when Georgian paramilitaries made another effort to retake the region; (2) in the fall of 2001,
when Georgian paramilitaries joined by Chechen irregulars entered
Abkhazia, before Russian air attacks forced them to retreat; and (3) again
in 2006, when Tbilisi—with the help of local militia—acquired control
over a very small slice of Abkhazia in the Kodori Gorge area, which had
previously been a no-man's land beyond the control of either Abkhazia's
government or Georgia's. After acquiring that strip of land, Georgia's
President Saakashvili further raised tensions between Tbilisi and the
separatist region by immediately announcing that the (Georgian-
dominated) Abkhaz government-in-exile, which had fled the region
when the war began in the early 1990s, would be installed in the newly
"liberated" area.[31]

Efforts to return Georgian refugees to their homes in the southern
part of the province—always an explosive issue—have likewise remained
stalled. Many Georgian refugees *did* return to the areas inside the region
near the Abkhazia-Georgia borders following the 1993 cease-fire and the
implementation of UN-sponsored return policies, but during the
renewed fighting in 1998 most resumed their status as displaced persons
in Georgia. Some 200,000 of them still remain there, despite the fact that
in 2003, as an encouragement to others to return, a small unit of United
Nations police was deployed in the Gali district near Georgia's borders

in order to protect those few Georgian refugees who have returned and to train a local police force to function in the area. Further progress is blocked by the Abkhaz fear that any significant return of the Georgian refugees would result in the Abkhaz people again becoming a minority in their homeland (those few Georgians who have returned constitute nearly a fifth of Abkhazia's thin population). Consequently, Abkhazia's leaders refuse to accept repatriation until, at the least, Georgia's removes all economic sanctions on the region. Tbilisi refuses to do that on the grounds that Abkhazia is a rebellious part of Georgia, and not an independent state.

In sum, the conflict over Abkhazia remains frozen, but still volatile. Paramilitary activity continues, and the likelihood of a renewed conflict between Tbilisi and Abkhazia has increased.[32] Like the others before it, the peace initiative launched by President Saakashvili a month after his election in January 2004, in which he offered to negotiate full autonomy for the province, was formally rejected by Abkhazia's leadership. Abkhazia's leader, Sergei Bagapsh, stated at that time, that Abkhazia had no intention of resuming talks with Tbilisi aimed at reintegration. Nor, he added, would Abkhazia consent to the return of any Georgian involved in the previous fighting, and those who might be allowed to repatriate would be allowed to settle only in the Gali district, near the border with Georgia.[33] In other words, Abkhazia remains, at the very best, interested in only a confederate arrangement of equals with Georgia, not in reintegration into the country as a federal state. That is not a negotiating stance that is likely to resolve the Abkhazia issue in the near future.

Particularism and Regionalism in Ajara

As already noted, language, ethnicity, and religion do not necessarily overlap one another in Georgia. According to the Central Intelligence Agency's *Factbook,* the country is 83.8 percent Georgian, in terms of ethnic identity. Yet only 71 percent speak Georgian as their mother tongue (9 percent cited Russian as their native language tongue, and Abkhaz is the official language in Abkhazia). Similarly, although the country is 83.9 percent Christian Orthodox, not all Georgians are. Nearly 10 percent are Muslims, including the ethnic Georgians in the Ajara region (also known as Adzharia, Adjara, and Ajaria) on Georgia's Black Sea coast, which was part of the Ottoman Empire until 1878. In fact, the Muslim nature of this ethnically Georgian area led Moscow to structure it, along with Abkhazia and South Ossetia, as an autonomous regional republic inside Georgia, and Ajara was one of only two oblasts in the Soviet system whose autonomy was justified because of a religious difference from the union republic's majority.

Ajara's ethnic affinity with the rest of Georgia largely explains why it took a different path from Abkhazia and South Ossetia when the latter declared their independence from Tbilisi. Rather than pursuing a separatist agenda when Georgia declared its independence, the political strongman in control of this region, Asian Abashidze, defined Ajara's interests in terms of a very high level of [federal] autonomy in the new Georgia state. To Abashidze, that meant an Ajara totally under his influence, and as far from the control of the country's capital as the separatist regimes in South Ossetia and Abkhazia. Faced with civil wars elsewhere in Georgia, Georgia's President Gamsakhurdia accepted Abashidze's view of Ajara's place in the country's political process—and so did Shevardnadze, when he replaced Gamsakhurdia as Georgia's leader. In return, although Abashidze ran Ajara as his private preserve for more than a dozen years, he steadfastly supported Tbilisi in its confrontations with the rebellious northern regions and stressed the Georgian character of Ajara's people just as consistently within his own region.

It was not until Shevardnadze's fall from power that Abashidze's authority—and Ajara's independence from Tbilisi's control—were challenged. The decisive confrontation occurred in 2004, shortly after the election of Saakashvili, who had campaigned on uniting his country (as had his predecessor). Four days after his January 8 election, the authorities in Ajara declared a regional state of emergency in an effort to seize the initiative before Saakashvili began to follow up on his campaign promise. When Ajara authorities prevented the country's newly elected president from entering their province two months later, Saakashvili's response was first to put Georgia's military on standby alert and then, when Abashidze refused to accept Tbilisi's authority, to impose severe trade restrictions on the province on March 15.

Political tensions between Ajara and Tbilisi escalated during the following several weeks. In the meantime, President Saakashvili's hand was strengthened when his supporters gained a majority of the seats in parliament in Georgia's legislative elections at the end of March. The end game began on May 2, when Ajarian forces destroyed the three principal bridges linking their region to the rest of Georgia in an action justified on the grounds that it would prevent any contemplated invasion of Ajara by Georgia's army. The action was too much for the regime's former supporters. Amid street protests in Ajara's capital, Russia's foreign minister, Igor Ivanov, intervened to negotiate an end to the spiraling conflict. Three days later, Abashidze was out of office by his own hand and on his way to Moscow. On May 6 President Saakashvili flew to the province to welcome it back into Georgia and to confirm its autonomy, bringing a peaceful end to a problem that had plagued Tbilisi since Georgia became independent.[34]

Georgia's Armenian and Azerbaijan Southeast

The Armenian and Azerbaijani people living predominantly in Georgia's southeastern region and constituting between 10 and 15 percent of Georgia's overall population have never been a separatist threat to Georgia. On the other hand, the general consensus is that this area has the potential to become the hottest political spot in the country, and that any virulent assertion of nationalism by the Armenians in particular could undermine the delicate regional peace currently existing between Azerbaijan and Armenia in their conflict over the Nagorno-Karabakh territory. Moreover, by 2004 allegations of police brutality against the Armenian and Azerbaijani communities in these regions were already producing a growing number of protests, along with a growing number of incidents involving reported ethnic violence and killings.

Although idiosyncratic issues have to some degree been driving this recent ethno-political assertiveness in the two communities, their general dissatisfaction with their rule by Tbilisi can be traced to two broadly shared factors. First, there has been little effort by Tbilisi to integrate either community into Georgia's political process, Georgian society, or the country's economic system. Many Armenians and Azeris do not speak Georgian as a second language because Georgia's educational system has rarely offered them instruction in formal Georgian (partly out of Tbilisi's fear that doing so would offend their respective cultural sensitivities and trigger protests against being Georgianized). As a consequence, they often face discrimination in applying for jobs. In turn, this discrimination has resulted in disproportionately high unemployment levels in both communities, and a general sense of being treated like second-class citizens because of who they are.[35]

Acerbating their situation and seeming to validate that perception is the second factor: Georgia's Armenians and Azeris are significantly under-represented in government and other spheres of public life, and thus they have rarely been part of the policy-making process in Georgia. Indeed, they have been cut off from Tbilisi to some degree physically, as well. Until recently, Tbilisi's inattentiveness to the infrastructure needs inside their regions was paralleled by the poor transportation network linking them to Tbilisi. Only during the last few years, with outside funding, has Georgia begun to invest in rehabilitating the roadway and other infrastructure networks in these minority regions. Tbilisi also recently created a Ministry for Civic Integration designed to train minorities for public administrative positions in the state.[36] But the fruits of those labors, if carried through, are still years in the future, whereas the frustration is now.

Of the two minority groups, the lesser challenge to Georgia's territorial integrity is posed by the country's approximately 285,000 Azeri. More than 75 percent of them live next to Georgia's predominantly Armenian region (Samtskhe-Javakheti) in the country's Kvemo-Karli southeast, which has a small border with Azerbaijan. There, they constitute a solid majority in several towns, but only 45 percent of the region's overall population. Hence, although they have serious grievances over such issues as discrimination against them in land privatization (although ethnic Azeris are predominantly farmers, absentee Georgian owners acquired much of the region's best land when it was privatized by Tbilisi) and abuse by local authorities, there have been few demands for regional autonomy. They would still be ruled by others. Nevertheless, clashes between the Georgians and the Azerbaijan community in this area date from 1989 and have intermittently continued to the present—and they have also recently become bloody. In December 2004, for example, an Azeri woman was killed and several Azeris were injured in a village protest demanding that half of the local Jockey Club's land be given to local farmers.

Finally, with respect to Georgia's Azeri community, the recent growth of (essentially defensive) Azeri national assertiveness can be ascribed to a growing collective sense of insecurity. Combined with the high unemployment levels and their general socioeconomic status, this sense of physical imperilment accounts for much of the current emigration of Azeris from Georgia. In fact, Azeris believe (as do the Armenians in Samtskhe-Javakheti) that there is a systematic effort to drive them from their region. They cite the "disappearances" that have involved some of their spokesmen, the heavy sentences that others have received for minor legal infractions, and the Tbilisi campaign against smuggling and black market activities in their region that has deleteriously affected the livelihood of many Azeris.[37] Thus, although President Saakashvili has made some effort to address the Azeris' grievances and fears, in the short term there remains a high probability that there will be more, not fewer, Azeri protests and confrontations with local authorities in this region's near future.

In the meantime, the demands for regional autonomy and the risks of heightened conflict remain far greater in Georgia's predominantly Armenian Javakheti region, where slightly more than half of Georgia's quarter of a million ethnic Armenians live. Located to the east of Ajara and north of the country's border with Armenia, this region was originally the homeland of Georgia's Meskhetian Turkish population before Stalin deported them to what is now Uzbekistan. Since Georgia's independence, the region has remained an Armenian majority area, despite the desires of many Meskhetians to return to it. Because it has an

Armenian majority (now approximately 55 percent), nationalist organizations tend to push for regional autonomy as a cure to the problems faced by the Armenians in the area. And the confrontations between these organizations and local, predominantly Georgian authorities have worsened in these early days of the twenty-first century. The replacement of ethnic Armenians by ethnic Georgians on the customs house staff in Akhalkalaki in December 2005, for example, produced an ugly confrontation with local leaders when protesters temporarily seized the customs house. Three months later, the killing of an ethnic Armenian by ethnic Georgian migrants generated several days of protests against the police authorities and local court system throughout the region.

Apart from the Armenians' general economic grievances and, especially, their dissatisfaction with their inability to use their language in public life, the Armenian community's chief complaint focuses on the changing demographics of their region and what they perceive to be Tbilisi's intention to "Georgianize" them, by forcing them to learn Georgian, and its desire to "Georgianize" the region. The heart of the issue is a population time bomb ticking away in their backyard. There are already an estimated 20 percent fewer Armenians in the region than there were at the end of the Soviet era, and Georgia's Armenians are continuing to leave for jobs elsewhere (primarily Russia and Armenia). During the same period, Tbilisi has been encouraging ethnic Georgians from other parts of the country to migrate to the area. Consequently—and underscoring the delicacy of Tbilisi's relationship with the region in current Georgian politics—in addition to demanding regional autonomy in a federal-style structure and better representation in the state's decision-making bodies, Armenian activists now demand that Georgian officials end the movement of ethnic Georgians into the Samtskhe-Javakheti region.

Georgia's National Separatism Problems: The International Dimension

Complicating the management of Tbilisi's conflicts with its ethnopolitically assertive, territorialized minorities is the broader international framework within which these conflicts have been, and continue to be played out. The more distant element here is the revived rivalry between the United States and Putin's Russia. The United States strongly, albeit mostly diplomatically, backs Tbilisi in its conflicts with Abkhazia and South Ossetia, and Russia generally, if unofficially, supports their separatist regimes. An unquantifiable element, this rivalry nevertheless complicates any management of the national separatist problems faced by Tbilisi, insofar as neither Georgia's government nor those in the two breakaway regions can be sure of how much support they can expect from the United States and Russia, respectively.

Tbilisi's more immediate problem with its breakaway regions is Moscow's material support of the regimes in South Ossetia and Abkhazia, however much Russia voices its neutrality in the matter of Tbilisi's conflict with them. Georgian paramilitaries bent on retrieving these lost areas must necessarily pass through the Russian peacekeepers deployed along their borders, which guarantees diplomatic conflicts between Moscow and Tbilisi. Additionally, these conflicts have intermittently escalated to the point where Russia has imposed economic sanctions on Georgia. On other occasions, charges have revolved around Russia spying on the Saakashvili administration and violating Georgian air space. These tensions have been exacerbated by Russia's concern with the Panski Gorge being used as a sanctuary by Chechen rebels and its declared willingness to send troops into that nominally Georgian, but generally uncontrolled territory to ferret out and destroy its enemies hiding there. Once launched, these diplomatic tiffs have sometimes developed a momentum of their own, further hardening Tbilisi's already firm unwillingness to compromise with the rebel regimes and adding an additional dimension to its conflicts with them. Thus, Georgia's confrontation with Moscow over Russia's alleged efforts to undermine Georgia's government and its arrest of four Russian military officers charged with spying in the summer of 2006 spiraled in multiple directions. For example, Moscow cracked down on Georgians living and operating businesses in Russia before Georgia's release of the alleged spies eased the situation.[38]

Still elsewhere, there is the impact of developments affecting Kosovo on the "frozen" conflicts in Abkhazia and South Ossetia—both of whom appealed to the United Nations in June 2007 to put them on the list for international recognition, after Kosovo. Meanwhile, hanging over the renewed unrest in Georgia's predominantly Armenian south are two international factors that as early as 2002 prompted one international think tank to describe Tbilisi's problems with its Armenian Samtskhe-Javakheti region as "the most delicate minority situation in the Southern Caucasus today."[39]

First, a considerable number of Armenians there have found relatively well-paying jobs in and around the Russian military base in the region. The closure of that base will result in loss of their jobs and will add a further depressing element to the area's already troubled economy. It is a situation ripe for exploitation by Armenian activists.

Second, and in the only slightly longer term, there is the previously noted political time bomb lying to Georgia's south: the Armenian-Azerbaijani conflict over Nagorno-Karabakh. Unintegrated into

Georgia's mainstream, Georgia's Armenians already have a greater affinity with the majority in Armenia than with the other citizens where they live. A new war between Armenia and Azerbaijan could stir that affinity into a nationalist desire for separation and merger with Armenia, rather than the political autonomy that they now demand. It could also lead to Armenian ultranationalists fixing their eyes on Georgia's most heavily Armenian areas across the Armenian border—a fear that has thus far caused Tbilisi to treat that border area as a security issue.

POLITICAL TURMOIL

Georgia had stature within the framework of the Soviet Union, if not necessarily significant political influence. The birthplace of Stalin, it was also known for its industriousness, and it was one of the centers of the country's black market. That underground economy made available the goods (such as knock-off blue jeans) produced after hours in its factories that prolonged the life of Soviet communism when Soviet citizens began to demand more in the consumer goods department and fewer commercially made films about the wonders of Soviet tractors and tanks. That economic panache died with the Soviet Union, and it has been well buried by the economic struggles that have plagued Georgia since its independence. Now Georgia is a net energy importer in an era of high energy costs, with 40 percent of its workforce in agriculture and the markets for their products shrinking. With the country running double-digit unemployment figures overall, and with more than half of its population living below the poverty level, Georgia has economically limped into the twenty-first century as a shadow of its former self.

Quite apart from the separatist challenges that have drained the state's resources, coping with such a long-term economic downturn would be hard enough on the political health of even long-established political systems, much less the nascent administration of a country emerging from a long period of rule by others (the Russians that dominated the Soviet government in Moscow) and seeking simultaneously to democratize its political institutions and restructure its economy. But in addition to the loss of the Soviet market, Georgia *has* had to cope with civil rebellions and successful separatist movements that have removed large parts of Georgia from Tbilisi's control. In addition, confrontations with Russia and the problems of political violence affecting the state's leadership have further undercut Georgia's ability to establish an effective political order and have contributed to the pattern of chronic political turbulence that has further debilitated the development of stable democratic government in independent Georgia. That pattern of turbulence, however, was already present by the time Georgia broke free from Moscow's rule.

A Violent Birth

It may have been the liberal policies of Gorbachev that encouraged Georgian nationalists during the late 1980s to demonstrate openly against further rule by the Soviet Union, but it was the repressive use of political force by Moscow that gave Georgia's nationalist movement its momentum. It began with the excessive force that Soviet troops under Russian command employed against the nationalist demonstrators in Tbilisi in 1989, which on one occasion alone resulted in the death of nearly 50 Georgian demonstrators, including 16 women and children.

Those killings further alienated mainstream Georgians from Soviet rule and fueled a sharp increase in Georgian nationalism. As a result, in the 1990 elections involving Georgia's parliament a bloc of parties led by a nationalist writer and former repressed dissident, Zviad Gamsakhurdia, defeated the incumbent candidates of the ruling Communist Party by garnering 64 percent of the vote to the latter's 29 percent. Supported by a majority in the newly elected legislature, Gamsakhurdia assumed the republic's chairmanship, and the following year he scheduled a referendum on whether Georgia should declare its independence.

When that vote was held—with some boycotting of the referendum in the minority regions—98 percent voted "yes," and in April 1991 Georgia declared its independence. A month later Gamsakhurdia won the presidency with 87 percent of the vote, and Moscow's largely quiescent acceptance of Georgia's departure was later cited as one of the factors that prompted Soviet military leaders to attempt to gain control of the Soviet Union in August of that year.

Independence: The Turmoil Continues

Gamsakhurdia's honeymoon with the Georgian people did not long survive the summer of 1991, and a great deal of the blame for his decline in popularity rests on his shoulders. Once elected, his rule became increasingly dictatorial. Moreover, as criticism of his regime mounted among Georgia's elites, a degree of paranoia crept into his rule and he increasingly accused his critics of being traitors. Matters came to a head in August of his first year in office when his prime minister, Tengiz Sigua, joined the mounting opposition to his rule and departed the administration, followed by the commander of Georgia's military force, Tengiz Kitovani, who took most of the country's national guard units with him.

Almost immediately thereafter, fighting broke out between the president's loyalists and the opposition, and a portion of Tbilisi still bears the scars of that conflict. Then, from late December 1991 until early January 1992, protestors gathered in large numbers to demand the president's resignation. Under a very real threat to his life, Gamsakhurdia fled Tbilisi on January 6. Two months later, as the tide of conflict in Abkhazia shifted in favor of the separatist region, the inheritors of power in Tbilisi—a ruling council composed of Sigua, Kitovani and Jaba Ionelani, a Georgian warlord commanding his own paramilitary—invited Shevardnadze to join them. Shortly thereafter, Shevardnadze resigned as the Soviet Union's foreign minister to return home, and he quickly emerged as the country's leader—first as speaker of its assembly, and later as president following Georgia's adoption of a new constitution and presidential elections in 1995.[40]

In the meantime, the drama involving Gamsakhurdia took an even more violent turn when the ex-president departed Russia to return to Georgia's Megrelia/Mingrelia region, where his family had its base. From there, he launched his own rebellion against the regime in Tbilisi. Moreover, before his supporters were finally crushed by Tbilisi's troops bolstered by Russian forces, the conflagration spread into full blown civil war in the ethnic Georgia heartland. The troops that Tbilisi sent to quell the rebellion engaged in widespread looting, further alienating the Mingrelians from the capital and gaining Gamsakhurdia the support of the Mingrelian minority inhabiting the eastern part of Abkhazia.

Political Turmoil and the Shevardnadze Years

By the end of Shevardnadze's first year as president, he had thoroughly consolidated power into his and his party's hands. The governing council that he had joined in 1992 was disbanded in May 1993, and Kitovani was removed as defense minister. By January 1995, Shevardnadze was strong enough to go one step further and have Kitovani arrested when, without the government's permission, he and approximately 1,000 of his supporters launched their own war to "liberate" Abkhazia. Later that same year, Shevardnadze was also able to eliminate Ioseliani's paramilitary as a threat to his rule, and Ioseliani himself was arrested that November after an assassin tried to kill Shevardnadze. By the mid-1990s the fighting was over, not only in central Georgia, but also in Abkhazia and South Ossetia. On the other hand, those two regions—along with Ajara—were also beyond Tbilisi's control, and Shevardnadze's inability to reverse that situation placed a heavy strain on his years in office. But Shevardnadze, like Gamsakhurdia before him, soon gave protestors other reasons to indict his administration.

Rumors of political corruption surfaced shortly after Georgia gained its independence, and they gathered strength following the April 2000 presidential election in which Shevardnadze won 82 percent of the vote, but which was faulted by OSCE observers for its many irregularities. By the time of the 2002 local elections, Shevardnadze's corrupt business connections had also become an issue, along with the government's inability to improve the country's general economic conditions. The election's outcome foreshadowed the drama that was to come. Shevardnadze's party not only continued to drop in the polls, but also failed to win a single seat on the Tbilisi city council.[41] Even before that time, however, charges of corruption and the administration's seeming inability to curb highly visible crimes—including the kidnapping of UN and Red Cross personnel, some of whom had to be ransomed back, and assassination attempts on foreign officials such as the December 1998 slaying of a Greek diplomat—had raised serious questions about the regime's ability to govern. So had a mutiny by 200 troops in October 1998, even though it had been quickly quelled, and a more serious mutiny over living conditions by 400 national guard troops stationed at a base only 25 miles north of the capital.

Responding to the outcome of the local elections and the mass demonstrations that took place later that year to protest corruption and government policies, Shevardnadze fired his cabinet. Seen largely as symbolic gesture to retain his own power, their dismissal bought him nearly another two years in office.

The Rose Revolution

Accounts of the Rose Revolution, which forced Shevardnadze from office and increased the power of the Georgian people, describe it as a peaceful one. If so, then the term "peaceful revolution" has become highly relative since Czechoslovakia's Velvet Revolution, when mass gatherings of Czech protestors playing Western rock music outside government buildings in Prague peacefully persuaded that country's communist rulers to step down. By comparison, the demonstrations-based revolution that led to Shevardnadze's resignation was, euphemistically, at the very least a rowdy one.

As the country approached its parliamentary elections in the fall of 2003, unemployment rates were stalled in the 30-percent range and per capita income was still only a fraction of what it had been when Georgia became independent. Dissatisfaction with the government's performance ran high, and the public opinion polls taken before the November 2 vote favored the government's opposition. The announced results, however, gave Shevardnadze's allies a narrow victory. Concurrently, European observers announced their finding that the election had been marred by widespread irregularities.

The opposition parties launched their protests of the results two days later, and the demonstrations gathered momentum rapidly, with the protestors soon multiplying to include thousands. On November 22 the protests moved from the street to occupy Georgia's legislature, when Mikhail Saakashvili and his supporters stormed the parliament while Shevardnadze was speaking. A mild altercation ensued, but only a minor one—principally because the assembly's guards had deserted their post. Amid demands for his resignation, President Shevardnadze hastily left the building.

The next day Shevardnadze resigned in order to keep Georgians from spilling Georgian blood yet again, and power passed temporarily into the hands of the leader of the United Democrats Party, who declared herself the country's acting president. On November 25, two days after Shevardnadze's departure, a new presidential election was scheduled for January 4, 2004. On November 26 Saakashvili, an American-educated lawyer, announced his intention to run for president as the consensus candidate of the opposition National Movement Party. Following less than six weeks of campaigning he was elected president on January 4, with more than 80 percent of the vote.[42]

Recent Political Turmoil

Saakashvili promised, as his predecessors had before him, to deal with the rebellious regions, and he had immediate success in Ajara. He also adopted a more pro-Western approach to foreign policy than Shevardnadze's, and instituted a series of economic reforms designed to make Georgia more attractive to outside investors and to curtail small-scale economic corruption and tax-paying delinquency. Two years later, however, the turmoil was back. In 2006, for example, 6,000 Georgians gathered in protest, many of whom were small business owners whose earnings had been adversely affected by the reforms aimed at gray market activity. The next year brought much of the same. Indeed, the political unrest that continued to grow across the country throughout the spring and into the early summer of 2007 prompted the International Crisis Group to put Georgia on its "deteriorating circumstances" list.[43]

In November 2007, Saakashvili ordered the arrest of a former foreign minister who was then the leader of the opposition, Irakli Okruashvili, on corruption charges following Okruashvili's accusation that Saakashvili had ordered the murder of a prominent businessman. The protests that immediately ensued were primarily by Okruashvili's supporters and focused on his arrest, but they also reflected the broader public's pent-up frustrations with the government in general and with Saakashvili's cronyism in particular. Tensions also continued to heat up in the separatist areas. Georgian forces and separatists in South Ossetia exchanged gunfire, and the leader of Abkhazia deployed heavy weapons and additional troops along the border with Georgia as rumors of another invasion by Tbilisi forces circulated.

President Saakashvili was in New York when the protests began. After returning to Georgia, he moved up the previously scheduled presidential election to the first Sunday in January 2008, but the demonstrations continued. Within a week, the president had his supportive majority in parliament declare a fifteen-day period of emergency rule, during which Georgian authorities aggressively cleared the streets of the protestors in a manner that observers described as a "repressive and disproportionate response to the peaceful protests."[44] And when the election took place, its outcome was marred by charges of fraud and a mixed review from international monitors, who found local irregularities but no systematic effort to control the election's outcome. More importantly, the vote indicated how very far downward Saakashvili's popularity had tumbled in only four years, with his percentage dropping from 85 percent in 2004 to only 51.75 percent in January 2008—barely enough to avoid a runoff election. In the election's aftermath, opposition protestors gathered again on the streets of Tbilisi, although in lesser numbers than in November.[45]

State Violence

The idea of "state violence" normally evokes images of Robespierre, whose Committee on Public Safety employed terror to intimidate a country of tens of millions into accepting his leadership for more than a year following the French Revolution. There are similar images of Stalin, whose ruthless rule led to the deaths of unknown numbers who were executed because he distrusted them and of the legions of non-Russia nations whom he deemed disloyal and who perished when he had them forcefully transplanted to Siberia and other remote regions of the Soviet Union. Such images bear no proximity to Georgian politics. However corrupt and willing to rig elections the government of President Shevardnadze may have been, it did not engage in the systematic use of state-sponsored violence to stay in office. Nor, despite the tumultuous nature of Georgian politics as the country has lunged towards democracy, has Georgia descended into a disorderly political equivalent of Chicago's gangland turf battles during the Prohibition era. Still, the proceedings of the government in Tbilisi and in the capitals of the de facto breakaway regions of Abkhazia and South Ossetia, and the functioning of government in other parts of the country, have been sufficiently punctuated by acts of political violence as to warrant concern for the future of a democratizing country. Shevardnadze, for example, not only had his motorcade attacked as he left the ceremony that signed Georgia's new constitution into effect in 1995, but he subsequently survived two assassination attempts in the late 1990s—one by a rocket-propelled grenade that struck his armored limousine in 1997 and killed two of his bodyguards, and the second by ambush a year later, when gunfire killed another of his bodyguards.

The new century has been no less violent. In 2004 there was the diagnosed accidental death by natural gas poisoning of Prime Minister Zurob Zhvania, one of the architects of the Rose Revolution, while visiting a friend's apartment. Then there is an additional short list of political violence in Georgia involving prominent politicians in the early years of the twenty-first century:

- The November 2001 death of a supporter of a candidate running in Abkhazia's presidential election, when demonstrators chose to storm government buildings in the region's capital of Sukhumi
- Tbilisi's early 2004 charge that the government of Ajara had hired four contract killers to assassinate Georgia's president
- A July 2005 incident involving the detonation of a grenade in Tbilisi on the occasion of President Bush's visit to that city
- The July 2007 grenade attack on Abkhazia's prime minister, Alexander Ankvab (the fourth attempt to assassinate him since he acquired power)
- The murder that same year of the leader of Georgia's opposition Faith, Fatherland, and Language Party, who was gunned down on the streets of Tbilisi

Compounding the situation, and making the future of Georgia even harder to gauge in this area, is the fact that in its withdrawal from Georgia, the Soviet army left behind a number of poorly guarded munitions depots.[46] Post-independence politics would seem to indicate that at least some of the grenades, napalm bombs, and other conventional weapons of that former superpower have found their way into the hands of political activists in Georgia.

RUSSIA

There can be no debate of the fact that Moscow's continuing troubles with its "autonomous" republics in the Northern Caucasus warrant Russia's inclusion in this volume. The major issue is whether, even without that violent political conflict, the European part of Russia would qualify as a hot spot in its own right. In turn, that question breaks down into two subsidiary considerations: (1) whether the drift away from electoral democracy toward a more directive form of democracy—if not authoritarian rule itself—during the era of Vladimir Putin's presidency renders Russia a trouble spot on the rim of the European union; and (2) whether such other issues as crime, corruption, and terrorism make Russia outside of the Caucasus a dangerous hot spot in its own right.[47] The answer here to both questions is no, but both warrant consideration—and certainly the spread of terrorism into other parts of Russia as a result of the troubles in the Caucasus is an issue in its own right.

Western critics of Putin's Russia have framed their warnings of the perils of contemporary Russia in terms of Putin's antipluralistic recentralization of power in the state's hands, willingness to silence his Russian and foreign critics by whatever means necessary, and manipulation of democratic elections in order to ensure his continued power in office. On all counts, evidence is not hard to find.

One dimension of Putin's drive for a more orderly Russia has clearly been to bring key state resources back under the state's control. The government of President Vladimir Putin has routinely employed legal proceedings to accomplish that objective, primarily by using the courts to prosecute the state's post-communist economic oligarchies on charges of embezzlement, tax fraud, and/or corruption. The legal process has been used similarly to gain control of key economic sectors through bankruptcy proceedings. In the energy field, for example, the owner of one of Russia's largest private oil companies was forced to flee the country to avoid prosecution for tax evasion and the umbrella crime of "illegal business practices," and bankruptcy proceedings forced the country's biggest oil company, Yukos, to close its doors in August 2006. Not infrequently, whether out of self-interest or conviction, the targets of these proceedings have also been ardent critics of Putin—for example, Boris Berezovsky, the former head of the Russian airline giant Aeroflot, who endorsed a coup to dislodge Putin and his entourage from power after being sentenced in absentia to six years in jail on embezzlement charges.

Of more concern to human rights groups has been the silencing of Putin critics by less legalistic and gentile means. The most celebrated case involved the alleged murder by radiation poisoning of a former Russian spy, a latter-day critic of Putin's Russia who was living in London's very large Russian community. Although they have gained less notoriety, the frequent and rough disruptions of anti-Putin protests by public authorities have also been widely criticized by human rights organizations.[48] So too have the forced closure of the offices of domestic and international human rights operations concerned with such issues as rights violations in Chechnya, and the pressure that has been brought to bear on foreign diplomats and on domestic and foreign news agencies, whose reports have offended public officials. In early 2006, four British diplomats were expelled for allegedly spying on Russia, and the BBC's broadcasts from Russia have occasionally been suspended by the state, generally in retaliation for stories in the British press alleging that Putin's government played a role in the London slaying of the former Russian spy who had become a Putin critic. Relations between Putin and the United States also worsened in 2006, when radio stations throughout Russia suddenly ceased to carry Voice of America broadcasts. More intimidating still to would-be critics of the Putin regime, a strikingly large number of journalists between 2004 and 2005 were murdered in Russia, with no convictions of anyone responsible for the crimes.[49] And these numbers do not include the mysterious deaths of journalists that have not been labeled murder. Such was the case of Ivan Safronov, a military correspondent for a business daily whose reporting was often critical of Russian military operations (such as the failed launch of a much-touted intercontinental missile in December 2005) and who died after falling down the stairwell of his Moscow apartment building in March 2006.

Western critics of the Putin government have also continually cited flaws in the elections that have given Putin his growing power base. The 2007 parliamentary elections in which parties pledged to Putin crushed his rivals have come under attack in particular, because of the intimidation that Putin's rivals faced, the difficulty that election monitors from Western Europe had in gaining entry to the country, the disruption of the rallies of opposition parties, the arrest of opposition candidates, and the widespread irregularities that surrounded the counting of ballots in an election that Putin's agents had reputedly told party workers would be a referendum on his rule. In addition, his agents also allegedly urged them to ensure that the parties backing Putin would win the 70 percent of the seats in the new parliament that were necessary to amend the Russian constitution.[50]

Finally, Putin's critics have also expressed concern over the orchestrated manner in which Putin prolonged his power in 2007. When precluded by the constitution from seeking a new term as president, he basically shifted his offices by first picking an obscure and semi-elderly (65 years old) long-time associate, Viktor Subkov, to be Russia's new prime minister, then touting Subkov's qualifications before eventually anointing Dmitry Medvedev to be his successor as president, and finally agreeing to heed the call of his countrymen and remain in government as

Russia's prime minister in a Medvedev presidency. The same critics have dismissed Putin's apparent popularity as "oil democracy"—the byproduct of his use of oil revenues to curry the favor of his countrymen in his private "march to czarism."[51]

Yet when all of these transgressions and criticisms are added together, they still bespeak a Russia more orderly than in the past—one that seems to be generally accepted by most of its citizens and is almost certainly less dangerous to the regions around it and to the West in general than the Russia of Yeltsin, a decade ago. Outside of the Caucasus, today's Russia is not a hot spot. Boris Yeltsin's Russia, on the other hand—a state on the brink of failure that could not contain the rebellion in Chechnya, police its weapons inventory, or control the economic oligarchs looting its resources and the corrupt politicians reaping the personal rewards of public office across its Eurasian expanse—may have been. To be sure, a more assertive Russia— rebuilding its arms, consolidating control over its energy resources by squeezing out foreign companies, commandeering Russian energy enterprises at a time when oil and gas wealth is international power, and pursuing a more independent foreign policy—is certainly not what Western democracies hoped would happen in post-communist Russia. In the long term, it may not even be in the best interest of the Russian people to alienate outside investment capital by returning to a more state-managed economy. But all this does not mean that Russia has returned to its former totalitarian system. Even if today's Russia may not be anyone's model of a beautifully democratizing polity, it is a safer country than it was during the Yeltsin years. And it is still, at least for the moment, a great deal freer than it was in all but perhaps the last days of communism, when Gorbachev's liberalization policies permitted open criticism of the state and even its communist leaders. Indeed, Gorbachev himself lavished praise on Putin at the same time Western observers were criticizing the country's 2007 national elections, lauding Putin for pulling "Russia out of chaos," spearheading the country's "resurgence" in world affairs and at home, and ensuring post-communist Russia's "place in history."[52]

There is also some question about how democratic Russia was under Yeltsin. Implicit in the criticism of Putin's government is that it has retreated on the democratic front; yet, Yeltsin's Russia also had its bloody political moments—for example, the 1993 confrontation between Yeltsin and his opponents in the Russian parliament. Likewise, despite all of the democratization advice Russia received from Western governments and civic-minded nongovernment actors, elections under Yeltsin were also criticized frequently for their undemocratic quality—especially the election that resulted in Yeltsin's reelection in 1996, and the 1999 parliamentary elections. Furthermore, their outcome was not a more democratic Russia, just a weaker one with so many political parties in the Russian parliament that the result was an anemic government incapable of effectively attacking the economic, security, and criminal challenges confronting the state. That weakness at the center also encouraged the country's elected regional governors to stray out of control and establish their own fiefdoms.[53]

Recentralization of power has allowed Putin more effectively to combat corruption across Russia and, by invoking anticorruption powers, to dismiss mayors and bring once again under Moscow's control the Russian cities that became increasingly corrupt and lawless during the 1990s of Boris Yeltsin. Similarly, Putin's move to have the country's governors appointed, rather than elected, has given Moscow the tool for cleaning up Russia's regional governments. That move has also enhanced Putin's personal power, to be sure, but in much of the country—and especially in Russia's east—it has not come at the expense of any politically accountable democratic system that citizens of consolidated democracies would readily recognize, and it has managed to create order out of what many Russians saw as chaos.

These gains have not been cost-free, either to the West, which found Yeltsin's Russia more malleable in international affairs, or to the Russian people. Problems linger in many areas. Weapon depots remain under-guarded, and St. Petersburg is still widely viewed as Russia's crime capital—a reputation it gained during the early years of the twenty-first century as a result of the wave of gangland killings that swept the city, the assassination of its most reform-minded politicians, and a high crime rate in which the theft of even petty property often results in violence. The criminal networks that grew in the immediate aftermath of the fall of communism still strike out violently against state prosecutors and other officials combating such illegal activities as money-laundering. Indeed, the danger of conducting courtroom proceedings against these criminals reached the point where the state purchased 12,000 semiautomatic handguns in early 2007 to arm its judges, in order to make courtrooms safer. On the economic front, pensions are now being paid regularly, but gains have often been at the price of enacting such unpopular reforms as those that allow the state to buy out, with one-time payments at bargain prices, such formerly long-term welfare entitlements as the free transportation and free medicine that Russia formerly extended to its pensioners. Perhaps most taxing, there are still the problems associated with fully pacifying Russia's autonomous republics in the Caucasus and ending the political violence that still travels out of that troubled area to threaten public safety in Russia's European heartland.

Russian soldiers patrol the ruins of Grozny. © Yuri Kochetkov/epa/Corbis.

CHECHNYA

The problems resulting from national sentiments take a variety of forms in Russia. There are Russian ultranationalists who are opposed to the presence of "foreigners" (including the non-Russian citizens of the country) in major Russian cities and who therefore often blur into the anti-Jewish neo-Nazi youth groups that are found in most Russian metropolitan areas. The ultranationalists also favor a more assertive foreign policy abroad, and they have been associated with politically violent acts against both institutions of the state and foreign critics of Russia.

There are also pockets of ethnic minorities throughout Russia who continue to clamor for more local autonomy than they currently receive or against the discrimination they perceive themselves to be suffering at the hands of the Russian majority ruling in Moscow. Nevertheless, since the breakup of the Soviet Union the most deadly conflicts faced by Moscow have emanated from the nationalist separatist movements spread across the Russian Caucasus (also known as the Northern Caucasus) in general, and in particular from Chechnya. Its majority population, Muslim since the eighth century, differs from its Russian rulers in terms of ethnic origin, language, and religion.

The Civil Wars in Chechnya

The Chechen people, like the Abkhaz in Georgia, have lived in their region since before recorded history. Also like the Abkhaz, the Chechens have not taken kindly to rule by outsiders. And quite apart from the two civil wars that have been fought in Chechnya since the fall of the Soviet Union, the Chechens have been grievously abused by the rule of others within the historical memory of Chechens still living.[54]

Origins of the Chechen-Russian Conflict

Although Russians began to settle in the Chechen region as early as the sixteenth century, conflict did not occur between Russia and the indigenous Vainakh (Chechen and Ingush) communities until the Czars began to annex the area into the Russian Empire nearly 200 years later. The first major clash occurred during the time of Peter the Great, who in 1722 dispatched forces to capture a disputed village. By the end of the century the Czars found themselves dealing with a large-scale rebellion against Russian rule. The conflict continued to escalate into the nineteenth century, when a Dagestani cleric, Imam Shamil, organized the first state in the area, and Dagestani and Chechen Muslim warriors fought the Russian army for nearly half a century (1817 to 1864) before being finally subdued. In the process, large numbers of Chechens and Dagestanis died in the fighting, and numerous Chechen villages were destroyed in that village-centered society. In the war's aftermath, the area's Chechen population was further reduced to less than two-thirds its former size by the massive deportation of Chechens to Turkey, Siberia, or the vast plains of Eurasian Russia.

History repeated itself to a certain degree in Chechnya following the Russian revolution. As with several other minority groups in the Caucasus that had fallen under communist rule in the 1920s, the Chechens briefly enjoyed a measure of autonomy under Chechen communist leaders, only to have that autonomy revoked by Stalin and to have their region merged with the Ingush people's territory to their west. When Stalin subsequently implemented his forced collectivization of agriculture policy in Chechnya, local revolts occurred in 1932–33. As a consequence, like other rebellious or distrusted national minorities under Stalin's rule, the remaining Chechens and Ingush were deported to Central Asia during World War II. In the wake of the territory's forced ethnic cleansing, the short-lived Chechen-Ingush Autonomous Soviet Socialist Republic (ASSR) disappeared, and its territory was divided among neighboring areas.

Following Stalin's death—and again, as in the case of other victims of Stalin's deportation policies—the Chechens were allowed to return to their territory and the Chechen-Ingush ASSR was restored, but this time under the control of Russians, rather than local communists. Chechens were routinely excluded from any position of authority, and Soviet rule focused on harvesting the oil that had been discovered years earlier around Grozny for the benefit of the Soviet homeland, not for the Chechen people. Consequently, little was done to develop the territory as a whole in its remaining years under Soviet rule.

Finally, and yet again following the pattern that developed in the Soviet Union's non-Russian union republics during the Gorbachev era of *perestroika*, the easing of political censorship opened the door to the open organization of Chechen nationalist groups. These groups initially demanded an end to the discrimination that Chechens faced because of their nationality, as well as financial support to revive and teach the Chechen culture. Leading the charge by 1989 was the Vainakh Democratic Party, and when the efforts to repress its activities failed to curb the rising tide of Chechen nationalism, the Russians switched tactics and tried accommodation by appointing a Chechen, Doku Zavgayev, to replace the Russian party boss who had been governing Chechnya.

The Road to Civil War

Zavgayev's goal was simultaneously to persuade Moscow to give the Chechen-Ingush ASSR real and substantial autonomy, and to co-opt Chechnya's intellectual and cultural leaders into supporting the idea of Chechnya remaining inside the Soviet Union. His strategy quickly disintegrated in the face of internal and external developments. Inside Chechnya, Soviet accommodation had come too late to abate the growth of Chechen nationalism; the goal of Chechen nationalists had become independence, not federal autonomy for their region inside the Soviet Union. Toward that end, and in the midst of demonstrations calling for Chechnya's independence, Chechen nationalist organizations fused into the Pan-National Congress of the Chechen People (PNCCP) at the end of 1990 and invited Soviet Air Force General Jokher Dudayev, a Chechen by birth, to assume its leadership.

From the outset there was little doubt that the PNCCP was prepared to pursue Chechnya's independence, by force if necessary, because almost immediately it began to arm itself with weapons purchased on the Soviet black market and to form its own paramilitary "national guard." Whatever its timetable for acquiring power may have been, the failed military grab for power in Moscow in August 1991, accelerated it. Organizing mass rallies on the square outside the Chechen-Ingush republic's legislature (Supreme Soviet), the PNCCP demanded that the body disband and that Zavgayev resign. When nothing resulted,

Dudayev's minions took control of the local television station and, when the police refused Zavgayev's orders to disperse the crowd, Dudayev went on the air to declare that the Chechen revolution was under way.

In short order it succeeded in grabbing control of political authority in Grozny, at least. On September 6 Dudayev's supporters stormed the region's assembly. When the fighting ended, one deputy was dead and Zavgayev had been "arrested" and forced to resign. Less than a month later the PNCCP formally declared itself the only government of the Chechen Republic, and by the end of October Dudayev had been elected its president in an election that almost certainly would not have passed the OSCE's "free and fair" test. On November 1, the Chechen Republic declared its independence, despite the fact that an earlier referendum had indicated that a majority of the people preferred to remain a part of the Russian Federation.

Unlike the union republics that declared their independence at the same time, Chechnya was a part of the Russian federation, an oil-producing part of it, at that. As a consequence, its declarations of independence received a different reception in Moscow than those of the Soviet Union's non-Russian union republics. With little planning beforehand, a unit of Russian troops was flown into the area, only to be surrounded by Dudayev's own military, taken prisoner, and sent out of Chechnya on buses—a quick triumph over Moscow's machinations that instantly made Dudayev a celebrity throughout Chechnya.

Thereafter a *modus vivendi* emerged between Moscow and Grozny, in which the former refused to acknowledge the latter's sovereignty but accepted Dudayev's regime as a fact of post-Soviet political life and dealt with it in order to keep the region's oil industry intact. As part of the arrangement, Russia also formally dissolved the Chechen-Ingush Republic and withdrew the last of its troops from Chechnya in June 1992, leaving behind a large cache of additional weapons for Dudayev's supporters. With a bit more skill on Dudayev's part the arrangement might have endured, and the province's future might have taken a different turn. Much like Georgia's independence president, however, Dudayev proved to be politically incompetent, venal, and dictatorial.

By mid-1993 the rivalry between Dudayev and his critics inside the Chechen parliament was an open one. His critics indicted him for mismanaging the republic and accused his cronies of being both corrupt and in league with organized criminal networks. In response, Dudayev disbanded the parliament, proclaimed presidential rule, and deployed his forces to crush all protest. By June, his control over the capital and its immediate environs was complete, but it did not cover all of Chechnya. His opponents regrouped in the north, near the Russian border, and organized themselves in December 1993 into the Provisional Council of the Chechen People (PCCP). With military assistance from Moscow in the form of equipment, money, training, and "volunteers," the PCCP established its own military bases. The political confrontation of the previous year evolved into warfare inside Chechnya between the PCCP and Dudayev's government in Grozny, with Moscow providing the PCCP forces with air support.

The First Russia-Chechnya Civil War

In November 1994, after enjoying some success in the countryside operations, PCCP forces launched an attack on Grozny itself, only to be beaten back. Among the prisoners of war put on parade by Dudayev were several Russian volunteers. Embarrassed yet again, the Yeltsin government made one last diplomatic effort to resolve the political impasse between Moscow and Grozny. When that effort failed, Yeltsin turned to his direct military option. On December 11, 1994, Russian forces entered Chechnya from its west, east, and north.

The war lasted approximately twenty months, from December 1994 until August 1996, with a quasi-lull between June and December of 1995. At the outset, Russian forces again underestimated the resistance they might encounter. Capturing the capital required two months of hard fighting, which took the lives of approximately 27,000 civilians and obliterated much of Grozny. Although parts of Chechnya still remained outside Moscow's control, an interim government was established in Grozny. By April 1995 matters had seemingly stabilized, and Moscow invited the OSCE to use its good offices to try to establish a cease-fire, which it did in June. Nevertheless, skirmishes of a guerrilla warfare nature with Russian forces continued on an isolated basis, even as negotiations continued to seek a diplomatic solution to the conflict. More famously, in mid-summer the Chechen field commander, Shamil Basayev, carried the war across Chechnya's border into the adjacent Russian province of Stavropol, where his unit captured a small town and took hundreds of Russians hostages, the last of whom were released only when Basayev and his men were safely again in the hills of southern Chechnya.

There seemed to be further progress in August, when the outlines of a tentative peace agreement were accepted by the Chechen negotiators in Grozny, whose legitimacy to negotiate on behalf of the Chechen people Dudayev denied. In October 1995, however, the talks exploded when the Russian general overseeing them was injured by a car bomb, and by the end of the year the full-scale warfare between the Russian military and the Chechen rebels had resumed.

Despite some military setbacks, matters seemed to be moving in Moscow's direction when a Russian missile struck and killed Dudayev in April 1996, but the principal outcome of his death appears to have been a hardening of the Chechen rebels' resolve and a lowering of the guard by Russia's military commanders. Thus, when the Chechen separatists counterattacked in August of that year, they were able to retake Grozny and several other Chechen towns before the Russian units—devastated by the attack—could regroup. To further compound its losses, throughout the conflict Russia had been unable to end the attacks on areas outside of Chechnya by such Chechen warlords as Basayev and Salman Raduyev. In short, twenty months after invading the country, Russia was where it had begun—no longer in control of the region's capital and fighting a tenacious nationalist movement that had effective paramilitary commanders. In response, Yeltsin chose to cut his losses and Moscow negotiated an end to the civil war with the Chechen military commander, General Asian Maskhadov, in the Dagestani city of Khasavyurt (the "Khasavyurt Accord").

The Interim

Between the end of the first war in August 1996 and the advent of the second civil war in October 1999, Chechnya became a quasi-frozen conflict from which Moscow again withdrew its troops. Moreover, following the elections held in Chechnya under OSCE auspices in January 1997, which resulted in Maskhadov being elected president with 65 percent of the vote, Moscow recognized Maskhadov as the legally elected president of the Chechen Republic of Ichkera—a move that helped normalize the region's dialogue with Moscow, but stopped short of recognizing the republic's independence or constituting a renunciation by Moscow of its claim to the region. Meanwhile, inside Chechnya, the region descended into anarchy.

Nearly six years of warfare, internal and with Russia, had left Chechnya even more impoverished. By some estimates, between half and four-fifths of its economic assets were destroyed during the warfare. Moreover, much of Chechnya was in ruins, and the Maskhadov government lacked the funds either to rebuild it or maintain effective order in it. Chaos resulted, organized criminal gangs multiplied, kidnapping and ransoming foreigners became a growth industry, and Grozny itself became so dangerous that in December 1998 the OSCE withdrew its mission from the capital and relocated it in Moscow. Meanwhile, the centers of power outside of Grozny became the region's warlords—still ubiquitous players in the politics of Chechnya and other points in the Caucasus, however incongruous the concept of warlords continuing to exist in twenty-first-century Europe may seem. Yet in Chechnya, it was the actions of one of these warlords, operating boldly with funding from outside Islamic groups, that triggered the second civil war between Russia and Chechnya.

The Second Civil War

In August 1999, Chechen warlord and former field commander Shamil Basayev led his Islamic "peacekeeping brigade," which had been trained with outside funding, into neighboring Dagestan with the intent of linking up with the Islamic separatists fighting there and ultimately uniting Chechnya and Dagestan into a single Islamic state. Dagestanis had repeatedly been victimized by Chechen raids throughout the 1990s, and a substantial contingent of Russian forces was on hand to repulse Basayev's invading force. Nevertheless, given the backdrop of the political chaos in Chechnya and Russia's experience with Islamic extremists in Afghanistan, Basayev's incursion was enough to convince Russian president Vladimir Putin that prophylactic action was needed before he had an out-of-control Islamic movement throughout Russia's Northern Caucasus.[55] Consequently, Putin once again sent the Russian military into Chechnya shortly after the raid, initially to establish a security buffer zone between Russia and Chechnya in the region's traditionally loyal northern lowlands.

Successful in achieving its initial objective, in November 1999 the Russia military expanded its goal into retaking all of Chechnya. Better prepared than in the past, they generally succeeded after several months of hard fighting, forcing the Chechen rebels to retreat into the mountainous area of southern Chechnya. There, they developed a hit-and-run counterattack strategy designed to lower the morale of their Russian enemy. The strategy was largely successful, and it also produced a dividend. Frustrated, the Russians often responded to the raids by attacking Chechen villages, a form of reprisal that made it easier for the rebels to obtain additional recruits eager to kill Russians. The number of refugees swelling into camps in neighboring, poor countries grew, and complete military success continued to elude the Russian military. On the other hand, Grozny and much of Chechnya were still in Russian hands, and as the new year began Maskhadov declared his willingness to engage in peace talks with Moscow, although it was clear to all that he could not control the warlords leading the fighting in the south.

In 2001 Putin shifted tactics and began to engage the separatists with Chechens, rather than with Russian soldiers. Making this possible was the defection of a Muslim cleric, Mufti Akhmad Kadyrov, who came over to the Russian side and who Moscow anointed as the leader of a new civilian administration in Chechnya. Kadyrov was allowed not only to establish his own Muslim court system, but also to recruit and arm approximately 15,000 militia to support his administration. With the tide no longer running in favor of the separatists, Putin essentially declared victory in April 2002 and pronounced the civil war at an end, with Grozny once again under the control of a pro-Moscow government. The truth was a little less rosy, however, and a war of attrition has subsequently continued, often taking large numbers of lives. On the other hand, unlike the acceptance of failure that marked the end of the first civil war, the second concluded favorably for Russia, with the separatists no longer controlling the region's government and too weak to dislodge the Russian-supported government in Grozny. That government was backed by the presence of more than 80,000 Russian troops, in a region holding only slightly more than a million people, when Putin pronounced the war at an end.

Contemporary Chechnya: The Conflict Continues

Despite a substantial amount of rebuilding financed by Moscow and international agencies since the end of the second civil war (some of which has actually reached its intended targets instead of being siphoned off by the corrupt practices that remain in place), Chechnya continues to be a dangerous place. Its separatists, fewer in number but remaining entrenched in the region's mountainous south, still threaten areas both near at hand and more remote, and shootouts between the rebels and Russian security forces have continued—including in the streets of Grozny. On a more orderly note, there *have* been gains for Chechnya on the political front, including the ratification by referendum of a constitution for Chechnya and Moscow's promise to give Chechnya special status among the autonomous areas within the Russian federation At the same time, the nature of day-to-day politics in the province has been far less savory—for example, the manner in which Akhmad Kadyrov cemented his control of Chechnya in the October 2003 presidential election, in which he reportedly won 80 percent of the vote. Neutral observers unanimously noted that the election took place in an intimidating environment, and that only Kadyrov was permitted to hold rallies and received media coverage. There was also the matter of a grenade being thrown into the headquarters of his chief rival in the presidential election.

Subsequent political change inside the province has likewise been driven at least as often by violent death among political players on both sides as by such orderly processes as elections and adherence to the constitutional rules of the game. On May 9, 2004, for example, a land mine planted beneath the dignitaries' stand at a Grozny football stadium was detonated during a parade, killing Kadyrov. His death put the republic's political system into the hands of caretakers until the late president's son, Ramzan Kadyrov, was appointed president in 2007. Like his father, Ramzan Kadyrov retains a large private militia whose actions have been linked to the killing and kidnapping of human rights workers in Chechnya, as well as his separatist enemies.[56] Meanwhile, the primary challenger to the political authorities in Grozny, former president Maskhadov (who joined the separatists in the south after losing power to Akhmad Kadyrov), was removed from the political scene when he was stalked and killed by Russian forces in March 2005. Perhaps even more important in terms of ending the violence in the region, Shamil Basayev was killed in the summer of 2006. Believed responsible for numerous terrorist acts, including planning the attack on a school in neighboring North Ossetia in which hundreds of children died, Basayev was a major player in the continuing political violence in Chechnya. Russian president Putin has frequently complained of the United States' double standard on terrorism—that the United States invokes the terrorist threat to its borders in order to justify its occupation of a country half a globe away, while condemning Russia's military action against separatists in Chechnya, whose radical groups have occupied schools in nearby provinces and bombed apartment houses in Moscow. His argument is not without foundation, but it deserves three qualifiers.

First, quite apart from its own military operations, Russia itself contributed significantly to the destructiveness of the conflict in Chechnya. As Stuart Kaufman succinctly summarized the issue, "By arming and training Chechen fighters [voluntarily] in Abkhazia, Russia sowed the seeds of its own problems when those same Chechens led the resistance to Russians in Russia's Chechnya wars of the 1990s."[57]

Second, the amount of criticism flowing from the White House with respect to Russia's heavy hand in Chechnya abated considerably after the terrorist attack on the United States on September 11, 2001.

Finally, nothing has so strengthened Moscow's hand in dealing with its Chechen problem than the U.S. occupation of Iraq, which has drawn Muslim extremists and would-be freedom fighters to Iraq to fight the American infidel, as they once flocked to Afghanistan to combat the Russians, who invaded the country in late December 1979. Without the U.S. decision to invade and occupy Iraq, at least some of those volunteers from around the Muslim world (including Western Europe's Muslim community) would almost certainly be lending their assistance to today's Chechen rebels. They were doing so in discernible numbers before September 11 and the subsequent U.S. actions, first in Afghanistan and then in Iraq.

INSTABILITY IN THE AUTONOMOUS REPUBLICS

Outside of Chechnya, the autonomous republics composing the rest of the Russian Caucasus have had their issues with Moscow and were a conflict-management problem for the Russian government before the civil wars began in Chechnya. They also have had their internal conflicts, given the large number of ethnic groups within them (Dagestan, for example, has more than thirty different national communities), as well as conflicts with one another. During the meltdown of the Soviet Union, for example, a brief war erupted in 1992 between North Ossetia and Ingushetia, and tens of thousands of Ingush in North Ossetia were forced to leave their homes. More importantly, a variety of destabilizing forces have continued to plague these small autonomous republics in the Russian federation, preventing their governments from establishing durable regimes. The mix varies from one autonomous republic to another, but the list of toxic ingredients accounting for the area's still volatile and often violent nature is substantially the same across the Northern Caucasus:

- The corruption prevalent in many of the governments
- The continuing presence of pockets of the Chechen rebels who fled to these neighboring areas
- The alienation and high level of unemployment to be found among the youth in these republics
- The generally depressed condition of their economies
- The revival of Islam (sometimes accelerated by the appeal of militant Islamic extremism)
- Longstanding grievances with Moscow
- Rival ethnic and national identities, sometimes aggravated by issues involving refugees from the fighting in Chechnya[58]

The resulting cocktail is a region of extreme political unpredictability in which, somewhere, political violence is likely to be very close to the surface or boiling over at any given time. The following summaries are brief, alphabetized snapshots of the political turmoil and violence that have unfolded in the area's principal autonomous republics since the "end" of the war in Chechnya.

Dagestan

Located to the east and south of Chechnya, Dagestan was a major supply corridor for outsiders who aided the Chechen rebels during the wars in Chechnya, and at times it was a victim of forays by Chechen rebels into adjacent areas during the war. Extremist groups, religious and otherwise, still operate widely within its territory, and kidnapping and hostage taking are a part of its economic life.

Ingushetia Republic

Ethnically akin to the Chechens and, like the Chechens, a people who do not have many good memories involving Russian rule, the Ingush have nevertheless not mounted any attempt to separate from Russia since the collapse of the Soviet system. Ingushetia has been a useful sanctuary for Chechen rebels, however, and those rebels have continued to pose a threat to the safety of its people, especially those affiliated with its pro-Moscow government. The major instance of violence in this republic since the winding down of the second civil war in Chechnya took place in 2004, when more than 500 armed Chechen rebels attacked the main government buildings in Nazran and killed ninety-three people, mostly government officials and security personnel. The political situation in the republic has remained tense ever since. In June 2006, seven people were assassinated by members of an Islamic underground organization with alleged ties to Chechens. The victims included the local official responsible for aiding Russians desiring to resettle in the republic and the senior police commander. Nor did the situation improve the following year, which ended with nearly three months of drive-by shootings, kidnapping incidents, and efforts to assassinate public officials.

Kabardino-Balkaria Republic

Located north of Chechnya, this republic too has suffered from growing instances of political violence since the end of the war in Chechnya. The most notable was in October 2005, when its capital city of some 275,000 people was the scene of a shootout between security forces and Islamic extremists that killed more than a hundred people. The attack has been subsequently attributed both to a widespread backlash against a government that is widely perceived as corrupt, and to its overzealous crackdown on Islamic militants, which alienated the region's more moderate Muslims and facilitated the growth of extremist Islamic groups.[59]

North Ossetia

The North Osseti, like their brethren in Georgia, are of Persian stock, and since the breakup of the Soviet Union they have had their own ideas about separating from Russia. Most of those ideas have not included merging with the South Osseti, who have established a de facto independence in their frozen conflict with the government in Tbilisi. North Ossetia's borders continue to be highly porous and vulnerable to raids from neighboring areas, as in 2004 when extremists commandeered Public School No. 1 in Beslan. They held more than a thousand school children hostage before security forces stormed the building in a rescue operation that resulted in hundreds of lives being lost. Internally, given the prevalence of criminal gangs and the remnants of Chechen separatists, securing the public safety has been a chronic problem. A typical example is the November 2007 bus explosion in the region that claimed five lives, wounded a dozen, and was simply attributed to "militants." Also inside the republic, the rumors that Ingush were among the perpetrators of the Beslan attack have notably increased tensions between the Osseti and the Ingush who remain in the region,

TERRORISM

There have been several watersheds in the evolution of terrorism, that mode of unconventional warfare that condones the indiscriminate killing of civilians in order to achieve its political aims. One of the first, and certainly one of the most important of these, was Robespierre's contribution to its development. Prior to the French Revolution, terrorism had essentially involved those who lacked political power lashing out in single acts against those who had power, in the hope of acquiring it themselves. If entire villages had to die from drinking the water of poisoned wells in order to kill a sultan, then so be it. Robespierre expanded terrorism as a work in progress in two ways. His lesser contribution was to use indiscriminate political violence as a tool of control by which a state could secure the obedience of the governed—at least for a while. His greater contribution to terrorism's evolution was tied to the lesser one. Robespierre understood that terrorism involves two elements: the physical act itself, and the psychological climate of insecurity that it can engender in the broader political community. By systematically using seemingly random acts of violence, he and his cohorts were able to intimidate France into accepting their dictatorial rule—until their time ran out, and they too got to meet Madame Guillotine. Until then, incalculable numbers of French citizens were dissuaded from plotting against Robespierre's regime. You never knew when the midnight rap at the door might be for you and your family, if you did not acquiesce to Robespierre's rule.

In the contemporary world, the second dimension of terrorism is the dominant one. Blowing up the twin towers with hijacked aircraft did not alter U.S. foreign policy with respect to Israel or produce a withdrawal of American forces from the Muslim world, but it did for some time result in abnormally high vacancy rates in other notable high-rise buildings in New York. In like manner, the terrorist attacks against Russian citizens have not altered Russian policy with respect to the Caucasus, but they have produced fears throughout Russia that the violence primarily localized in Chechnya and adjacent areas might be visited on Russians elsewhere. Indeed, those fears were being noted by foreign journalists from the beginning of the first civil war in Chechnya, when Muscovites—made jittery by Dudayev's talk of holy wars against Russia—flooded the newly established terrorist hotline to report suspicious, swarthy-looking people typical of those persons living in the Caucasus.[60] In fact, Russians had more to worry about on the terrorist front than just the Chechens.

Homegrown Terrorism

The Chechnya Connection

Since the collapse of the Soviet Union, the Russian Federation outside of Chechnya has been, and continues to be the scene of numerous terrorist acts committed by citizens of Russia, even though the vast majority of those acts and threatened actions—and certainly the most dramatic and lethal ones—have been perpetrated by Chechen operatives. The most notorious of these is the 2004 attack on the Beslan school mentioned earlier, in which more than 300 school children died and which has been painfully chronicled on film in the documentary *Three Days in September*. That attack, however, was only one part of a decade-long series of terrorist acts and attacks targeting Russian citizens outside of Chechnya, beginning with Shamil Basayev's November 1995 threat to detonate a dirty bomb in Moscow. Giving the threat its credibility was the fact that he gave Moscow authorities the coordinates to unearth a container of radioactive cesium 137 that his operatives had buried in a Moscow park. He claimed to have three additional canisters of the element, but if he did, they were never used. Other deadly attacks on Moscow and other Russian cities have been carried out by the Chechens, however.[61] The most notable of these were the September 1999 series of bombings involving two Moscow apartment buildings and a third in Volgodonsk that collectively killed more than 230 people, and the October 2002 takeover of a Moscow theater by approximately 50 Chechen militants (including several "Black Widow" suicide bombers wired with explosives). The theater incident resulted in the deaths of 129 theatergoers when Moscow's security forces used a debilitating gas compound to liberate the hostages.[62] Although less publicized abroad, the Chechen war has also resulted in a number of other highly visible and intimidating terrorist attacks that were perpetrated in Russia, including the May 2005 torching of a Moscow theater. In the same month, the terrorists also claimed responsibility for a power outage that left thousands trapped on Moscow subways.

The Other Russian Terrorists

A common byproduct of terrorist acts is the encouragement of others to engage in terrorist tactics in order to achieve their objectives. So it has been in Russia, where the dramatic terrorist acts executed inside and outside Chechnya by Chechen terrorists appear to have inspired a variety of actors to use terrorism in order to achieve their objectives. In some instances, the practitioners have apparently not even had a political agenda. The gas attack that sickened scores of Russian shoppers at a St. Petersburg home supply store near the end of December 2005, for example, has been filed as either an attempt to extort money from the store or as payback in some commercial dispute involving the store and its contractors. Similarly, the explosion that destroyed a bus in the Volga River city of Togliatti, killing eight and wounding fifty, was attributed not to political terrorists but to gangland feuds in an area with a history of such rivalry. Yet clearly some Russians—primarily ultranationalist youth groups—do see themselves as revolutionaries, and numerous terrorist acts have been attributed to them. Such acts include the 2005 derailing of a Chechnya to Moscow train with a bomb that detonated with the force of six pounds of TNT, and the derailing of an express train linking Moscow to St. Petersburg with a similar bomb in August 2007. Similarly motivated groups have been implicated in a series of assassination attempts against such public figures as the director of Russia's state-controlled electric power monopoly. The perpetrators' objectives may remain vague, but their manner of pursuing their goals clearly falls into the category of terrorism.

Al Qaeda and Chechnya

Finally, there is the question of whether any of the separatist groups employing terrorist tactics on behalf of Chechnya in the Soviet Union today are part of a global war of civilizations pitting Russia and the West on one side against al Qaeda and its Muslim extremist allies on the other. The issue, in fact, remains just that: a question without a definitive answer. There is little doubt that Muslims from outside Chechnya journeyed there to fight the Russians during the Chechen civil wars. An April 1996 ambush that killed 73 Russian troops, for example, was led by a field commander from Jordan, and the investigation into the 1999 apartment building bombings concluded that the operations were planned by Arabs, not Chechens. Nor does there appear to be any doubt as to whether Muslims connected with al Qaeda, if not necessarily al Qaeda soldiers, were in Chechnya when the war ended. Quite apart from the boast by Afghanistan leaders in 2000, on the occasion of Afghanistan's formal recognition of the Chechen Republic's independence, that Taliban fighters were resisting the Russians in Grozny, Georgian President Shevardnadze in June of the following year acknowledged the presence of (presumably) al Qaeda–trained Chechen fighters among the Chechen refugees in Georgia when he requested American assistance to dislodge them from Georgia's Panski Gorge region. There is, however, no recent evidence to support the proposition that al Qaeda operatives are currently a part of the struggle in Chechnya or elsewhere in the Russian Caucasus. There is, on the other hand, considerable evidence that documents their presence in Afghanistan, Iraq, and Pakistan in assisting the local groups fighting United States forces, America's international allies, and the units of the host governments allied with the United States. Unfortunately, al Qaeda's absence does not make the Russian Caucasus any less a hot spot in the contemporary world.

Timeline

95–55 BC	Reign of King Tigran I, the greatest Armenian king.
301–314 AD	Armenia becomes the first country to adopt Christianity as national religion.
c. 700 AD	Arabs conquer Armenia, introduce Islam to region.
1008	Georgia unified under Abkhazian ruler Bagrat III.
14th–18th century	Armenian principalities in Karabakh enjoy autonomy under Persian rule.
17th century	Abkhazia gains independence from Georgia; principal Ossetian migration to Georgia occurs.
1801–10	Russia annexes Georgian principalities and Abkhazia.
1813–28	Russia annexes Azerbaijan and Armenia.
1831	Russia encounters stiff resistance in the Islamic northeast Caucasus.
1835–59	Chechens rebel against Russian rule.
1866–77	Abkhazian uprisings against Russia lead to mass expulsion of Abkhazians from region.
1905–06	Armenian-Tatar War; guerrilla conflict between Armenians and Azerbaijanis.

1915	Ottoman-organized genocide of Armenians during World War I begins.
1918	Georgia gains independence during Russian civil war, fights rebellions in Abkhazia and South Ossetia.
1918–20	War begins between independent Armenia and Azerbaijan over Nagorno-Karabakh region.
1920–21	Soviet Russia annexes Armenia and Azerbaijan, gives Nagorno-Karabakh to Azerbaijan; Georgia annexed by Soviet Russia; Abkhazia set up as separate Soviet republic.
1922	Chechen Autonomous Republic established.
1923	Predominantly Armenian Nagorno-Karabakh Autonomous Oblast created in Soviet Azerbaijan.
1931	Abkhazia passes to Georgia as autonomous republic.
1934	Checheno-Ingush Republic established inside Soviet Russian federation.
1944	Chechens and other Caucasian nationalities deported to Central Asia.
1957	As part of de-Stalinization process, Chechens allowed to return to Chechnya.
1986	*Glasnost* era leads to demands in Nagorno-Karabakh for its transfer to Armenia.
1986–88	Georgian and Abkhazian nationalist movements resurface.
1988	Mass nationalist protests in Armenia and Nagorno-Karabakh combine with anti-Armenian riots and lead to waves of ethnic cleansing in both Armenia and Azerbaijan.
1989	First round of ethnic violence in Abkhazia and South Ossetia.
1990	Georgian elections bring nationalist leader Gamsakhurdia to power; South Ossetia declares independence from Georgia; Georgia dissolves South Ossetian autonomy; riot in Baku, Azerbaijan crushed by Soviet troops; in Chechnya, a national congress held in Grozny.
1991	Georgia proclaims independence in April; later, collapse of Soviet Union leads to Soviet withdrawal, independence of Armenia and Azerbaijan, outbreak of war for independence in South Ossetia, and establishment of new

	autonomous government in Abkhazia in Georgia; Djohar Dudayev is elected president of Chechnya.
1992	In aftermath of Soviet Union's collapse, a full-scale war develops between Azerbaijan and Armenia over Nagorno-Karabakh area; in Georgia, Gamsakhurdia is ousted, sparking intra-Georgian civil war; Shevardnadze's return to power ends fighting in South Ossetia, even as the government launches assault on Abkhazia to establish its control there. In Russia, Chechen Republic declares its independence.
1993	War in Abkhazia ends with Abkhazian victory over Georgia's troops and most Georgians fleeing region. In Azerbaijan, a former Communist Party leader seizes power. In Chechnya, Dudayev decrees presidential rule.
1994	Cease-fire established in Azerbaijan, producing de facto Armenian military victory over Baku and control of Nagorno-Karabakh. Russia invades Chechnya to regain control over that secessionist region; Russian/CIS peacekeeping force deployed in Georgia.
1995	Russian troops take Grozny.
1996	Chechen separatists recapture Grozny and other cities; first Chechen civil war ends with de facto success of separatists in creating an independent Chechnya.
1998	Remaining Georgians flee Abkhazia as fighting renewed there; kidnapping and other criminal activities increase; Armenian president Ter-Petrosian forced to resign for making concessions to Azerbaijan in peace negotiations.
1999	Chechen rebels invade Dagestan, igniting a second civil war between Moscow and Russia. Vladimir Putin era begins in Russia; Russian troops re-invade Chechnya and attack Grozny.
2000	Afghan Muslims reportedly fighting Russians in Chechnya; Chechen rebels forced to abandon Grozny; Putin elected Russian president.
2001	Shevardnadze claims that Chechen militants are in Georgia's Pankisi Gorge; American presidential spokesperson states that al Qaeda terrorist organization is active in Chechnya.

2002	United States troops sent to train Georgian forces to combat al Qaeda in Pankisi Gorge.
2003	Pro-democracy Rose Revolution occurs in Georgia; Shevardnadze steps down.
2004	New Georgian president reestablishes Tbilisi's control over Ajara; tensions increase between Tbilisi and Georgia's two breakaway regions, where conflict had been previously "frozen."
2005	Arms race begins to heat up between Armenia and Azerbaijan.
2007	Putin negotiates replacement president and agrees to become Russia's prime minister, signaling a possible shift in constitutional power in Russia toward a parliament that was overwhelmingly composed of his party's members following Russia's 2007 election. Georgia's government clamps down on protests and declares short-term state of emergency in a move many see as a step backward toward a more authoritarian form of government.

Notes

1. For further research on the breakup of the Soviet Union and the establish-ment of the independent countries formed out of the former union republics, including those spread across the much troubled Caucasus region, the beginning points are Daniel C. Diller, *Russia and the Independent States* (Washington, DC: Congressional Quarterly, Inc., 1993) and the excellent series of essays by Graham Smith, ed. *The Nationalities Question in the Post-Soviet States* (New York: Longman, 1996). More recent works on both Russia and the hot spot areas of Georgia, Armenia, and Azerbaijan are included in the case studies that follow this introductory section on politics in this region.

2. Evgeny Gontmakher, "Close the Gap: Long-term Economic Plans Must Be Structured to Bridge the Socio-Economic Divide," *The Washington Post* (December 20, 2007: "Russia behind the Headlines" insert).

3. See Irina Titova, "Russian Life Expectancy on Downward Trend," *St. Petersburg Times* (January 17, 2003; Website of Johnson's Russia List).

4. Other criteria commonly used in identifying failed or failing states include human flight from them, economic factors working against stability, presence of external intervention in their affairs, and demographic pressures undermining the state's effectiveness. The World Bank uses a composite of twelve such indicators to identify failed states and states leaning in that direction, all with the potential of affecting the political stability of neighboring areas in their failure. By those composite criteria, neither Russia nor any of the states in the European Caucasus

were listed on the World Bank's Failed States Index as late as 2007, although human rights-abusive Belarus, and Moldova with its still unsecured Transnistria region, were on the lower end of the list. The 2007 Index and a full explanation of how it was derived are available at http://www.foreignpolicy.com.

5. The quotation from Kaufman is taken from page 213 of his essay on the "Soviet Union: The Nagorno-Karabakh Conflict," in Joseph R. Rudolph, ed. *The Encyclopedia of Modern Ethnic Conflicts* (Westport, CT and London: Greenwood Press, 2003: 207–214). For additional reading on the conflict and other cases of ethnic conflict in the former Soviet Union, see also Stuart J. Kaufman, *Modern Hatreds: The Symbolic Politics of Ethnic War* (Ithaca, NY: Cornell University Press, 2001). For further research on the Nagorno-Karabakh conflict and Armenian and Azerbaijani politics in particular, see especially Michael P. Croissant, *The Armenia-Azerbaijan Conflict: Causes and Implications* (Westport, CT: Praeger, 1998); Levan Chorbajian, ed. *The Making of Nagorno-Karabakh: From Secession to Republic* (New York: Palgrave, 2001); and the early report by Human Rights Watch, *Azerbaijan: Seven Years of Conflict in Nagorno-Karabakh* (Helsinki, Finland: Human Rights Watch, 1991).

6. See Kaufman, "Soviet Union: The Nagorno-Karabakh Conflict," op. cit., 209–210. The direct quotation is found on p. 209.

7. International Crisis Group, "Nagorno-Karabakh: Viewing the Conflict from the Ground" (ICG Europe Report No. 166, September 14, 2005: 1–2; http://www.crisisgroup.org).

8. According to Armenia's 2001 census, the country was 97.9 percent composed of ethnic Armenians. In terms of religion, the country was 94.7 percent Armenian Apostolic, and Armenian was the mother language of 97.9 percent of its people. Azerbaijan's 1999 census reported similar figures, listing that country's population as 90.6 percent ethnic Azerbaijani (Azeri), 93.4 percent Muslim in religion, and 90.3 percent speaking Azeri as a mother tongue. All figures are taken from the Central Intelligence Agency's *World Factbook* (https://www.cia.gov/library/publications/the-world-factbook/index.html, accessed July 23, 2007).

9. In 2007, for example, the Berlin-based corruption-monitoring group, Transparency International, ranked Azerbaijan 150th out of the 180 states (listed from best to worst) that it evaluated. By contrast, Armenia ranked 79th and was seen as having slightly improved its efforts to combat its own, not trivial level of corruption. See Gayla Leshchinskiy, "Corruption Getting Worse in Central Asia—Report" (Eurasia Insight, October 1, 2007; http://www.eurasianet.org).

10. International Crisis Group, "Nagorno-Karabakh: Viewing the Conflict from the Ground," op. cit., pp. 11–12.

11. See International Crisis Group, "Azerbaijan's 2005 Elections: Lost Opportunity" (ICG Europe Briefing No. 40, November 21, 2005; http://www.crisisgroup.org).

12. See Fred Hiatt, "Armenians Who Need Help Today," *The Washington Post* (October 15, 2007). The quotation is taken from a Freedom House report that Hiatt cites.

13. International Crisis Group, "Nagorno-Karabakh: Risking War" (ICG Europe Report No. 187, November 14, 2007: 15).

14. "Azerbaijan's 2005 Elections", op. cit., p. 26.

15. The current population bears little resemblance to the population of the area when the conflict between Armenia and Azerbaijan began to build during the late 1980s. The last Soviet census of the area, conducted in 1989, reported that Nagorno-Karabakh had a population of 189,085, of which 145,500 (76.9 percent) were Armenian and 40,700 (21.5 percent) were Azeris. It is estimated that not only have all Azeris subsequently left the area, but that approximately 70,000 Armenians who lived there before the war have also moved to other areas. The latter number has been offset by Armenians moving to the Nagorno-Karabakh Republic from outlying districts and by the arrival of "refugees" from other parts of Azerbaijan. Observers confirm Baku's frequent charge that Armenia has encouraged many of its citizens or those who fled there from Azerbaijan to resettle in Nagorno-Karabakh to bolster an Armenian claim to the area, even if the more than 40,000 Azeris who left are returned in any future settlement agreement. [The Organization for Security and Cooperation in Europe (OSCE) has appointed a commission to investigate these "ethnic-stocking" charges.] Also substantially modified has been the population of the Lachin area of Azerbaijan that lies between Nagorno-Karabakh and the Armenian border and which the Nagorno-Karabakh Republic currently treats as an essential part of itself. Prior to the war, the area contained more than 47,000 Azeris and Kurds; today it houses approximately 10,000 Armenians and none of its former Azeri residents. All data is taken from ICG, "Nagorno-Karabakh: Viewing the Conflict from the Ground," op. cit., pp. 4–7.

16. Ibid., pp. 9–10.

17. Jill Shankleman, *Oil Profit and Peace: Does Business Have a Role in Peacemaking?* (Washington, DC: United States Institute of Peace, 2007).

18. "Nagorno-Karabakh: Risking War," op. cit., pp. 12–13.

19. Ibid. The direct quotation is from page 1 of the executive summary.

20. Ibid., pp. 12–14, for a more detailed discussion of the balance of power in the area.

21. See International Crisis Group, "Armenia: Internal Instability Ahead" (ICG Europe Report No. 158, October 18, 2004; http://www.crisisgroup.org).

22. For background reading on the history and birth of the contemporary independent state of Georgia, see especially Ronald Grigor Suny, *The Making of the Georgian Nation* (Bloomington, IN: Indiana University Press, 1988), and Shireen T. Hunter, *The Transcaucasus in Transition: Nation Building and Conflict* (Washington, DC: Center for Strategic and International Studies, 1994).

23. Tax collection figures were reported in the Central Intelligence Agency's *World Factbook* under "Georgia" (https://www.cia.gov/library/publications/the-world-factbook/index.html, accessed July 20, 2007).

24. See the coverage of the Transparency International Report by Keti Khachidze, "Corruption Index Improves But More Work Still Needed," *The Georgian Times* (October 1, 2007; http://www.geotimes.ge).

25. Associated Press, "NATO Chief Calls for Transparency, Judicial Independence in Georgia" *The International Herald Tribune* (October 4, 2007).

26. For a concise analysis of the causes of the 1990–92 war and the conflict itself, see International Crisis Group, "Georgia: Avoiding War in South Ossetia" (ICG Europe Report No. 159, November 25, 2004), released shortly after the resumption of hostilities in the cease-fire zone.

27. For a detailed discussion of the refugee issue as an obstacle to achieving a lasting peace between Tbilisi and South Ossetia, and of the status of the refugees from the South Ossetia conflict, see International Crisis Group, "Georgia-South Ossetia: Refugee Return the Path to Peace"(ICG Europe Briefing No. 38, April 19, 2005; http://www.crisisgroup.com).

28. "Georgia: Avoiding War in South Ossetia," op. cit., Executive Summary and Recommendations, p. 1.

29. For a thorough analysis of post-2004 events affecting the South Ossetia conflict, see International Crisis Group, "Georgia's South Ossetia Conflict: Make Haste Slowly" (ICG Europe Report No. 183, June 7, 2007) and "Georgia: Avoiding War in South Ossetia," op. cit.; http://www.crisisgroup.org).

30. Stuart Kaufman, "Soviet Union: The Ethnic Conflicts in Georgia," in *Encyclopedia of Modern Ethnic Conflicts*, op. cit., pp. 199–202.

31. News dispatch from Tbilisi, "Georgia to Take Over Part of Breakaway Area," *The Washington Post* (July 26, 2006). For an assessment of the conflict following this incident, see International Crisis Group, "Abkhaz Today" (ICG Europe Report No. 176, September 15, 2006; http://www.crisisgroup.org).

32. See International Crisis Group, "Abkhazia: Ways Forward" (ICG Europe Report No. 179, January 18, 2007; http://www.crisisgroup.org).

33. Apsnypress (Abkhazia's state press agency) report from Sukhumi, issued in Russian and made available in translation by BBC Worldwide Monitor, "Abkhaz Leader Rejects Georgian President's Proposals" (http://80-web.lexis-nexis.com.researchport.umd.edu/2250/universe.printdoc, accessed April 21, 2005).

34. For additional reading on Ajara regionalism and Saakashvili's successful policy of reintegrating the region into Georgia, see International Crisis Group, "Saakashvili's Ajara Success: Repeatable Elsewhere in Georgia?" (ICG Europe Briefing No. 34, August 18, 2004).

35. For a comprehensive discussion of the status of Georgia's Azeris and Armenian communities and the recent political conflicts involving them, see International Crisis Group, "Georgia's Armenian and Azeris Minorities" (ICG Europe Report No. 178, November 22, 1996; http://www.crisisgroup.org).

36. Ibid., "Executive Summary and Recommendations," p. 1.

37. Ibid., pp. 4–6.

38. See the coverage of the confrontation by Peter Finn, "Russia Recalls Envoy to Georgia: Move Follows Officers' Arrest on Spy Charges," *The Washington Post* (September 29, 2006), "Dispute Between Georgia, Russia Escalates," *The Washington Post* (August 30, 2007), and "Georgia Returns Four Russian Officers: Release of Alleged Spies Intended to Cut Tensions, but Russia Continues Retaliatory Measures," *The Washington Post* (October 3, 2006).

39. Cornell Caspian Consulting, "The South Caucasus: A Regional Overview and Conflict Assessment: Conflict and Security Assessment" (report from 2002: p. 5; http://www.cornellcaspian.com/sida/sida-cfl-2.html).

40. Kaufman, "Soviet Union: The Ethnic Conflicts in Georgia," op cit., 200–202.

41. United States Institute of Peace, "Online Training Course for OSCE, Including React: Module 7. Caucasus," (April 2004: 21–24; http://www.usip.org/training/online/osce.html).

42. For an outstanding, on-the-spot analysis of Georgia's Rose Revolution, coupled with the careful discussion "Why Georgia Matters," see International Crisis Group, "Georgia: What Now?" (ICG Europe Report No. 151, December 3, 2003; http://www.crisisgroup.org). On the state of despair among Georgia's people that drove the Revolution, see Arnold R. Isaacs, "Post Soviet Blues: Georgian Sketches" (Dart Center for Journalism and Trauma Special Report, 2005; www.dartcenter.org).

43. International Crisis Group, "ICG Crisis Watch No. 49" (September 1, 2007; www.crisisgroup.org).

44. For a detailed discussion of the factors leading up to the November 2007 demonstrations, and the government's response to them, see International Crisis Group, "Georgia: Sliding Toward Authoritarianism? (ICG Europe Report No. 189, December 19, 2007; http://www.crisisgroup.org). The quotation is from the Executive Summary of the study, p. 1. For accounts of the November demonstrations as they occurred, see C. J. Chivers, "Georgia Leader Declares Emergency Over Protest: Riot Police Sweep Crowds Off Tbilisi Streets," *The New York Times* (November 8, 2007), and Tara Bahrampour, "Georgia's President Moves Up Election Date," *The Washington Post* (November 9, 2007).

45. Tara Bahrampour, "Vote in Georgia Produces a Thin Margin: Saakashvili's Opponents Seen Likely to Challenge Presidential Election Results," *The Washington Post* (January 7, 2008).

46. See Peter Baker, "A Former Superpower's Hazardous Legacy," *The Washington Post* (May 26, 2004).

47. There is no shortage of books on post-Russian politics, and most are excellent for further reading. Two of the best and most recent, and highly recommended here, are Vicki I. Helsi, *Government and Politics in Russia and the Post-Soviet Region* (Boston: Houghton Mifflin Company, 2007) and Lilia Shevtsova (trans. Arch Tait), *Russia—Lost in Transition: The Yeltsin and Putin Legacies* (Washington, DC: Carnegie Endowment for International Peace, 2007). Also highly recommended are two other, somewhat earlier Carnegie Endowment publications: Michael McFaul, Nikolai Petrov, and Andrei Ryabov, *Between Dictatorship and Democracy: Russian Post-Communist Political Reform* (2004), and on the specific subject of Russia's problems in Chechnya, Dmitri V. Trenin and Alexei V. Malashenko, *Russia's Restless Frontier: The Chechnya Factor in Post Soviet Russia* (2004).

48. See, for example, Peter Finn, "Russian Police Beat Democracy Activists: Dozens Detained During March in St. Petersburg," *The Washington Post* (March 4, 2007), and Peter Finn, "Dozens Arrested as Riot Police Beat Anti-Kremlin Protestors in St. Petersburg," *The Washington Post* (April 16, 2007).

49. Douglas Birch, "For Journalists, Russia Remains a Perilous Place: Group Says Country Failed to Fully Probe Murders of 12 Reporters, Editors," *The Baltimore Sun* (July 9, 2005).

50. For on-the-spot coverage of Russia's 2007 parliamentary elections, see Peter Finn's reports published in *The Washington Post,* especially "Russia Pursues Crackdown" (December 4, 2007).

51. See, for example, the editorial on Russia's 2007 parliamentary elections, "In Russia, the Backward March to Czarism Continues," *The Washington Post* (December 4, 2007) and the lead editorial, The Russian Lesson," *The Baltimore Sun* (December 4, 2007).

52. Cited in Doug Struck, "Gorbachev Applauds Putin's Achievements," *The Washington Post* (December 5, 2007). Other long-time critics of politics in Russia, including Aleksandr Solzhenitsyn, have also praised Putin's accomplishments.

53. See, for example, the op ed piece by Eugene B. Rumer, a senior research fellow at United States National Defense University's Institute for Strategic Studies, "Not Another Soviet Union," *The Washington Post* (September 24, 2004).

54. For further research on Chechnya and its struggle for independence, see James Hughes, *Chechnya: From Nationalism to Jihad* (Philadelphia: University of Pennsylvania Press, 2007); A. V. Malashenko, et al., *Russia's Restless Frontier: The Chechnya Factor in Post-Soviet Russia* (Washington, DC: Carnegie Endowment for Peace, 2004); John Russell, *Chechnya: Russia's "War on Terror"* (London: Routledge, 2007); and Sebastian Smith, *Allah's Mountains: The Battle for Chechnya* (New York: Tauris Parke, 2005).

55. For additional background reading on Basayev's raid and the interim between Chechnya's two civil wars, see Stuart J. Kaufman, "Soviet Union: The Conflict in Chechnya," *Encyclopedia of Modern Ethnic Conflicts,* op. cit., pp. 192–198, esp. pp. 194–196.

56. Human rights organizations have also indicted the Russian forces in Chechnya for continuing to commit—on a far lesser scale than during the war—human rights violations involving the "disappearance" of critics, instances of torture, and "executions" conducted without judicial authorization.

57. Kaufman, "Soviet Union: The Ethnic Conflicts in Georgia," op. cit., p. 206.

58. For an overview of Russia's troubled North Caucasus, see Peter Finn, "Chechen War's Regional Reach," *The Washington Post* (March 10, 2005). For a more in-depth examination, see Domitilla Sagramoso, "Violence and Conflict in the Russian North Caucasus," *International Affairs,* 83.4 (July 2007: 681–705).

59. Peter Finn, "Crackdown Provoked Shootout in Russia: Gunmen Sprang from Region's Alienated Muslims," *The Washington Post* (October 15, 2005).

60. "Moscow Gripped by Terrorism Fear," *The Washington Post* (December 16, 1991).

61. Kaufman, "Soviet Union: The Conflict in Chechnya," op. cit., pp. 193–94.

62. The "Black Widows" are a much-feared auxiliary of Chechen terrorist organizations. Composed of women widowed as a result of the struggle in Chechnya, they have been part of several suicide operations since the official end of the second Chechen civil war.

CHAPTER 7

WESTERN EUROPE

To no small degree, the discussion here of the Europe-wide potential for political violence emanating from the European-born Muslim communities in Western Europe is testimony to how quickly matters can change in the contemporary world, and in a dangerous direction. Only a few years ago, the only significant sources of political violence in Western Europe continued to be the seething ethno-regional conflicts rooted in Northern Ireland, Basque Spain, Cyprus, and the French island of Corsica. There were, of course, objective reasons to believe in the *possibility* that the frustration with second-class status within Western Europe's immigrant communities might erupt periodically into violent protests, but such violence on a widespread scale did not then seem probable in the advanced democratic world. Then came the terrorist attack on the commuter trains in Madrid; the assassinations of a critic of Islam and an anti-immigrant party leader in Holland by Dutch-born Muslims; and the attack on London commuters—all during the 2004–05 period.[1]

Given the dramatic nature of these attacks, and the security issue that they have collectively injected into the "foreigner" debate in Europe, the broader conflicts between the hosting European communities and their immigrant and foreign worker communities that began arriving in Europe during the 1950s has too often been ignored. Nevertheless, apart from the dangers posed to the public safety by radical European Muslims or Muslim extremists entering Europe to commit terrorist acts, there continues to be a significant danger that political violence will emerge from those economic and social underclasses—living in Europe, but non-European in origin—simply because of their underclass status. Moreover, in many instances the security threat posed by Muslim extremists is at least as much traceable to their long-term underclass status as to the inspiration, encouragement, and perhaps assistance they have received from al Qaeda and other internationally structured, anti-Western terrorist organizations. Indeed, the relationship between a minority's status and the danger that it poses to the public safety may be particularly significant in two of Western Europe's largest countries. France is the state with Western Europe's largest Muslim community and, to date, has been the scene of the largest eruption of prolonged political violence by a young, restless, and largely unemployed "foreigner" underclass. In Britain, radical Islamic activity takes place against a backdrop of forty years of racial unrest between the native British people and Britain's immigrants from its "Coloured Commonwealth." The threat to public safety confronting these states is explored in greater detail in the sections of this chapter devoted to France and the United Kingdom. To some degree, however, the "foreigner" issue has now become a significant enough challenge to the maintenance of public order throughout Western Europe that—as in the case of Spain and the Netherlands—almost any country may find itself to be a hot spot of politically motivated violence.

ANTI-FOREIGNER VIOLENCE

The arrival of ethnically and culturally distinct foreigners, usually at the bottom of the established social and economic order, has frequently been accompanied by an upsurge in political violence in the immigrant-receiving world. The post-9/11 world may have redefined the terms of that conflict, and it has certainly given anti-foreigner parties and interest groups new arguments with which to bolster their case against further immigration. But the post-9/11 outlook scarcely created either those arguments or the conflict between host and immigrant communities in the advanced democratic world.

Defining the Problem: Popular Terminology and the "Foreigner Problem"

The "foreigner" issue takes many forms. In the United States it focuses on immigration—in particular, the presence of millions of illegal immigrants. In Germany, it is a foreign worker issue, rooted in the postwar buildup in what was then West Germany of workers from southern Europe (chiefly Turkey), at a time when West Germany's economic recovery and expansion were creating a minus 1 percent unemployment rate, measured against the available domestic work force. Still elsewhere, it is often simply a "them" issue, especially in small-population states where the growth of immigrant communities from culturally remote areas is seen as a threat to the existing way of life.

In whatever form it manifests itself, the "foreigner" issue is popularly defined less in terms of those who are *legally* foreigners for census purposes (that is, citizens of other countries residing abroad) than those who are perceived to be "foreign" because they do not share a European point of origin. Consequently, the term "foreigner" in quotation marks is used initially as a blanket designation to refer to this element in contemporary Western European politics. In some instances, "foreigners" are in fact citizens of the countries in which they live, as a result of having been naturalized or having acquired citizenship by virtue of their birth in a country such as France or the United States, where place of birth is the standard criterion for determining citizenship. They may also be a regular part of the electorate, and—as in Britain—may have seen some of their members attain high public office. Nevertheless, to a large number of native Europeans, they still stand apart in their "otherness," and although that otherness varies with the locale, it is generally at the heart of the "foreigner" issue throughout a Western Europe whose citizens previously had little or no prior exposure to, or experience with racial or other forms of profound ethnic and cultural diversity.

The "Foreigner Issue" in Pre-9/11 Western Europe

The arrival of foreign workers and immigrant communities and the emergence of the "foreigner issue" in Western Europe followed a common pattern in the receiving states, differing from state to state only in terms of timing (that is, when the non-Europeans began to arrive in large numbers) and the legal status of those arriving (that is, whether they were foreign workers subject to deportation after loss of employment; immigrants expected to naturalize; or the children of foreigners entitled to citizenship in many European states because they were born in those countries).

In most instances, the arrival and buildup of these communities can be traced to Europe's post–World War II need for additional manpower. In virtually all instances, the European states recruited or otherwise admitted ever-growing numbers of people from culturally and geographically remote areas without making any serious commitment to settling them into their new countries or preparing their own native populations for a multicultural future. As a result, most of these communities developed identities apart from the host populations. The new arrivals overwhelmingly accepted jobs at the low end of the economic spectrum, thereby reinforcing the host population's perception of them as inferior, because they were willing to do jobs that native Europeans would not do at the wages being offered. The immigrants also settled in affordable, but overcrowded and substandard housing in the crime-ridden, declining outskirts of European cities. Family unification programs and procreation gradually increased their ranks, and sometimes antidiscrimination laws were enacted to combat the more egregious discrimination they faced. Throughout the process, however, little was done to integrate them into the host populations.

Some groups particularly, whose members are not surprisingly found in disproportionate numbers within Muslim terrorist cells in today's Europe, were left out of the mainstream. More than a generation ago, for example, academic researchers warned that the disproportionately high levels of unemployment and failure rates in the schools of Europe's Moroccan communities boded ill for Europe's future tranquility.[2] That future has now arrived, and Moroccans—despite their access to the generous social welfare programs of countries such as Holland—have figured prominently in the terrorist attacks in Holland and Spain in the early years of the twenty-first century.

By the late 1960s, the buildup of a large number of culturally diverse immigrants and foreign workers in Britain and several countries on the continent of Western Europe had led to the gradual emergence of anti-immigrant sentiments and political parties. In fact, even before the economic downturn of the early 1970s spawned by the sudden, fourfold increase in the price of imported OPEC oil in 1973, both Germany and Holland had decided to cease recruiting any additional foreign workers, despite the fact that their still rapidly expanding economies could have absorbed them. Nevertheless, it was the recession of the mid-1970s and the deeper recession of the 1980s, combined with the unwillingness of the host governments to deport large numbers of their foreign workers, that provided Europe's growing number of anti-immigrant parties with an issue upon which to increase their share of the vote. Soon, the pressure that those parties were placing on their mainstream competitors prompted established leaders throughout Europe to legitimize anti-foreigner rhetoric by aping the language of the anti-immigrant parties, in order to protect their own parties' electoral flanks. Deportation of the workers, however, was not an option. By then the immigrant and foreign laborers had already become necessary components of their countries' domestic workforces.[3]

The failure of the countries hosting the first wave of immigrants, foreign workers, and (later) refugees and/or asylum seekers to pursue assimilation policies toward these new groups resulted in their failure to develop second-generation "hyphenated Europeans." By contrast, the Irish-American and German-American sons and daughters of European immigrants had emerged in the United States a century before and paved the way for the full integration of America's European immigrants into American society. The European governments' failure to prepare their native populations for the long-term presence of non-European peoples and cultures in their midst led to overt displays of intolerance, discrimination, and sometimes political violence directed against Europe's immigrant communities long before 9/11.

Often, the more insular or closed the host society was, the greater the violence that was directed against the outsiders. Thus, anti-foreigner protest in Germany was more explosive in the former East Germany than in West Germany during the 1990s, in part because of the isolated nature of East German society under communism. Instances of violence nevertheless occurred throughout Germany, where law enforcement is left in the hands of the states rather than a central police force, and where local authorities occasionally looked the other way. In fact, because of the numbers involved, Germany in general has usually received the harshest criticism of any country for its failure to come to terms with the foreigner issue and with the violence that has been directed against Germany's minority communities. The principal indictments have been (1) the failure of its government, media, and other opinion leaders to promote programs involving an interaction between the host population and the foreign communities, and (2) its government's tendency to deny the existence of problems related to the foreigner issue, even when that evidence has been indisputable, as in the 1992 firebombing of an apartment in Moelin, a small town outside Hamburg, that left children and the elderly dead. Still, the anti-foreigner violence extended throughout Western Europe, as did the discriminatory and restrictive policies aimed at the foreigner communities well before 9/11 (see Timeline).

HOMEGROWN TERRORISM

The militancy of Europe's Muslim communities, as opposed to that of its non-Muslim "foreigners" from Africa, Asia, and the West Indies, has often been explained as the result of the secular attitudes of Europeans colliding with the nonsecular attitudes of many Muslim immigrants. Another factor is that Europeans display less inclination to accept diversity than is typical in settler societies such as the United States, with their large immigrant populations (albeit mostly from Europe initially) and their melting-pot concepts of society. Consequently, there is perhaps a greater tendency for European Muslims to see themselves as outsiders because their faith connects religion with all other aspects of life.[4] Certainly Western European news reports of Muslims being arrested for planning terrorist activity, raising money for radical groups, and attempting, conducting, or abetting terrorist activities have become common since 9/11. Given these developments, Western European countries have even become nervous about hosting events (such as the World Cup finals) that might draw militant Muslims and/or result in violent confrontations between Muslim visitors and their own mobilized, anti-"foreigner" groups. It is hard to attribute such security-related attitudes to unfounded alarmism. Since the September 11, 2001, attack on the United States, Western European countries have monitored a rising effort on the part of Muslim activists to recruit Muslim prisoners in European jails and Muslim youth in schools, mosques, and social clubs, as well as a constant Internet contact between European Muslims and radical Islamic organizations urging them to become a part of the global war against materialistic-hedonistic Western civilization. Some have actively joined the cause by journeying to fight for Muslims in Bosnia during the civil war there, training for their *jihad* against the West in Afghanistan and the Sudan, and—more recently—becoming activists in attacking the coalition forces and personnel of international organizations in Iraq.

By mid-decade Western Europe itself had been the scene of several ugly instances of political violence. The most notorious were the 2004 attack on commuter trains in Madrid, subsequently linked to Moroccans; the 2005 bombing attack on London's transit system by British-born Asians; and the murder of a Dutch film maker (also by a man of Moroccan ancestry), whose works were highly critical of the manner in which women are treated in the Muslim world. To these acts of violence may be added the fall 2005 riots by Muslim youth in France, which caused so much damage throughout that country over a month-long period; the evidence linking conspirators in Germany and Spain to the 9/11 attacks on New York and Washington; and the revelation that such countries as Belgium, which has long billed itself as the "crossroads of Europe," have now become crossroads of terrorist activity and breeding grounds for home-grown terrorism in Europe. As one commentator summarized the situation, "the front lines of Europe's war on terror can [now] be found in the outlying slums and mosques of cities like Paris, Leeds, Madrid, Rotterdam, and Malmo."[5] Consequently, even a snapshot of a representative sample of Western European states produces a picture of life within the European Union that is, viewed from a security perspective, potentially grave:

- Belgium, the capital of the European Union, has recently acquired the reputation of also being the capital of extremist Muslim groups operating in Continental Europe, given its traditionally weak security system and the ease with which bogus Belgian passports have been obtainable by outsiders.

- France, the country with the largest concentration of Europe's Muslims, has also been the scene of Europe's longest Muslim demonstrations against their perceived second-class status. An assimilationist state that is militantly secular, France has particular problems in assimilating millions of people for whom religion and political behavior are inseparable, and it is thus particularly vulnerable to future violence, such as the month-long rioting that it experienced in the fall of 2005.
- Germany continues to be another center for international terrorist activity, although significant counter-terrorist progress has been made there since the revelation that Hamburg was one of the staging grounds from which the 9/11 attacks were planned.
- Greece, which is usually under the radar in terms of Muslim terrorist activity, has otherwise been a long-term center of anti-Western, anti-United States activity so intense that at the end of the twentieth century, Greece ranked second only to Colombia in the number of anti-American attacks committed annually within its jurisdiction.
- Italy has recently been active in interdicting illegal immigrants from Africa and is best known in the anti-terrorism field for its struggle in the late 1970s and early 1980s against one of Western Europe's most notorious urban terrorist organizations, the Italian Red Brigade. The country has also achieved a recent reputation for becoming yet another Western European center for al Qaeda and other Islamic extremist organizations, most of which currently appear to be buried within its large Muslim population in the northern city of Milan.
- The Netherlands was where film maker Theo Van Gogh, who had been critical of the status of women in the Islamic religion, was stabbed to death by a second-generation Dutch citizen of Moroccan origin. The killer was a member of the Hofstad Network, an Islamic organization with cells in Holland, Spain, Morocco, Italy, and Belgium, which at the time was allegedly planning a string of assassinations of Dutch political leaders and an attack on a Dutch nuclear power installation. His arrest came at the same time as the murder of the leader of Holland's principal anti-immigrant party on the eve of the country's national election, and has understandably raised long-term fears for their future safety among Dutch politicians and civilians.
- Spain, the scene of the fatal 2004 terrorist attack on Madrid's public transportation system that killed 191 people and injured 2,000, has now shifted the focus of its anti-terrorist fight from its long war against the Basque separatist organization, the ETA, to monitoring the dangers posed to its security by its Muslim community. Most of them are Moroccans living as second-class citizens in substandard housing, and employed in menial jobs.

- The United Kingdom was the scene of the bloody 2005 attack on London's commuters by radical British-born Muslims of Pakistani descent, and of numerous lesser or failed attacks. The country has long been plagued by conflicts between its native white and immigrant non-white communities, and more recently it has become a haven for radical Muslim activity—both in "London-stan" and in England's older industrial cities—because of the British government's pre-9/11 inclination to avoid interfering in the way of life of its Muslim communities.

MUSLIM CULTURES

Quite apart from the home-grown terrorist security issue, there is little real, short- or middle-term prospect for a meaningful decline in the likelihood of political violence in Western Europe, or for an improvement in the relationship between European governments and their native communities, on the one hand, and the militant, hard-core radical elements in their "foreign" (albeit often European-born) communities on the other. For the most part, these actors remain separated not only by religion, lifestyle, and social class, but also quite widely by their respective perceptions of the world in which they live. In a study released in 2006, for example, the Pew Center's Global Attitudes Survey found that a relatively significant percentage of Muslims in Britain (19 percent), Spain (23 percent), and France (35 percent) agreed that in order to protect Islam, suicide bombings directed against civilian targets are justified, at least on some occasions. Even more shocking from a Western perspective, 35 percent of Spanish Muslims, 44 percent of German Muslims, 46 percent of French Muslims, and 56 percent of British Muslims answered "no" when asked if Arabs carried out the 9/11 attacks. Meanwhile, on the other side, pollsters found that only 36 percent of Germany's non-Muslims and 29 percent of Spain's non-Muslim population viewed Muslims favorably, and that even in the United States and Britain, where multiculturalism has been accepted, the percentages for those who viewed Muslims favorably were only in the 50- to 60-percent range.[6]

Invariably, these differences in perception have led to conflicts that have spilled violently into the streets and have sometimes spread to other countries, as in the case of the demonstrations resulting from the publication in Denmark of cartoons depicting Muhammad. Before the uproar subsided, the cartoons had triggered violent demonstrations among Muslims in Europe and throughout the world, and they led a Pakistani cleric to offer a $1 million bounty to anyone who would kill the cartoonists responsible for the caricatures of the prophet.[7] Unfortunately, prudence requires that the Danish cartoon case, like the murder in Holland of an author critical of Islam, should be treated more as a harbinger of future violence than an isolated event in contemporary Western European politics.

On the other hand, to say that street protests, isolated violence, and the danger of home-grown terrorism are perhaps now a part of life in Western Europe does not mean that European governments should curtail their efforts to attack the social and economic conditions that breed radicalism, or—where warranted—that they should not apologize to or otherwise try to mollify hostile Muslims when Western insensitivity to Islam provokes angry reactions. Quite the contrary, even though the public safety issue has necessarily become a part of the policy-making equation throughout the region. Finding the proper balance between accommodation and security is a tricky challenge that is not likely to result in elegant policies. Denmark's response to the fury unleashed by the publication of the Mohammad cartoons illustrates the point. As a conciliatory gesture, Denmark hastily decided to donate funds to a United Nations agency charged with fighting prejudice, and the country scheduled a Muslim cultural exposition to educate its own citizens about the Muslim world. At the same time, though, the Danish government also began to frame more restrictive, if vaguely worded legislation aimed at punishing anyone instigating acts of terrorism or offering advice to terrorists. The likely target of the proposed legislation was perfectly obvious to Denmark's Islamic communities.

Nor should Western governments slow down their efforts to reach out to and establish close ties with, or even cultivate, moderate Muslim factions within their borders. Nevertheless, these governments must recognize that voices of moderation do not always reach the ears of the radicalized and alienated. In the near future, these accommodation efforts are unlikely to avert further acts of political violence. After all, France's December 2002 creation of an advisory Muslim Council, composed primarily of religious leaders drawn from moderate Muslim communities, did not avert or mute the nationwide rioting in France by Muslim youth in the fall of 2005, or the temporary seizure of a Paris train station in the spring of 2007. The French council was patterned after one long in existence in Britain, where the transit system was targeted by radical, British-born Muslims in the summer of 2005, and where Glasgow's airport was attacked two years later by professionally-educated would-be doctors from the Middle East who chose to be suicide bombers for Islam.

Meanwhile, in turn, such outpourings of Muslim anger with the West—even when falling far short of the violent protests Muslim youth have staged in France, or the terrorist attacks on Madrid and London—invariably provoke backlashes in the host communities. For example, the Muslim attacks on Danish embassies abroad inspired the desecration of Muslim graves outside Copenhagen.

In short, whether the focus is on the transplanted minorities or on the host populations, the general ambiance of politics in Western Europe on the immigrant issue remains a volatile one. Furthermore, at least a trio of factors are currently at work that are likely to make the "foreigner" issue even more dangerous as Western Europe edges into the second decade of the twenty-first century.

First, for the "foreigner" minorities throughout Europe an enough-is-enough element is at work, and it is playing out in those parties involved on both sides of the conflict. The reasons given by the native British, French, and other Western Europeans for resenting or fearing their minority communities still vary somewhat from country to country. In some instances the focus of this hostility is on Muslims' failure to assimilate, in others the fear that their growing numbers may swamp the cultures of the less-populous European countries. In still other countries the security issue may loom the largest, and in other cases it may be just a sense of disquiet with the changing nature of the culture into which the people were born. Whatever the reason or combination of reasons, there is a passion at work that is rooted in local frustration over the failure of their government's efforts to curb the "foreigner" culture or to halt the influx of growing numbers of illegal immigrants after more than a generation of trying to do stop it.

Meanwhile, the perspective of the minority communities is that they have struggled too long or have seen their less-fortunate contemporaries struggle at the bottom of the social and economic ladder too long, and that they have been discriminated against in the countries they migrated to or where they were born, and perhaps where even their parents were born. To now have their neighborhoods—already often potentially explosive racial ghettoes—subjected to security-inspired raids and crackdowns only adds additional insult to their sense of ill-treatment. Such attitudes do not lend themselves to patient searches for policy solutions to the complex issues embraced under the "immigrant" umbrella. Rather, confrontational politics and occasional violence are more likely to grow out of such rising frustration with disappointed expectations in any society, and in the advanced democratic world the outlook is no different.

Second, there is the cat-is-out-of-the-bag problem. Often, militancy begets militancy. Prior to the 2004 terrorist attack on Madrid's commuter trains and the nationwide rioting in France the following year, disquiet hung over Europe—a feeling that something *might* happen, that the local rioting, firebombings, and incidents of street confrontations and arson some countries had experienced might get out of control. There was a fear that Europe might experience something similar to the 9/11 attacks. Now that both kinds of incidents have occurred, host populations wait for the other shoe to drop and push their governments to take preventive action that is often confrontational. And now, radicalized Muslims in Europe who are possibly already alienated from and isolated in their own moderate Muslim communities have precedents to inspire them, and "role models" to follow.

Finally, for Europe's Muslims there is the international connection—a global network offering advice and encouragement to the alienated. It is one of the ironies of the current age that the excessive violence of the 9/11 attacks by a global terrorist organization and the subsequent attacks in Madrid and London—which can be credited at least in part with having had a dampening effect on the extremism of such European-based terrorist organizations as the IRA and the ETA (discussed *infra*)—may have inspired the alienated youth in Europe's Muslim communities to commit more assaults on the societies in which they are imbedded. For some, such as those involved in the Madrid and London bombings and those who planned the abortive car bombing attack on London's Hyde Park and Piccadilly districts in June 2007, the lure of being part of a global struggle has become a powerful force *pulling* them in a radical direction, even as the second-class status of their living conditions in Western Europe has *pushed* them in the same direction. And beyond those who

Burned out cars in a Renault showroom in the Paris suburbs in 2005 mark the eleventh consecutive night of rioting by Muslim youth in France. The riots spread throughout France and lasted for nearly a month. © Jean-Michel Turpin/Corbis.

are inspired by radical clerics and their Internet screens are those European Muslims who have already been mobilized, trained, and given experience in urban warfare in the Afghanistan and Iraq theaters. They will be returning to their homes in Western Europe when those wars end, or when they have sufficient expertise to be useful in a *jihad* at home.

FRANCE

Modern France has historically defined itself in terms of its language, its secular nature, and its religion. To be French was to be French-speaking, to be at least nominally Catholic, and to subscribe to the utterly secular nature of the state.

To be sure, France has always had its agnostics and atheists, but they have traditionally represented a small number of its people and have not espoused alternative religious outlooks. It was not always so, however. Once upon a time, France had a sizable Protestant Huguenot minority, but approximately 1,200 Huguenots were massacred at Vassy on March 1, 1562, and another 8,000 or more in Paris beginning on the night of August 23, 1572. Thirty years of religious warfare from 1562 to 1598 led to the killing of perhaps a quarter of a million French Huguenots over-all, and to the massive emigration of others to America, South Africa, and Protestant European states. By the time of the French Revolution, few of them remained in France.

In the same sense, the commitment born in the French Revolution to a self-consciously secular French state—the ideal of *laicité*—has had its detractors. For nearly a century after that revolution, which had been, among other things, against divine-right monarchs, the proponents of a continued union of church and state fought a delaying action against the adoption of a secular state. By the twentieth century, however, they had lost their case, and their departure from the scene has been just as complete as that of the Huguenots, although it was achieved in the less traumatic form of a 1905 law that excluded religion from all public institutions.

France has also historically been an underpopulated country by European standards, if not by those of North American countries, and therein lies the germ of what many French now see as a serious threat to France's culture and traditional nature. Even today, the United States and Canada have exceptionally low population densities (30 per square kilometer in the United States and only 3 per square kilometer in Canada), but with an overall population density of 110 per square kilometer in France as a whole and a much lower number outside of Paris and the areas north and east of the capital (where a quarter of the

French population lives), France's population density has historically been only a half or a third that of its neighbors. Indeed, underpopulation has been a long-standing problem for France. A series of wars abroad in the name of empire, including the long war in Indochina from 1947 to 1954, and three major wars with Germany between 1870 (the Franco-German war) and the end of World War II (1945) left the size of the French population almost unchanged—hovering around 40 million—from 1840 until the 1950s. World War I was particularly costly, leaving a third of the country's young men ages 18 to 35 either dead or wounded, and thus unable to procreate at normal levels. The fear of another great war also inhibited French families from having children as early, or in the same numbers, as might otherwise have been expected in a country of Catholics and small farmers interested in raising their own workforce.

In part because of its underpopulated condition, France has been willing to serve as an immigrant (or destination) country, and historically it erected few obstacles to deter immigrants from coming to it. If largely to find the needed troops for its military, France also adopted liberal naturalization laws during the nineteenth century and defined citizenship liberally in terms of where a child is born (*jus soli*), instead of following the restrictive German model of focusing on parentage (you are a German citizen only if born of German parents, no matter how long your ancestors may have lived in Germany). Still, France did not historically receive large numbers of migrating people, and before 1955 those who did arrive in sizable numbers came in only two waves: Russians, after the successful communist takeover of their country in 1917, and Vietnamese loyal to France, after the fall of the French Indochina empire in 1954. In all instances, the expectation was the same: that the power of French culture, and of French as the language of diplomacy, of literature, of the great chefs, and of the courts of Europe until the nineteenth century, would cause those acquiring French citizenship to assimilate by adopting the French language and faith, if they had not already done so. In most instances, the immigrants did. The Indochinese, however, were the last major wave of foreign nationals entering France to fit that model.

IMMIGRATION AND ETHNO-CULTURAL CONFLICT[8]

Postwar France had a greater need for labor than those arriving from Vietnam could provide, even when augmented by the arrival of perhaps several hundred thousand North Africans who had supported Paris against the rising tide of nationalism in their countries during the waning days of French imperialism.[9] Consequently, the governments of France during the 1950s began to recruit foreign workers from France's overseas department of Algeria and neighboring areas across the Mediterranean Sea. Even if they were so ungrateful as to want to shed their rule by Paris, Algerians and Tunisians had the advantage of being near at hand and frequently spoke *some* French. They were therefore more attractive as additions to the French labor force than the workers from Turkey and elsewhere in southern Europe that West Germany was then recruiting to meet its massive, post–World War II reconstruction needs. The fact that they were also most certainly not Catholics, but rather Muslims, was largely ignored at the time. They were to be only temporary members of the French workforce, who would stash money away while working in France to support a better life once they returned to their homelands and their Arab and Islamic ways of life.

The perception that these recruits were temporary, or short-term, members of the French workforce who were there only on renewable work visas rather than as immigrants destined to become permanent members of French society had important policy implications. First, and in retrospect foremost, their arrival and gradual growth in numbers occurred with little or no consideration of what impact the presence of a large number of Muslims might have on French society and politics. Second, no effort was made to settle them on arrival. They had to search for what was inevitably substandard housing, separated from their French hosts in deteriorating urban neighborhoods, and take the menial jobs that the French disdained if they were to stay. Eventually, these foreign workers became an economic and social underclass who were physically and ethnically separated from their hosts. Finally, no effort was made to prepare a French society, inexperienced in melting pot interactions with distinctly foreign peoples, for the coming reality of a France in which millions of non-assimilating Muslims would become a part of the daily landscape, as well as the workforce.

The major change in those early years occurred within the foreign worker communities themselves, however. Most scholars agree that the majority of those recruited from North Africa in the late 1950s and early 1960s shared the French belief that their stay would be temporary. However, the wages they received in France proved to be substantially less than anticipated, and saving became difficult. When the loneliness of being a single male in a strange land became unbearable, they took advantage of France's family reunification programs, sent for their wives, and began to raise families in the land of their work. Gradually, and almost imperceptibly, they had ceased to be temporary help and had become in practice, if not by law, a permanent and culturally quite distinct element in the French population.[10]

The issues raised by the development of a large Muslim community in France have evolved over time, with each new reason for opposing their presence augmenting, rather than supplanting, the earlier arguments raised by the country's anti-immigrant Front National (FN) party and others opposed to their growing presence.

The Visibility Problem

The basic issue is the *presence* of a large Muslim population openly practicing a faith that joins religion and state, despite the premium placed on the secular nature of the state in the native French political culture. Or, to phrase the matter slightly differently, France's large Muslim (ethno-class) minority is itself the issue. It is impossible to date precisely when this came about, because it has occurred at different moments in different parts of France. It probably began in southern France, where a large contingent of France's Muslim immigrant population settled amid large numbers of expatriate French nationals (*les pieds noirs)* who had been driven back to France during Algeria's war for independence and—having left everything behind in Algeria—were predisposed to dislike the workforce arriving from former French North Africa. Conversely, because of its cosmopolitan nature, size, and the geographical dispersion of the Muslim community on its periphery, Paris was perhaps the last part of France to develop a strong, anti-foreign cadre among its residents, most of whom did not begin to mobilize politically on the matter until 1989. Then, the unwillingness of Muslim schoolgirls to shed the *hijab*—the scarves Muslim women traditionally wear to cover their hair—while attending a public (hence, secular) school in the town of Creil, north of Paris, became a national *cause célèbre*. In between was the rest of the country, as the foreign workers reached a critical mass of visibility in an increasing share of provincial France. By the end of the 1970s, Arab women attired not just in the veil, but from crown to toe in long, flowing robes, could be daily and incongruously seen strolling along the streets and in the shadow of the cathedral in Strasbourg, France's most Germanic city, in the heart of the Alsace-Lorraine region.

Those years were not entirely hapless ones for France's growing workforce from North Africa and, gradually, from beyond. As their lives stabilized, their housing improved in at least a relative sense, from makeshift camps of tents to overcrowded apartments like those in the innercity minority neighborhoods of the United States. Moreover, before 1973 job opportunities seemed secure in France's expanding economy, as postwar France not only rebuilt but belatedly industrialized. Prior to World War II, France's chronic underpopulation, absence of fossil fuel resources, lack of indigenous investment capital, and overprotected agricultural sector had combined to leave France out of the industrial revolution. Britain's economy had expanded 350 percent, and Germany's

500 percent, between 1870 and 1940, whereas France's economy grew only a little more than 70 percent. After World War II, immigrant labor filled the initial manpower void and capital became available, first in the form of the United States government's Marshall Plan funds and then from American corporations investing in Europe. Meanwhile, the economic integration in Europe that began during the 1950s and gave France access to German coal, as well as to the inexpensive Middle Eastern oil that was then flowing into Europe, forced France by the mid-1960s to abandon its protectionist agricultural policies. In that economic glow there was the growing unlikelihood of another war, as both the United States and Soviet Union looked for ways to avoid confrontation after the Cuban Missile Crisis of 1962 brought them—and the world—to the brink of a nuclear holocaust. France's foreign workers, as well as the native French people, began to have children in numbers France had not seen in at least a century—but the foreigners were definitely having more children per family than their hosts.

What was economically good for the foreign workforce, however, soon became politically bad for them. As they became more numerous and visible, their presence became a political issue, and an unrest in regard to their growing presence began to set in, especially at the bottom of France's socioeconomic ladder. For the French, economic expansionism was creating new jobs at the top and in the middle of the French economy, leading to a growing French middle class. But at the bottom, where the number of jobs was proportionately shrinking, France's unskilled and semiskilled native workers were feeling squeezed. The foreign workers gradually became not only a political target of groups seeking to limit or reduce their number, but also the targets of street violence where their neighborhoods abutted the poorer neighborhoods of their French hosts. Those areas were usually on the outer "red belt" edges of the country's growing industrial cities, where its normally Communist-voting, unskilled French laborers lived. By the early 1970s, street fights and other violent incidents involving Algerians had grown sufficiently in number for the government of Algeria to announce that it was suspending the emigration of Algerians to France until the situation improved.

At that time, it is important to note, the conflict and violence were social, not political in motivation. More often than not they resulted from the frustration of a downwardly mobile native French working class combined with the cultural shock of a host population that suddenly found itself confronting unprepared a rising tide of very different people in its own slipping neighborhoods. And the foreign workers arriving in growing numbers during the 1950s, 1960s, and 1970s *were* very different from those who had preceded them. First, they were non-European, and in rising numbers they would continue to give France a multicultural character it had not had before. Indeed, by 1990 the Europeans (principally Spanish, Italians, and Portuguese), who had constituted more than half of France's foreign residents as late as the mid-1960s, accounted for only a little more than a third (36.9 percent) of them, whereas the Muslim North African contingent had grown from a third of the foreign residents in 1975 to nearly half (45.8 percent) by 1990.[11] Second, unlike the Europeans who previously dominated France's foreign population, not only were the North Africans not Catholic, but they visibly displayed their foreign nature in their attire, and—as they acclimated to their permanent presence and began to erect markets and mosques—they proclaimed their intent to continue to adhere to it.

Above all, to those concerned with their presence, they appeared to be a monolithic threat to the French way of life. Moroccans, Tunisians, and Algerians were all Arab, all Muslim, and hence foreign—man, woman, and child—even if that child had been born in France and was eligible for French citizenship. In fact, however, neither then nor now have those communities been monolithic—neither individually nor, much less, collectively. Not only did they not all arrive from the same country, but even if the focus is only on the "big three" lender countries—Algeria, Tunisia, and Morocco—the foreign workers came in different years and often entered the economy at different levels. Moreover, within each country's Muslim immigrant population are to be found divisions of faith, from moderate interpretations of Islamic law to fundamentalism.

The Algerians, the largest group, arrived the earliest and over a far longer period of time, not just during the 1955 to 1974 era when France's foreign worker population acquired its visibility, but subsequently as well. The initial Algerian arrivals—unlike those currently entering France at the high end of the workforce because they possess professional skills that France still needs and are allowed to migrate on temporary work permits—were young males willing to take any job at wages well below what a French worker would demand for the same, usually dirty work. They essentially defined the image of the foreign workers from Arab and Muslim North Africa that became permanently fixed in the minds of their hosts. Moroccans did not arrive until the 1960s, when that image was already fixed, and they fell into it even though they were much more likely to have a small amount of working capital on arrival, and often started small businesses in France. The Tunisians were the last to arrive in large numbers legally, entering France from the mid-1960s until 1974, when a changing economy and mounting pressure against the foreign workers led the French government to end the legal immigration of new foreign workers. Like the Moroccans, the Tunisians were more likely to establish small businesses and shops than the Algerians, who overwhelmingly found their niche in the wage economy. Nevertheless, by the early 1970s all three nationalities were one very "foreign" collective in the mind of the average native French worker, and well before the first oil crisis forced France to reevaluate its manpower needs, the notion was already building that there were too many of "them" in France.

Economic Stagflation and the Politicization of the "Foreigner" Issue

The sharp downturn of the global economy in the aftermath of the 1973 and 1979 oil crises made France's "foreigner" problem into a salient political issue. The nearly thirty years of sustained economic growth that France had enjoyed following World War II (*les Trente Glorieuses*) ended abruptly when the October 1973 Yom Kippur war erupted between Israel and its neighboring Arab states. The short war, during which the United States directly aided Israel, led to an Arab oil embargo of countries friendly to Israel and gave the members of the Organization of Petroleum Exporting Countries (OPEC) their long-awaited opportunity to take over ownership of the oil fields formerly leased indefinitely to Western petroleum companies. The price of their oil on the world market immediately quadrupled, from less than $3 per barrel to nearly $12 per barrel. Hysterical buying followed, as Western oil-importing countries competed against one another to purchase future deliveries, driving the actual price of oil to more than $20 per barrel for a short time before it eventually stabilized in the mid-teens. The process repeated itself in 1979, when the fall of the Shah of Iran in January and the beginning of a decade-long war between Iraq and Iran that September combined to tighten the oil market and boost OPEC's posted price of oil to $36 per barrel—a twelvefold price increase in six years for an imported commodity that was supplying more than half of France's total energy by that time.

Throughout the oil-consuming world, high inflation and governmental counterinflationary policies followed, and with those policies came a substantial rise in unemployment rates. In France, unemployment rates jumped from less than 7 percent of the workforce in 1973 to 12 percent by 1979, and 15 percent a year later. Thereafter, the rate of increase in France's unemployment rate slackened, but unemployment continued to grow to the point that, by 1993, approximately 3 million French workers were unemployed—twice the number who were out of work a generation before. Apart from the foreign workers themselves, the hardest hit were those men and women under twenty-five who had entered the workforce between 1983 and 1993 and for whom the rate of unemployment by 1993 was nearly one in three for women (31.6 percent) and one in four for men (24.2 percent).[12] It was not until the late 1990s that France's number of unemployed began to drop appreciably to the 2.3 million unemployed (a rate of 9 to 10 percent) that defined its economy in the early years of the twenty-first century.

The bad economic news for French workers, which reinforced the already existing hostility to the "foreigner" presence in many quarters, quickly translated into new votes for Jean-Marie Le Pen's National Front party, and hence very bad political news for France's foreign workers. In fact, all evidence indicated that they suffered disproportionately high levels of unemployment during France's prolonged recession, routinely accounting for a fifth of the unemployed even though they represented only 6 percent of the workforce. The recession, however, was not a time when the French unemployed were feeling particularly reasonable and objective.

Le Pen's *Front National* (FN, or National Front) party has been described as a combination of the worst in French protest politics: "racial and religious prejudice, anti-establishment rhetoric, populism, [and] know-nothingism."[13] Le Pen and other members of the post-war, neo-Fascist New Order Party founded FN on the eve of the first oil crisis in 1972. As a party of the far right with an ultranationalist stripe, its focus from the beginning has been on France's foreign worker community. Indeed, at the heart of its platform from the outset has been the demand that France close its door to new immigrants from North Africa and expel those already working in France. Yet during the first decade of its existence, the National Front enjoyed little election success because the lingering French belief that the foreign workers would leave or assimilate merged with their hope that the economy would soon revive to blunt the FN's appeal. Similarly, the French electorate shifted away from the parties of the right to ask the Socialists for new leadership in the early 1980s. Although not a part of the Gaullist-led coalition of the right that had governed France's Fifth French Republic (1958 to the present) from its inception, the National Front was a small and new party on the right at a time when the electorate was moving to the left in response to hardening economic times.

By the mid-1980s the economy was still tight, but the number of foreign workers in France had grown even larger. The primary effect of the 1974 decision by the French government to cease issuing work visas for new workers had essentially been to shift the inflow from abroad into illegal channels. A miserably paying job in France's stagnant economy's black (illegal) labor market was better than no job in Algeria or elsewhere, or even a low-paying job in a third-world economy. Gradually, Le Pen's party and its anti-immigrant message began to find receptive audiences. Its electoral breakthrough came in the local elections of 1983, when FN garnered nearly

10 percent of the vote, and during the period between 1984 and 1999, when it persistently attracted 10 to 15 percent of the overall vote in France and 25 percent in cities with large North African populations—very significant numbers in the context of France's multiparty system.

The electoral success of the FN, in turn, had a profound impact on the behavior of France's principal political parties, and on French public policy as well. As a result of the FN's gains and the impact of public opinion polls persistently showing more than 70 percent of the French population believing that there were too many Arabs in their country, by the 1990s anti-immigrant rhetoric and policies had been adopted by the major parties of both the French Left (the Socialists, led by President Francois Mitterrand, President of France from 1981 to 1995) and the Right (the Gaullists, led by Jacques Chirac, who succeeded Mitterrand as president in 1995). Valery Giscard d'Estaing, former president and titular leader of the Gaullists' principal ally on the right, equated the immigrant presence with the Nazi occupation of France. He urged the expulsion of all unemployed foreign workers and the preferential hiring of native French workers to fill future job vacancies. For his part, President Mitterrand spoke of the French people's reaching their "threshold of tolerance" and abandoned his prior advocacy of voting rights for immigrants in local elections. Leading the charge was Chirac, who as mayor of Paris and leader of the Gaullist Party unequivocally argued that France must "not accept any new immigration . . . [and must] severely curb illegal immigrants, rigorously apply the laws of the Republic, systematically expel those whose status is irregular, and . . . promote a policy of encouraging return immigration."[14]

This rhetorical mainstreaming of the foreigner issue was particularly telling in the case of the French Socialist Party, which during its first turn at controlling the French Assembly had adopted a multicultural approach to dealing with diversity in France. It had passed legislation favorable to both the linguistic minorities in such French regions as Corsica and Alsace-Lorraine and the ethnic minorities arriving in France from abroad. Favoring the immigrants, but grievously misreading the pulse of France, the Socialists enacted legislation that liberalized naturalization requirements, subsidized minority cultural associations, and attempted to equalize the wages and other employment benefits of the foreign and indigenous workforces. Not surprisingly, the next election put the Gaullists and their allies on the right in solid control of the French legislature once again.

The End of *la belle France*?

The drift toward ever-increasing anti-foreigner rhetoric and policies on the part of France's mainstream political leaders reflected above all the emergence of yet another dimension in the French perception of the "foreigner" problem. By the 1990s, the debate had become less about their numbers or even their relationship to France's unemployment problem, and more about the threat they posed to the nature of the French nation. The numbers from North Africa were continuing to grow. By the mid-1990s, the foreign nationals from Tunisia, Algeria, and Morocco accounted for nearly 1.5 million (or nearly 3 percent) of those officially estimated to be living in France. To those can be added the *illegal* foreign population, estimated by most scholars at approximately 5 million immigrants, 70 percent of whom come from North Africa.[15] And those numbers are likely to continue to grow, even if the border could somehow be sealed. By the mid-1990s, the foreign population in France was responsible for one out of eight (12.7 percent) births in the country, although foreigners represent only one-sixteenth (6.3 percent) of the population.[16]

More importantly to the French, the immigrants were continuing to transplant their culture, their children were being raised in a North African ambience in France itself, and at *their* volition the cultural distance separating them from the French was widening, at least for large numbers that included the young. Streets accommodate their markets. Halal butchers (those sanctioned by clerics to slaughter animals) do a thriving business in immigrant neighborhoods. Mosques and prayer rooms have been multiplying—from approximately a dozen in the 1970s to more than 1,000 today, including eight large mosques with the capacity to hold more than a thousand of the faithful at a time. And even though fundamentalist clerics have been giving inflammatory speeches against the secular French state and Western policies in the world, French Muslims have demanded both state funding for Muslim schools akin to that already being given to Catholic and Jewish schools, and the sanctioning of Muslim holy days as state public holidays.[17]

Even when the focus was on the numbers (too many) of Muslims in the country and the later charge that they were stealing jobs from the French, the subtext of the FN's campaign against the presence of the "foreigners" had always been the effect that their culture would have on France. In that context, Le Pen long claimed that he was only saying what everyone else thought. By the 1990s, the unwillingness of the Muslims to assimilate—defined by, but not limited to the wearing of the scarf and the establishment of mosques and prayer rooms—and the "colonizing" efforts of the Muslims to Islamize France had become the lead issue in the "foreigner" debate. In that context, others were now saying what Le Pen had long said, including (by the twenty-first century) the adviser on immigration to the French Minister of the Interior. In his words, it was for France's Muslim communities to change, not France, for "when somebody emigrates, he changes not only his country but also his history. Foreigners arriving to settle in France must understand that from henceforth their ancestors are the Gauls and that they have a new homeland."[18]

The Security of the State and Its People

In the past, most notably because of its government's support of the regime ruling Algeria, France has experienced isolated, if highly publicized acts of terrorism, almost always intermittent and perpetrated by a radical fringe in its domestic Algerian community. That broad community itself had never been seen as a threat to the state or to the general safety of the French. But the September 11, 2001 attacks by al Qaeda terrorists, followed by the 2004 attack on commuter trains in Madrid and the 2005 terrorist bombings of buses and the subway system in London, did more than just give the FN another issue to add to its list of reasons for expelling France's "foreign community"—a platform that by then included the revocation of naturalized Muslims' citizenship, if not that of Muslim children born in France. It added a compelling security dimension to the "foreigner" issue.

Although the attack on the United States was executed by foreigners entering the country for that purpose, the Madrid and London attacks were committed wholly or in part by self-financing young Muslim militants who had grown up in the country whose citizens they targeted. The danger that France might harbor similarly alienated, dangerous terrorists within its Muslim communities had to be faced, especially given the fact that the country-of-distant-origin featured prominently among those accused of the Madrid bombing was Morocco. France's 1999 census had revealed that Moroccans (already one-eighth of the foreign population) constituted one of the fastest growing elements among its foreign residents.[19]

The Prospect of Additional Violence

Throughout the past nearly half a century, the debate—and the policies that have been implemented—concerning France's Arab and Muslim workers (and citizens, in many instances) have been decidedly one-sided. Antidiscrimination associations such as S.O.S.-Racism have lobbied on their behalf and organized rallies against the flagrantly discriminatory government policies aimed at them. On occasion, the French parties and unions on the left have also championed their cause. For the most part, however, those workers and France's smaller, non-Muslim "foreigner" communities have been on the receiving end of policies treating *them* as the problem, rather than treating their substandard living conditions or the often daily discrimination against them as the problem. During the 1970s, while many continued to live in shanty towns known locally as *bidonvilles* or were in the process of relocating to the decaying suburbs of French cities, the government was primarily concerned with closing the door to further immigration of foreign workers from outside the European Communities, increasing border patrols against illegal entrants, and offering those already legally in France the singularly unattractive payoff of a free ticket home and a $2,000 bonus to leave France. Fewer than 5 percent of France's *unemployed* foreign workers took advantage of the offer. During the 1980s, except for a brief hiatus provided by the well-meaning multicultural policies of the Socialist Party, the screw continued to turn. Borders were further tightened against illegal immigrants, the loss of a job frequently led to deportation, and those subsidies that the Socialists had made available to foreign cultural associations quickly dried up when the Gaullists and their allies on the French right returned to office in the mid-1980s.

The picture further darkened for the "foreigners" in the 1990s. The head-scarf issue in 1989 and a riot in Lyons staged by frustrated Muslim youth the following year mobilized a broad spectrum of the native French republic behind the restrictive policies advocated by the FN, and Paris responded accordingly. New laws, including a constitutional amendment, were enacted in 1993 to curb illegal immigration and expel the illegals from France. Three years later, at the same time that a United Nations study conducted by its Human Rights Commission was condemning the "wave of xenophobia and racism in France," the government enacted laws that restricted the access of France's legal immigrants to health care, education, and other public services. And, even before debate on the foreigner issue took its post-9/11 turn toward security concerns, the French government had already begun deporting individuals—chiefly Muslim clerics—on the vague grounds that they constituted a threat to the public order. Since that time these deportations have accelerated; the head-scarf issue has been revived; national legislation has been passed to ban the wearing of obvious religious attire in France's secular school system; and raids on Muslim neighborhoods in the name of security have become unexceptional events, if not common ones. There is also a rather unsettling statistic related to law enforcement, even allowing for the fact that economic underclasses are frequently disproportionately forced into illicit crimes. Although they represent only 10 percent of France's population, the country's Muslims make up at least half of France's prison inmates.[20]

Paris has extended some gestures of accommodation to its "foreigner" communities, but a growing sense of too little, too late envelops them. The long-contemplated Muslim Council (*le Conseil francais du culture musulman)* that was finally created in 2002 to advise the French govern-ment, for example, has been widely interpreted by many of France's diverse Muslim communities as more of an effort on the part of Paris to co-opt and control Muslims than to empower them. Its authority is advi-sory, the members appointed to it have favored the moderate wings of Muslim thought in France, and a central role on the Council was ascribed to the Paris Mosque that had long been known for its liberal interpreta-tion of Islamic teachings. Under these conditions it was perhaps inevitable that many French Muslims would suspect the Council of hav-ing too close a relationship with the French government at a time when the government was converting the long-standing philosophy of *laicité* into an aggressive policy aimed at combating the religious activism affect-ing the state. Those suspicions seemed confirmed when France's moder-ate Muslim clerics and the leaders of its more moderate associations failed to object strenuously when, on July 3, 2003, President Chirac established a commission to study the implementation of *laicité* principles in France and later steered through the French Assembly a secularization law that bans all religious symbols, including the veil, from French public schools. Subsequently, and again with minor protests from the moderate Muslim leaders who have access to the French government, then Interior Minister and current President of France Nicolas Sarkozy has spoken openly about extending the Muslim Council's control over such areas as "cemetery plots, places of worship, [and] the designation of prison chaplains" in pursuit of the "imperious necessity to *organize Islam in France*" (italics added).[21]

In truth, both the French government and France's foreign communi-ties have objective cases to make—in contrast to the Le Pen faction. All states have an interest in protecting their inner ethos, and for many coun-tries in Europe the core of that ethos is the hard-won right to be secu-lar—to maintain the strict separation between the religious realm and the political sphere that Islam does not recognize, even though the more pro-gressive states in the world of Islam have found a way of living with it. Especially on such matters as the controversy over the wearing of the tra-ditional Muslim head scarf, the state can mount a compelling defense that it has a right to ban religious wear, because the mission of French schools is to neutralize the religious differences separating the French people while immersing everyone in the attributes of French civilization and the glories of French history. Beyond this objective, the advocates of shaping Islam to France point to the need to secure with affirmative action directed toward the Muslim communities such traditional French values as liberty and equality—which today means equality between the sexes—but without negating the French Muslim's right to a distinct cul-tural identity within the state.[22] To do less would be to fail in both the schools' and the state's mission to maintain the French nation and its core principles.

For their part, France's Muslim community can legitimately argue that the French nation has never wanted them—certainly not on a permanent, equal, and multicultural basis—and that after two generations of facing social and economic discrimination, even as French-born citizens, it is time to shout "enough!" They believe it is also time to reject actively the French efforts to integrate them on France's terms, not theirs. The culture of France in many ways continues to be an affront to peaceful Islamic fundamentalists, from the presence of alcoholic beverages everywhere, even (watered down) at children's place settings, to the licentious way in which barely clad French women present themselves in public. But when France's devout Muslims try to shield their culture from Western vulgarity and materialism by wearing the veil and refusing to study Darwin in schools, by abstaining from public pools and beaches where the sexes commingle, and by refusing to permit Muslim women to be examined by male doctors in the public health system, they are blamed for not assimilating. Hence, from the vantage point of the Muslim communities, the fact that a segment of France's previously nonreligious and disaffected Arab youth is now embracing Islam is scarcely a cause for alarm, and certainly not a reflection of religious extremism among French Muslims. Rather, it is explicable in terms of the youths' search for a sense of community and identity in a still-hostile land—a France that still marginalizes them and their parents. And from their vantage point it continues to be a very hostile land, indeed. Quite apart from the recent tightening of security, France is still, after two generations, a country where occupational mobility remains blocked by laws limiting various jobs in the public sector to French citizens, and where daily life for the majority of "foreigners" is played out against a backdrop of drab housing and unemployment, or unchallenging jobs.

For those "foreigners" growing up in contemporary France, rising expectations have thus given way to increased frustration. More importantly, to date it is that frustration that has led to a threat to France's public order, not the plotting of radical Arabs to commit terrorist acts against the French state and French society. That fact of contemporary French political life was most vividly underscored by the month-long, spontaneous rioting across France by Muslim and non-Muslim youth in France's "foreigner" communities in the fall of 2005. Although triggered by the shooting of two Muslim teenagers being chased for petty crimes by French police, the riots revealed a wide, deep, and volatile sense of alienation from native French society within the new generation of young "foreign" adults, which previously had only been suspected. It is not surprising that some have felt provoked to violent protest, given that alienation and some of the recent—and sometimes insensitive—actions by the French government to protect the security and/or secular nature of the state. A short list includes

- The deportation of popular but radical Muslim clerics, of non-citizens involved in the 2005 riots in Paris, of law-abiding but illegal immigrants, and of foreign students at the end of their academic terms
- The silencing of a Hezbollah television station in France for its anti-Semitic programming
- The denial of security permits to Arab workers at Charles de Gaulle airport
- The laws requiring French schools to give more attention to the positive benefits of colonialism, and to expel Muslim girls who wear the veil to class

But the resentment flows both ways in contemporary France, which makes the situation even more explosive. The native French resent the not-so-creeping multiculturalism that seems to be taking over their country. North African Muslim Arabs, joined often by the Muslims from scores of other countries that have also migrated to France, resent the French government for targeting their leaders, culture, and practices for what appears to them to be opportunistic political gain, as well as for its more recent willingness to categorize France's Muslim communities in general as "suspect" in this age of international terrorism. At the same time, they find themselves in an ambiguous position in a France now composed of two societies, each distinct in appearance and clearly defined in ethno-religious terms, and each viewing the other through the cultural prism of its own experience and outlook.

The overwhelming majority of France's Muslims are law-abiding, political moderates, as the current government-defined concept of French Islam assumes. At the same time, they are also residents of an assertively secular state in which they adhere, even if only nominally, to a religion whose comprehensive guide to life does not include the Western concept of the separation of church and state. Moreover, the government has compounded their dilemma, in a sense, by placing them in a zero-sum game. The more they embrace their religion and wear it on their heads and body in public, the more they separate themselves from French society. The more they succumb to the state's pressure to assimilate into a French society still none-too-hospitable toward them, the more they have reason to question their commitment to their faith. Violence breeds in those conditions, and from time to time it will continue to erupt. The rioting in the fall of 2005 was foreshadowed earlier that year, when the growing tension and clashes between two French underclasses in the south of France—the Romani and thousands of local Muslims—produced heated demonstrations and left two people dead.[23] It has had its echoes since.

If the Muslims of France, even those from North Africa, were as monolithic and cohesive as the French frequently view them, the tension might be defused at the ballot box. Now constituting a tenth of the population and approximately 8 percent of the electorate, France's Muslims represent a growing voting bloc. Indeed, French politicians—most notably former President Chirac—have occasionally tempered their anti-immigrant rhetoric long enough to appeal to them when running for office, albeit carefully, so as not to produce the type of French voter backlash that punished the Socialist Party for its dip in the waters of multiculturalism during the 1980s. But such cohesiveness does not exist among French Muslims. Already divided in terms of national origins and religious persuasion inside the Muslim faith, they have become more divided than ever on how to protect their interests in the French political process since the French government instituted its aggressive secularization policy in the early twenty-first century. Some have seen the Muslim Council as a possible avenue for inclusion, but others have seen it as a tool in the war against Islam in France. Yet for the moment, the Council is their major means of access to the French government.

Meanwhile, there is growing frustration on the part of the French government and native French society with its non-assimilating Muslim minority, and the frustration of the minority with their lot in France also continues to grow. For those at or near the socioeconomic bottom in both societies, violence lurks not too far from the surface. Is there a chance that France will explode into cultural civil war? Despite the lengthy rioting by Muslim youth in 2005 and the shorter outbursts of disorderly protests in those quarters subsequently, the answer remains an emphatic no. Apart from everyone's vested interest in preserving the French economy and the normally prevailing sense of decorum in the debate between the government and France's moderate Muslim leadership, the splintered nature of the North African communities makes a concerted response to the secularist targeting of those communities improbable. The most likely scenario is that the combustible mixture of alienation and disillusionment inside the Muslim community will periodically explode into violent protest, perhaps punctuated in the years ahead by thoroughly radicalized Muslims following the lead of their brethren in Spain and Britain and executing a terrorist act. It can be lethal, but it is not the stuff of communal civil warfare.

On the other hand, in a security-conscious age the government increasingly defines the "Muslim issue" in France, if not the "foreigner" issue, in zero-sum terms. Either the North Africans adopt the image of secular Islam (perhaps a contradiction in terms) endorsed by the state, or else. Framed in that way, does the issue then have enormous *potential* for disrupting French politics and unleashing sporadic political violence? The answer to that question is an equally emphatic "*Oui!*"

NATIONALISM AND SEPARATISM IN CORSICA

Unlike many of the politically sensitive regions chronicled in this volume, the island of Corsica *is* also a major vacation hot spot in Europe, with lush woodlands, hillsides, a mountain peak towering a mile and a half over the island, gorgeous beaches, historic sites, quaint picturesque towns, and—in the summer—enough different languages being spoken to give it a cosmopolitan air. In those hills, however, Corsica's native tongue not only dominates, but is apt to be saying less-than-kind things about those speaking French down below. French has been the language of Corsica's rulers since 1768, when France acquired it from a Genoa happy to be rid of a quarrelsome island that it had not fully controlled for generations.

France has yet to find itself in a similar position, but for at least thirty years the island's native population has flirted with separatism and has, on occasion, voted in significant numbers for the candidates of Corsican nationalist parties. Moreover, for at least that many years a network of separatist organizations has clandestinely attacked the institutions of metropolitan France and the vacation homes of French citizens on the island. It is a low-intensity conflict that has claimed few lives, unlike the "The Troubles" in Northern Ireland, but it is also a conflict that shows little immediate likelihood of abating.

The Survival of Corsican Identity

As is true of so many of the islands off Europe's coastline, Corsica has been at the crossroads of history for thousands of years. One of its principal cities, Aleria, was founded by the Phoenicians in approximately 562 BC. Greek civilization, Roman conquest, and invasions by the Vandals, Goths, and Moors have all left their mark. Nevertheless, its history and culture since Medieval times have been most shaped by its geography. Located only fifty-eight miles west of Italy (approximately half the distance separating it from southern France), the Corsicans speak an Indo-European language of Romance or Latin origin heavily influenced by the Tuscan tongue of Northern Italy. Their language is not a dialect of French, even though it has absorbed a considerable number of French words and phrases over the centuries. More importantly, for nearly five centuries (1284–1769), Corsica was under the sometimes firm, sometimes nominal control of Genoa.

The years under Genoa's rule were turbulent ones for both Genoa and Corsica—a time when disease, including the plague in the fourteenth century and malaria epidemics in the sixteenth century, shortened lives and led to the exodus of many Corsican people. But it did not inhibit the French, Barbary coast pirates, and other outsiders from raiding the island and/or continuing to meddle in its affairs. It was not until the mid-fourteenth century that Genoa consolidated its rule over the island's poor and diseased people, and another 200 years passed before that rule was secured from foreign intervention by the creation of a series of fortifications and towers along Corsica's coastline. Elsewhere on the island, though, by the end of the sixteenth century Genoa's heavy hand was already provoking the first stirring of insurrections against its rule.

By the eighteenth century, the sporadic rebellions had evolved into a full-blown independence movement—what would now be called a low-intensity war for independence. Really a series of four consecutive insurrections beginning in 1729 and spanning forty years, Corsica's war for independence gradually led to the emergence of a sense of national identity among its sparse population, produced a genuine national leader in Pascal Paoli, and led to the island's de facto independence. Genoan rule collapsed in 1753, and the island began fifteen years of self-government under Paoli as general-in-chief of the Corsican Nation. In 1768, after failing to gain the assistance of either Austria or France in quelling the rebellion, Genoa deeded the island and its rebellious people to France.

The arrival of French rule was as acrimonious as the end of Corsica's relationship with Genoa. When Paris acquired the island it agreed to give the Corsicans a wide measure of political autonomy. After the deal was sealed, however, French troops arriving on the island quickly vanquished Paolo's government and within a year put an end to Corsica's war for independence. By 1769 French rule had been established, and in those days that meant, in the words of Louis XIV, one Faith, one language, and one indivisible state. For the Corsicans, that axiom soon translated into no local autonomy and no respect for, nor official tolerance of the Corsican tongue.

The French Revolution twenty years later did nothing to change that long-term policy under which Corsica and France's other peripheral and ethno-linguistically distinct regions (most notably Brittany in France's northwest, Alsace-Lorraine on its eastern border with Germany, and the Basque areas along its southwestern border with Spain) were governed. In the short term, however, the chaos that engulfed France for several years during the 1790s—when France had four constitutional systems within ten years—gave Corsica a measure of freedom. Corsica very quickly proclaimed its independence (again), and Paoli returned from twenty years of exile in England to establish an Anglo-Corsican kingdom on the island between 1794 and 1796. But French troops re-entered Corsica in force in 1796, and the kingdom fell quickly. On the other hand, the ascent to power by Corsican-born Napoleon Bonaparte within a year of renewed French rule on the island provided Corsicans with a previously missing link to France. Corsica's independence movement gradually faded away with the turn of the new century and Napoleon's pursuit of empire for France.

The importance of those eighteenth-century days of independence, the island's national leaders, and Italian and French perfidy to contemporary Corsican nationalism can scarcely be overstated. The tales of those days and events continue to be nurtured and retold on the island, and they have provided the foundation for Corsica's contemporary nationalism and demands for freedom from French rule. Thus, even today it is Paoli and his revolution that evokes the image of freedom and liberty on Corsica, not the French Revolution and fall of the Bastille on July 14, 1789. In fact, it was not until several months *after* the French Revolution, on November 30, 1789, that Corsica was decreed an integral part of the French empire.

Corsica and the Assimilationist State

Despite the bond that the people of Corsica felt with Napoleon as a fellow Corsican, neither Napoleon nor the regime he fashioned proved to be a friend of Corsican autonomy. Not only did Napoleon reestablish Paris' control over Corsica—rule that has since been interrupted only twice, when Germans and Italians occupied the island during World Wars I and II—but it was Napoleon who introduced the highly centralized prefect system by which all of France was administered for the next 175 years. Under that system, political control over the island passed into the hands of a Paris-appointed administrator (*prefect*), whose primary duty was to ensure that what was enacted in Paris would be fully implemented in Corsica. No special allowances were to be made for local customs or languages. The system thus spelled an end to local hopes for autonomy, even if in practice Paris frequently had to tolerate Corsican and other regional languages simply because its appointed agents were unfamiliar with them (no Corsican served as prefect for more than a century). Consequently, those agents needed the assistance of local citizens to administer French law in those regions of France whose languages and dialects were unknown to them.

Hard as the prefect system was on the dreams of Corsican nationalists, the greater threat to the island's culture came from the assimilation policies that Paris aimed at its linguistically self-differentiating regions during the first century after the French Revolution. As a general rule, Corsica's location as an island more than 100 miles off the coast of France gave it an advantage in withstanding these assimilationist efforts, even as the nature of its language put it at a disadvantage—compared to most of France's other regionalized linguistic minorities—in regard to receiving special dispensation in the twentieth century.

The government's first foray into assimilating, and thereby fully civilizing, these regionalized communities followed on the heels of the French Revolution. Prior to then, Paris had little interest in the cultures of France's periphery and equally little interest in developing policies to integrate the country's non-French-speaking peoples into the French culture. Their ways of life were often the subject of plays in the theaters of Paris and marionette productions in its parks, but so long as they disarmed their regional armies, vowed loyalty to Paris, and paid their taxes, they were generally left to their "backward" lifestyles. After the French Revolution, the principle that government rested on the popular sovereignty of one indivisible nation meant that local cultures rooted in other languages had to go. The most radical of the revolutionaries believed that some of the population would also have to go—in particular, the German-speaking French people of Alsace and Lorraine, who were seen as likely candidates for expulsion across the Rhine because they were not thought capable of being assimilated. For the more moderate, however, the focus became language.

On January 27, 1794, less than five years after the Revolution, France established a centralized education system with the intent of deploying teachers to France's periphery like soldiers, there to propagate the French language. Regional languages were to be tolerated, not forbidden, however, on the assumption that when people learned to speak French, the language of the Revolution, local dialects would gradually fade away to a slow death. That assumption proved to be false. Four generations later, the Third French Republic (1870–71 to 1940) was born in the aftermath of France's defeat by Germany in the Franco-Prussian War, which left Alsace and Lorraine in Germany's possession for nearly half a century. At that time the regional tongues were still thriving, and France launched a second, more intense effort to assimilate its regionalized minorities.

The Ferry Laws, enacted between 1881 and 1884 at the urging of Jules Ferry, who was then both the premier of France and its minister of education, were the centerpiece of the new campaign. For the first time, free and compulsory primary school education was mandated for all children in France between seven and thirteen years of age, and that education was to be conducted *in French*. It was also to be offered through a system of public schools, not the Catholic schools that had previously provided so much of French schooling and were often closely attuned to the regional cultures—and just as often opposed to the secular, often militantly anti-clerical governments of France. The focus of the policy, however, was continental France, meaning that Corsica, with its remote locale and sparse, widely spaced rural population, was once again spared the full brunt of the assimilation mandates of Paris. Corsica's people were less aggressively steered toward the language and culture of (Paris-defined) France. Consequently, Corsica was slower than other parts of France to mobilize in defense of its culture and create modern nationalist parties along the lines of those that emerged in France's Basque areas (1893), Catalonia (1901), Occitania (1907), Brittany (1911), and—after its return to Paris following World War I—Alsace and Lorraine (1928).

Corsica and Post–World War II France

By the 1950s, regional cultural associations and, frequently, regional parties throughout continental France's linguistically distinct areas were demanding regional linguistic autonomy. At a minimum, they wanted the right to speak the regional tongue in their public schools, and preferably to teach some classes in that language or at least teach the history of their regions in their public schools. In response, the French government in 1951 enacted the Deixonne Act (still without officially conceding that there were any ethnic minorities in France, only linguistic minorities). The statute in no way diminished the importance of the French language or Paris's commitment to the full assimilation of France's peripheral communities, but for the first time in modern France it did officially permit the study of regional languages in four of its regions: Brittany, the Basque lands, French Catalonia, and Occitania.

As an exercise in accommodation, the Deixonne Act requires several qualifications. First, by the time of the law's passage (1951), most of the areas that had been linguistically distinct at the time of the French Revolution had achieved integration with France as a result of the late nineteenth and early twentieth-century creation of national communication grids and a national economy, and through their service in the name of France during the Empire and in two world wars. Although lying outside France's internal communication and transportation grids, Corsicans also participated in these developments, serving as "in many cases, the primary administrators of France's colonial empire and often its main engineers, farmers, and builders—especially in Indochina."[24]

Second, the Deixonne Act most definitely was not a step toward the regional political autonomy that regionalists desired. Those requests continued to fall on deaf ears throughout the twentieth century. In 1963 Paris *did* create Regional Economic Development committees that tended to coincide with the boundaries of the country's peripheral minority communities, and while in power in the 1980s the Socialist Party somewhat decentralized authority into the hands of regional councils by way of promoting "regional and minority culture." Nevertheless, throughout these years French remained the sole language for radio and television broadcasting, government business, and public documents, and by the late twentieth century the number of people taking classes in their regional languages was decreasing throughout France. Furthermore, much of the modest encouragement of regional languages that resulted from passage of the Deixonne Act was later neutralized by policies implemented to combat the spread of English into French, because the statutes forbidding the use of any language other than French for official purposes or business activity also applied to the regional tongues. Only the languages of France's Muslims and other foreign communities were exempted from such provisions.

Finally, the Deixonne Act did not apply to all of France's ethnolinguistic minority communities. Those regions speaking "allogenous" (other) languages (Corsican, Alsatian, and Flemish dialects) were excluded on the grounds that their languages were variations of the languages spoken in other European countries. It was thus not until 1974, when Corsican was added to the list, that Corsicans began to benefit from the Deixonne Act. On the other hand, in both Alsace and Corsica, where the local languages *are* the languages of daily use inside and outside the household, those benefits were hardly necessary for the regional tongues to survive. Estimates involving language use in Corsica, for example, persistently concluded that during the 1970s more than 70 percent of those living on the island still spoke *Corse*.[25] Moreover, by then both Corsican nationalism and the principal Corsican ethno-nationalist organizations had also become a feature of life in Corsica, along with the growing presence of political violence.

Contemporary Corsican Nationalism and Political Violence

Because of their insulation from Paris's more intrusive efforts to bring France's peripheral linguistic communities into the French cultural regime, modern Corsican nationalist organizations may have developed later than those of Alsace-Lorraine and Brittany, but they have had a much greater impact on French politics than their older counterparts in continental France.

The formative years for the development of both contemporary Corsican nationalism—defined broadly in terms of a desire to escape Parisian rule—and its nationalist organizations stretch from 1962, when France was finally forced after a lengthy military campaign to concede independence to Algeria, to 1967, when the last of Corsica's principal eth-nopolitical organizations (*Action regionaliste corse*) was founded. Algerian independence resulted in large numbers of the French citizens formerly living in Algeria migrating to Corsica, where they settled on significant portions of the island's land and consumed the largest amount of the economic subsidies that Paris was then extending to its less-economically developed regions. The result was local resentment toward both the new arrivals and toward Paris, for encouraging them to migrate to Corsica. A measure of that dissatisfaction was tallied a few years later in 1969. A ref-erendum that proposed administratively reorganizing France on a regional basis failed in France as a whole, but it carried in Corsica, as well as in most of France's other linguistic minority regions.

With the government of France still unwilling to concede political autonomy to these regions, the 1970s witnessed in Corsica and elsewhere a blossoming of quasi-terrorist organizations dedicated to forcing the local home rule concessions from Paris that it seemed otherwise unwill-ing to make. In the truest sense of the word, these were extreme measures being undertaken by extremist groups driven to extremes by the French government's persistent unwillingness even to concede the presence of ethnic minorities in France, much less grant them a measure of regional autonomy. On the other hand, when political violence and assassinations were marking the struggle for Basque separatist autonomy in Franco's Spain, as well as the conflict between the Protestant and Catholic com-munities in Northern Ireland, the term "extremist" needs to be qualified when applied to the clandestine regional organizations committed to the cause of Breton, Alsatian, and Corsican nationalism at that point in time. Rather than people, the targets of France's clandestine nationalist organ-izations have overwhelmingly been the physical symbols of the French state (its national banks and its radio and television stations) or, especially in Corsica, the vacation homes of absentee French owners.

Such tactics have produced few concessions to regionalists in mainland France, and for the most part even these minor episodes involving polit-ical violence have faded away there, along with the groups utilizing such methods to extract concessions from Paris. In the case of Corsica, how-ever, these tactics have been pursued more aggressively and longer, and on an island that is a tourist cash cow for the French economy. They have to some degree succeeded in calling attention to the special case that Corsica's demand for autonomy represents. The island *is* physically removed from the rest of France and can thereby legitimately claim a greater need for local autonomy for its citizens and their unique culture and distinct way of life—a life that occasionally revolves around an extended-family clan system interwoven with "strongly-differentiated gender roles, codes of honor and the vendetta, and occultism."[26] In any event, by the 1970s the combination of Corsica's distinctiveness, economic deprivation compared to France as a whole, and a long-standing perception of Parisian insensitivity to its needs had produced both a strong home rule movement, led by two popular ethno-regionalist parties, and a degree of political mobilization around nationalistic themes that was unequaled in France's other minority regions.

Faced with rising nationalist sentiment and the problems of law and order posed by Corsica's quasi-terrorist, separatist organizations, during the 1980s the French government began to make a greater effort to accommodate the regionalist orientations of Corsica's people than it was willing to make in order to placate continental France's restive regionalist movements. Hence, beginning with the 1982 creation of an essentially advisory Corsican Assembly, the French government abandoned its previous efforts to ignore and/or repress Corsican separatism and embarked on a twenty-year effort to accommodate ethno-regional sentiment on the island.

The government's efforts to reach a mutually acceptable *modus vivendi* with Corsican nationalists were based on the formula of cultural autonomy, economic development packages, and political decentralization that has been largely successful in accommodating regionalist sentiment elsewhere in France. In addition, and largely because these policies were less successful in Corsica than elsewhere, Paris has been willing to extend to the Corsicans a measure of home rule.

The first step was the establishment in 1982 of Corsica's first directly elected Assembly, which had executive (that is, primarily administrative) decision-making authority in a wide range of areas, including education, economic development, agriculture, and housing. In addition, in deference to Corsican history, a new university named for Pasquale Paoli was to be created in Corsica, and the house that had served as the seat of his government was to become a Center for Corsican Studies.

The second round began in April 1991, when the citizens of Corsica were officially recognized as a distinct "people" inside France. The process expanded in 1993 with a set of institutional reforms that augmented the Corsican Assembly's authority and created a second Corsican executive—this one elected by the island's councillors. The round culminated in 1999 with promises by both Paris and the European Union to launch massive regional development programs in Corsica in order to close the economic gap separating Corsicans from most other French citizens. Still, political turbulence continued on the island, albeit with Corsica's clandestine nationalist organizations functioning, for the most part, more like lobbying groups than guerrilla separatist movements of the Basque ETA variety. As one reporter summarized the situation, by mid-decade the bombings had become "a form of communication with more impact than a fax."[27] Then, despite the economic and political concessions that the island had received and the promises of more to come, the level of political violence sharply escalated during the late 1990s, most notably with the 1998 assassination of Claude Erignac, the island's Paris-appointed governor, while he was attending a concert in Ajaccio with this wife.

Despite these events, Paris embarked in 2000 on the third step of the plan to decentralize political authority in Corsica. Socialist premier Lionel Jospin launched the process by concluding an accord that would merge executive authority on the island into a single office, still further expand the Assembly's power, widen the opportunities for women to hold public office by introducing a quota system, and mandate the teaching of the Corsican language in the island's public schools. Although the Corsican Assembly overwhelmingly ratified the agreement, its implementation first required approval by Corsican voters in a non-binding referendum scheduled for early July 2003, and then its passage by the French Assembly. The latter appeared to be a given, inasmuch as the proposal originated under a Socialist government and was given the active support of Gaullist president Jacques Chirac's interior minister, Nicolas Sarkozy, who personally campaigned in Corsica in support of the referendum.

The Likelihood of Future Violence

The Corsicans said "non," despite the efforts of Paris to persuade them to vote "oui" on the referendum, and despite the referendum's endorsement by the island's principal nationalist party, the *Corsica Nazione*, on the grounds that the accord represented a positive step toward future independence from France—an interpretation most definitely not Sarkozy's. Polls had indicated during the run-up period that the vote would be close, and it was. When the final votes were counted, the referendum failed by 2,190 votes out of the 12,090 cast, or by a 51 percent to 49 percent majority. The biggest surprise was the high level of no-shows on election day, when almost 40 percent of Corsica's eligible voters chose to stay home, making the referendum not just a policy disappointment but a public relations disaster for the Chirac-Sarkozy government.

The reasons for the referendum's failure are debatable. The core of the opposition consisted of the island's established elites, especially its political cadre (councillors and Assembly personnel), who feared that the accord's implementation would erode their authority or mandate that they share it with others. A second tier of opposition came from the nationalist camp, which divided over endorsing the accord and was generally suspicious of anything originating in Paris. Many in this camp seem to have followed the *Corsica Nazione*'s lead and grudgingly supported the accord. A large bloc of the "no" voters were from nationalist groups, however, and the French government may have only itself to blame for that development. In the last days of the campaign a well-known Corsican nationalist was arrested by a special unit of the French police force and charged with Erignac's 1998 murder, thereby propelling perhaps even a majority of the nationalist camp into the "no" column. Still, the pivotal or swing vote against the referendum appears to have come from islanders who were just confused as to what the details of home rule would be and/or were fearful that a "yes" vote might compromise their access to the welfare system that the government in Paris provided.

Whatever the reasons for the referendum's failure, it immediately led to a souring of the relationship between Paris and the island's nationalists that had preceded the vote, and a return to the days of tension and periodic political violence that continue to make Corsica "the only region [of France] still employing sporadic violence to draw attention to its ethnic demands."[28] For its part, the Chirac government accepted the defeat with minimal grace and a promise to return to a hard-line approach to controlling the island, by force if necessary—in other words, an approach similar to those that had failed in the past and had led to the development of clandestine separatist organizations. Nor did France have to wait long for the nationalists' response to its declaration. Already angry at the arrest of a popular Corsican nationalist for Erignac's assassination, a banned separatist organization (the Corsican National Liberation Front) declared an end to its seven-month truce with Paris on July 18—less than two weeks after the defeat of the referendum. By then, four holiday homes of French nationals and a nightclub complex popular with the island's tourists had been *plastické*—that is, bombed with plastic explosives.

The violence has not subsequently abated, although there have been lulls in it—most notably between late 2003 and March 2005, when the island's main separatist group, the FLNC-Union of Combatants, adhered to a self-imposed ceasefire. Attacks on police stations and the villas of French nationals, and the occasional attack on tourist facilities, continue to mar the Corsican image of tranquil beaches and good food that tourist agencies advertise to sun-starved Northern Europeans. Much of the time these attacks have averaged three per week, have been spread across the island, and have been conducted almost always when the targets were empty. In the process, there has been an inevitable hardening of the uncompromising positions held by both the government in Paris (which cannot afford to look weak in the eyes of the continental French, many of whom continue to stereotype Corsicans alternately as lazy farmers or Italianesque thugs) and the separatist organizations on an island where most polls continue to show nearly 90 percent of the population identifying themselves as Corsicans (compared to fewer than 60 percent who think of themselves as French in any sense).[29]

Finally, even if a very substantial degree of fence-mending were to occur between the Corsicans, their nationalist spokesmen, and France's central government in Paris, there is only a modest likelihood that politically related violence will end on the island in the near future. One of the less savory by-products of the long struggle for some form of meaningful self-rule has been the splintering of the island's clandestine separatist organizations and their subsequent competition for the funds necessary to sustain their operations. When there were few of them, Corsicans generally could be counted upon to contribute much of their operating capital. Unfortunately, as the price of plastic explosives has increased on the world market and the thug element that is frequently attracted to terrorist organizations has infiltrated their ranks, several of Corsica's once-nationalist organizations have essentially become extortionists offering "protection services." For a fee, tourist agencies and hotel and café owners catering to tourists can be reasonably assured that their establishments will not be targeted by separatist groups (or at least by the separatist group offering the services). This seamy side of the nationalist movement in Corsica was exposed dramatically in the summer of 2004, when the French government arrested two veterans of Corsica's nationalist struggle (one of whom headed the pro-independence *Unione nationale* party in the Corsican Assembly) for using sports associations and other front organizations to raise money for the separatist cause—and for themselves.

The offering of such "protection services" and related extortion did not end with the court cases against these men—nor did political violence on Corsica, for whatever cause.

SPAIN

On March 22, 2006, the Basque paramilitary organization *Euzkadi Ta Askatasuna* (ETA) announced that it was unconditionally abandoning its long, terrorism-centered campaign to achieve an independent Basque state in the European Union.[30] If the cease-fire endures and a lasting peace emerges, it will mark the most significant change in Spain's political landscape since the 1975 demise of its long-term dictator, General Francisco Franco, and the subsequent creation of a democratic political system in Spain. Despite the fact that democratization entailed structuring a federal form of government in which most of Spain's Basques received a measure of political autonomy in return for their support for the new system, the Basques' often-violent struggle for independence had continued. Moreover, prior to the March 2006 pledge, more than 800 people had died at the ETA's hands over a forty-year period dating from the late 1960s, including some of the most prominent members of Spain's government in Madrid.[31]

BASQUE NATIONALISM AND SEPARATISM

The driving force behind Basque nationalism has been, and continues to be the Basques' sense of their uniqueness as a people. As perceptions go, theirs is unusually well founded.

Occupying a geographical homeland on opposite sides of the rugged Pyrenees mountains that separate Basque France (now administratively organized as the Department of the Atlantic Pyrenees) from the four historic Basque territories of Alava, Vizcaya, Guipuzcoa, and Navarre in Basque Spain,[32] the Basques are widely believed to be the oldest community in Europe and to have inhabited their mountain region since the Stone Age. Even more fundamentally, Europe's Basques possess a cultural, biological, and linguistic distinctiveness that separates them from the people who later settled the continent. Large numbers of Basques still speak a non-Indo-European language (Vasco) that linguists view as the oldest language in Europe, and unlike any other spoken there.[33] Then there is the blood evidence of their uniqueness. Unlike the solid majority of other Europeans, whose blood is Rh-positive, 85 percent of the Basques have the relatively rare blood type O that is Rh-negative.[34] Legends have been born from these linguistic and "geo-genetic" factors, including tales that trace the Basques to the survivors of the lost continent of Atlantis. To be sure, no evidence has ever bolstered that theory, but the sense of ethnic and national identity is not so much in the eye of the beholder as in the mind of the holder. The Basques of Spain have long seen themselves as unique, and thus entitled to the right to govern themselves.

State-Making and the Emergence of Modern Basque Nationalism

The first union of the Spanish Basque areas occurred in 1029—more than 800 years before the development of modern Basque national consciousness—when the King of Navarre, Sancho the Elder, acquired the Basque-occupied lands to the west of his kingdom (approximately the area of today's Basque Autonomous Community comprising Alava,

Vizcaya, and Guipuzcoa in contemporary Spain). Even before then, however, there had been agreements (*fueros*) between ruled and ruler that conferred on the Basques the right to a large degree of local self-rule. That system not only survived the area's union under Navarre rule, but it also continued largely unmodified from the mid-twelfth century into modern times.[35]

The union of 1029 lasted for more than 170 years, but beginning in 1200, Castilian incursions into the region began the process of fragmenting the Basque kingdom and bringing its components gradually under Castilian rule through a combination of conquest and dynastic marriage. For the most part, though, rule by Madrid was at arms length, and the Basques enjoyed a degree of autonomy. And when that autonomy was temporarily suspended, it was usually at a cost to Madrid—as in 1717, when the inclusion of the Basquelands in a common tariff policy with the rest of Spain led to a bloody revolt in Basque Spain and Madrid's revocation of the tariff policy for another century and a half.

It was not until the latter third of the nineteenth century, therefore, that the reestablishment of a common tariff system and Madrid's policies affecting life in the Basque provinces produced the first stirring of modern Basque nationalism and demands for autonomy. Also at issue was the Basques' feeling that Madrid was exploiting their homeland, one of Europe's earliest to industrialize and most prosperous areas by the late nineteenth century, for the well-being of Castilian Spain. Finally, there was the negative "us versus them" Basque reaction to the migration of other Spaniards into their region. In response to these developments, the titular father of contemporary Basque nationalism, Sabino Arana, founded the Basque Nationalist Party (PNV) in 1895 to defend Basque interests in the Castilian-dominated state.

The Rise of Basque Militancy: The Spanish Civil War and Life under Franco

There followed a forty-year struggle by the Basques to regain their lost right to autonomy, which reached its short-lived fruition only in 1936 when the First Basque Autonomy Statute was passed by the Madrid government on the eve of the Spanish Civil War. Unfortunately for the Basques, that war between fascist-leaning, conservative Catholic forces under Franco (abetted by Italy and Germany) and the Popular Front on the Republican side ended with Franco's success. Even before the war ended there were disastrous consequences for the Basques, who sided with the Republic. Perhaps the most notorious days of that war, which resulted in 750,000 deaths, occurred in the Basquelands on April 26, 1937, when the German Cordon Legion supporting Franco bombed the

Basque city of Gernika, causing an enormous loss of life. Two months later, when Bilbao fell, the war essentially ended for the Basques. It was two years later, however, when the war officially ended, that the full cost of being on the losing side fell upon the Basques. As Roland Vazquez, then of the Basque Study Center at the University of Nevada, summarized the situation in 2003, "Vizcaya and Guipuzo were declared 'traitor provinces.' Executions and property confiscation were rampant. The number of Basques in exile approached 150,000."[36]

Retribution did not end there. The display of Basque flags, the celebration of Basque holidays, and the public use of the Basque language and its teaching in schools were all forbidden. So, too, was the christening of babies with non-Castilian Spanish names. Basque nationalism, however, gradually grew as a result of the resentment fostered by the hardships imposed on the Basques and the suppression of their culture.

EUZKADI TA ASKATASUNA (ETA) TERRORISM

World War II completely overshadowed developments in Spain in general, and the fate of Spain's non-Castilian, Republic-supporting minorities in particular. When the war in Europe ended with the defeat of Germany's and Italy's fascist regimes, Basque nationalists read their defeat as an opportunity to lobby an anti-fascist West for its support in prying its lost autonomy away from the fascist-friendly regime in Madrid. That may have been a sound strategy in 1945, but then came the Cold War, and with it the United States' willingness to tolerate Franco's regime in return for air bases in Spain, and Spain's participation in NATO. By the late 1950s the complete failure of the nationalist diplomatic strategy was obvious, and Basque nationalists turned to other options. On July 11, 1959, the ETA (*Euzkadi Ta Askatasuna*, Basque Homeland and Freedom) was born when a group of young nationalists affiliated with the Basque Nationalist Party (PNV) broke away from that party to pursue Basque interests more aggressively.

At the time of its birth, the ETA was only one of numerous nationalist organizations functioning in Spain's Basquelands, including a network of clandestine Basque language schools for primary and secondary students, which substantially contributed to the cultural revival of Basque identity after World War II.[37] Yet from the moment of its birth, the ETA and its political arms have been at the heart of both the Basque nationalist movement in Spain and the European groups willing to employ political violence in quest of their goals. Assassination by a gunshot in the neck and by car bombs became the ETA's signature stock in trade, and although its operations were initially directed against Madrid's "occupying army" in the Basquelands themselves, it very quickly developed active cells in Madrid, Barcelona, and other major cities in non-Basque Spain. By the 1970s, in fact, some of its most notorious successes were occurring outside of its base. In turn, the ETA's growing terrorist activity resulted in additional repression of the Basque provinces by Madrid, which over the years included the torture of ETA suspects and—even in democratic Spain—the creation by Madrid of "dirty war" assassination squads to retaliate against ETA sympathizers and to hunt down ETA operatives.[38]

Post-Franco Spain and the Continuing Politics of Violence

The death of Franco on November 20, 1975, marked the end of a repressive regime and launched a constitution-drafting process that by 1979 had resulted in the creation of a federal parliamentary democracy in Spain, in which the Catalans, Galacians, and Basques were recognized as "historic regions" entitled to special treatment and receiving a measure of federal autonomy over their affairs. In the case of the Basques, the federalization process centered on creation of the Basque Autonomous Community (BAC) that included three of Spain's four Basque provinces.

Although most Basques at the time were not content with the initial transfer of federal autonomy they received, the creation of the BAC, complete with its own elected legislature, executive branch, and police force, substantially changed the political environment in which the ETA functioned. Violence no longer seemed essential to large numbers of Basques, or even a proper way to pursue additional autonomy. Acknowledging these changes, the ETA began periodically to offer cease-fires in return for the government in Madrid recognizing the sovereignty and right to self-determination of Spain's Basque people. In the process, the ETA itself split into separate factions, one militant and the other more moderate. Freed from the restraining influence of the moderate faction, the militants gradually grew more and more extremist in their activities. They offset the members they lost when the ETA divided by organizing a violence-prone youth group that subsequently engaged in such street-level activities as burning buses and throwing Molotov cocktails at select state targets.

Ironically, the 1978–89 years during which the Basque Autonomous Community consolidated its constitutional autonomy produced more politically-motivated murders (nearly 70 per year) than any decade during the ETA's struggle again Franco's regime.[39] This upsurge in part reflected the fact that after the initial grant of autonomy to the Basque

A video showing masked ETA terrorist group members declaring a permanent cease-fire to come into effect on March 24, 2006 in San Sebastian. © Javier Echezarreta/epa/Corbis.

areas and the earlier, 1976 offer of amnesty to ETA operatives, the government in Madrid abandoned further accommodation efforts. In fact, the number of ETA members in Spanish prisons grew substantially between late 1978 and the end of 1980. But the rise in political violence also reflected an internal debate between moderates and the lingering, pro-violence diehards within the ETA, which resulted in the split within the ETA and an intensification of the campaign of violence by its most militant splinter factions. As a result, the original ETA targets—public officials (most famously Spain's prime minister and Franco's designed heir, Admiral Luis Carrero Blanco, who was killed in Madrid in December 1973 by a bomb planted under his car) and members of the Spanish military and police—were expanded to include delegates to the Spanish Parliament and local city councils, journalists, businessmen, and teachers. In the wave of violence that stretched across the 1980s and into the 1990s, civilians including children were also targeted at random, and died, in ETA terrorist acts such as the 1979 bombing of the Madrid train station and airport on the same day and, a decade later, the bombing of a supermarket in Barcelona that left twenty-one dead and forty injured.[40]

The Prospects for a Lasting Peace

The ETA cease-fire declared in March 2006 was undone less than nine months later by a bomb detonated at the Madrid airport. An extremist ETA cell was quick to take credit for the action, which led to protests against the ETA throughout Spain and the government in Madrid declaring that, for its part, the war against the terrorists was not over. The government's official rhetoric aside, the bombing did not destroy the prospects for peace between Madrid and the ETA, but it did leave those prospects in doubt once again.

On the positive side of the ledger, several factors continue to work against a return to the very violent, final decades of the twentieth century. Generalized fatigue from violence, as in Northern Ireland, and even in some Basque areas an anger at the ETA's radical turn and continued terrorist activity long after the democratization process had taken root in Spain, continue to be the best reasons to believe that sustained campaigns of ETA violence will remain a thing of the past. Particularly alienating were the ETA's alleged effort in 1996 to assassinate Spain's widely popular head of state, King Juan Carlos, and its 1997 murder of Migel Angel Blanco. A counselor who was kidnapped in the Basquelands, Blanco was executed when the government of Spain refused to negotiate with the ETA on its demands, despite the protests of millions across the country urging his release. The border with France has long been closed to Basque extremists as the result of an agreement between Madrid and Paris and the French willingness to arrest and extradite ETA operatives found in France's Basque region. Consequently, ETA activities absolutely depend upon a logistical support network on their side of the border. That network has continued to dry up, all the more rapidly since the March 2004 terrorist bombing by al Qaeda operatives of commuter trains in Madrid, which left behind a general abhorrence of violent political methods throughout Spain. Even before that attack, however, the ETA had begun to cut back on its terrorist activity in the early years of the twenty-first century, in recognition of its weakened position and the growing distaste for its methods, even in Basque Spain.

Nor is it easy to see how the ETA might rebuild its support base, inasmuch as the vast majority of the Basques in Spain have no interest in either independence or the merger with Basque France to form a new state in the European Union, which was one of the ETA's founding goals. That, too, is a fact of political life in Spain in these early years of the new millennium, and it has been widely seen as the primary reason for fewer acts of political violence attributed to the ETA in the years prior to its announced "permanent cease-fire" in March 2006.[41]

The prospects for a permanent peace can also be enhanced considerably if, despite the isolated incidents involving diehard Basque extremists that are perhaps inevitable, Madrid is willing gradually to cede more financial and decision-making autonomy to the BAC. Madrid has thus far been willing to negotiate such issues with its Catalan region since the initial devolution of authority to that region during Spain's democratization process, but it has used the continuing violence in the Basque movement as a justification for not doing the same for its Basque region, on the grounds that it would reward extremism. With that extremism now narrowed to such a small cadre of rejectionists, more conciliatory moves by Madrid might not only further isolate those extremists, but might also contribute to putting an end to the violence that has made Spain one of Western Europe's widely recognized hot spots for half a century.

Until that future day, Spain's Basque problem clearly remains a thorny one, even if Basque terrorism now ranks a distant second to the fear that home-grown Islamic terrorism now inspires in Spain. Nevertheless, an ETA bomb was detonated at 9 a.m. at Madrid's international airport in the last days of 2006, approximately nine months after ETA spokesmen declared they were abandoning such tactics. That incident illustrates the point that at least some ETA members have yet to abandon their violent pursuit of Basque independence, and there are reasons to believe they will not do so soon.

Aside from the obvious fact that Madrid is not going to cede independence to its Basque lands—either under the threat of isolated violence or otherwise—the Basque problem persists at least in part because Madrid seems to lack a coherent game plan for accommodating mainstream Basque desires for more autonomy. ETA violence gives Madrid a convenient excuse to delay tackling that desire by saying that it will not negotiate with murderers, but even among the ETA's most ardent Basque critics, that excuse will eventually wear out. There is some hope that a truly lasting peace might be built by enacting for Basque Spain a statute similar to the one passed for Catalonia. As approved by the Catalan voters in a June 2006 referendum, that statute not only gave Spain's Catalans greater autonomy over their region's affairs, but it also recognized their status as a distinct nation.[42] Even if extended to the Basquelands, however, such a concession may no longer suffice to satisfy Basque aspirations. National identity remains stronger in the Basque region than in Catalonia, perhaps because the latter has been exposed to a host of cosmopolitan influences that have not affected the more remote Basque north, ever since Barcelona hosted the Olympics games and was subsequently anointed—deservedly so—by the European Union as a "European City." The Catalan language that was so pervasive on the radio and in the streets of Barcelona only a generation ago has significantly faded, at least in public, and the city's main street, the Rambla, now reverberates in English, French, and other tongues of the world. Meanwhile, Basque continues to be widely heard even in relatively urbane San Sebastian and Bilbao, and perceived slights and attacks on Basque nationalism are still met with large, if peaceful protests.[43] The BAC regional government's proposal to Madrid—that Spain allow the region to have its own courts and exist as a "free state" with a loose association with the rest of Spain—continues to be not only utterly unacceptable to the government of Spain, but also far removed from the much more limited concessions made to Catalan nationalism.[44]

Moreover, conciliatory moves of any sort by Madrid toward the Basque region are sure to be opposed by those groups throughout Spain who find it impossible to forgive the ETA for its prior crimes—groups such as Spain's Association of Victims of Terrorism, which condemned the ETA's declaration of a permanent cease-fire in March 2006 as a "new trick by the murderers to achieve their political objectives."[45] In a sense, that sentiment was also shared by some Basques, whose reaction to the ETA's March declaration did not so much involve jubilation as a continuing unease. There was a feeling that the violence that had gripped the Basque provinces for forty years would continue after a brief holiday, as had occurred in the case of so many of the conditional cease-fires declared by the ETA in the past.[46] And with the bombing of the Madrid airport, most people on all sides (Basques and non-Basques) seemed confirmed in that belief.

Finally, there is the danger that the ETA violence, like violence in Northern Ireland, may not end until the last terrorist who has devoted his or her life to the cause is exiled or in the grave, from natural or unnatural causes. They may be diminishing in number, but as long as they can plant a bomb they continue to have the ability to block or at least slow down a peace-building process, and without their cause after a lifetime of commitment to it, too often they have no other identity, and hence no reason to step aside and let peace have its proverbial chance. From this vantage point, it may be that the decrease in ETA violence from 2003 to the March declaration in 2006 was not so much a retreat by the ETA from its violent ways as it was a result of the increasing effectiveness of Spain's security forces in ferreting out its personnel and preempting its attacks. Those security forces and others in Western Europe have exercised greater vigilance since the 9/11 al Qaeda attacks on the United States, and even more since the 2004 attack on Madrid's railway commuters. In the same vein, the ETA's downplaying of violence during this period may be viewed more as a reflection of its leaders' recognition of the alienating effect of ETA extremism on the Basque community at large in the aftermath of those terrorist attacks. Or it may be that both forces were at work, but individually or in combination they did not end ETA violence, even during the 2004–06 period. Thus, the ETA's answer to the Spanish government's rejection of the autonomy plan being proposed by the BAC was to detonate a bomb in February 2005 in a Madrid office park, where King Juan Carlos was scheduled to appear. The blast injured nearly 50 people, and three months later another bomb exploded during rush hour in Madrid, with even greater injuries.[47] Then came the March declaration of nonviolence, perhaps by the ETA's principal leaders, followed by the Madrid airport bombing, perhaps the work of disgruntled ETA diehard extremists whose principal target was the peace process.

THE UNITED KINGDOM OF GREAT BRITAIN AND NORTHERN IRELAND

GREAT BRITAIN: RACIAL UNREST AND HOMEGROWN TERRORISM

The July 7, 2005, attack on London's mass transit system, which claimed 56 lives and injured approximately 700, was by no means London's introduction to the world of terrorism. Between 1980 and 2000, the Irish Republican Army was responsible for at least a dozen different terrorist incidents in London, as well as occasionally lethal attacks on civilians elsewhere in Britain. Nor was the London attack the most deadly suffered to date by Western European democracies at the hands of Muslim extremists. The previous year's attack on commuter

A view of the bus destroyed by a bomb in Woburn Place, London. Over 50 were killed and 700 injured during the morning rush hour. © Peter Macdiarmid/epa/Corbis.

trains in Madrid claimed nearly four times as many lives. Yet far more than the Madrid attack, or the brewing tension between Europe's Muslim communities and their hosts in France and elsewhere in the West, the July 7 attack and the failed effort six days later to repeat the same type of bombing of London's buses and subway system signaled a new threat to British society. Unlike the Madrid bombers, most of those responsible for the July 7 and subsequent efforts to kill civilians in London were home-grown fundamentalist Muslim terrorists, either born and raised in Britain or immigrant residents. They were not foreign nationals or international operatives deployed into a Western state to commit terrorist acts.[48]

In Britain, as on the Continent, violence and the prospect of political violence involving immigrant communities has its roots in the unstructured, post–World War II buildup in Western Europe of large numbers of foreign workers, immigrants, refugees, and asylum seekers drawn from areas culturally remote from the secularized Western states in which they find themselves today.

The Development of the Race Issue in Britain

The gradual buildup of these communities' presence began with the liquidation of Britain's overseas empire in the early years after World War II, beginning with the 1947 partition of the Indian subcontinent into India and Pakistan upon Britain's departure and the granting of independence to Ceylon (now Sri Lanka) that same year. At the end of empire, former subjects of British rule took advantage of their citizenship in the British Commonwealth (a loose association of former colonies) to seek residency and economic opportunity in the former mother country. The numbers mounted quickly, from the 2,000 new Commonwealth immigrants who arrived in Britain in 1953 to an average of 40,000 per year entering the United Kingdom between 1955 and 1960. By the end of that decade, approximately 800,000 had arrived, with most of the newer arrivals taking menial jobs.[49] In the long term they would permanently alter the shape of British society in a multicultural direction. In the short term, their large-scale arrival was neither planned nor expected, and even after they began to grow into a significant ethnic minority in Britain, little systematic thought went into integrating them into their new country. Rather, it was assumed that many of the early arrivals were familiar with English and would assimilate into the Britain that was receiving them.

In the early years this assumption did not seem so terribly naive, inasmuch as some of the first to arrive were professionals who merged relatively seamlessly into British society as doctors and other medical personnel in the National Health Plan that had been created in postwar Britain, and into other middle-class positions in the British economy. As their number grew, though, they found their employment and living arrangements in a working-class Britain much less inclined to accept their cultural differences. Still, their arrival did not become a significant political issue until the late 1950s, when the end of Britain's postwar economic boom coincided with the still-rising tide of immigration. At that point the immigrants—despite their willingness to accept the most menial of jobs—began to be seen as job competitors in a shrinking working-class job market. The result was a significant upsurge in racial tension during the late 1950s and the 1960s, a decade before the era of economic stagflation following the oil crises of 1973 and 1979 led to the intensification of the foreign worker/immigrant issue on the European continent.

By the 1970s the race issue had penetrated into mainstream British politics, led by the burning rhetoric of Enoch Powell, a well-known member of the Conservative Party who is widely credited with making racism respectable in Britain during the late 1960s and early 1970s. He later came to share that distinction with Margaret Thatcher, who frequently integrated references to the unique nature of the British people and other code words for white Britain into her speeches during the 1979 general election campaign that led to her first term as prime minister. By then, the laws under which immigrants could enter Britain had already been substantially narrowed, much as the politicizing of the foreign worker issue on the European continent had led to a spate of legislation designed to close the door to further legal influxes of foreign workers.

Race, the Immigration Issue, and British Exceptionalism

The parallels between the development of the race/"foreigner" issue in Britain and elsewhere in Europe can be pushed too far. When the end of the colonial era began, Britain possessed a global empire. Consequently, those migrating to Britain at the outset came from widely dispersed areas, unlike immigrants arriving in countries on the Continent. There, the bulk of the foreign workers in each country arrived initially from, and continue to be largely drawn from specific areas—North Africa supplying France, for example, and Turkey sending foreign workers to Germany. To be sure, most of Britain's initial post–World War II immigrants in general, and its Muslim arrivals in particular, came from the Indian subcontinent. The wave of immigrants who entered Britain from 1947 to 1960, however, also contained large numbers from the West Indies and Sub-Saharan Africa.[50] Only much later did Britain's Muslim population receive an additional boost from those arriving from East Africa, often as asylum seekers and refugees. The communities have all become large, and in the process there has been strife as often between these immigrant communities as between Britain's immigrants and its native born.

In addition, those entering Britain from its former empire arrived earlier, in most instances, than the foreign workers recruited by France, Germany, and other continental countries after World War II. Hence, they have had a longer history in the land to which they migrated than Europe's "foreigner" communities have had. Unfortunately, it is often a history marred by overt discrimination against them and racial riots involving them. That history now spans nearly half a century, from the fighting in Nottingham and the Notting Hill district of London in August 1958, which involved approximately 1,500 black and white rioters and left 8 injured; to the 1995 riots in Brixton ignited by the death at police hands of a black burglary suspect; to the riots in Oldham in 2001, which started with a fight between a white and an Asian teenager and ended with Asian youths turning on the police. Also dotting that history are the acts of racial hatred directed at immigrant communities, ranging from the "Pak-bashing" of the 1970s and early 1980s (when young British thugs [the "teddy boys"] in areas such as Manchester and Liverpool would tire of snapping antennae off premium cars and would head to the docks and factory areas to beat up Asian workers), to fire-bombings, attempted murder, and murder by the time of the 2005 bombing attacks on London. There was a pronounced upward trend in the frequency and gravity of race-based and/or faith-based hate crimes following the September 11 attack by al Qaeda terrorists on the United States. As a result of such acts of violence, Britain's immigrants in general, and especially its Muslim communities, have tended to self-segregate themselves from broader British society in their search for personal security and acceptance.

Finally, Britain's Muslim and other immigrant communities have been having children in Britain for generations, making many of those still seen as "foreigners" and "immigrants" in the eyes of the Enoch Powells and the followers of the anti-immigrant British National Party full-fledged British citizens by birth. They are thus, even in the heightened security-conscious days of the early twenty-first century, immune from deportation, unlike those not yet naturalized under British law or holding only foreign worker visas on the Continent. It is a legal fact of British life foreseen by Enoch Powell in his much-publicized 1968 "River of Blood" speech, in which he urged his countrymen to close the gates to immigrants before it became too late to prevent Britain from becoming the multicultural society that he feared, and which it has now become— and which has been generally accepted, albeit with some unease, by the majority in contemporary Britain.[51]

By the time of Powell's call to arms, the immigrant issue and the outbreaks of periodic violence associated with it were already producing responses in Britain beyond the nationality laws that were crafted to halt the further influx of Commonwealth citizens. To protect the immigrant communities, anti-discrimination statutes were being placed into effect by the 1960s, although they usually lacked strong courtroom enforcement. Likewise, by the early 1970s attention was at last being given to the impact of immigration on British society and, later, to the status of immigrants in Britain—most notably with the passage in 1976 of a widely acclaimed Race Relations Act that recognized the multicultural nature of the country and the right of each community to preserve its distinctive culture. Unfortunately, considering the discrimination many of the immigrants have felt and the competition for jobs and housing that they have had to face from members of other immigrant communities, by the end of the twentieth century the act already appeared to have contributed—on balance—more to the growth of communal separateness and intracommunal cohesion, interethnic tensions, and conflict in Britain than to the racial harmony it was meant to produce.

That picture has become even more stark in subsequent years, as the "9/11" factor has worked its way into British outlooks and politics, separating even more those people of Muslim identity from the other immigrant communities and the native British.

An "Israelization" of British Life?

By the time of the July attacks on London's mass transit system, Britain's immigrant communities constituted approximately 6 percent of the country's population and were its fastest-growing component. More than one out of three of that 6 percent—between 1.5 and 2 million people—were Muslims, overwhelmingly concentrated in England.[52] More importantly, by that point the feelings of separateness and alienation affecting British Muslims had become so great that a survey taken by *The Daily Telegraph* found that one out of four sympathized with those committing the attacks, and 56 percent said that they understood and at least in part could relate to the motives they ascribed to the attackers (including calling attention to discrimination and the denigration of Islam in Britain).[53]

The London attacks thus signaled a sharp shift away from the earlier riots involving working-class members of immigrant and native British societies and toward a new era of potential terrorism pitting British-born Muslims against the country of their birth. As later revelations indicated, however, Britain had already been under attack by home-grown radical Muslims for years prior to the July assaults on

London commuters. According to London's mayor, Ken Livingstone, terrorists had tried to attack London on eight occasions between September 11, 2001, and July 7, 2005.[54] To these attempts can be added the discovery of myriad terrorist plots by British-born Muslims to attack nightclubs, trains, and other targets, including one plot to assemble and detonate a "dirty bomb" (conventional explosives wrapped in radioactive materials), as well as efforts to use England as a launching pad for elaborate attacks on U.S. airlines.[55] It is consequently little wonder that after the 2005 London transit attacks some Britons were openly worrying about an "Israelization" of British life—that is, a "steady stream of bus, café, grocery, mail and street bombings."[56] With the announcement of each new plot unearthed, each radical arrested, and each danger averted, that anti-immigrant sentiment has continued to grow, along with anxieties in the native-born and immigrant communities about their future in the country.

Leaning against the Wind: The Struggle to Regain Normalcy

The attacks by radical, home-grown terrorists on British targets have been broadly attributed to three factors. First, there is the alienation of and growing strength of radical Islam within Britain's immigrant underclasses. Second, the radical messages of clerics and other hate-mongering elements within the Muslim community in Britain and beyond, via the Internet, incite violence even as they make British Muslims feel a part of the struggle against Western culture and imperialism.[57] Third, there is resentment of Britain's collaboration with the United States in the overthrow of Saddam Hussein's regime in Iraq in 2003, and the subsequent occupation of Iraq. Of the three, the most toxic and least treatable is the first, and it is not likely to be neutralized by the Blair government's steps since July 2005 to enact tough anti-terrorist laws, incarcerate or expel Islamic radicals, open a broader dialogue with British Muslims, and introduce citizenship exams. As a new part of the British naturalization process, these citizenship exams establish a "Britishness" test designed to ensure that future citizens will be deeply steeped in British culture, by including questions involving the queen's ceremonial duties, the rituals of Boxing Day, and the information required on a dog's collar in Britain. Even without leaders inciting hatred, either out of a sincere belief in the corrupt ways of the West or for their personal advantage—a problem that is unlikely to evaporate, even with an aggressive deportation policy aimed at those leaders—the sense of alienation in some quarters of Britain's "foreign" population may have already reached irreversible levels. Unlike in the United States, where the first response of friends and family upon learning of a horror perpetrated by some individual is usually to express shock ("He was always such a polite young man . . ."), the neighbors of those involved in the July bombings in London expressed little surprise, given the widespread anger among young people at the discrimination they have experienced, the interethnic tensions among the immigrant communities, and the poverty that is a part of their daily lives.

Even Britain's withdrawal from Iraq is unlikely to quell that anger, as long as Britain continues to foil British-born plots to attack the United States and its citizens. Moreover, given the high level of alienation, even daily irritants can nurture existing animosities. And for those predisposed to look for them, such irritants are not hard to find. Britain, like many countries in Western Europe, has banned the wearing of the veil by Muslim women in public schools. A bitter debate ensued when a teaching assistant refused to remove her veil in the presence of men, and public officials argued for her firing. Muslim schools, meanwhile, have been raided in search of evidence of possible terrorist activity, and Muslims maintaining radical Websites can be deported. Elsewhere, the mosques of radical fundamentalist clerics are closed, but British juries have refused to find the leaders of the anti-immigrant British National Front guilty of inciting racial hatred. Those leaders referred to Islam as a "wicked, vicious faith," and the British government has refused to prosecute the officers who shot and killed an unarmed Brazilian immigrant they mistakenly identified as a suicide bomber in the aftermath of the London bombings.[58]

Then there is the uneasy feeling of native Britons in regard to the still-changing face of Britain in an age of Muslim extremism. An August 2005 survey found that 62 percent of all respondents and 87 percent of British Muslims have favorable views of the country's multicultural character, but it also found that more than half (54 percent) agreed that "parts of the country don't feel like Britain any more because of immigration."[59] Meanwhile, those within the "foreign" population who have moved to the more rural areas of England have not only failed to escape racism, but have also found that they are three to four times more likely to experience "overt racism" than those dwelling in the more heavily urban and cosmopolitan parts of the country.[60] Nor are the minorities without their own discriminatory tendencies. Within the immigrant communities, those who came to work in Britain reportedly harbor their own anti-immigrant sentiments against the asylum seekers who came as refugees.[61]

None of this is to say that England is about to become Europe's Israel. There is far more alarmism than analysis being expressed by those who worry about the coming Israelization of life in Britain. Israel is a country surrounded by enemies, many of whom have grown up and become bitter living on land that Israel took from Egypt and Jordan in a 1967 war. Britain is an island surrounded by water, whose Muslims and other immigrants chose voluntarily to enter after Britain peacefully withdrew from their native lands and those of their parents. Still, Britain is a country with a Muslim community that exhibits budding frustrations, increasing radicalism, and a demonstrated willingness by some of its members to undertake acts of terrorism—a nation with a history of white-black violence and increasing instances of what the British now refer to as "black-on-black" violence between, for example, West Indians and Somalis. Accordingly, Britain is apt to remain a hot spot of sporadic, but potentially serious political violence for at least the immediate future.

NORTHERN IRELAND: PARTITION OR LONDON RULE?

It has often been said that the root of Britain's problems in Ireland was its inability to decide whether that island was the British political system's most remote component or its nearest colony. Unlike Wales, which fell under England's rule during approximately the same centuries-long period, but which was gradually integrated economically, socially (with some English disdain for its lower-class ways), and politically into the United Kingdom, Ireland was settled before it was conquered. Consequently, for most of its history with London it was ruled, rather than integrated into the broader political process of which it was an important component—as well as a perennial trouble spot. Even when politically integrated with Great Britain (i.e., England, Scotland, and Wales on the central island) by the Act of Union of 1801, which gave birth to the United Kingdom of Great Britain and Ireland and provided Ireland with representation in Parliament, the large Catholic majority in Ireland remained disenfranchised, inasmuch as Catholics were still prohibited from holding seats in Parliament at the time of the Act of Union.

More than two centuries have now passed since Ireland and Great Britain were politically united, and three quarters of a century have elapsed since the tensions in that relationship led to the Anglo-Irish Civil War that separated most of Ireland from Britain in the 1920s. Six counties of Northern Ireland, known as Ulster, were heavily settled by Protestant immigrants from Britain and chose to remain a part of the United Kingdom when Ireland was partitioned. In today's United Kingdom, "Ireland" continues to be very much a problematic issue on Parliament's agenda, despite considerable international efforts to assist

London in managing it. To be sure, much progress has been made in normalizing life in Ulster, but what the British have long called "The Troubles" still linger there. Moreover, as long as there are diehard rejectionists in the Catholic camp who are willing to kill in the name of reunification with Ireland, and their equally violent counterparts in the Protestant-Unionist camp who refuse to share power with Ulster's Catholic minority, Northern Ireland will likely remain a hot spot in the United Kingdom. And although they are aging groups, and the temperature of Ulster politics *is* gradually cooling, they remain obstacles to consolidating the peace process in Northern Ireland fully, and they negatively affect the security of life in that region to a degree quite disproportionate to their number.

Ireland as Empire

The "Irish problem" has been a fixture of British politics, in one form or another, for a hundred years, but its roots stretch much further into the past—to the Norman conquest of Ireland, which was complete by 1171. For our purposes, however, its origins can best be dated from 1534. It was then that England's King Henry VIII simultaneously (1) broke the bond between the British monarchy and the Catholic Church and declared the Anglican Church to be the official church of all of his realm—including an Ireland which by then had been devoutly Catholic for more than a thousand years—and (2) asserted a regal claim over the lands of Ireland, which entitled him to distribute them as he saw fit.[62] By the century's end, a plantation system controlled by an Anglo-Protestant nobility was rapidly being established in Ireland, displacing the Irish landholders and breeding local resentment.

Next came Britain's colonization of Ireland, which was expanded following Britain's interim rule by Oliver Cromwell and a series of Anglo-Saxon/Protestant military victories over the indigenous, ethnically Celtic, religiously Catholic people of Ireland during the seventeenth century. The capstone events were the decisive Battle of the Boyne in 1690, when the English defeated Ireland's last Catholic king and took full control of the island, and the subsequent Treaty of Limerick, in which James II formally surrendered to William II (of Orange). In short order the Irish aristocrats who had supported James II were stripped of their estates and titles. In a land where historical memories run deep, the Battle of the Boyne's outcome is still discussed in Irish pubs as though it were last week's rugby football contest, and its annual celebration by militant Protestant organizations such as Ulster's Orange Order still frequently results in unruly demonstrations, and sometimes bloodshed.

Colonizing and Controlling Ireland

Long before the Battle of the Boyne, the island's early contact with British traders, the creation of English outposts along its eastern coastline that began during the Middle Ages, and especially the growing size of the English presence in Ireland during the sixteenth century resulted in conflict between the indigenous Celtic Irish and the English interlopers. During the early seventeenth century, rebellions in isolated areas became more frequent. Although they were usually quickly quelled, their growing tenacity convinced Oliver Cromwell in the middle of the seventeenth century that Ireland first needed a strong taste of coercive control, and that Britain then needed to colonize Ireland more thoroughly in order to secure its hold over the island. Cromwell himself saw to the coercive control. It is estimated that his army killed, at the very least, tens of thousands of Irish Catholics in the name of Protestantism during the 1640s, when he also put a good number of Catholic churches in Ireland *and* Britain to the torch. Cromwell's successors followed his advice in regard to colonizing Ireland. As the seventeenth century came to a close, a steady stream of settlers from Great Britain were establishing roots in Ireland, with London's encouragement.

Many of these settlers were English, but from the early seventeenth century onward, the majority of those arriving in Ireland came from Scotland, a Protestant land whose immigrants were useful and loyal colonists for Ireland. In religious faith, however, they were nonconformists (that is, Presbyterians rather than worshipers in the official Church of England). As a means of easing interfaith tensions between England and Scotland, which were by then joined under a common king, the Scots were encouraged to migrate. They did so, altering Ireland's geopolitical circumstances and setting the stage for a conflict that continues in some form to this day.

The trek of their migration from western Scotland southward landed them in Ireland's northeastern quadrant, which is today's Northern Ireland, or Ulster. There, and there alone, the Protestant settlers became the majority of the regional population. In the remainder of Ireland the indigenous Celts, who were Catholics, accounted for more than 95 percent of the population. Sensitive to their minority status, the Protestants passed harsh laws to protect the political control of the island that they had won on the battlefield. Beginning with the Penal Codes, passed in 1695 in the immediate aftermath of Britain's victory in the Battle of the Boyne, laws were enacted that required village priests to register their parish or be branded. Other laws forbade Catholics from owning guns, receiving a foreign education, or marrying Protestants. Eventually the Gaelic culture was attacked through laws forbidding a Catholic education and mandating the teaching of English. Thus, although the colonial relationship between Britain and

Ireland officially ended in 1800 with the Act of Union, a semicolonial relationship between occupier and occupied continued throughout the nineteenth century. Not surprisingly, when Catholics were allowed to hold seats in Parliament, Irish representatives were soon demanding greater Irish control over Irish affairs—a demand that intensified after the Great Potato Famine of 1844–48 almost halved Ireland's population and nearly obliterated the Gaelic culture that had managed to survive despite the British laws affecting it.[63] The numerical totals were staggering. One and a half million Irish fled their land and emigrated, most to the United States. Another million starved to death in Ireland. The southern, overwhelmingly Catholic region, with its agrarian economy, was especially devastated. Ulster, with its linen and ship building industries, was less affected—a situation that only intensified the growing animosity between the Catholic peasants in the south and their British conquerors, landlords, and rulers.[64]

To the island's Protestant minority at the beginning of the twentieth century, the idea of Irish Home Rule—that is, autonomous lawmaking ability in assigned areas—was anathema. It would have meant surrendering political control to those whom they had been exploiting and oppressing for more than a century, and the idea of being on the losing side of a democratic, majority-rule lawmaking process had zero appeal. Accordingly, the late nineteenth century witnessed not only the flowering of a significant home rule movement in Ireland but also—a sign of things to come—the growth of communal strife between the island's two communities, most frequently taking the form of guerrilla-style attacks by Irish nationalists on the countryside estates of the island's British landlords ("the plantation wars"). The indigenous "Catholics" demanded a local parliament responsive to the will of Ireland's majority—that is, themselves. The imported "Protestant" minority—with some timely encouragement from the British Conservative Party, which was implacably opposed to home rule—organized itself to fight, if necessary, to preserve the existing system of direct rule by London.[65]

What emerged in Ireland and at least somewhat continues to define Ulster politics today was not, as often popularly described by the U.S. press, a "sectarian" conflict based purely on religion. It was a protracted communal conflict between two groups of people separated by multiple, reinforcing fractures in their society. The conflict was defined by the desire of one group—the Protestant Ulstermen—to remain a part of the United Kingdom, and the desire of the other—the Irish Catholic Nationalists—to achieve independence from British rule. By the dawn of the twentieth century, both communities had developed their own paramilitary organizations, as well as mainstream political parties and spokesmen committed to their respective goals. The most famous paramilitary groups were the Irish Republican Brotherhood (founded in 1858, the predecessor of the Irish Republican Army), which had already been fighting for Irish independence by that time, and the Orange Order, a militant Protestant organization that was founded in Ulster in 1795, committed to Protestant rule of Ireland, and named after William II of Orange.

After the Irish Republican Brotherhood's Fenian Uprising was quickly crushed in 1867, Irish nationalists began a prolonged and repeatedly frustrated campaign to acquire home rule by parliamentary means. That effort, which resulted in Ulster's Protestants uniting behind a militant campaign to prevent Ireland from achieving home rule, by violence if necessary, was interrupted by World War I.[66] After the war ended, and with home rule still unlikely, the quest for Irish autonomy became a military struggle. Fueling the intensity of that struggle was a mid-war event in Dublin—the Easter Rising of April 24–29, 1916—when Irish nationalists staged an insurrection and proclaimed Ireland's independence, expecting German aid to secure it. Until that moment, the British had been generally careful to deny the IRA martyrs whose death for Ireland could be used to mobilize the Catholic masses. Nationalist leaders who were captured and sentenced to death for treason were invariably not executed but exiled—upon pain of death should they return to Ireland—to either North America or Australia, where many of them used their political talents to prosper. The Easter Rising, staged at the moment when Britain's sons were dying for the United Kingdom in Europe's World War I trenches, was seen as unforgivable. Thus, although the uprising was quickly ended when British warships shelled Dublin, its architects were tried and executed. Many were in their mid-teens, and another was unable to walk and had to be tied to a chair for his execution by firing squad. With their deaths, home rule lost its appeal, and an uprising that originally had little support became a rallying point for Irish nationalism and a trigger for the battle for a free Ireland. Consequently, almost as soon as World War I ended the largely guerrilla-style Anglo-Irish War for Ireland's independence (1918 to 1921) began.

From Partition to London Rule: The Return of Political Violence

Partition: Relocating the "Irish Problem"

Faced with a mass movement demanding independence in most of Ireland and violent opposition to an independent Ireland in heavily (two-thirds) Protestant Ulster, the government in London split the difference—and Ireland—in 1922. The six northeastern counties (Ulster) were separated from the remainder of the island, which became known as the Irish Free State (now the Republic of Ireland) and was set on the path toward full independence. Ulster (also known as Northern Ireland) received an elected assembly of its own and special autonomy status inside the United Kingdom, which the Protestant Unionist (or

Loyalist) majority was quick to use to protect its privileges in the region, with little concern for the rights of Ulster's Catholic minority. Catholics remained at the lower end of the socioeconomic ladder in Northern Ireland, received their public education at inferior schools, and had to wait longer for less-desirable public housing than their Protestant counterparts. Even in those local areas where Northern Ireland's Catholics constituted a majority, local districts were normally gerry-mandered in such a way as to prevent the Catholics from controlling local districts.

Consequently, partition did not end Britain's "Irish Problem"—it only moved the center of the struggle between Catholics and Protestants to Ulster, where for the next half century separate school systems, separate social and political organizations, and separate socialization processes at mother's knee reinforced the divisions between the region's one-third Catholic minority and two-thirds Protestant majority. Nevertheless, the half-century following partition was generally quiet in Ulster. In fact, a call to arms by IRA operatives as late as 1962 fell largely on deaf ears within the minority population. The Ulster Catholics continued to express a collective desire for merger with the Republic of Ireland, but they eschewed violence as a means of achieving it—perhaps because of lingering memories of the violence that preceded partition.

In the 1960s, however, the political culture and political life in Ireland began to shift. Inspired by the increasingly successful civil rights movement of African Americans in the United States, Northern Ireland's Catholics launched a civil rights movement of their own. Peaceful demonstrations were held during 1968 and 1969, in which the Catholics demanded such civil rights objectives as access to better schools, control over local governments in Catholic majority areas, and an end to the discrimination they faced in obtaining employment and public housing. Then, when the regional government of Ian Faulkner's Ulster Unionist Party initially seemed inclined to accom-modate many of these demands, the result was a backlash in the Protestant community. Counter-demonstrations were organized by working-class Protestants opposed to entertaining any of the Catholics' demands. There was demagogue rhetoric from local Protestant politicians such as Ian Paisley, and sometimes violent clashes between Catholic and Protestant demonstrators in the streets. Faulkner was defeated in his bid for reelection, and the adamantly uncompromising Ulster Ultra Unionist Party rose to power.

By the end of the decade, the Catholics were increasingly turning to militant organizations such as the IRA to represent their interests, and the paramilitary Ulster Volunteer Force (UVF) had reconstituted itself within the Protestant communities. The fisticuff confrontations in the streets between Catholics and Protestants had been replaced by tit-for-tat killings, in which the death of a Protestant at Catholic hands was quickly followed by the death of a Catholic at the hands of Protestant extremists, and vice versa. No longer able to ignore Ulster's drift into chaos under the Protestant-dominated home rule government it had acquired at partition, London in 1969 deployed British troops in the region to restore order and keep the peace. Three years later the region's civilian government was suspended, and Northern Ireland fell under the direct rule of the United Kingdom's government in London.

London Rule: "The Troubles" Continue

The dispatching of British troops to Northern Ireland in 1969 was initially greeted with relief by both the Protestant and Catholic communities. The Protestants saw the troops as arriving to strengthen Ulster's membership in the United Kingdom, whereas the Catholics saw them as a source of protection from the Protestant community in general, and from the Ulster police force in particular. Unfortunately, in the crucial years between 1970 and 1972, British troops became identified with "the other side" by both Protestants and Catholics, and their ability to function as peacekeepers while maintaining their personal safety was severely compromised.

Problems developed when the troops were used to enforce *regional* laws. Because these laws were enacted by the Protestant-dominated Ulster assembly, their enforcement by the British troops resulted in Ulster's Catholic-nationalist community gradually associating the troops with Ulster's Protestant-unionist majority. The process began in July 1970, when troops began to enforce an unpopular curfew in Belfast, and it gathered momentum thereafter, rapidly accelerating after the often-indiscriminate roundup of IRA leaders throughout the region in August 1971. As a consequence, even before the "Bloody Sunday" episode of January 1972, when British troops fired into a crowd at Derry ("Londonderry" on Protestant maps) and killed fourteen peacefully demonstrating Catholic civilians, British troops had become targets for IRA assassins. They remained so for at least the next twenty years, as the Provisional IRA (the IRA's extremist wing) shifted its tactics from "enforcement terrorism"—that is, terrorist operations aimed at Catholics collaborating with the Protestant enemy—to "agitational terrorism" aimed at assassinating British and Protestant Ulster politicians, police, and military personnel.[67] The campaign began on another Bloody Sunday, this time in July 1972, when the IRA detonated more than twenty bombs in Belfast's city center. Meanwhile, the suspension of Ulster's civilian government in March 1972 had alienated Britain's forces from the region's Protestant majority as well, especially when it became clear to the Protestants that the restoration of civilian rule would occur only within the framework of the bi-communal power-sharing arrangement proposed by London in the early 1970s. The proposal had died twice between 1972 and 1974 when Protestants refused to participate in the elected Assembly and the Protestant working class staged a general strike in opposition to power sharing. By the time London signed the Anglo-Irish Treaty of 1985, which conferred on the Republic of Ireland a recognized right to be part of the negotiating process involving the future of politics in Ulster, Protestant alienation from London's directives was almost complete, and the conflict in Ulster had become defined by the strife between Catholic and Protestant paramilitary forces.[68]

Pacifying Ulster and the Search for Peace

In 1974 London abandoned its efforts to restore civilian government in Northern Ireland and placed the region under the rule of a cabinet-level member of the British government. Ten tumultuous years of paramilitary activity followed, including bombings and killings that stretched from Northern Ireland to England itself and which were almost equally the work of extremists in both the Catholic and Protestant communities. Meanwhile, IRA prisoners engaged in hunger strikes to protest their incarceration and Britain's unwillingness to accede to the IRA's nationalist demand that the two Irelands be rejoined under Dublin rule. Eventually, ten inmates would die in these protests.

In the early 1980s, Prime Minister Margaret Thatcher's conservative government launched a new approach to ending the impasse between the two communities and trying to lower the level of violence in Ulster. To allay the fears of Ulster's Catholics, Thatcher negotiated an agreement with the Republic of Ireland (the Anglo-Irish Agreement) under which the Republic would guarantee the minority's rights in any governing arrangement that might be fashioned for the province. Still, progress was slow between the 1985 agreement and the Good Friday Agreement of 1998, which established the basis for subsequent government-building in Northern Ireland, despite the on again-off again cease fires declared by various Catholic and Protestant paramilitary organizations. The longest of these stretched from 1994 to 1996, when frustration with the absence of progress at the negotiating table led the IRA to resume its terrorist activities with a bombing attack in London's Canary Wharf district.

The British Labour Party's return to power at Westminster in the 1990s played a major role in restarting the peace-making process, but outsiders also played an important role. The U.S. president, Bill Clinton, personally visited Ireland on a peace-making mission and subsequently permitted the president of Sinn Féin, Gerry Adams, to enter the United States, while urging Protestant leaders in Ulster to include Sinn Féin—the IRA's political wing—in the negotiating process. Clinton also appointed former senator

George Mitchell as his representative in the on-going talks to stabilize politics in Ulster. Mitchell later played an important role, both in the launching of the multi-party peace talks that led to the Good Friday Agreement and in the subsequent creation of an international Independent Monitoring Commission. The commission was charged with overseeing the decommissioning and disarmament process involving the Catholic and Protestant militias in Ulster, and with monitoring terrorist activity in the region during its transition back to civilian rule.

The centerpiece of that transition was the Good Friday Agreement, in which the leaders of the major parties involved in the Northern Ireland conflict accepted a broad, comprehensive plan for restoring civilian rule in Ulster. The plan took the form of an elected legislative assembly and a fourteen-member executive body based on power-sharing formulae. Although approved by large majorities (85 percent overall) in referendums held in the Republic of Ireland and in Ulster, the implementation of the Agreement stalled almost immediately. For years, the central issues revolved around (1) the presence of certain parties in the Assembly, especially Sinn Féin, the Assembly's second largest party, (2) the decommissioning requirement, and (3) Northern Ireland's continuing communal violence, which was largely the product of actions by the extremists in both camps who opposed the Good Friday Agreement. The British Parliament, pursuant to the Agreement, formally transferred power to Ulster's new regional institutions in December 1999, but for years it was impossible to form a civilian government in Northern Ireland because the largest party in the elected Assembly, the Ulster Unionist Party (UUP), refused to cooperate with the Catholic minority throughout the Assembly's term in office, ostensibly in protest of the IRA's delay in turning in its arms and decommissioning its units.

Meanwhile, violence continued in a province still policed by the British peacekeeping forces more than thirty years after their arrival. Official figures place the number killed by fire bombs, pipe bombs, assassinations, and tit-for-tat killings at approximately 3,900 in Ulster between 1969 and 2000, with another 20,000 injured and as much as 80 percent of the province's population affected by the violence, in some areas.[69] The actual numbers may be slightly lower, because these figures probably include family feud and grudge killings that had little to do with the motivations of the Catholic Nationalist and Protestant Union Loyalist activists, but were made to appear to be part of that political violence. Moreover, to Americans jaded by the homicide rates of many American cities of half a million or more, even the 3,900 death figure may not seem very high for a thirty-year period in a region of more than 1.5 million people. Baltimore, for example, averages approximately 300 homicides per year—a rate that will result in more than 9,000 homicide deaths over a thirty-year period, if unchecked. *But*—and this is an

The peace line separating the Protestant and Catholic communities on the west side of Belfast remains a part of Ulster's political fabric. Courtesy of Martin Melaugh. Copyright CAIN (cain.ulst.ac.uk).

important exception—in the U.S. cities most deaths are localized in drug-infested areas that are identifiable and, for most urban residents, avoidable. Northern Ireland's homicides were not. Living in Northern Ireland meant that violence might find you at any time, on any bus, or in any pub. Life went on, but tension was always a large part of it.

Political Violence and Contemporary Ulster

The inclusion of Gerry Adams in the peace process, and the pressure subsequently placed on him to contribute to it, began to pay important dividends on April 7, 2005, when he urged his IRA paramilitary supporters to end their violent resistance to implementation of the Good Friday Agreement. A month later the leadership of the IRA assented and agreed to disarm. A year later, the impasse over creating a civilian, elected executive in Northern Ireland was also overcome, in part because of Adams' action when Protestant hardliner Ian Paisley dropped his objection to the participation of Sinn Féin in the government and a power-sharing executive composed of the major parties of both the Protestant and Catholic communities finally came into being. Hence, the good news is that the violence in Ulster, which was already falling in the early years of the twenty-first century, has an excellent likelihood of continuing to decrease. It is very good news indeed for those who have lived in a world of random terrorist violence for nearly two generations.

There are other factors at work in providing for a more peaceful Northern Ireland, in addition to the IRA's pledge to disarm and the formation of an executive in which Catholics and Protestants share governing authority. Two other factors may be even more important in the long term in regard to searching for a lasting peace in Ulster. First, there are the demographic changes occurring there. The 2001 census indicated that Catholics had grown to constitute nearly 45 percent of Ulster's population, and that they continue to have larger families than their Protestant neighbors. Consequently, in another generation or even a decade they may become the majority in Ulster, making the retention of a power-sharing approach to governance an arrangement that is even more attractive to Ulster's Protestants.[70] Second, there is the fatigue factor. Local residents may have reached the point where they will no longer abet the militants in their camps or provide them with the logistical support network needed to conduct successful terrorist activity. In fact, it appears that this factor more than any other finally prompted the IRA to agree to disarm in the summer of 2005. Other problems persist, however, and although international watch groups began to characterize Northern Ireland as an "improving situation" in 2007, they have not dropped this long-standing hot spot in Western Europe from their lists.

The bad news begins with the quite different levels of commitment to the peace process that are found in Northern Ireland's two communities. Polls held in Ulster since the referendum on the Good Friday Agreement indicate exceedingly high support for the Agreement (96 percent) among Catholics, but only a slight (52 percent) majority of Protestants favor it. Thus, despite the demographic changes occurring in Ulster, its Protestants remain lukewarm in supporting the power-sharing arrangement in place of the pre-1972 majority rule system.[71] Such disparities are likely to change only gradually in the near future, reflecting as they do a still existing, albeit unofficial, system of apartheid that separates the two Northern Ireland communities in terms of residency, schooling, and commerce. So prevalent is this system in day-to-day activities that a relatively recent survey conducted by the University of Ulster found that 73 percent of Protestant youth have never had a significant conversation with a Catholic contemporary.[72]

Despite the decommissioning process and the restoration of civilian rule, a durable peace remains hostage to the continuing presence of rejectionist elements in both camps who are not only unwilling to accept the Good Friday Agreement and the power-sharing arrangement, but are still ready to use violence to undermine both. They may no longer enjoy wide support in their respective communities, but Northern Ireland still has its career extremists who have made conflict their reason for being for so long that they can find little identity beyond it, and therefore they are reluctant to let it go.

Beyond these diehard elements, there lies a broader, but still small number of citizens in both communities who have, since 1972, been co-opted into the dynamics of intercommunal warfare. It is not a problem limited to Northern Ireland, as the sections in this chapter on Corsica and Basque Spain attest. When the threshold leading to a high level of sustained political violence is crossed, communal conflicts tend to accelerate at a very fast rate measured in terms of instances of violence, increasing casualty figures, clashes per time interval, and so forth. Too often, such traditional institutions for conflict resolution as the local police and courts become contaminated to the point where they can no longer contribute to the containment of violence. In short order, the dynamic nature of the situation thus becomes a problem in its own right, and reversing the flow to reestablish local institutions of conflict control that can replace peacekeeping forces or other outsider brakes on the violence is a difficult and time-consuming process. That process began in earnest in Northern Ireland only in the mid-1990s, and only the slightest headway has yet been made in redesigning and rebuilding the cross-communal confidence in Ulster's police force that was shattered during "The Troubles." Part of the reason is the overlap between some of its members and their membership in Union paramilitaries, but also simply because it was a 93-percent Protestant police force, which Northern Ireland Catholics inevitably identified with the interests of the Protestant community. The prospect of random political violence will thus be a long time departing from Ulster.

The duration of that departure will also be prolonged by the sheer number of militant organizations and splinter groups that multiplied in both camps between 1972 and the Good Friday Agreement, all of whom are expected to disarm completely under the terms of the peace settlement, although many still continue to drag their feet on the matter. Thus, as late as October 2005, several months after the IRA's decision to lay down its arms, the Independent Monitoring Commission was still uneasy with the activities of several organizations, including

- The Irish National Liberation Army (INLA)
- The Loyalist Volunteer Force (LVF)
- The Provisional Irish Republican Army (PIRA)
- The Ulster Defense Association (UDA)
- The Ulster Volunteer Force (UVR)
- The Red Hand Commandos

- The Continuity Irish Republican Army (CIRA), which had become increasingly active in acquiring more weapons
- The Real Irish Republican Army (RIRA), which was still actively training new recruits and attacking police[73]

In short, although the mainstream communal militias seem to be cooperating and disarming, robberies, vandalism, pipe bombings, and even murders continue to be part of the environment of Northern Ireland, though a smaller part than in the past.

Moreover, the communal violence involving the area's Catholics and Protestants is no longer the only political violence in Ulster. Perhaps because of the pervasiveness and deep roots of the culture of violence in the region, the new millennium has also witnessed outbreaks of violence against the foreign workers drawn to Northern Ireland by its recent economic growth. Unlike the conflict involving foreign workers on the Continent and immigrants from Asia and Africa in Britain, in most instances race has not been a factor in Northern Ireland. In fact, the most common early targets were workers of Lithuanian origin, not a group usually associated with global troublemaking or trouble spots. Nevertheless, they have been seen as a threat to local wage structures because of their willingness to work for less than the wages normally paid working-class Catholics and Protestants, and therefore they have been targeted for economically motivated attacks in a region where political violence remains a tradition.

Finally, and perhaps most discouraging of all in terms of the prospects for Ulster to eradicate that tradition, there is the simple fact that the long-standing conflict between the province's opposing cultures is kept alive by the nature of life in Northern Ireland. Monuments and wall art depicting the symbols and the historical and more contemporary struggles of the communities are everywhere. There are the always well-organized and executed "celebrations" of anniversaries that are emblematic of the differences separating the communities, such as the annual Protestant fete on July 12 in honor of the Battle of the Boyne, and the Catholic vigils that mourn the victims of Bloody Sunday each year. These observances are regularly used to renew fervor in the faithful and to reach out to new activists, and any of them can lapse quickly into a nonrandom, calendar-based moment of political violence in those neighborhoods where the celebrations are meant to be most provocative. Scarcely had the IRA agreed to lay down its arms in 2005, for example, than Northern Ireland was shaken by three nights of Protestant rioting as a result of the British decision to prevent the Orange Order from marching into a disputed area of Belfast. Before the violence passed, Protestants had attacked police and British soldiers with firebombs, homemade grenades, and clubs; the fighting had spread to include altercations between Catholics and Protestants; and more than sixty people had been injured.

Timeline

1029	First Basque union, achieved by Sancho the Elder, will last until Castilian conquests begin in 1200.
1171	Norman "Conquest" of Ireland; Anglo-Norman rule gradually erodes over next 350 years.
1512	Castile control over Basque provinces essentially completed with absorption of Navarre by Castile.
1533–1603	Re-conquest of Ireland by Tudor England; initial plantations of English Protestants established.
1689–91	Battle of Boyne and Treaty of Limerick bring Ireland under full British control.
1695	Penal Code limits religious, social, and political freedoms of Irish Catholics.
1717	Efforts to bring Basque territory under Spanish tariff system cause bloody revolt in Basquelands.
1752	Corsica acquires nominal independence but is still officially a possession of Genoa.
1768	Genoa cedes Corsica to France, concluding state-building process of modern France.
1789	French Revolution ends old order in name of popular sovereignty.
1795	Orange Order founded in Ulster.
1798	Irish (Catholic) insurrection dedicated to making Ireland an independent republic fails.
1800	Act of Union is passed; Irish parliament dissolved and Ireland now ruled from London, where only Irish Protestants are initially eligible to hold seats in House of Commons.
1844	Potato crop fails; resulting famine causes mass emigration of indigenous Irish.
1858	Irish Republican Brotherhood, committed to achieving Ireland's independence, is founded.
1867, 1884	Changing UK suffrage laws give many Irish Catholics the vote and representation in Parliament.
1879	"Land wars" begin in Ireland against Protestant landlords who evict their tenants.
1889	Irish Parliamentary Party (Catholic) at Westminster begins campaign to achieve home rule.

1895	Basque Nationalist Party (PNV) and Basque nationalist movement founded.
1905	Ulster Unionist Council (Protestant) founded to oppose home rule for Ireland.
1907	Sinn Féin founded on commitment to make Ireland a "modern Catholic state."
1913	Second Home Rule Bill passes in House of Commons; Ulster Volunteer Force forms to resist any attempt to implement the policy; World War I begins, tabling home rule issue in Parliament.
1916	Easter Uprising; Irish Republic is proclaimed, but rebellion quickly subdued and leaders executed.
1917	Communists seize control of Russia; Russian refugees arrive in Paris in large numbers.
1918	Anglo-Irish War for Ireland's independence begins.
1920	Government of Ireland Act passes, authorizing creation of parliaments in Dublin and Belfast.
1922	Anglo-Irish Treaty creates Irish Free State out of twenty-six of Ireland's thirty-two counties; partition under way.
1925	Boundary between the Irish Free State and the British province of Northern Ireland established.
1936	Second Spanish Republic restores Basque autonomy on eve of Spanish Civil War.
1939	Spanish Civil War ends with Basques on losing side; Franco retaliates against Basques.
1939–45	World War II. Ireland declares policy of neutrality; Northern Ireland enters war against Germany.
1945–50	Buildup of non-European people in Western Europe begins, as European countries rebuild after World War II and liquidate—or are forced to liquidate—their overseas empires.
1948	British Nationality Act confirms that citizens of colonies and Commonwealth are British subjects entitled to enter Britain; migration of significant numbers of nonwhites to Britain begins.
1949	Republic of Ireland declared; Northern Ireland remains part of United Kingdom.
1956–62	IRA campaign to unite Ireland; called off in 1962 due to lack of support.
1958	"Race" riots erupt in Nottingham and Notting Hill, London.

1959	ETA is founded to gain independence for Spain's Basquelands and their union with Basque France.
1960s	Foreigner issue emerges in Western Europe as number of immigrants and foreign workers grows.
1962	Algeria achieves independence; many French Algerians immigrate to Corsica; in United Kingdom, the Commonwealth Immigrants Act restricts rights of nonwhites to immigrate to Britain.
1965–67	Principal nationalist organizations emerge in Corsica.
1968–69	Catholic civil rights movement grows in Ulster; violence results. Enoch Powell's 1968 "Rivers of Blood" speech warns Britain of need to curb immigration. ETA draws first blood in Spain
1969	British peacekeeping troops deployed in (London)Derry and Belfast in Northern Ireland
1970s	Birth of anti-immigrant parties and growth of anti-immigrant violence throughout Western Europe; Germany, Holland, and France respond to domestic pressure by shutting doors to more foreign workers.
1972	Bloody Sunday in Ulster; 14 die when British troops fire on peaceful Catholic demonstrators; London subsequently assumes direct rule of Ulster; civil liberties suspended.
1972	France's *Front National* (FN) anti-immigrant party founded by Jean-Marie Le Pen.
1973	ETA assassinates Franco's apparent heir to power, Spanish Prime Minister Carrero Blanco.
1975	Franco dies and King Juan Carlos succeeds him; process of democratizing Spain begins.
1978	Conservative Party leader Margaret Thatcher helps legitimize British racist rhetoric by discussing public's fears of Britain being "swamped" by people of a different culture.
1979	Autonomy Statue for Basque Spain is approved; Basques acquire their own state in a federalizing Spain.
1980s	Global recession further intensifies anti-foreigner issue; Britain further narrows eligibility of former subjects to enter country as (1981) youth riots occur in minority areas of multiracial English cities.

1982	By special statute, Paris establishes a Corsican Assembly.
1983	Madrid initiates brutal campaign to eradicate ETA, deploying its own paramilitary force to Basque region.
1985	Anglo-Irish Agreement establishes the basis for limited sharing of governmental responsibilities in Ulster between the British and Irish governments.
1989	National furor occurs in France when Muslim students refuse to remove their head coverings.
1990s	Success of anti-immigrant parties, domestic public opinion, and slow recovery from recession prompt many states to deny illegal immigrants access to social welfare systems.
1992	European Charter of Regional Languages proposes safeguards for Europe's minority tongues.
1994	New cease-fire established in Ulster; first official British Government meeting with Sinn Féin.
1995	Jacque Chirac is elected French president on a plank stressing new toughness toward illegal immigrants.
1995	Riots involving Caribbean youth in Brixton (England) follow police shooting of a black burglary suspect.
1996	German states pressure Bosnian refugees to leave, consider expelling those refusing to go.
1996	Mitchell Report recommends six principles of nonviolence to govern all-party talks on Ulster. IRA's cease-fire ends with bomb explosion in Canary Wharf, London.
1997	New IRA cease-fire. International decommissioning body established to oversee militia's disarmament. Sinn Féin enters all-party talks, Protestant Democratic Unionists leave in protest.
1997	ETA execution of a Basque councillor alienates many moderate Basques who once supported it.
1998	Germany: "foreigner-free" zones are in effect in at least twenty-five East German towns. "Good Friday Agreement" reached, with conditions for new power-sharing government in Ulster; Republic of Ireland renounces constitutional claim to Northern Ireland. Citing peace

progress in Northern Ireland, ETA declares cease-fire in Spain.

1999   Macpherson Report documents "institutional racism" within London Metropolitan police force. ETA resumes conflict against Madrid, but with slipping support among Basques.

2000   Austria: anti-immigrant Freedom Party becomes part of governing coalition. Italy: leading Italian cardinal urges limiting Muslim immigrants to preserve state's Catholic character.

2001   Britain: riots occur in Burnley, Leeds, and Oldham during general election; al Qaeda attack on United States adds security concerns to immigrant debate everywhere.

2002   Anti-immigrant parties continue to do well in elections in Austria, Denmark, Norway, and France. Germany enacts first-ever law to regulate immigration, and tightens its asylum law. Assassination of anti-immigrant Dutch populist in Holland results in new laws to limit immigration. In France negotiations begin on the devolution of additional authority to Corsican institutions.

2003   Corsicans reject proposed autonomy statute. In continental France, new education law requires schools to emphasize colonialism's positive aspects.

2004   Anti-immigration politics continues to mount. Austria's anti-immigrant Freedom Party candidate narrowly loses Presidential race, 52 percent to 48 percent. In Britain, tensions rise over arrest of Muslims. In Germany, a bomb blast in Turkish part of Cologne injures nearly 20 Turks. In Holland, the murder of critic of Islam causes violent backlash, including arson at a mosque. In Spain, the bombing of Madrid commuter trains by home-grown terrorists results in crackdown on Muslim population. In Britain, five home-grown terrorists are arrested for planning to bomb London nightclubs, power plants, and shopping malls. In France, the parliament bans Muslim headdress and other religious symbols and apparel from French schools.

2005   In France, fall rioting by Muslim youth sweeps
                       entire country following fatal shooting of
                       teenager by police. In Britain, scores die and
                       nearly a thousand are injured when home-grown
                       suicide bombers attack London's mass transit sys-
                       tem; three months later new requirements for nat-
                       uralization, including a "Britishness" test, are
                       adopted by Parliament.

2006   In Spain, ETA announces abandonment of terror-
                       ism, but extremists announce they will continue
                       struggle with arms until Basques are independent.
                       In United Kingdom, Protestant extremist armed
                       with gun and pipe bombs breaks into Ulster
                       Assembly; English police charge 25 with attempt-
                       ing to blow up planes bound from London to
                       New York. In France, Muslim youth continue to
                       riot throughout summer and into fall in protest of
                       injustice; a rash of fatal anti-immigrant fires
                       occurs in Paris.

2007   Northern Irish Protestants agree to form govern-
                       ment with Catholics; civilian government sworn
                       in Ulster. In Britain, a terrorist attack with al
                       Qaeda ties targeting London with car bombs is
                       averted, but suicide bombers crash flaming van
                       into Glasgow airport terminal.

Notes

1. For background reading on racism in Europe's past, see Benjamin P. Bowser, ed., *Racism and Anti-Racism in World Perspective* (Thousand Oaks, CA: Sage Publications, 1995). For more general reading on Europe's immigrant and foreign worker communities, see in particular Martin O. Heisler and Barbara Schmitter Heisler, eds., "From Foreign Workers to Settlers? Transnational Migration and the Emergence of the New Minorities," Special Issue of the *Annals of the American Academy of Political and Social Sciences*, 465 (1986). The conflict between hosts and these foreign-rooted groups, both before and after September 11, 2001, is discussed comparatively in Joseph Rudolph, "Chapter 5: Ethnopolitics in France in a Comparative Perspective" in *Politics and Ethnicity: A Comparative Study* (New York: Palgrave, 2006: 74–100, esp. 85–100). For a more pointed view of the dangers that Europe's Muslim communities might pose to security on the Continent, see Bruce Bawer, *While Europe Slept: How Radical Islam Is Destroying the West from Within* (New York: Random House-Doubleday, 2006).

2. See Eugeen Roosens, "Migration and Caste Formation in Europe: The Belgian Case," *Ethnic and Racial Studies*, XI.2 (1988: 207–17), and H. Stuart

Hughes, "The Torment of a Foreign Underclass" in *Sophisticated Rebels: The Political Culture of European Dissent, 1968-1987* (Cambridge, MA: Harvard University Press, 1988: 34–48).

3. In addition to the economic subsidy that low-wage immigrant laborers provide to the economies of advanced developed states today, there is the broader, future need of developed states for workers to continue to perform low-wage, generally unpleasant jobs (street construction, sewer maintenance, and so forth) for their aging infrastructures and to support their welfare systems at a time when their indigenous population is aging and its younger members are not reproducing at even a replacement level. In fact, the numbers here throughout the Western world are statistically shocking. As Robert Samuelson has summarized the situation, "On average, women must have two children for a society to replace itself. The number of children per woman is called the "total fertility rate," or TFR." Yet, as of 2005, the estimated TFR for Germany was only 1.4, and it was even lower for heavily Catholic Italy (1.3) and Spain (1.3). Robert J. Samuelson, "Behind the Birth Dearth," *The Washington Post* (May 24, 2006).

4. See, in particular, Kristin Archick, John Rollins, and Steven Woehrel, "Islamic Extremism in Europe" (Washington: Library of Congress, Congressional Research Service Report, July 29, 2005: order code RS22211), and Akeel Shah, "Why Europe Has Less Success Integrating Muslims Than North America" (Blogcritics.org, February 14, 2006).

5. Duncan Currie, "Over There, Over Here: What the European Crisis Suggests about Democracy, Fanaticism, and the War" (WeeklyStandard.com, November 10, 2005).

6. Pew Global Attitudes Project, "The Great Divide: How Westerners and Muslims View Each Other" (June 22, 2006; available online). Thirteen percent of even Germany's more secularized, largely Turkish Muslim population was also willing to condone suicide bombings against civilian targets under some circumstances.

7. See John Lancaster, "Pakistani Cleric Announces Bounty for Killing of Danish Cartoonists," *The Washington Post* (February 8, 2006); Paul Watson and Zulfiqar Ali, "3 Afghans Die During Protest over Cartoons: 4 NATO Soldiers Are Hurt in Clash at Base as Demonstrations Spread," *The Baltimore Sun* (February 8, 2006); Associated Press, "40,000 in Karachi Protest Cartoons of Muhammad," *The Washington Post* (February 12, 2006).

8. In France, as in much of contemporary Western Europe, the "foreigner" issue is popularly defined far less in legal terms or those used for census purposes (that is, citizens of other countries residing in France) than in terms of those who are perceived to be "foreign" by the native population, even though they may have acquired citizenship. Hence, quotation marks are used here and elsewhere in this section, and elsewhere in this volume, to refer to the "foreigner" factor that has become so important in contemporary French and European politics.

9. Many of these refugees were rewarded with a decade-long refugee camp existence upon their arrival in France. It gave them little beyond sanctuary in return for their aid, which made them traitors to their own people and gave them

little opportunity to relieve France's worker shortage. When the foreigner issue became politically sensitive, there was even less public opportunity to thank them for their aid or to integrate them into the French economy at the middle-class level that they had enjoyed in Algeria and Tunisia. Indeed, it was not until 1998 that a president of France acknowledged the large numbers of Algerians who had fought on behalf of France alongside the French, in both World War I and World War II.

10. See the chapter by H. Stuart Hughes, "The Torment of a Foreign Underclass," in his *Sophisticated Rebels: The Political Culture of European Dissent, 1968–1987* (Cambridge, MA: Harvard University Press, 1988: 34–48, esp. 35–37).

11. See Kimberly Hamilton, "The Challenge of French Diversity" (http://www.migrationinformation.com/Profiles/display.cfm?ID=2, accessed August 16, 2004). The remainder of the foreign population consisted of people from the culturally remote areas of Sub-Saharan Africa, the Middle East, and Southeast Asia.

12. Ronald Tiersky, *France in the New Europe: Changing Yet Steadfast* (Belmont, CA: Wadsworth, 1994: 33–38).

13. Tiersky, op. cit., p. 110.

14. Jacques Chirac, "Jacques Chirac on French Population Issues," *Population and Development Review*, xi.1 (March 1985: 163–64).

15. See Milton J. Esman, *Ethnic Politics* (Ithaca, NY: Cornell University Press, 1997: 97).

16. Official statistics can be found at http//www.France.diplomatic.fr/ France/geo/popu.gb.html. The mid-1990s figures were available as of July 1, 1997.

17. See John Rossart, "France: Praying Ties to the Arab World," *Business Week* (September 20, 2004: 52).

18. Jean-Claude Barreau, cited in Martin Peretz, "Revenged," *New Republic* (February 23, 2004: 38).

19. Hamilton, op. cit.

20. See Migration News, "France, Benelux," which synthesizes a variety of news sources (http://www.migration.ucdavis.edu/mn/comments.php?id=3077_0_4_0).

21. See Paul J. White, "France's 'New Secularism': The French War on Islam?" available online at http:www.famsy.com/salam/French%20secularism%201203. htm. The Sarkozy citation is attributed to Le Monde, July 4, 2003.

22. "The Melting Pot That Isn't," *The Economist* (July 28, 2001: 50).

23. "'Race Killing' Sparks French Riot" (BBC News online, May 31, 2005: http://news.bbc.co.uk/2/hi/europe/4594019.stm).

24. Peter Ross Range, "France's Paradox Island: Corsica," *National Geographic*, CCIII (April, 2003: 56–75), available online.

25. Sue Ellen Charlton, "France: Ethnic Conflict and the Problem of Corsica," in Joseph R. Rudolph, Jr., ed. *Encyclopedia of Modern Ethnic Conflict* (London and Westport, CT: Greenwood Press: 69–78, @ 72).

26. Ibid.

27. Lewis Dolinsky, "Where Nationalism Is a Blast," *The Baltimore Sun* (December 21, 1996).

28. Charlton, "France: Ethnic Conflict," p. 70.

29. "Corsica Insula: Corsica from the Inside" (www.corsica-insula.com/island.htm).

30. The initials stand for *Euzkadi Ta Askatasuna*: Basque for Basque Homeland and Freedom. The ETA followed its March 22 announcement the next day with a call for compromise and a peaceful settlement of the Basque conflict directed at the governments of both Spain and France. See "ETA Calls for Fresh Peace Moves" (BBC News online, March 23, 2006; http://news.bbc.co.uk/2/hi/europe/4835906.stm).

31. For more detailed discussions of the often violent struggle by Basque groups to achieve their political goals in contemporary Spain, see Daniele Conversi, *The Basques, the Catalans and Spain: Alternative Routes to National Mobilization* (Reno: University of Nevada Press, 1997); William A. Douglass, et al., *Basque Politics and Nationalism on the Eve of the Millennium* (Reno: Basque Studies Institute, 1999); Francisco J. Llera Ramo, "Basque Polarization: Between Autonomy and Independence," *Nationalism and Ethnic Politics,* V (Autumn-Winter, 1999: 101–120; Goldie Shabad and Francisco J. Llera Ramo, "Political Violence in a Democratic State: Basque Terrorism in Spain," in Martha Crenshaw, ed. *Terrorism in Context* (University Park, PA: Pennsylvania State University Press, 1995: 410–69).

32. In the federalization process that accompanied democratization and constitution-writing in post-Franco Spain, Alava, Vizcaya, and Guipuzcoa were united by 1979 statute into the single Basque Autonomous Community of Pais Vasco. The largest of the provinces, Navarra, was left out for myriad reasons and received its own autonomous community status in another statute enacted that same year. On the constitution-making process in general and the allocation of autonomy status to the Basques in particular, see Robert P. Clark, "Spanish Democracy and Regional Autonomy: The Autonomous Community System and Self -Government for the Ethnic Homelands," in Joseph R. Rudolph, Jr., and Robert J. Thompson, eds. *Ethnoterritorial Politics, Policy and the Western World* (Boulder, CO: Lynne Rienner, 1989: 15–43, esp. 18–21).

33. See Terry G. Jordan-Bychkov and Bella Jordan-Bychkov, *The European Culture Area: a Systematic Geography* (New York: Rowman & Littlefield, 2001: 146). Basque is classified as an agglutinative tongue, alone in its family. Some linguists have found its closest match among Native Alaskans. In Europe, its "only possible relative" is to be found in the northern Caucasus. See also Roland Vazquez, "Spain: Basque Nationalism and Conflict in Democratic Spain," in Joseph R. Rudolph, Jr., ed. *Encyclopedia of Modern Ethnic Conflicts* (Westport, CT: Greenwood Press, 2003: 215–223, esp. 216).

34. Jordan-Bychkov, op. cit., pp. 149 f.

35. Vazquez, op. cit., pp. 216–217.

36. Ibid., p. 218.

37. Ibid., p. 219.

38. The initials stand for *Grupos Antiterroristas de Liberacion*: Antiterrorist Liberation Groups.

39. See Enric Martinez-Herrera, "National Extremism and Outcomes of State Policies in the Basque Country, 1979–2001," *International Journal of Multicultural*

Studies, IV (2002) (available online at http://unesdoc.unesco.org/images/0013/001390/139048E.pdf#page=18).

40. Vazquez, op. cit., p. 220.

41. See Keith B. Richburg, "Long Basque Rebellion Losing Strength: International Effort Squeezes Underground Separatist Group," *The Washington Post* (December 11, 2003). Richburg cites figures showing a sharp drop in ETA activity from the high-water years between 1977 and 1980, when it still had legitimacy. Spain was then in the process of restructuring itself after Franco's death, and ETA attacks were then responsible for from sixty to more than eighty deaths per year. In contrast, despite the short-term upsurge in ETA activity in the early 2000s, the number of deaths attributable to its bombings and shooting shrank to an average of fewer than five a year.

42. See John Ward Anderson, "Catalan Voters Endorse Greater Autonomy: Backers Say Measure May Ease Tension in Spain; Opponents Call It Slippery Slope," *The Washington Post* (June 19, 2006).

43. See, for example, "Basques Protest Spain's Attempt to Outlaw Party," *The Baltimore Sun* (June 16, 2002) regarding the tens of thousands who protested Madrid's moves to outlaw the Batasuna Party, which was then the political wing of the ETA.

44. See Pamela Rolfe, "Spanish Leader Rebuffs Basque: Autonomy Plan Called Illegal," *The Washington Post* (January 14, 2005).

45. Cited in "Eta Calls for Fresh Peace Moves," op. cit. See also "Spaniards Protest Offer of Talks with Basques," *The Baltimore Sun* (June 5, 2006) on the hundreds of thousands who protested the government's qualified offer to meet with the ETA to discuss future peace moves following the ETA's declaration of an unconditional cease-fire in March of that year.

46. See Renwick McLean, "In Basque Region's Capital, Fear Lingers Despite a Truce," *The New York Times* (March 25, 2006).

47. See "Madrid Bomb Injures 43 in Apparent ETA Attack," *The Washington Post* (February 10, 2005), and "Car Bombing in Madrid, Blamed on ETA, Injures 52," *The Washington Post* (May 26, 2005).

48. Of the four young men involved in the successful July 7 attacks, three were British-born and of Pakistani descent. The fourth was an immigrant from Jamaica who had recently been converted to Islam. As for the unsuccessful bombers of the following week, three were immigrants from East Africa (one each from Somalia, Eritrea, and Ethiopia).

49. See Anthony Mark Messina, "United Kingdom: The Making of British Race Relations," in Joseph R. Rudolph Jr., ed. *Encyclopedia of Modern Ethnic Conflicts* (London and Westport, CT: Greenwood Press, 2003: 243–249).

50. For a long time, the English, Scots, and Welsh tended to lump all such people under the now very much out-of-fashion rubric of "colored," with "black" reserved only for those coming from Africa.

51. In Powell's words, in 1969, "Already by 1985 the native born would constitute the majority [in the "foreigner" community]. It is this fact which creates the new urgency of action now, of just the kind of action which is hardest for politicians to take, action where the difficulties lie in the present but the evils to be prevented or minimized lie several parliaments ahead." The full text of the

speech is available at the Website of *Sterling Times* (http://www.sterlingtimes. org/text_rivers_of-blood.htm).

52. Ataullah Siddiqui, "Muslims in Britain: Past and Present" (Islam for Today; http://www.islamfortoday.com/britain.htm).

53. Antony King, "One in Four Muslims Sympathises with Motives of Terrorists," *The Daily Telegraph* (July 23, 2005) and Philip Johnston, "50,000,000 and Growing: Immigration Pushes England's Population to New High in Biggest Rise since the 'Baby Boom' Years," *The Daily Telegraph* (August 26, 2005).

54. Reported from the news services in *The Washington Post* (November 27, 2005). No specific details were given.

55. See, in particular, John Ward Anderson and Karen DeYoung, "Plot to Bomb U.S.-Bound Jets Is Foiled: Britain Arrests 24 Suspected Conspirators," *The Washington Post* (August 11, 2006) and Kevin Sullivan, "Britain Arrests 8 for 'Facilitating Terrorism Abroad,'" *The Washington Post* (May 25, 2006).

56. "London, Again: A 21st-century threat; 19th-century Laws" (July 22, 2005; OpinionJournal.com), an opinion editorial posted following the failed second attack on London's mass transit system.

57. See "Britain a Breeding Ground for Hate Fed by Militant Muslim Preachers," *The Baltimore Sun* (July 10, 2005), a *New York Times* wire release.

58. See, respectively, Kevin Sullivan and Mary Jordan, "Blair Acts Against Muslim 'Fringe,'" *The Washington Post* (August 6, 2005); Kevin Sullivan, "British Jury Clears Two of Racial Charges," *The Washington Post* (February 3, 2006); and Kevin Sullivan, "Britain Declines to Prosecute Officers in Subway Shooting," *The Washington Post* (July 18, 2006).

59. Cited in Kevin Sullivan, "Poll: Britons Support Multiculturalism," *The Washington Post* (August 11, 2005).

60. Reported in Jay Raymer, "Divided Britain: Race—Still the Hate Grows," *The Observer* (March 27, 2005).

61. See, for example, Charlotte Edwardes, "International Tension in Britain 'at worst level in 50 years;' Black-on-Black Violent Confrontations Are Endemic in Some Areas, Television Documentary Claims," *The Sunday Telegraph* (August 8, 2004).

62. Michael Kronenwetter, *Northern Ireland* (New York: Franklin Watts, 1990: 25–26). Kronenwetter provides excellent background reading for additional details on the evolution of Britain's "Irish Problem." For a more concise summary of Ireland's relationship with Britain prior to partition, see Sean P. Duffy, "United Kingdom: The Irish Question and the Partition of Ireland," in Joseph R. Rudolph, Jr., ed. *The Encyclopedia of Modern Ethnic Conflicts* (New York and London: Greenwood Press, 2003: 251–58).

63. Official statistics indicate that between 1850 and 1871, the proportion of Ireland's population that still spoke Gaelic dropped from more than 25 percent to only 14 percent.

64. See Kronenwetter, op. cit., p. 43 f. As a result of the famine, emigration, and English land-holding policies, by 1900 the indigenous Irish Catholics had become an underclass that owned only about 7 percent of their native land.

65. Subsequently, the terms "Catholic" and "Protestant" have functioned as a convenient shorthand for referring to two distinct communities in Ireland that

are divided from one another by three reinforcing factors: ethnic origin, religious orientation, and political goals. The Catholics are those of Celtic origin who are indigenous to the island, Catholic in religion, and nationalist in their desire for home rule, originally, and now independence from Britain and the reintegration of Ulster into the Republic of Ireland.

66. The home rule proposal passed the British House of Commons on two occasions, in 1893 and again in 1913. In each instance its passage was blocked or delayed to death by the more conservative House of Lords. Nevertheless, the possibility of its passage on both occasions galvanized the Protestants in Ulster to mobilize. In 1905, for example, the Ulster Unionist Council (UUC) was organized to resist home rule, and by 1910 it was seeking arms abroad to resist violently, if necessary, any home rule measures affecting Ulster. Similarly, in 1912, with another measure pending, 400,000 Protestant Unionists signed a "Solemn League and Covenant" to resist home rule, and the following year another organization, the Ulster Volunteer Force (UVF), emerged with goals and orientation toward violence similar to that of the UUC. See Duffy, op cit., pp. 251–52 and 256–57.

67. See Charles Townshend, "The Process of Terror in Irish Politics," in Noel G. Sullivan, ed. *Terrorism, Ideology, and Revolution* (Boulder, CO: Westview Press, 1986: 88–114, 100–102). Townshend maintains that this shift away from enforcement terrorism, which had a long tradition in Irish history, toward agitational terrorism was one of the major developments in the Irish Question between 1969 and 1985.

68. The Treaty also recognized that no decision would be made without the approval of a majority of the other side (i.e., Ulster's Protestant community), but that recognition of reality did little to appease Protestant extremists.

69. The figures are drawn from Joseph Ruane and Jennifer Todd, *The Dynamics of Conflict in Northern Ireland* (Cambridge, UK: Cambridge University Press, 1996: 1), cited in Duffy, op. cit., p. 261.

70. See James E. DiLisio, *Ireland in Transition: A Geographical and Historical Interpretation* (Baltimore: Burren Press, 2003: 255).

71. See Paul Sussman, "Breaking the Cycle of Violence" (http://www.cnn.com/SPECIALS/2000/n.ireland/overview.htm).

72. Cited in John O'Farrell, "Payback Time in Belfast," *New Statesman,* CXXXIV.4758 (September 19, 2005).

73. The full text of the Seventh Report of the Independent Monitoring Commission (London: HMSO, October, 2005) is available online (http://www.justice.ie/en/JELR/IMCRpt7.pdf/Files/IMCRpt7.pdf) as are the earlier and more recent of the Commission's regular, at least bi-annual reports.

North America

CHAPTER 8

CANADA

NATIONALISM AND SEPARATISM IN QUEBEC

The separatist tide has receded somewhat since Quebec voters narrowly failed to authorize their provincial government to pursue a separatist agenda in the mid-1990s, but the prospect of the political upheaval that its revival might cause remains close to the surface of Canadian politics. In Quebec, pro-independence parties continue to enjoy support and Quebec drivers continue to put Quebec license plates on their cars that bear the vaguely disquieting slogan, *Je me souviens* (I remember).

The Birth of Quebec Nationalism

Canada is not without its ethnic diversity. It houses an African American population dating from the underground railroad days of the pre–Civil War United States, augmented by the later arrival of immigrants from the French West Indies. Its western provinces are laced with Asian immigrants and their descendants, and Jewish refugees from interwar and early World War II Europe founded a large community in Montreal, from which many later migrated to the United States. Nevertheless, as a result of comparatively restrictive immigration policies and the unattractive prospect of settling in the inhospitable climates of northern Canada, Canada has never developed the widely dispersed, ethnic heterogeneity of its assimilationist English-speaking neighbor to the south.[1] Instead, it has developed as a bicultural state containing both English and French-speaking communities, the largest concentration of the latter (approximately 30 percent of the country's total population) being concentrated in one of its ten federal units, eastern Canada's restive province of Quebec.

Quebec and the Birth of Canada

This situation and its continuing implications for Canada's political stability have their roots in the compartmentalized origins of the modern Canadian state. Canada's eastern provinces, central provinces, and—eventually—its western provinces were settled by English colonists and other immigrants drawn largely from the United Kingdom, with Labrador and Newfoundland being explored by John Cabot as early as 1497 and becoming two of Britain's earliest outposts in North America. Meanwhile, the French were establishing settlements at an early date in the "New France" region lying along the St. Lawrence River, which Jacques Cartier began to explore in 1534.

It was 225 years later, and only by force of conquest, that New France began to fall into British hands with the victory of the British army in the 1759 Battle of Quebec [City] on the Plains of Abraham. The French were able to retake Quebec City the following year, but only temporarily before having to retreat to Montreal in the face of advancing British reinforcements. When the British captured Montreal as well in 1760, essentially all of New France fell permanently under British control. It was nearly fifteen years later, however, before Britain developed a comprehensive strategy—in retrospect, perhaps an ill-chosen one—for governing its new acquisition.

The policy, spelled out in the Quebec Act of 1774, entailed governing Quebec apart from English-speaking Canada, which was being managed from Ottawa in the adjacent province of Ontario, to Quebec's west. More importantly for the future development of Quebec-Canada relations, instead of continuing the initial effort to assimilate Quebec's people into English-speaking Canada, which had been resisted and resented, the Quebec Act allowed Quebec to preserve its French character. French civil codes and property laws were retained, and—despite its role as a carrier of both French culture and the faith—the powerful status of the Catholic Church in Quebec was not altered. In a sense, the Quebec Act of 1774 was a North American variation of the "indirect rule" system that the British were then developing to administer their empire on the Indian subcontinent—a low-cost way to govern utilizing indigenous local officials as agents of the British empire, whenever possible. But the indirect rule system always came with a price. In Quebec, as in India, it allowed the local community to retain its cultural identity; indeed, it legally conferred that right on them.

Three generations later, Quebec's French-speaking majority had not only failed to adjust fully to British rule, but were increasingly resistant to it. In 1837 their restiveness turned into open rebellion. Led by Louis-Joseph Papineau, French activists demanding that Britain cede greater political autonomy to French-speaking Quebec fought a brief, losing battle with British forces. The rebellion convinced Canada's governor-general, Lord Durham, of the need to give Quebec greater internal self-government. It also convinced him, however, of the need to couple such administrative reforms with serious efforts to anglicize Quebec's French population. Toward that end the Act of Union of 1841 merged English-speaking Ontario and French-speaking Quebec into a single province. By that time, though, it was too late to alter Quebec's deeply rooted, Francophone culture. Consequently, when the saber-rattling talk of those post-Civil War expansionists in the United States (who were openly discussing the annexation of parts of Canada) temporarily drowned out provincial opposition to union and prompted Canada's various provinces to unite under the British North American Act of 1867, Quebec was once again given separate province status as a still overwhelmingly French-speaking state in the newly created Canadian federation.

The "Quiet Revolution": The Reawakening of Quebec Nationalism

Quebec's sensitivity to rule by Canada's approximately 70 percent English-speaking majority (currently) did not disappear with the Act of Union. Nevertheless, for most of the next 80 or more years it rarely appeared in a separatist guise. Rather, as one of today's respected analysts of nationalism in the Western world, Saul Newman, has observed, after the Act of Union the emphasis shifted, both in Quebec and in the minority French communities in other provinces, from self-rule to the survival of the French culture (*la survivance*) in a predominantly English-speaking country whose symbolic head of state continued to be the British monarch. It was a quest that "entailed a glorification of rural French Canadian agrarian life, the conservative social dominance of a Catholic Church and an attempt to maintain a social and economic isolation from all things Anglophone, urban and industrial."[2]

In general, the survival strategy also meant downplaying an active French political agenda, except for a short-lived rebellion in the 1880s and active opposition in Quebec to being conscripted into "Britain's wars" during World War I and World War II. That approach was most conspicuously apparent in the provincial government given Quebec by its longtime premier, Maurice Le Noblet Duplessis (1936 to 1939, and again from 1944 to 1959). He not only supported a highly conservative political agenda that underwrote the Catholic Church's conservative influence on Quebec's agrarian French society (for which Duplessis received the Church's support and open endorsement at election time), but he also invited English-speaking capital and workers into Quebec to keep its French community out of industries, labor unions, and other activities and memberships that might have led to their active politicization.[3] In that way the province's resources fell under the control of outsiders during Duplessis's leadership, and British immigrants entered the province in large numbers.

In the end, Duplessis's efforts to limit change in his province were overcome by developments beyond his control, as well as by his own actions. He rose to power by exposing the corruption and patronage of the Liberal government that had preceded him and the party he founded. By the mid-1950s, however, his own misconduct—favoring English firms over French firms; using strong-arm tactics to block the development of unions; and permitting patronage, election fraud, and other forms of corruption to permeate his administration—had undermined his political support. Meanwhile, the strong economy that his conservative practices fostered had led to far-reaching economic change in Quebec from which its French citizens could not be shielded. To the contrary, they participated in and accelerated it as they moved in large numbers from rural areas into the metropolitan areas, where their province's economic, industrial, and financial domination by English-speaking Canadians was obvious to them. So, too, was the disparity in average income between their province's English-speaking residents and its native Francophones—a state of affairs that gradually produced political resentment against both the Quebec politicians and the Catholic clergy who were blamed for the development. The result was Quebec's "Quiet Revolution," a significant but largely peaceful rebellion against the *Union Nationale* party and its allies and beneficiaries in Quebec's Catholic clergy and English-dominated economic sector. In 1960, the Quebec Liberal Party, under the leadership of Jean Lesage, returned to office on a platform of change, promising to develop Quebec's economy for Quebec's French-speaking people and, politically, to make Quebec's indigenous French-speaking people the masters of their own house.

Nationalism, Separatism, and Liberation Fronts: Politics Heat Up

The Quiet Revolution, with its emphasis on secularizing the education system, re-establishing local control over the province's natural resources, promoting French-owned industry, protecting unions, and establishing a modern welfare state in Quebec was the gestation period for the birth of modern, often independence-minded, Quebec nationalism. It was the period when the Quebec-born French speakers living in the province ceased thinking of themselves as French-Canadians and began to consider themselves *Quebecois* (that is, members of a French-speaking Quebec nation). Schools remained in the hands of the Catholic and Protestant religious bodies that had previously run them, but they were brought firmly under the jurisdiction of Quebec's provincial government, which asserted control over the classroom even as it was expanding free public education through the eleventh grade and making school mandatory until the age of sixteen. The province's electric companies were nationalized and placed under the direction of the Liberal government's minister of natural resources, Rene Levesque. And shortly thereafter, public companies were also created in such sectors as forestry, mining, and steel. Capping the fast pace of change, 1963–64 saw the beginning of a province-based social welfare system with the creation of a Quebec pension plan.

The FLQ and the Politics of Violence

Setting the Stage

The political assertiveness of the Liberal government whetted the *Quebecois* appetite for more political autonomy, even as it generated tensions between the provincial government and Canada's federal government in Ottawa. From the outset, however, some factions in Quebec wanted to go beyond the goals of the Quiet Revolution and pursue independence. While the Liberals were launching their revolution inside the province, for example, another cadre of Quebec's French-speaking citizens was founding the *Rassemblement pour l'independance nationale* (RIN [Assembly for National Independence]). Moreover, not all *Quebecois* were willing to wait to see how far peaceful change could take the province. Thus, when three years later the RIN began to turn itself into a purely political party and dedicated itself to achieving a free and independent Quebec through the ballot box, its militant, Marxist wing broke away to found a clandestine terrorist organization committed to gaining Quebec's independence by whatever means necessary. It was called the *Front de liberation du Quebec* (FLQ [Front for the Liberation of Quebec]).

Quite apart from the stimulation it was deriving from the Liberal Party's Quebec-centered programs and rhetoric, the growth of nationalism in Quebec, and in some instances its radicalization, was also abetted by a brace of other developments during the 1960s and 1970s. First, before the Liberals could fully reap the electoral benefits of giving the *Quebecois* greater control over their province, they found themselves out of office. This turn of events was the result of the province's 1966 elections, in which the Liberals woefully misjudged their chances of losing and ran a lackluster campaign against the RIN, other nationalist parties, and the still well-organized *Union Nationale*—which itself adopted a nationalist, albeit pro-business stance on the conservative right. While the Liberals were touting the qualities of their leader, the party's competitors put their emphasis on a nationalist agenda that was in tune with and able to feed the rising tide of nationalist sentiment in Quebec. When the votes were counted, even though the *Union Nationale* won only slightly more than 40 percent of the vote, Quebec's single-member-district, winner-by-plurality electoral system enabled it to win a six-seat majority in Quebec's parliament. For their part, the Liberals finished first in the popular vote, but their 47 percent was down drastically from their previous showing. In a sign of things to come, most of the votes lost by the Liberals went to the pro-independence nationalist parties.

Second, the federal government's policies toward Quebec during this period tended to be woefully out of tune with political developments in Quebec. Instead of accommodating the *Quebecois'* desire for greater federal autonomy and recognizing Quebec as an essentially monolingual, French-speaking state in the Canadian federation, Ottawa offered all of French-speaking Canada the image of Canada as a truly bilingual state, in which French would be accorded the same status as English for all official purposes and students throughout Canada would henceforth learn both tongues. The policy, pushed especially during the Liberal Party governments of Quebec-born Pierre Trudeau between 1968 and 1979, appealed to the French-speaking minorities in the other Canadian provinces, but it grievously misread mainstream *Quebecois* thinking. Being masters in one's own home had come to mean making French the *sole* language of politics and business in Quebec Province, not forcing English-speaking Canada to give greater access to public employment to its French-Canadians. Hence, one of the first items on the Liberal Party's agenda when it routed the *Union Nationale* and regained control of the provincial government in the next provincial election by embracing *Quebecois* nationalism was to pass Proposition 22, a controversial (to Quebec's English-speaking minority and English-speaking businesses throughout North America) language bill that mandated the use of French by all commercial establishments doing business in Quebec.

The FLQ

In the meantime, the 1966–70 era was marked by a sharp, if brief, turn toward the politics of violence in the evolution of Quebec nationalism, spearheaded by the *Front de Liberation du Quebec* terrorist organization.

Though such organizations are rare in the advanced democratic world, in today's era of globally organized terrorist organizations, the FLQ emerged in the age when most terrorist organizations were home-grown. In fact, although terrorism (a tool of unconventional warfare that uses sometimes indiscriminate political violence to achieve political objectives) has been around since at least the days of the Society of Assassins in the Saudi Arabian peninsula of the late tenth century, transnational terrorism and terrorist organizations are a relatively recent phenomenon. They made their first significant appearance only in 1972, when Palestinian terrorists attacked the Israeli team at the Olympic Games in Munich. Until then, most terrorist organizations in North America and Europe still fell into one of two basic categories. One of these was composed of leftist, urban terrorist organizations such as the Baader-Meinhof gang in West Germany and the Red Brigade in Italy—groups focused on bringing down the established order and creating a vaguely defined, socialist future. The other category included regional-ized separatist groups of various ideological persuasion, or of no partic-ular doctrinal inclination, who were willing to use terrorism to advance the cause of the territorialized national communities that they purported to represent. Some, like the bombers in the German-speaking region of Northern Italy and those in Brittany and Corsica in France, tended to eschew human targets and concentrated on arson and bombing attacks on the institutions of the central governments controlling their regions. Others, most notably the terrorist organizations in Northern Ireland and the extreme Basque separatist organizations in Spain, did not draw the line at taking human lives.

The FLQ bridged these two categories. Founded by far-left extrem-ists in 1963, the FLQ was a leftist, urban-focused terrorist organiza-tion comprising several cells uniformly committed to Quebec's separatism from Canada. Toward that end, from the mid-1960s until 1970 the FLQ—either to raise money or to target English-speaking businesses and the offices and officials of the Canadian government in Quebec—committed at least 200 violent crimes, including bank robberies, bombings (most notably the Montreal Stock Exchange in February, 1969, injuring 27), kidnappings, and murder. Added to these were such lesser crimes as arson, breaking and entering industrial and military buildings, and robbing the homes of wealthy English-speaking residents in Quebec. Throughout, the FLQ conducted a psychological warfare campaign that stressed that there was more to come. The resulting atmosphere of intimidation drove a few English-speaking companies from Quebec and led the officials of numerous others to buy armored automobiles, hire bodyguards, and travel as infrequently as possible.

The October Crisis

FLQ cells multiplied over the years, but so too did the number of their members who were apprehended and jailed for the specific crimes that they committed, and/or for engaging in terrorism. Nevertheless, although few people publicly condoned its actions and the FLQ's more violent acts drew criticism, few *Quebecois* politicians at the time argued that it deserved to be ostracized. In late 1970, however, its leaders went too far. Known in Canadian politics as the October Crisis, the events began with the October 5 kidnapping in Montreal of the British trade commissioner, James Cross. Demands for his release included the freeing of twenty-three "political prisoners" (the FLQ activists then imprisoned in Canadian jails), the publication of the FLQ's manifesto on creating a free and socialist Quebec, an aircraft to fly the kidnappers to safe asylum in either Cuba or Algeria, and half-million-dollar ransom fee, to be paid in gold. Over the next three days, while federal and provincial authorities cooperated in trying to solve the crime, the FLQ's manifesto was read on Canadian radio and published in part in several newspapers throughout Canada. Five days after the kidnapping, however, the Canadian government formally rejected the demands involving the gold ransom and the freeing of FLQ prisoners. A few hours later, the FLQ took a second hostage: Pierre Laporte, Quebec's vice premier and minister of labor.

The double kidnapping prompted the Liberal Party governments in Ottawa and Quebec province to collaborate closely in responding to the FLQ's specific threat to kill its hostages if its demands were not met and to the broad threat to public safety that it posed. Moreover, the ruling and opposition parties in Quebec closed ranks, condemning the FLQ and requesting that the federal government deploy military forces to assist the government of Quebec in restoring order. The following day, October 16, at the request of Quebec's premier, the federal government went one step further and invoked the World War I-era War Measures Act in response to the "insurrection" in the province. Under the terms of that Act, the federal government was given the power to declare martial law, suspend the writ of *habeas corpus*, and engage in wide-ranging police activity normally left in the hands of the provinces under Canada's federal system. The next day, the FLQ cell holding Laporte announced that it had executed him. His body was subsequently recovered in the trunk of a car abandoned near the Montreal airport.

Six weeks passed before investigators located the hiding place where Cross was being held. In the interim, 118 FLQ members, supporters, and sympathizers with communist backgrounds had been arrested under the War Measures Act, and some were charged with Laporte's murder. Cross himself was released unharmed in return for government assurances that his captors would be allowed to leave Canada without imprisonment, and shortly thereafter they were allowed to do so. By then, even the most ardent nationalists in Quebec had largely turned against the FLQ, and the end of 1970 also essentially marked the end of the FLQ as an important champion of Quebec nationalism and the terrorist route to sovereignty.

The PQ and the Peaceful Pursuit of Separatism

Although the FLQ received most of the publicity involving Quebec's pursuit of independence during the 1960s, nationalist sentiment was growing quietly but significantly within the province's French-speaking majority throughout the decade. It was a mood that French President Charles de Gaulle captured perfectly, if not very diplomatically, when in 1967 he used his invitation to speak at the Expo 67 celebration that Canada hosted to commemorate its one hundredth birthday to proclaim *"Vive le Quebec libre!"* (roughly, "Long live free Quebec!") to a cheering Montreal audience. And it was a mood Rene Levesque read equally well when, following the Liberal Party's defeat in Quebec's 1966 provincial elections, he quit the Liberals to form a separate nationalist party. After the next two years spent negotiating with the existing nationalist parties and organizations, Levesque had accomplished his mission with the founding of the *Parti Quebecois* (PQ) in 1968. It was a new force in Quebec politics that was composed of many of the RIN's followers, those who had supported other nationalist parties in 1966, and Quebec nationalists who had previously voted for the Liberal Party.

The PQ's 1970 electoral debut was impressive, but it was overshadowed by the Liberal Party's total victory over the incumbent *Union Nationale*. The PQ's victory six years later in Quebec's 1976 elections, however, left Ottawa fearful of Canada's future when the final tally gave the PQ a dominating majority (71 of the 110 seats) in the Quebec Assembly. Prime Minister Trudeau's Liberal Party wing in the province, in contrast, managed to hold onto only 26 of its seats, and the *Union Nationale's* presence in Quebec's parliament shrank from 56 seats in 1966 to only 13 a decade later. Ironically, it was the Liberal Party's policy of courting the nationalist vote by passing Proposition 22 that had rebounded to the PQ's advantage. The hostile reaction to the measure in the English-speaking community inside and outside Quebec had further fed Quebec nationalism to the point where, in 1976 at least, the Liberal Party's continuing emphasis on a strong Quebec in the Canadian federation could no longer enfold it.

Four of the suspected members, in 1971, of the Quebec Liberation Front charged with the murder of the Quebec minister of labor, Pierre Laporte. Copyright Brian Smith/Corbis.

The Sovereignty Issue Intensifies: Referendums, the *Quebecois*, and the "Quebec Problem"

The First Referendum

The PQ's success in acquiring control over Quebec's government led immediately to further provincial legislation (the Charter of the French Language). It was designed to enshrine French as not just the primary language of Quebec, but also the tongue of public discourse, complete with provisions forbidding immigrants, their children, and the children of French-speaking parents from receiving a public education in Quebec's English-language schools, which henceforth were to be only for the province's English-speaking population. More troubling to Ottawa, the PQ's electoral victory was read by many in the party as a mandate to push forward with its pronounced goal of detaching Quebec from Canada. In making that interpretation, the party stumbled badly.

The latter part of the 1970s produced an uncertain economic climate in most advanced industrial countries, primarily because of the sharp increase in the price of imported oil. It quadrupled, from less than $3 a barrel in 1972 to nearly $12 a barrel in late 1973, and then rose again in 1979 to approximately $36 a barrel. Inflation soared in most oil-importing states, and their counterinflationary policies drove up unemployment rates as well. Corporate profits, consumer spending, and government revenue declined as "stagflation" gripped the developed economies of North America and Western Europe. It was not an auspicious time for any region to sell the argument of going it alone, especially one such as Quebec, whose programs were being partially financed by transfers from the central government. Nevertheless, the PQ pushed forward with precisely that agenda in 1980, holding a referendum on whether the province's leaders should begin to negotiate the terms governing Quebec's departure from, and subsequent associational arrangement with, Canada. The result was a resounding, nearly 60-percent vote against the proposition on May 20, 1980. Nevertheless, the following year a weakened PQ was reelected to another term in office. Nationalist sentiment remained strong in the province, despite the fact that a cost-benefit analysis of going it alone had caused a majority of even French-speaking voters to oppose the referendum.

The PQ's fortunes declined visibly when its founder and leader, Levesque, resigned in 1985. Almost immediately thereafter the party failed to win reelection in Quebec's provincial elections. The Liberals' return to power, however, was not accompanied by any evident waning of the desire by a majority of the province's French-speaking population to achieve at least some constitutional recognition of Quebec's special status in the Canadian federation. Quite the contrary; when Trudeau essentially worked around Quebec to renegotiate Canada's constitution

License plate of the Province of Quebec. The "Je me souviens" plate was introduced amid growing Quebec nationalism in 1979, replacing the "La Belle
Province" motto. Photograph courtesy of Eric Belgrad.

and sever its last formal, albeit symbolic link with Britain by replacing
the Queen with a governor-general as Canada's head of state, the diplomatic slight further fueled Quebec nationalism and Quebec's demands
for the special treatment that Trudeau had promised the province in 1980
when campaigning against the pending referendum on sovereignty.

Mollifying Quebec: The Lake Meech and Charlottetown Accords

Despite Trudeau's pledge, efforts to accommodate Quebec with
institutional adjustments did not begin in earnest until 1987, when the
Progressive Conservative Party won control of the Canadian government. Under the leadership of Brian Mulroney, who was himself Quebec
born, and in collaboration with the Liberal Party Premier of Quebec, an
agreement was negotiated among the Canadian and provincial prime
ministers at Lake Meech in the Province of Quebec. It recognized
Quebec's special status as a "distinct society" in the Canadian federation
and guaranteed Quebec—and the other provinces—such enhanced influence in Canadian politics as formal input to the appointing of Supreme
Court judges. To became valid, however, the constitutional changes
proposed in the Lake Meech Accord had to be unanimously endorsed by
Canada's provinces, and from the beginning there was a public opinion
backlash both in Quebec, where the accord did not seem to go far enough

in institutionalizing Quebec's special status, and in English-speaking Canada, where it was criticized for a variety of reasons, including the failure of the Lake Meech conference to include representatives of Canada's Native Americans. In the end, at the eleventh hour for ratification in 1990, Newfoundland and Manitoba refused to ratify the agreement. Far from mollifying *Quebecois* sentiment, the failed Lake Meech Accord intensified nationalist feelings in the province to the point where, for the first time, polls showed that a majority in Quebec favored the sovereignty-independence option.

With talk of a second referendum on the sovereignty issue gaining momentum in Quebec, Ottawa made a second attempt to accommodate Quebec nationalism that same year by appointing a study commission to make recommendations that became the core of an agreement struck in 1992 at Charlottetown, Prince Edward Island. This time the accord covered a much wider area, including a series of social issues involving health care, education, the environment, and collective bargaining. The heart of the Charlottetown Accord, nevertheless, was the "Canada Clause," which attempted to identify the core characteristics that Canada incarnates, including respect for diversity and recognition of Quebec as constituting a "distinct society" within the Canadian federation. Toward that end the accord proposed to enshrine constitutionally some long-standing practices designed to accommodate Quebec, such as the appointment of three of the nine justices on the Canadian Supreme Court from that province.[4] Unlike the Lake Meech Accord, the Charlottetown Accord was to be submitted to the people in separate referendums to be held in each of Canada's ten federal provinces and its two autonomous territories (the Yukon and the Northwest territories).

The Charlottetown Accord's greater specificity compared to the language of the Lake Meech Accord quickly translated into greater controversy, which in Quebec centered on the "distinct society" provisions of the agreement. The *Parti Quebecois* campaigned for a No vote in the 1992 referendum on the accord, on the grounds that it did not go far enough toward granting Quebec the additional autonomy it deserved, given its special status in Canada. Also opposing the proposal was former Canadian prime minister Pierre Trudeau, who had spent most of his career in the government of Canada focusing on the Quebec issue, as either minister of justice (1967) concerned with the FLQ or as Canadian prime minister (1968–1979; 1980–1984). He urged his colleagues in the Quebec wing of the Liberal Party to reject the referendum, because it gave so much to Quebec that it threatened the survival of the Canadian federation. The intensity of both the debate and the nationalist sentiment in Quebec can be read in the electoral turnout—which at 82.8 percent was far higher than the all-Canada average (71 percent)—and in the decisiveness of the No vote, 56.7 percent to 43.3 percent against the accord. Yet elsewhere in Canada the Charlottetown Accord did not fare much better. Overall, six of the ten provinces rejected it.

The Second Referendum

Two years later the 1994 provincial elections in Quebec returned the PQ to power, and the party immediately began preparations for holding a second referendum on the sovereignty/independence issue. As in the case of the 1980 referendum, a Yes vote would not mean immediate secession; it would only authorize the government of Quebec to begin consultations with the federal government in Ottawa toward that end. Should those negotiations fail, however, a Yes vote in this second referendum would essentially authorize the government in Quebec to unilaterally declare the province's independence. Consequently, the proposal alarmed Quebec's English-speaking community even more than the previous sovereignty referendum had. And there were sound reasons for their concern. The unwillingness of two English-speaking provinces to ratify the Lake Meech Accord recognizing Quebec's special status was still a sore point among the *Quebecois,* and this time around the cost of leaving Canada was no longer as high. Not only was the global stagflation of the 1980s a thing of the past, but the recent negotiation of a North American Free Trade Agreement was widely interpreted to mean that even if Quebec were separated from Canada, it would still be part of a free trade zone encompassing not only the rest of Canada, but all of North America.

Thanks to an extremely vocal and tense debate, election turnout for the referendum was more than 90 percent of the province's eligible voters. This time around, however, the final tally was neither definitive nor satisfying to either side. The vote was extremely close, with the No votes adding up to 50.6 percent of the total vote and 49.4 percent voting in favor of the proposal. Furthermore, Quebec's linguistic communities split over the measure. English-speaking Quebeckers voted overwhelmingly against the referendum, but in contrast to the first referendum, a majority of the French-speaking *Quebecois* voted in favor of the measure. Another observation is that the determining balance of votes appears to have been cast by members of the immigrant community in Quebec, who were allowed to vote on the measure. Looking to Ottawa with thanks for their admission to Canada and for the protection of their rights, the immigrants voted preponderantly against the measure, allowing the PQ to blame the outcome on the votes of interlopers who did not understand Canadian history or appreciate Quebec's unique character. Protests over the referendum's outcome, even among the most ardent Quebec nationalists, nonetheless remained peaceful.

Evading Quebec

The 1995 vote's immediate impact on Canadian politics was principally on the political party front. The narrow victory of the "no" vote did nothing to undermine support for the PQ and may have even solidified it in the short term, insofar as the party won re-election to another term and governed Quebec until losing to the Liberals eight years later, in 2003. Combined with the outcome of the Lake Meech and Charlottetown Accords, however, the "no" vote on the 1995 referendum convinced Quebec nationalists of the need to push their cause more aggressively in the Canadian Parliament in Ottawa. Toward that end the *Bloc Quebecois*, whose political life began in 1990 as an informal coalition of Progressive Conservatives and Quebec Liberals in Ottawa and which ran for the first time as the voice of Quebec in the 1993 federal elections, broadened its base after the 1995 referendum by incorporating the PQ into the *Bloc.* Since then, the *Bloc Quebecois* has normally garnered 40 percent or more of Quebec's votes in Canada's federal elections, and it has usually held at least 50 seats in the 308-seat Canadian assembly. Given the often divided nature of the vote in Canadian elections and the not-infrequent failure of any of Canada's system-wide parties to gain an outright majority in the Canadian parliament, it is a sufficient enough presence to qualify the *Bloc* as a legitimate coalition partner, whose support of a Progressive Conservative government might be exchanged for legislation favorable to Quebec.[5]

Prior to the Progressive Conservative victory in Canada's 2006 elections, the Bloc had found few sympathetic ears in the Liberal Party cabinets that governed Canada between 1993 and 2006. Quebec has traditionally been a Liberal stronghold, and its support is critical to the Liberals having a parliamentary majority in Ottawa. Quebec's departure from Canada would greatly reduce the Liberals' chances of governing the country. Consequently, Liberal leaders spent much of the 1990s seeking to block any third referendum, on the reasoning that the Canadian federation is indivisible and that referendums on sovereignty are therefore unconstitutional, and cannot be held. The early twenty-first century found the Liberals still clinging to that position when the heat was somewhat reduced by the PQ's loss and the Liberals' return to power in Quebec.

Future Prospects for Peace and Turmoil

Public opinion polls in the early twenty-first century indicated some waning of nationalist sentiment in Quebec, but the Quebec Francophones had by no means abandoned their desire for enhanced autonomy. Thus, the future of politics in Quebec, and hence for Canada, looks neither altogether rosy nor entirely bleak in these early years of the new millennium.

On the plus side, there are currently no signs that Quebec will return to the days of FLQ violence. On that count, Quebec may be the most tenuous of the hot spots included in this volume. At the same time, emotions still run very high on both sides—among those who would move Quebec out of Canada and those in English-speaking Canada and Quebec's shrinking English-speaking community who remain utterly opposed to, and actively seek to block, any such action.[6] A new referendum effort would thus guarantee a heated debate in Quebec, in which that province's English-speaking minority and immigrant communities would likely be singled out as obstacles to Quebec achieving its national self-determination. And were Quebec to begin the process of withdrawing from Canada, the losers inside and outside of Quebec would become quarrelsome at the very least—whatever that might mean in a country not noted for having a particularly violent political culture.

For now, ardent Quebec nationalists remain frustrated, and the Quebec issue remains an unresolved and important dimension of Canadian politics. Nor has the slight decline in support for the sovereignty option in early twenty-first-century polls been accompanied by a notable reduction in tension. Although distinctly a fringe movement in contemporary Quebec politics, the FLQ still makes headlines. In 2001, for example, it targeted seven McDonald's stores and a coffee chain operating in Quebec under its English name (Second Cup) for firebombings because of their un-*Quebecois* nature and/or audacity in not adopting French logos and names. Short of a coalition government at the center depending on *Bloc Quebecois* support to govern, Quebec's nationals are not likely to see any significant olive branches extended in their direction by English-speaking Canadians. The compromising spirit of the late 1980s and early 1990s, which led the premiers of the other provinces to agree to the language and substance of the Lake Meech and Charlottetown Accords in order to accommodate Quebec separatists, appears to be gone for at least the foreseeable future. Indeed, it essentially disappeared during the mid-1990s, when so many of the premiers agreeing to the accords were swept out of office and Gallup Polls were already recording a solid 75-percent majority of English-speaking Canadians preferring to risk separation rather than grant additional concessions to the *Quebecois*.

Timeline

| 1534 | As British settle upper Canada, Jacques Cartier claims region around the St. Lawrence for France. |

1759	British defeat "New France" in battle at Quebec City; French empire in Canada soon vanishes.
1774	Quebec Act formalizes British control of Quebec in framework that preserves distinctive French civil codes, the system of landholding, and the authority of the Catholic Church as preserver of Quebec's culture.
1837	Rebellion of French Canadians seeking greater political power fails.
1841	Act of Union unites Ontario and Quebec into one province, and efforts to assimilate French Quebec begin.
1867	British North America Act creates the confederation of Canada; Quebec becomes a separate federal province.
1917	Conscription for World War I is bitterly opposed by French-Canadians.
1941–45	World War II causes a new political crisis involving French-Canadian opposition to conscription.
1960	Jean Lesage of the Liberal Party is elected premier of Quebec; the Quiet Revolution begins.
1968	René Lévesque forms the *Parti Québécois* (PQ), committed to achieving Quebec's sovereign independence.
1970	The *Front de Libération du Québec* (FLQ) kidnaps and kills Quebec's Minister of Labor. Canada activates War Measures Act, suspending some civil liberties in Quebec; FLQ loses public support in Quebec.
1976	The PQ wins Quebec provincial elections; René Lévesque becomes premier.
1977	Quebec Assembly enacts bill designed to make French the language of business and social mobility in Quebec.
1980	Quebec holds its first referendum on renegotiating its relationship with Canada; nearly two-thirds of Quebec's voters vote against doing so.
1987	Meech Lake Accord is negotiated, giving Quebec recognition as a "distinct society."
1990	Unable to receive ratification from all provinces, the Meech Lake Accord dies; support for sovereignty soars among *Québécois*.

1992	Second attempt to negotiate a new constitutional arrangement in Canada fails.
1995	Second Quebec referendum on Quebec negotiating its separation from Canada loses narrowly (50.6 percent to 49.4 percent).
2000	Enthusiasm for independence moves to the back burner of Quebec's early twenty-first century public agenda behind economic concerns and public safety issues posed by revelation of homegrown terrorists among Canada's Muslims.

Notes

1. Although Canada is larger than the continental United States in area, its current population is only approximately a tenth of the U.S. population, and more than 90 percent of those people live within a narrow, 50- to 100-mile-wide belt spanning the Canadian side of its border with the United States.

2. Saul Newman, "Canada: The Nationalist Movement in Quebec," in Joseph R. Rudolph Jr., ed. *Encyclopedia of Modern Ethnic Conflicts* (Westport, CT: Greenwood Press, 2003: 27–36).

3. Ibid.

4. The practice had initially been justified on the grounds that Quebec's legal system, unlike that of the remainder of Canada, does not recognize the English concept of common law (i.e. judge-made law), but is built on the French system of civil laws and codes.

5. In the January 2006 vote, for example, the Progressive Conservatives won the election, but with only 124 seats in the 308-seat Assembly. The Liberals retained 103 seats, the *Bloc Quebecois* won 51 seats, and the remaining 30 seats went to an independent candidate and the New Democratic Party.

6. The decrease in the population of English-speaking Quebec residents began with the language laws of 1971, and their number did not stabilize again until the 1990s. English speakers in Quebec are now slightly more than 10 percent of Quebec's population, although only 3 percent of the people now indicate that they are British in origin. In contrast, the figures for both categories were approximately 14 percent in 1971. See the demographic study of Quebec's population from Marianopolis College, "Quebec History" (http://www2.marianopolis.edu/quebechistory/stats/angpop41.htm, accessed June 16, 2005).

CHAPTER 9

THE UNITED STATES

Just as antiglobalization protests can be a threat to the peace on a rotating basis, depending on where such targets of antiglobalization sentiments as the IMF, the WTO, and the G-8 leaders hold their meetings, so single-interest groups that advocate extreme action can raise issues of political violence within the United States depending on where individual groups see the primary threat to their interests and developments affecting the targets of their wrath, be they logging industries, petrochemical plants, cosmetics firms engaging in animal testing, or doctors assisting suicide or performing abortions. In the words of former House of Representatives Majority Leader Tip O'Neill, "all politics is local" to some degree, and within the framework of our definition, "hot spots" can be local as well.

To be sure, aggressive interest groups are by no means limited to the United States. The phenomenon of single-interest politics is to be found in some form throughout the economically developed, advanced democratic world. Indeed, it is a product of that world, whose increasingly educated and politically aware citizenry possess the economic resources and time to pursue issues far broader than those bread-and-butter economic interests (minimum wages, the right to unionize, welfare services) central to industrializing societies. Some of these interests—such as stopping the globalization process—are transnational in nature. Others, such as controlling immigration, primarily manifest themselves inside the political processes of individual countries. And still others are more idiosyncratic to the rules (taxation systems, access to abortion, use of capital punishment, parental rights of unmarried fathers, civil rights of homosexuals) and the concerns and conditions (pursuit of stem cell research, drilling for oil on public lands, the harvesting of forests by construction companies, love of dogs) that are found in individual societies. Not all issues have thus far given birth to extremist interest groups, but some have. Thus, interest group Websites urging criminal acts against those perceived to be engaging in such activities as harming the environment or hunting animals for sport are scarcely rare in today's world. Even those with peaceful orientations can cross the line. The more extreme members of the Father's Rights group in Britain, for example, hatched a plot in early 2006 to advance their cause somehow by kidnapping the son of British Prime Minister Tony Blair. Similarly, usually nonviolent groups opposed to nuclear power in France and Spain nonetheless have amassed long records of contemplating or engaging in violent action against the nuclear power industries in their countries.

Nevertheless, over the last several decades the most passionate pursuit of single-interest objectives and the most conspicuous use of violence by single-interest groups and their extremist devotees have been found within and throughout the United States.

SINGLE-INTEREST EXTREMISTS

Antiabortionists

Although not the oldest of the violence-prone organizations or movements in the United States, the antiabortion organizations are surely among the most interesting and active single-issue groups to have emerged since the Vietnam War era. At first blush, the idea of people carrying pro-life banners who are willing to endorse or otherwise participate in not just violent, but murderous activities seems highly paradoxical, and not a little surreal. To date at least, gun control activists have not been known to engage in shootouts with chief executive officers of arms manufacturing companies, and most of the violence associated with the antiwar movement during the Vietnam era has been attributed not to the pacifists, but to far-left-wing, quasi-anarchist groups attaching themselves to the Peace Movement. Likewise, although groups opposing capital punishment—for example, Amnesty International and the American Civil Liberties Union, as well as more specialized foes of the death penalty such as Fast and Vigil—have engaged in various civil disobedience demonstrations, they have logically shunned confrontations likely to result in injuries. Yet the willingness of pro-life extremists to condone, urge, and employ political violence in the name of their cause—far from being paradoxical—is actually understandable, *and* it explains much of the danger to the public safety posed by single-interest extremists in America.

Those drawn to the extremist wings of single-interest movements, like the movements themselves, are a diverse lot. Charlatans and opportunists are no doubt a part of the crowd, exploiting the interests and beliefs of others for personal influence and/or financial gain. Fanatics, too, are frequently present, motivated by intense hatreds or passions bordering on the psychotic. And some are perhaps drawn to movement politics out of boredom. Most, however, tend to be neither the dispossessed, the psychotic, nor the downtrodden. Timothy McVeigh, the architect of the Oklahoma City Federal Building bombing that claimed 168 lives in April 1995, was more disciplined and willing to die for the cause than most, but by all accounts he was a quiet, polite son of middle America's middle class. Moreover, most activists feel passionately about the issue that has brought them into the political arena, and none more so than those drawn to antiabortion groups out of a sincere belief that life begins at conception and that abortion is state-licensed murder. Indeed, to those anchoring their convictions to a religious base, not to use whatever means necessary to try to stop those working in abortion clinics and performing "mass murder" might seem not only wrong, but immoral. Consider, for example, the case of Eric Rudolph, who was sentenced in 2005 to life in prison for his 1998 bombing of a women's clinic, which resulted in the death of an off-duty police officer and the maiming of a nurse. By way of explanation, Rudolph said, "What they [in the clinic] did was participate in the murder of 50 children a week. Abortion is murder, and because it is murder I believe deadly force is needed to stop it." In short, if "the state is no longer the protector of the [unborn] innocents," others must act.[1]

A History of Political Violence

Viewed from a perspective such as Eric Rudolph's, it is not surprising that following the Supreme Court's judgment in the landmark 1971 case of *Roe v. Wade*—which upheld a woman's right to terminate pregnancy during the first trimester, thus launching America's antiabortion movement—antiabortion activists established themselves for nearly two decades as the country's most violence-prone single-interest group. According to MSNBC tallies, between 1977 (when the first clinic was firebombed) and 1994, antiabortion activists committed more than 1700 acts of violence directed at doctors, nurses, and clinics providing abortions.[2] More recent figures gathered by the National Abortion Federation are similar, indicating that between 1985 and 2005 antiabortion extremists— sometimes as the inadvertent result of bombings, and on other occasions by design—killed 6 people, attempted murder in 15 other instances, committed more than 200 instances of bombing or arson, made approximately

750 death or bomb threats, and engaged in hundreds of acts of vandalism, robbery, and stalking, and related acts of intimidation.[3]

To state the obvious, by no means do all of those opposed the *Roe* decision engage in such practices. Record keepers usually distinguish between the antiabortionists, who are willing to engage in violent action in order to prohibit a practice currently deemed constitutional, and the pro-life organizations such the National Right to Life Committee,[4] who advocate working within the political system. The pro-lifers' objective is to limit access to abortion through legislation, such as that requiring parental notification in the case of minors, and to reverse *Roe* some day by influencing the nomination of new justices to the United States Supreme Court. On the other hand, until 1994 the most common tactic of pro-life organizations was blocking access to abortion clinics to doctors, nurses, and prospective patients—an in-their-face mode of political activity, laced with emotion on all sides, that under the best of circumstances was a form of physical intimidation of those seeking to cross the line and enter the clinic. This tactic often resulted in violent confrontations between the pro-life protestors, on one side, and the pro-abortion groups, clinic personnel and patients, and the police on the other.

It was the violence associated with these blockades that persuaded Congress to pass the Freedom of Access to Clinic Entrances Act of 1996 (FACE), with its very stiff penalties ($100,000 fines and up to a year in jail) for even first-time offenders. Since then, blockades of clinics have become negligible (only 20 were reported between 2001 and 2004), and those few that have been staged have been brief and largely symbolic, resulting in no arrests. In place of the blockades, however, moderate pro-life organizations have turned with increasing frequency to picketing clinics—an activity that also attracts the deeply committed and hence carries its own risk of turning violent. Some groups, such as Operation Rescue and the Pro-Life Rescue League, have become so militant that the federal government has been driven to apply the Racketeer Influenced and Corrupt Organizations (RICO) Act to curtail their practices. Although RICO was specifically intended for use in combating organized crime, its language is broad enough to cover any illegal criminal acts committed on an ongoing basis by any organization. Consequently, those who persistently blocked access to abortion clinics during the 1990s fell within its reach.

Changing Tactics and the Hard-Core Antiabortionists

The movement of more moderate pro-life groups away from blockades and other confrontational and conflict-laden modes of advancing their cause was not entirely out of fear of federal prosecution. The murder, arson, and bombing campaigns of the antiabortion extremists also had a dampening effect on the activities of moderate pro-life activists, who were alternately repelled by such violence and fearful of being identified with the actions of such extremists as Eric Rudolph. Consequently, the violence associated with the antiabortion movement has increasingly been committed by a small percentage of those who belong to the most extreme antiabortion groups. At the same time, these are precisely the ones who are most inclined to commit the most violent acts, perhaps in part because they feel that the cause has been abandoned by those opposed to abortion who have moderated their activities.

Nor is it possible to dismiss extremists such as Rudolph as homicidal criminals, acting entirely on their own and bringing disrepute to the entire antiabortion movement—at least, not in the current age. For one thing, as the Canadian-based Consultants on Religious Tolerance organization has noted, "recent cases involving the assassination and attempted murder of abortion providers, in both the United States and Canada, have shown that perpetrators appear to be sheltered by a network of sympathizers."[5] Simply stated, like all terrorists whose attacks indiscriminately affect innocent civilians, antiabortion extremists require a logistical support base in order to hide, arm themselves, and conduct their activities beyond their own locales. Many appear to have just such a network, or to be in the process of developing or locating one.

In that network-building endeavor, a principal ally of these groups has been the World Wide Web, which has enabled antiabortionists to develop that supportive network more easily—and less traceably—than would have been true otherwise. For antiabortion extremists, as well as for their counterparts in other single-issue movements that periodically engage in acts of political violence, the Web has significantly blurred the lines separating lone wolf criminals, groups advocating extremist action, and organizations abetting acts of violence. Indeed, even experts in tracking antiabortion activists have yet to decide how to classify perhaps the most significant antiabortion organization in the contemporary United States—Michael Bray's Virginia-based Army of God.

The most benign conjecture is that the Army of God is only a religiously motivated, ultra-antiabortion organization that encourages violence against those performing, assisting in the performance of, or seeking abortions, and whose cause and name have repeatedly been invoked by individuals convicted of committing those acts. On the other hand, it may actually be what it clearly aspires to be—an established, underground network of people joined together by their common conviction that violence is a legitimate means of ending the practice of abortion. What is indisputable is that its well-circulated underground manual goes beyond a general advocacy of violence against abortion

Army of God and other anti-abortion activists protest the forthcoming execution of Paul Hill in Starke, Florida, in September 2003. Hill killed Dr. John Britton and James Barrett in 1994 outside a Pensacola, Florida, abortion clinic. Hill was the first person executed in the United States for murdering a doctor who performed abortions. © David Kadlubowski/Corbis.

clinics. It provides instructions on how to build homemade ammonium nitrate bombs and C-4 plastic explosives, recommends the maiming of clinic doctors by removing their hands, and even defines the murder of clinic personnel as justifiable homicide.[6] It is equally clear that the Army of God is not alone in its fight, and for those seeking directions toward targets, the information is often only a mouse click away. Although sometimes fined and even closed down by federal authorities as illegally threatening abortion providers, the Website of the Army of God and such affiliated or related sites as those of the Christian Gallery regularly post photos of aborted fetuses, the "heroes" in the struggle against abortion (often convicted felons and even murderers), those entering abortion clinics, and those working in the clinics. The names, telephone numbers, and addresses of clinic workers are frequently attached to the photos.

Animal Rights and Environmental Terrorism

Meanwhile, the organizations most prone toward political violence as a means of pursuing their objectives in the United States in the early years of the twenty-first century have been those dedicated to protecting animals and the environment.[7] According to the National Memorial Institute for the Prevention of Terrorism—created in Oklahoma City to honor the victims of the Federal Building bombing there—a total of twenty-three terrorist incidents occurred in the United States from early 2003 to January 2005. Of these, all but three were perpetrated by such militant environmental groups as the Earth Liberation Front (ELF) and the underground Animal Liberation Front (ALF).[8] Few of these incidents were trivial, although none resulted in fatalities. ELF's arson attack on a San Diego housing development in 2003, for example, did damage estimated at more than $160 million.[9] And beyond their acts of arson and sabotage, these groups have launched numerous Internet campaigns aimed at those engaged in animal testing and hunting, including sending monthly emails to hunters with identifiable religious backgrounds, carrying such salutations as "Dear Christian Murderer."

The most disturbing element involving these groups has been the steady escalation in the nature of their activities. Although ALF's origins can be traced to the early 1970s, the first act attributed to it did not occur until 1979, and that only involved vandalism—the illegal entry into New York University's Medical School and the release of five animals then being used for medical research and testing. By the mid-1990s, ALF's "leaderless resistance" (it has no official membership) and the activities of such fellow travelers as People for the Ethical Treatment of Animals (PETA) and—on the environmental side—ELF and its kin had been credited with hundreds of acts of arson, bombings, and vandalism that included attacks on such diverse targets as cosmetics manufacturing facilities, federal power stations, and cell phone towers. Moreover, the real escalation in their activities was still to come, especially in California, Oregon, Washington state, and New York state—still the favorite targets of the environmental and animal rights groups. Thus, although ecoterrorism had not taken a human life as late as mid-2006, most analysts did not foresee that record lasting much longer. As John Lewis, the deputy chief of the FBI's counterintelligence unit, summarized the situation in 2005, "When you are burning homes, buildings, and ski slopes, it's just a matter of time."[10]

Antigovernment Citizen Movements and Armed Militias

Whereas both the antiabortion and white supremacy movements often lay claim to, and draw from a Christian religious base, many of the most virulent right-wing movements of the post-Vietnam era did not do so. Indeed, some were avowedly secular and (again unlike the antiabortion movements and most racist groups) were less opposed to specific policies than broadly antigovernment in orientation. Of these, none was more influential on future developments on the political right than the West Coast's Posse Comitatus.

The Posse Comitatus

In a political landscape crowded with right-wing tax protest groups during the 1960s, many of whom were particularly incensed by the federal surtax added in mid-decade to help finance the Vietnam War, the Posse Comitatus stood out because of its well-developed antigovernment philosophy. Its name combines a Latin term referring to the "power of the country" and a name for the system by which local authorities called upon the people for help in enforcing the laws of early England and the American West. The Posse Comitatus that emerged in California and Oregon in approximately 1970 built its ideology around the principle that ultimate political power lies with the county and its local community. For Posse members and those who would later embrace its philosophy, the derivative argument was that the emergence of an ever-stronger central government, with the power to tax and otherwise control local people and agents, represented an unconstitutional usurpation of authority that was spearheaded by decisions of the federal judiciary. The corollary was that supreme power remained with the people, whose duty it is to restore their sovereign republic by unilateral action, under the leadership of their local sheriffs.

From the outset, subscribers had a self-interest in being a Posse member. At a minimum, it provided them with a convenient rationale for not paying their taxes—the counties had not been given a formal role in the ratification of the Sixteenth Amendment, which authorized the federal income tax. Nevertheless, it was during the farm crisis of the early 1980s, when large numbers of besieged farmers increased its ranks, that the Posse peaked in terms of membership, breadth of support, and violent impact on the American political landscape. Over the next decade, its members—including those with connections to hate groups— were involved in shootouts with authorities (most notably in North Dakota and Arkansas in 1983) as well as standoffs and other confrontations with federal authorities over their refusal to pay taxes, and as a result of their involvement in a variety of fraudulent activities and other crimes.[11] By the end of the decade, however, many of its leaders had died, either in those shootouts (Gordon Kahl) or naturally (William Potter Gale and Henry Beach), and with other leaders in jail, the Posse largely faded away as a significant antigovernment movement. Its philosophy, however, has continued to endure, reincarnated in the Sovereign Citizen

Movement and in various militias opposed to the "dictatorial" nature of the American political process.

The Sovereign Citizen Movement

The Sovereign Citizen Movement was born and developed during approximately the same period (1970 into the 1980s) as the Posse and also attracted several white supremacy elements to its cause by virtue of its antigovernment rhetoric. Unlike the Posse Comitatus, though, it has developed as a network of local units and—having long outlived the Posse—has continued to wage its war against the U.S. government through both violent and nonviolent (but highly illegal) means into the twenty-first century, and throughout the country.[12] In fact, some of its most infamous members and units have achieved more notoriety than most recent practitioners of political violence in U.S. politics. Timothy McVeigh's cohort in the bombing of the Oklahoma City Federal Building, Terry Nichols, was strongly linked to the Movement years before that day in April, 1995. The year following that attack, Sovereign Citizens were in the news again in one of the most publicized standoffs between federal authorities and anarchists, when for eighty-one days the Montana Freemen stood off the federal agents sent to arrest them on numerous charges. Elsewhere, extremists associated with the movement murdered police officers, assaulted state employees, shot volunteer firefighters, and kidnapped ordinary citizens in retaliation for the arrest of one of their cell's members.

Such violent action has continued into the new millennium, but the most conspicuous activity currently associated with the Sovereign Citizen Movement is its nonviolent but highly illegal activity aimed at state authority. Dubbed "paper terrorism," the activity has now spanned nearly two decades and has involved Citizen units in a variety of criminal acts. They have staged "common law courts" and issued threatening "orders" against officials found guilty of acting unconstitutionally, and they have filed frivolous lawsuits against public officials to clog up the court system. Citizen activists have pursued fraudulent schemes designed to bankroll the movement's activities and have posted boilerplate forms on their Websites for fellow citizens to use in their paper wars against public officials. In most instances, their presence is not likely to result in political violence, but the potential remains—and it is a nationwide potential.

State Militias

In a similar manner, the more violent antigovernment movements of the 1990s, the various state militias, have likewise ceased to pose the same violent threat to the public order that they once did. Indeed, compared to their activities both before and since that time, the decade of the 1990s was (to date) decidedly the high-water mark for these antigovernment organizations.

Compared to the Sovereign Citizen Movement and other right-wing antigovernment movements of the late twentieth century, the militia movement ranks as the youngest, dating not from the Vietnam era of the 1960s but from the early to mid-1990s. To be sure, right-wing paramilitary political groups have existed in America's past—for example, the pre-World War II neofascist organizations and such Cold War-era groups as the California Rangers—and white supremacist and survivalist organizations have occasionally organized themselves into military-style units. The militias of the 1990s differed from these forerunners both in terms of their nationwide scope of operations and the emphasis they placed on their highly developed "take back America" antigovernment ideology.[13]

A series of factors fueled the growth of these pro-gun, antigovernment movements, the most important of which were those federal standoffs with heavily armed dissident groups that occasionally turned both violent and tragic. In particular, the shootings at Ruby Ridge (Idaho) in 1992[14] and the fatal fire that ended the fifty-one-day standoff at Waco, Texas between the Bureau of Alcohol, Tobacco, and Firearms (BATF) and David Koresh at the compound of his Branch Davidian religious cult. The Branch Davidian incident on April 19, 1993, cost eighty lives (including 25 children).[15] Both of those tragedies were interpreted by the militias as clear "examples of a government willing to stop at nothing to stamp out people who refused to conform."[16]

As broad and rapid as the growth of these militias was in the early 1990s, the ebbing of these movements occurred almost equally quickly in the late 1990s and the first years of the following decade. In part, their decline is attributable to the steady pressure placed on them by federal authorities and the arrest of some of their more notable leaders, more often than not on weapon charges. The militia movement was also hurt by the failure of militias elsewhere to come to the aid of (i.e., to "rescue") those "under attack" by the federal government, most conspicuously during the lengthy standoff involving the Montana Freemen movement in 1996. Yet probably nothing damaged the militia movement as much as the bombing of the Oklahoma City Federal building, which its perpetrators in part justified as retaliation for the Waco "murders." It happened two years to the day after the fatal end of the siege at Waco, and along with the early, mistaken rumors that it was committed by militiamen, the Oklahoma City bombing alienated many who had been drawn to the militias and derailed further recruitment efforts.

Nor have subsequent events been conducive to a turnaround in the militias' fortunes. The millennium virus prophesied by the conspiracy doomsayers failed to materialize when the twenty-first century began. Then, with both Congress and the White House in the hands of the Republican Party from 2001 to 2006, and with the anti-Clinton rhetoric temporarily focused no wider than on the junior senator from New York, there was less general rabble-rousing on the political right to inspire antigovernment extremists. More importantly, the wellspring of patriotism unleashed by the terrorist attack on America by foreign extremists diminished the appeal of antigovernment politics and extremism in general in the United States. Nevertheless, the militias—along with their bombing plots, threatening rhetoric, and frequently illegal pursuits—continue to be an active part of the American landscape. Moreover, most analysts note that their waning has not been evenly distributed across the country. The militias in Michigan, Ohio, Indiana, Illinois and, in particular, the Kentucky State Militia remain nearly as strong as before. They continue to meet regularly, recruit widely (several militias have widened their recruitment activities to include women and minors), and train as paramilitary units for possible war against the enemy.

Hate Groups and Supremacists

Antiabortion violence remains a relatively recent development, largely from the political right in American politics. Right-wing extremist groups are scarcely new or novel actors in American politics, however. In fact, they are as old and American as the Ku Klux Klan (founded 1866), if not older. Their contemporary manifestations, however, differ from their predecessors in one important way.[17] At its peak, local branches of the Klan—which sprang up in the immediate aftermath of the United States Civil War—were normally composed of local public officials championing its cause. It was thus, at its core, a state-sponsored terrorist organization systematically employing random political violence at the local level to preserve a dominant white and Protestant status quo in the post-Civil War United States. In much the same way, Robespierre and his euphemistically named Committee on Public Safety used terrorism as a tool of politics to sustain (temporarily) their rule during post-Revolutionary France's Reign of Terror.

Organizations in the United States that are rooted in their respective memberships' shared hatred of others—principally Jews and those of African ancestry—and/or the supremacy of the white race are currently numerous, and they span the American continent. Their number, however, reflects their disorganized and decentralized nature, not a deep and continuing racial element in American society. Along with their generally thin ranks, their disorganization limits their ability to disrupt the contemporary U.S. political process, despite the inclination of many of their members to engage in political violence. Nevertheless, they continue to be extremist mainstays of the political scene, and although not all of the organizations falling under this heading advocate violence, those attracted to them often collaborate with one another and continue to pose real, if intermittent threats to the country's political system and its public officials.

In terms of number, recent calculations by the Poverty Law Center identified approximately 750 different hate groups operating in the United States in these early years of the twenty-first century.[18] Most tend to be small in membership, localized in their activity, and generally obscure in the national political process. Some, however, stand out from the crowd, albeit usually for quite different and often surprising reasons. The KKK, for example, is interesting precisely because of its contemporary weakness. "Passed over by most young white supremacists, who consider Klansmen to be ineffectual and faintly ridiculous old-timers," as one source put it, the KKK today consists of only a few thousand people distributed among more than 100 nominally independent units and scores of competing factions.[19] It still has some larger chapters—most notably in Kentucky, Indiana, and Texas—but its primary contribution to political violence in America now lies in its ties to, and frequent participation in the demonstrations of such active contemporary supremacist groups as the Aryan Nations.

Other white supremacist organizations are particularly noteworthy because of their success in growing while toning down their hate rhetoric and—following the advice of former KKK Imperial Wizard David Duke—mainstreaming their message, currently over the Internet. Stormfront.org, founded in 1995 by Don Black (a Duke protégé, former Duke campaign worker, and disillusioned Klan supporter), was the first white nationalist Internet Website. It concentrates on running members-only message boards that reinforce its members' sense of belonging by placing each in the context of a broader association. Messages are posted in polite terms (profanity, personal attacks, and racial slurs are expressly prohibited), and recruiting occurs by permitting "guest" access to the site and offering new members such collateral benefits as dating advice and the opportunity to post personal ads. In its first ten years of operation, its membership jumped from fewer than 10,000 members to more than 60,000, its daily Website hits rose from 1,700 to 30,000, and by 2005 approximately 4,500 members were logged onto its site at any given time. As one student examining Stormfront.org concluded, the organization seems content to spread its euphemistic message of hate "one computer at a time."[20]

Finally, there are the overtly violence-prone hate movements, with their message of white superiority over the "mud races." These organizations span the country and often find followings among like-minded, predominantly young white males in foreign locales. Prominent in this group are (1) the Idaho-based Aryan Nations/ Church of Jesus Christ Christian, (2) the National Alliance, now headquartered in West Virginia, and (3) the rejuvenated Creativity Movement, which was initially founded as the World Church of the Creator (WCOTC) in 1973 by Ben Klassen. Given the internal divisions in *and* the recent death of the leaders of both the Aryan Nations and the National Alliance, the Creativity Movement is now perhaps the most significant of the three.[21]

Klassen was a right-wing political drifter who once had been a member of the John Birch Society and a campaign worker in George Wallace's 1968 bid for the presidency. His call for a Racial Holy War ("RAHOWA"), his newsletter, and his *White Man's Bible*, with its anti-Semitic prescription for preventing the mongrelization of America, gradually attracted a following in the United States, Canada, Sweden, and South Africa during the 1980s. By the early 1990s, however, the arrest of many of its extremist members for crimes ranging from bombings to murder, and Klassen's own suicide in 1993, had left the WCOTC flat in the water. Then, three years after Klassen's death, the movement was re-energized under the direction of a young law graduate, Matt Hale. That reawakening was in no small part the result of publicity the movement received from Hale's efforts to obtain the license to practice law that Illinois denied him on the basis of his bigotry, and from the July 1999 "shooting spree" by one of his ardent supporters, which left two dead and nine wounded.

Violence continues to surround both Hale and his organization. In March 2005, for example, the mother and husband of the federal judge (Joan Lefkow) whose murder Hale had been convicted of soliciting were murdered. The Creativity Movement openly endorses violence (Klassen's *Bible* unequivocally states, "We of the CHURCH OF THE CREATOR are not hypocrites. We openly state that some people need killing"), and its followers have been involved in instances of assault against minorities, robbery, and murder. On balance, however, its primary activities have involved the staging of protests and demonstrations to spread its message, and the running of Internet and local membership drives aimed at attracting women and children, as well as alienated white males.[22] That path has often led the Creativity Movement and its fellow travelers, such as the Aryan Nations, into volatile situations. Over the course of the last quarter of the twentieth century, however, the violence of these successors to the KKK in the world of hate and racism was outstripped by the activities of the militia groups with whom they some-times shared an interest.

In the cluster of threats to the public order described in this volume, it is tempting to dismiss the United States' single-issue extremists as inconse-quential, at least comparatively. Unlike Quebec's separatists or the Chechens fighting Russia's army, white supremacy separatists dreaming of Aryan empires in the northwest or crusading against "mud people" pose no comparable threat to the survival of the country. The violence caused by antiabortionists and ecoterrorists affects only a small portion of the popu-lation, and it is easy to overlook. Even the assassination of public officials and other crimes carried out by militia groups are sporadic events, often buried beneath international headlines and other domestic stories in U.S. newspapers and rarely gaining their thirty seconds of coverage on prime-time news programs the day they occur. Yet when the cumulative effect of the various extremists is totaled, there is scarcely a part of the country or month of the year that has not been touched by their actions during the past decade, or one that can be safely excluded from episodic violence in the years ahead. In fact, even where existing organizations are in a state of decline, there are several reasons for future concern.

First, the dynamic environment of contemporary U.S. politics is, in terms of its political implications, a two-way street. Some events work against extremist activity, whereas others can work to its advantage. Continued population growth in general and in the American northwest in particular, for example, implies further development of the timber industry and the construction of new, sprawling housing tracts in envi-ronmentally untouched or thinly populated areas. Either scenario is as much an affront to ecoterrorists as the equally likely future development of gas and oil resources on federally owned parks and other properties of a country still too dependent on energy imports from the volatile Middle East, at ever higher prices. Meanwhile, Republican appointees to the United States Supreme Court during George W. Bush's presidency (2001–09) have inspired new hope among pro-life activists that the *Roe v. Wade* ruling may yet be overturned. In a country where 1,365,000 women get an abortion each year and one in six citizens remains opposed to abortion under any circumstances,[23] those appointments have height-ened the likelihood both of future picketing and other legal actions designed to call public attention to the abortion issue and of renewed violence by antiabortion extremists if they are disappointed by future Supreme Court decisions. Indeed, President Bush's two conservative nominees to the Supreme Court in 2005 had scarcely begun to hear cases before the South Dakota legislature in 2006 set the ball in motion for a challenge to *Roe v. Wade* by outlawing the performance of abortion by a doctor except to save the mother's life.

Second, the extremist organizations involved in single-interest politics are themselves of a dynamic nature. Consequently, those currently in decline or without leaders bear watching as much as those in the forefront of the public eye. Where leadership positions are up for grabs, aspirants are not only likely to emerge, but also to try to gain followers by outbidding one another in terms of proposing or undertaking extremist action. Where membership is declining, outreach programs may seek to broaden the membership base and establish liaisons with extremists committed to other causes. Intelligence gathered by extremist monitoring agencies suggests that many groups were doing precisely that in the early years of the twenty-first century. Women and young children, for example, are not just being recruited more aggressively by the militias and other far-right-wing movements; evidence suggests that they are becoming increasingly involved and energetic participants in the activities of these groups. Meanwhile, many extremist organizations of the political right are also reaching out to fringe groups on the left in a common bond of antigovernment action, most visibly in the tactical alliances emerging between the more militant antiglobalization groups on the left and the militias and other antigovernment, frequently conspiratorially inclined groups on the right, especially those inclined to believe in a host of government conspiracies against them and the American people.

Third, there is the changing nature of the threat posed to society by activists in hate groups and other single-issue extremist movements. As already noted, the activities organized and carried out by extremist organizations have recently been somewhat eclipsed by the more violent actions of "lone wolf" activists of the Timothy McVeigh ilk. These activists have been encouraged or have drawn support from the networks of extremist groups loosely linked together via the Internet, and they have frequently committed acts that transcend the interests of any single-interest movement. The prosecution of Eric Rudolph for his multiple acts of political violence has reflected this "crossover" development. Charges against him were related both to the bombing of abortion clinics *and* to the bombing of the 1996 Olympic Games in Atlanta, in the name of another, as yet undetermined cause. Whatever his motives, the actions of such quasi-loner terrorists are harder to track and preempt than those of identifiable organizations, and such men and women are often more mobile in their activities. They move from one region to another, and consequently they are more difficult to apprehend and punish than the members of extremist cells with an easily identifiable geographical base.

Other lights warning of future danger are blinking as well. The link between extremists and criminal activity, for example, is an old one, but it is developing a new twist. Racist, prison-based organizations of all hues have become perhaps the most violent groups in American society, either inside or outside of the prison walls, and their members regularly take their attitudes beyond those walls when they are paroled or otherwise released into the general population. Government efforts to arrest the development of these groups by aggressively prosecuting their members for crimes they commit inside prisons have been stepped up. Still, the groups have become ever more violent and dangerous while in custody; they have developed elaborate means of communicating with one another, even between maximum security prisons; and—as one Anti-Defamation League analyst noted—their members "continue to serve their organization from the outside. That's probably where the greatest danger to the community lies."[24]

Meanwhile, the danger to society also continues to rise from the single-interest extremists normally dwelling in the broader community, and in particular from those who in the early twenty-first century have indicated a willingness to employ anthrax and other forms of bioterrorism. For example, in the 1998 to 2000 period prior to the 9/11 attacks, the threat of bioterrorism on American soil had yet to make its way into popular anxieties. At that time, however, antiabortion activists threatened more than eighty different abortion clinics in sixteen states with anthrax attacks if they did not end their operations.

For political authorities, then, the problem of combating domestic terrorists pursuing *their* political agendas is similar to that of combating foreign terrorists in an age when fewer, but more dramatic terrorist acts can culminate in high numbers of civilian casualties. In both instances, such rights as association, freedom of speech, and privacy must be balanced against the commitment to protect the public safety. It is not an easy or simple balancing act. Even peaceful demonstrations that are pursued in a volatile context can provoke violent reactions in their audiences. That fact of political life has often been exploited by single-interest groups as a strategy, and it can be as dangerous to localized publics in the contemporary United States as direct action by the extremists themselves, when crowds get out of control.

IMMIGRATION

In the early spring of 2006, the illegal immigration issue that had long been simmering on the back burner of U.S. politics and furnishing a staple of conservative talk shows burst into the open. Congress took up the topic and drafted a measure that would have simultaneously criminalized illegal immigrants and authorized the construction of a wall along the entire U.S. border with Mexico. The pending legislation received widespread coverage on American news networks and quickly became an issue in Mexico's presidential campaign at the time, where it was

universally condemned. For those who might have missed the legislation's non-stop news coverage north and south of the border, legal and
illegal Hispanic immigrants dwelling in the United States offered an even
more-publicized addendum to the debate on immigration policy. Taking
matters into their own hands and taking to the streets, immigrant groups
staged nationwide public protests in opposition to the pending legislation
over a five-week period from late March through early May. The culmi-
nating event was a boycott of schools enrolling Hispanics and
workplaces employing them, which was staged to underscore their
importance in American society and to the American economy.

On balance, the protests were well organized and executed in a remarkably short period of time in more than a dozen targeted U.S. cities, including Los Angeles, Chicago, and Washington and in such state capitals as
Phoenix, Arizona and Austin, Texas. Moreover, they were overwhelmingly
peaceful, especially when compared to the turbulent, often violent demonstrations being staged at the same time by French students and young
French workers protesting a proposed labor law in France that would have
made it easier for French firms to fire new workers during their first
two years of employment. To be sure, these pro-immigration protests were
not free of controversy. The presence of foreign (mostly Mexican) flags
among the demonstrators in the initial rallies, in particular, drew considerable criticism from those supporting the proposals pending in Congress,
and the banners were carefully pruned from most subsequent rallies. Nor
were those opposed to the proposed legislation unified in their choice of
strategy. Many, for example, felt that the boycott was a bad idea. More
importantly, the efforts to organize the protests often revealed important
and potentially debilitating or explosive ethnic, racial, religious and [legal]
status divisions within both the Hispanic community and the immigrant
community in general, and between the immigrants and other minorities in
American society.[25] Still, on the whole events unfolded more or less tran-
quilly. Over the long haul, however, both the proposals to try again to curb
the flow of illegal immigration into the country and the open and vocal
opposition to them among those targeted by those proposals reflected a
volatile issue where emotions still run high on both sides, and are likely to
continue to do so for years ahead. It is a climate unlikely to remain
violence-free, even if it could actually have been entirely characterized as
such at the time of the spring 2006 demonstrations.

A Country of Immigrants

In both the established mind-set of its citizens and in historical reality,
the United States is an immigrant country that owes its prosperity and
prominence as much to those who came to it as to the natural wealth that

awaited them on the American continent. It was settled by, among others, religious refugees from Europe seeking to escape persecution by the majorities holding different faiths in their countries and by ordinary blokes willing to indenture themselves for a fixed time to escape the debtors' prisons of Britain. They worked off their debts and the cost of passage to America for the chance to start a new life there, if they survived the passage and their years of indentured service. The country blossomed in the late nineteenth and early twentieth centuries by accepting some 44 million immigrants, mostly from Europe. Their number was larger than the total population of France, at a time when that country was the largest state in Western Europe (excluding Eurasian Russia). Those people from diverse lands provided the human resources that enabled the United States first to fulfill its "Manifest Destiny" by expanding from the Atlantic to the Pacific and then to settle and hold that land against the challenges of nature and, less laudably, the native tribes who temporarily stood in their way. Later immigrants, in turn, helped launch the industrial revolution that by the time of World War I had made their country one of the great powers in the world. And the Jewish Germans who sought refuge in America from Nazi Germany during the years leading up to World War II paid their debt to their new country and saved incalculable lives by presenting the United States government with the secret of the atomic bomb—the weapon that would end the war against Japan without the costly invasion that otherwise would almost certainly have been necessary.

So said, it is equally true that both the arrival of immigrants from culturally diverse areas and the immigration policy created to deal with them have been controversial issues in the American political process since the inception of the republic forced the consideration of such matters on the Founding Fathers. As noted by Matthew Crenson, a political scientist at Johns Hopkins University, Alexander Hamilton even had doubts about the wisdom of admitting the Protestant Scotch-Irish for fear that they were too different from the new country's English to permit the development of a common nationality. Thomas Jefferson, on the other hand, felt that they would pose no problems, but he had his doubts about admitting large numbers of Germanic people. Indeed the resistance to assimilation exhibited by second- and third-generation German Americans—still dwelling in their German-oriented towns and in the *Kleindeutschlands* of older American cities—was still a point of contention in mainstream U.S. politics during World War I.

Meanwhile, the entry of people ever more removed from the fabled white Anglo-Saxon Protestant (WASP) prototype of the original settlers spawned anti-immigrant organizations such as the pre–Civil War Know Nothing Party and the clandestine post–Civil War Ku Klux Klan. The

KKK was often as much activated against the Jewish and Catholic immigrants moving into the southern United States as by the prospect of the freed slaves acquiring political influence. Elsewhere, long before the United States closed the door to unrestricted immigration from Europe during World War I, both the American government and numerous states had enacted discriminatory legislation barring Asians from entering the country or—if already present—from acquiring United States citizenship through naturalization proceedings. Even the U.S. Supreme Court, which had affirmed the citizenship of U.S.-born Chinese, ruled in 1922 that Japanese immigrants could constitutionally be declared ineligible for citizenship. As for Mexican workers in the United States, their treatment and conditions of employment in Texas by the time of World War II had become so bad that between 1943 and 1957 the Government of Mexico directly intervened and prohibited its citizens from working there.[26]

This scant inventory of immigrant communities in America suggests that although immigration has been a persistent concern in U.S. history, the groups targeted at any given moment have varied—usually on the basis of who was entering the country in large numbers and their cultural distance from the Northern European prototype at any particular time. On the other hand, a half-century ago the growing presence of Japanese and Korean war brides brought home from occupied Japan, and from Korea during the 1950s, combined with the collateral benefits that other cultural and racial minorities derived from the African American civil rights struggle of the 1950s to alter significantly the framework for approaching racial and ethnic diversity in the United States. What emerged was a general acceptance of *multiculturalism* as the normal configuration of twentieth-century American society. An equally widespread belief in the compatibility of multiculturalism with membership in the American nation defused any nationwide concern with the immigrant issue during much of the last third of the twentieth century—even as the number of refugees (especially from Vietnam in the 1970s), asylum seekers, and illegal immigrants from Mexico and points south continued to grow.

The Immigrant Issue Heats Up (Again)

The re-emergence of immigration as a significant, nationwide political issue in the early years of the new millennium—both with its echoes of old anti-immigration refrains and with the presence of some new and important twists—is best explained in terms of the abrupt convergence of a quintet of factors, any one of which might have eventually projected the immigrant issue into a national debate on public policy.

The local newspaper in Rogers, Arkansas, reports in July 2005 the Mexican election results as front-page headlines for its changing readership in the town where Sam Walton built his first Wal-Mart. Courtesy of Eric Belgrad.

Critical Mass

First and foremost, the re-surfacing of the issue was the direct result of both the growing size and visibility of the immigrant communities in American society, and the obvious impact of those developments on life in contemporary America. The statistics alone are daunting, whether the focus is on the total number of foreign-born people now living in the United States, the number of illegal immigrants in the country, or the size of the Hispanic community.

According to a relatively recent study by the Pew Hispanic Center, approximately half a million illegal immigrants were entering the country each year by 2005—more than the number now entering the United States legally.[27] Overall, the number of illegal immigrants in the United States more than doubled between 1995 and 2005, with eight out of ten of the more than 12 million illegal immigrants estimated to be in the United States by then coming from either Mexico or another Latin American country, and nearly six out of ten (57 percent) of them were Mexicans.[28] In part because of this steady flow of illegal immigrants from the south, by the time the United States held its 2000 census its Hispanic population had surpassed African Americans as the country's largest minority group. Moreover, its share of the population continues to grow, often as much a result of procreation as of immigration. Much more youthful than the population of non-Hispanic whites (half of the Hispanic population is under 27 years old, whereas half of the non-Hispanic white Americans are over 40), the Hispanic population is likely to increase in number for biological reasons, as well as for cultural ones. Indeed, although representing only 14 to 15 percent of the U.S. population in 2004 (41.3 million, out of a total population of approximately 293.7 million), Hispanics were doing just that in the early years of the twenty-first century. They accounted for 49 percent of the total growth in the U.S. population between 2000 and 2004, and Hispanic births in the United States outnumbered the total legal and the illegal Hispanic immigrants who entered the United States during those years.[29]

With their rapidly expanding numbers, the United States' foreign-born community has acquired greater visibility, both in the people's daily lives and in the daily news. Asians from the Indian subcontinent are ubiquitous behind convenience store counters at home and motel desks on the road. Iranians run Exxon and Mobil stations in large areas of the mid-Atlantic region. Gardeners on our college campuses are Asians from the Far East, and Hispanics continue to do domestic work and are increasingly evident in the construction crews of cities. And what the public does not witness, it reads about, as this partial list suggests:

- The importance of Hispanic workers, not native New Orleans residents, in the post-Katrina reconstruction of that city
- The growth of Hispanic television and radio media
- The explosive growth of Hispanic-owned businesses
- The discovery of a half-mile-long tunnel under the border separating Mexico from southern California
- Such "changing society" stories as the emergence of Muslim Girl Scout troops and sororities, the new face of the funeral business, and the scheduling of ethnic beauty contests

Even more important in terms of issue emergence, the growing number of legal and illegal immigrants has forced American society and its governments to confront a growing set of new problems. Welfare resources *have* been stretched in states with large numbers of illegal immigrants, and school resources have been strained in accepting their children. Local police forces have sometimes been forced to recruit in Puerto Rico to find enough of the Spanish-speaking officers suddenly needed to police Hispanic neighborhoods, where few immigrants are fluent in English. Libraries have had to rethink their holdings and services. These problems, too, have drawn media attention and have contributed to the evolution of the "immigrant issue"—in particular the "Hispanic issue" in twenty-first-century America.

On the other hand, the buildup in size and visibility has been unevenly distributed across the country, occurring in the Southwest and pivotal urban areas more quickly than elsewhere.[30] Thus, a decade before immigration again became a nationwide concern, California's voters in 1994 solidly approved, by a 59 percent to 41 percent majority, a statewide referendum (Proposition 187) denying illegal immigrants access to public services and their children access to education in the state's public schools. Six years later they also voted overwhelmingly to abolish bilingual education in California's public school system. Their action was an echo of past state action when Californians—faced with large foreign-born populations—used their legal systems to deny Asians the right to inherit property in the early twentieth century. When California's governor, Pete Wilson, tried to ride the immigration issue to the White House in the 1996 presidential election, however, his campaign for the Republican Party's nomination died in the winter snows of New Hampshire's primary, where he was soundly defeated.

With the growing size and countrywide spread of the immigrant community, the world of immigration politics has now changed. Public opinion is still ambivalent on the issue of what to do with foreign-born people who are in the United States illegally. Few would criminalize it; some would issue temporary work permits to the illegal immigrants; and a small percentage would deport them summarily. A solid majority, however, continues to perceive these workers—and especially the Hispanics among them—in a positive light, as decent people who work hard for a day's wages.[31] Unrestricted immigration is another matter, however, and the issue of continued illegal immigration in general and the insecure U. S. border with Mexico in particular has begun to resonate politically across the country to the same degree that the issue of illegal immigrants prompted anti-immigrant policy in California during the 1990s. The impact of these minority communities on matters such as welfare services, and the political conflict surrounding their growing presence, has likewise become country-wide. Nevertheless, with Congress generally at odds over what to do, the response to the immigrant issue largely fell upon state and local governments as late as 2007. By May 2006, for example, forty-three of the fifty states were considering legislation involving immigrant access to health and social services, education, or employment within their borders.

Job Insecurity in a Changing Economy

Two themes resonate throughout the history of both immigration in general and immigration as an issue in the United States. First, people have been and continue to be drawn to America in order to achieve a better way of life, defined as much in terms of economic well-being as civil liberty and individual rights. Sometimes there were specific catalysts underlying the movement—the persecution of religious minorities, the "Potato Famine" in mid-nineteenth-century Ireland, political turmoil in the land of origin—but often it was just the lure of free land or jobs that drew them. In that sense, the immigrant waves of the nineteenth century find their reflection in those of recent times, only now the foreign born normally come more from the south than from across the oceans separating America from China to the west and Europe to the east. The dynamics are the same as those that have drawn large numbers from the south of Europe, the Middle East, and Africa to Western Europe since World War II. As Milton Esman has summarized it, highly developed economies and societies, with their low birth rates, usually have a need for outside laborers, especially in eras of rapid economic growth. Developing countries, with their low income structure and high population growth rates, normally have labor surpluses.[32] It is a push-pull dynamic—from poverty and sometimes repression toward the promise of a better way of life—that continues to fuel global migration in the contemporary world.

At the same time, the perception of economic opportunity is quite different among those who have little or nothing than it is for those who live in the relative affluence of life in the developed democratic world. Consequently, migration from low- to high-opportunity areas has seldom ceased, even when the high-opportunity areas have experienced economic downturns, and this fact of global economic life has usually resulted in greater scrutiny being given to the immigrant issue in adverse economic times. Indeed, labor-importing areas typically try to halt or reverse the flow of immigration during such times, fearing—with justification or otherwise—that foreigners will take jobs from nationals. Thus, during the early years of the Great Depression, California undertook the mass deportation of Mexican laborers from the state in 1931. More recently, the global recessions of the 1970s and 1980s prompted France and other European countries—often under pressure from highly nationalistic, anti-immigration political parties—to halt further immigration, tighten their borders against illegal entrants, deport illegals and, in some instances, offer legal foreign workers cash incentives to return to their countries of origin.

The recent, visible impact of economic globalization on the American economy has resulted in a contemporary manifestation of this pattern, driving the immigrant issue upward on the political agenda to the point where it was firmly rooted in second place, behind only the war in Iraq, by the time of the U. S. Congressional elections in 2006. With such terms as "outsourcing" becoming a part of Americans' daily vocabulary, the continuing, unrestricted flow of approximately 1,000 illegal immigrants per day across the border between the United States and Mexico was ripe for politicization. On the other hand, as a self-consciously immigrant nation the United States does not have a strong anti-immigrant party like France's National Front, with its catchy, vote-getting slogan of the 1980s: "2 million unemployed French is 2 million foreign workers too many." There are, however, American media voices and think tanks on the conservative right. They have not been shy about spreading the word that illegal immigrants are stealing jobs from Americans at home at the very moment when, in their view, American industry is being driven to relocate jobs abroad because of the government- and union-imposed costs (corporate taxes, social security contributions, health care and pension fund contributions) of operating in the United States.[33]

As a point of fact, it is highly unlikely that even those illegal immigrants willing to take jobs at extremely low wages are causing higher unemployment overall among American workers in the United States, French workers in France, or German workers in Germany. Rather, the frequent pattern is for foreign laborers to perform, at least initially, the jobs that nationals will rarely take, and almost never at the wages that foreign workers accept. By taking those jobs they subsidize the economy, thereby enabling marginal firms to stay in business, so that domestic workers retain their jobs and society as a whole enjoys lower prices than would otherwise prevail.

On occasion, individuals in the domestic workforce may suffer. It is no secret why firms hire illegal foreign workers when they feel that they can get away with it. Hiring illegals saves employers the extra wages they must otherwise pay and the social security contributions they must make when hiring workers in the legal economy, as well as the cost of fringe benefits such as health and dental insurance. The same considerations lie behind corporate decisions to outsource jobs abroad, including the recent decisions of U.S. firms that once moved to Mexico to find cheap labor and are now outsourcing jobs to India, where the cost of skilled labor is cheaper still.[34] To blame illegal immigrants for large-scale domestic unemployment is another argument, and a difficult one to sustain. Politics, however, is frequently more about perception than reality—especially complicated realities—and the coincidence of a spurt in illegal immigration at the same moment that Americans are fearful of losing their jobs has contributed its part to widening and intensifying the immigration issue in early twenty-first-century America.

The Immigration Issue, Hispanic Voters, and Party Politics

The relationship between the growing importance of the immigration issue and U.S. party politics is also a complex one, but it is indisputably another factor that has added further heat and publicity to the debate over immigration policy. On the one hand, courting the immigrant vote, and especially that of Hispanics—the fastest-growing minority community in the United States and already a sixth of the country's population—has become a high priority for both the Republican Party and the Democrats during the past decade. Moreover, given the desire for cheap labor by the business community, which generally supports Republican candidates, supporting a guest worker policy makes particular sense for the Republican Party. For both parties, though, the immigrant issue is a hot-button topic, all the more so because the immigrant vote is concentrated in big, key electoral college states such as California, New York, Texas, and Florida and is thus crucial to winning the White House. Consequently, each party recognizes that the cost of alienating the Hispanic vote could be disastrous. The Republican Party, for example, has seen its competitiveness in California's statewide races fade away since a Republican governor pushed for the adoption of the anti-immigration measure Proposition 187 in the early 1990s.

On the other hand, the strongest proponents of taking a hard line on immigration (for example, by sealing the border and denying services to illegal immigrants) are to be found within the Republican Party's conservative core in the southwestern border states that now receive large numbers of Hispanic immigrants in general, and illegal Mexican immigrants in particular. Caught in the dilemma of trying to satisfy this core and the expanding number of U.S. voters already concerned with the immigration issue[35]—without alienating the Hispanic vote—the Republican Party has split on this matter. To a lesser extent, the Democratic Party has also split with its own, albeit smaller, hard-line element. Hence, at a time when the United States needed a coherent immigration policy capable of deflecting the growing volatility of the issue, its major parties were divided on the issue at mid-decade, with the Democrats the more inclined of the two to support amnesty for those already illegally in the country. Congress has also split on the matter, between the Senate, where the conservative, small-population states have more representation, and the House of Representatives. As a result, not only has the government failed to manage the potentially volatile issue of illegal immigration, but partisan debate has exacerbated the conflict over immigration. Nor is any legislation that may be passed apt to satisfy those involved with the issue. It is sure to be a compromise measure, offering stronger border security to appease anti-immigrant groups and some framework for regularizing the illegal immigrants in the country, that is designed to garner the votes of liberal House and Senate members that are essential to passing any immigration legislation.

The September 11 Factor

Giving the immigrant issue yet another dimension and greater saliency in early twenty-first century U.S. politics is the much publicized "9/ll factor." The impact of the terrorist attack on September 11, 2001 has permeated so many areas of U.S. policy that it is hard to identify those areas most affected. Energy policy, for example, has once again taken center stage, nearly as much because of the perceived need to reduce dependency on potentially hostile oil suppliers as because of the high price of gasoline. Foreign policy has been radically altered by the post-9/11 Bush Doctrine of preemptive war. Five years later, the stock market was still struggling to reach its level at the time of the attack. Nevertheless, few areas were as directly affected by the country's altered political agenda as immigration policy. Without the 9/11 factor it is doubtful that the immigration issue would have become so prominent in the 2006 national elections, or even an important concern outside of the Southwest and perhaps a few of the other parts of the country experiencing a rapid growth in their foreign-born population.

The enhanced concern with domestic (homeland) security following those attacks simultaneously drew national attention to the growing numbers of non-European immigrants in the U.S. population in general, and to the issues of illegal immigration and border security in particular. As a consequence, the activity of foreign workers in sensitive posts has come under greater scrutiny, although usually with results that have had nothing to do with the al Qaeda network responsible for the 2001 attacks—for example, foreign scientists have been arrested for sending secrets to China. Security sweeps on and around such sensitive areas as U.S. ports and airports have found large numbers of illegal aliens on the job, although the vast majority of these have been laborers in menial positions, and none with terrorist ties. Furthermore, arrests that directly involved plots to attack future U.S. targets have all involved legal and illegal residents from only the Muslim world (principally the Middle East and Pakistan), or U.S. citizens.[36] Still, once the spotlight focused on the immigrant question, the continuous arrival of illegal aliens from Mexico and points south across the United States' 2000-mile-long and inevitably porous border with Mexico could scarcely escape notice, despite the fact that the only known terrorist operatives seeking entry into the United States via its land borders were coming from Canada. Likewise, it is the

United States' northern neighbor, not Mexico, that has its own, home-grown problem with domestic terrorists who have al Qaeda links or aspirations.

Border Violence, Death, and the Immigrant Issue

Violence and coercive government action directed against and/or involving immigrant groups is at least as old as the local battles for political influence between the Irish and Italian immigrants who settled into adjacent neighborhood in mid-nineteenth-century America. As late as the 1930s, Italians in New Jersey were being attacked because of their ethnicity by the 1930s version of American skinheads, and Italians were rounded up along with Japanese Americans to be sent to interment camps during the early years of World War II. The local struggles for power in the nineteenth and early twentieth centuries occurred before the prying eye of television cameras was a factor, but the violence associated with immigrants in the contemporary United States gets that attention-generating and issue-hardening coverage, and there is no shortage of stories to cover.

Most of the newspaper and photojournalism accounts of immigration-related violence and death are focused on the Mexican-American border. Even with the deployment of National Guard troops to the area in June 2006, and the subsequent decline in the number of illegal immigrants interdicted daily, that border remains anything but tranquil. It is crossed by drug dealers and the so-called "coyotes," who smuggle immigrants into the United States for a fee that rises with the numbers patrolling the U.S. side of the border—and all carry guns.[37] Border duty has proven to be especially hazardous for the Mexican officials who take their obligations seriously,[38] but it has also proven to be deadly for those immigrants who are successfully smuggled into the southwestern desert areas or cross on their own, only to face the danger of crossing large tracks of sand with inadequate water supplies, just as the harsh morning sun is rising.

The dangers at the Mexican border are not the only problems faced by the illegal aliens entering the United States. Throughout the country they are often prey to violent muggings. Their physical traits and imperfect English signal their presence, and because they are part of the illegal economy they usually are paid in cash and they are unlikely to report being attacked to authorities, for fear of deportation. Indeed, even legal immigrants often do not report thefts or seek welfare services, lest their names lead authorities to the illegal immigrants they know and often shelter. As a consequence, the immigrant community is far more likely to suffer from inadequate health care and disease than the U.S. population as a whole is. This is also true of their children, 93 percent of whom are estimated to have been born in the United States and hence are U.S. citizens.[39]

Finally, as every viewer of *CSI: Miami* and other American crime shows knows, illegal immigrants sometimes bring crime with them. Drug dealers come from the South American countries, and the Russian mafia is widely seen as being responsible for a variety of crimes, including the botched car theft that cost the life of comedian Bill Cosby's son in Los Angeles in the 1990s. Today there is the notorious MS-13 (the Mara Salvatorucha), the largest and certainly one of the most violent Hispanic gangs in the United States, with an estimated 2000 members in Washington's Virginia suburbs alone.[40] Television episodes, movies, and newspaper accounts of such matters undoubtedly lead to exaggerated views of the prevalence of criminal elements among America's recent immigrants, but they also spread the word and contribute their part to keeping the policy debate on immigration hot in the contemporary United States.

Many of the arguments raised by those advocating the immediate expulsion of illegal immigrants and greater limitation of those legally admitted to the country have historically been a part of past debates over immigration in the United States. The two most common of those old refrains cite the danger posed to the jobs of American citizens by the availability of cheap, often illegal labor, and the resistance of immigrants to assimilation. In today's continuing discourse, the latter argument is sometimes given a novel spin: that in the current era of global terrorism, security considerations do not afford the United States the luxury of waiting the several generations that it previously took for some former immigrant groups to lose their old allegiances and shed their hyphenated status (Italian Americans, German Americans, etc.). The essence of the argument, however, is not very different from those quasi-hysterical moments in American politics involving yellow perils, red scares, and World War I rumors (spread by Prohibitionists) that German American brewmasters were addicting the country's youth to demon alcohol in order to make them more vulnerable to the armies of Imperial Germany.

At the same time, there are several dimensions to the contemporary debate over immigration that were largely lacking in the past and which give it, especially with respect to the immigrants from Mexico, a more volatile character than would otherwise be present. First, there is the shared border between Mexico and the United States, which offers easy access to American soil for those migrating from the south and— contrary to the hopes of border wall advocates— cannot be fully sealed. Such access did not exist for immigrants coming from more remote lands in the past. Second, the focus is not on who to admit and which groups to keep out, but on what to do with the more than 10 million illegal immigrants—at least 20 million people from Mexico altogether—who are already in the country.[41] Third, there is the territorial argument—that the illegal immigrants from Mexico are, in a sense, not so much migrating as *returning* to land that once was Mexico's (hence, "theirs") or Spain's (and therefore was originally Spanish-speaking territory). That argument, of course, ignores the historical reality that even earlier— before the Spanish arrived— it was the land of the Apache, Hopi, Navajo, and other native tribes, but the territorial argument still is the basis for anti-immigrationist fears that a plot is afoot to (re)-Mexicanize the American Southwest. And finally, giving some credibility to the less shrill arguments for curtailing immigration, there is the sheer size of the Hispanic immigrant community, both legal and otherwise.

It is the combination of the size and territoriality of the legal and illegal Hispanic (especially Mexican) communities that gives the "difficult to assimilate" argument against illegal Hispanic immigrants its biting edge, and which makes the U.S. Southwest a potential political hot spot in the years ahead. Historically, the vastness of the territory receiving them spread out the nineteenth- and twentieth-century waves of immigrants as they moved westward, weakening their ability to hold onto the Old World languages, customs, and identities that they brought with them to America. The United States thus solidified its claim to being an immigrant country at that time, but also as a country of *widely diffused immigrant communities.* Today's situation is different in the southwestern United States, if not necessarily for the Hispanic communities elsewhere. The nineteenth-century European, and later Asian, immigrants tended to settle in linguistic polyglots that made it necessary for the newcomers to learn English as a link language for local communications, thus facilitating at least a linguistic assimilation. More recently, the large concentration of Spanish speakers in the Southwest has made it possible for the immigrants to develop their own economically viable communities in their native language.

Similarly, for their predecessors the prescription for vertical social and economic mobility was straightforward and easy to follow, if also strict. Also clear were the rewards for following that prescription in a relatively new country that was endowed with so much natural and industrial wealth available to the incoming masses during the nineteenth century. The principal rules, for those who wished to profit, were learn the English language, dress conventionally, send your children to the free and obligatory primary and secondary schools, and be loyal to the government. Most immigrants followed them, even though in practice not all groups found assimilation equally easy, and not all efforts were rewarded. For most immigrants, however, a better life did follow, at least from one generation to the next, and that, in turn, provided a reason for being loyal to the U.S. government. Meanwhile, cross-cultural socio-economic mobility facilitated the emergence of a common nation out of an increasingly pluralistic population, and cross-cultural marriages gradually became common, gnawing away at the individual ethnic differences separating the members of American society.

In the contemporary Southwest, a different picture of settlement dominates the region. Learning English is not necessarily the same high priority. The Hispanic economy and community are large enough to afford *some* opportunity for upward mobility and middle-class status without acquiring English fluency in the shortest possible time, and making it one's mother tongue over a generation or two. Hence, although the evidence to date is fairly strong that Hispanic children outside of the Southwest are assimilating at approximately the same pace as the children of earlier immigrant groups, it *is* equally possible that in the southwestern United States the process of cultural assimilation may occur—as the immigration hardliners argue—at a much slower pace than usual.

The bottom line, then, is that short of an effective expulsion of the majority of Hispanic illegal aliens from the country and a tight sealing of the border—actions that are politically and logistically improbable, given the growing political power of the legal Hispanic community, the opposition of most U.S. civil rights groups and religious organizations to summary deportation, the length of the border with Mexico, and the sheer numbers involved—the immigrant debate is almost certain to continue and perhaps intensify in the immediate future.

Political Ethos and the Immigration Question

As a land settled by minorities and outcasts, the United States has a history of tolerance toward diversity. To be sure, this commitment has offered minorities no guarantees of justice, and there are moments in U.S. history when you must search hard to find either tolerance or the just treatment of specific minorities. Still, to reemphasize an earlier point, this self-recognition of the origin and nature of American society provides a daily, continuing buffer against extremism taking hold in the field of immigration policy-making, despite the fact that U.S. history is also the story of ethnic turf battles by local immigrant communities seeking a foothold, and of periodic violence against immigrant minorities.

On the other hand, it is not a question of whether the contemporary immigrant issue will become violent; it already is, to a degree. Here, however, our concern is not the criminal violence of MS-13 and its ilk, but rather politically motivated violence, or violence resulting from policy developments. The focus is on whether violence will expand, where it is most likely to occur, and what groups will be affected by it. In this context, there are some ominous signs of a more turbulent future, especially in the southwestern cities with large, primarily Hispanic immigrant communities, and in the border area with Mexico.

Growing Numbers, Growing Conflict

There is a close fit between the broad objectives of white supremacist organizations, militia organizations, and other hate groups on the one hand, and the more narrow objectives of those who oppose permitting illegal immigrants to remain in the United States and favor closing the border to further immigration from the south on the other hand. That relationship increases the likelihood that random political violence may occur throughout the United States in the future, if the hate groups become more involved in the immigrant issue. By around 2005, they had already placed themselves in provocative settings by stationing observers along the frontier to detect illegal crossings and by staging counter-protests in favor of tighter immigration control during the large-scale rallies that immigrant groups staged in the spring of 2006 to oppose such legislation. Nevertheless, the greatest likelihood of conflict in the near future undoubtedly lies where it has already manifested itself: in the conflicts that result from the growing size of the immigrant communities and generate issues between them and the others living in those areas.

In some instances, these conflicts involve conservative, upper-middle-class or wealthy Americans seeking to protect the property values and/or perceived ethos of their communities. For example, tensions have been building with the changing population pattern in Washington, D.C.'s outer Virginia suburbs, whose predominantly immigrant minorities are expected to become a majority in the general population, and eventually dominate the voting-age population. Among other reactions, local governments have raided the places where workers gather for day labor in order to identify illegal immigrants and report them to federal authorities. They have enacted local ordinances prohibiting the employment of illegal immigrants and the renting of business property to them, and they have banned extended families from living together in a common residence. Meanwhile, laws designating English as the official language of government have gained momentum across the country and, for their part, states have also passed voter identification legislation. Conversely, government proposals to create a day labor center where migrants could go to seek temporary employment have led to hate calls to local talk radio shows and to the electoral defeat of local officials who supported the measure. The danger of much of this action is not just its dubious constitutionality, inasmuch as the federal government has exclusive authority over immigration; it also creates a sense of unwelcomeness that can—if it lasts for a long time—embitter the immigrant communities to the point where the anger spills out into the open in violent protests against a perceived second-class citizen status, as happened in France in the fall of 2005.

A more immediate potential source of political violence is the brewing and sometimes already existing conflict between new immigrant groups who seem to be prospering at the expense of the older groups that are socio-economically stuck below them in the system. To date, most conflicts have involved an African American underclass still populating many urban areas and a propertied immigrant community—usually Asian—that has acquired stores in their neighborhoods. The most famous of these incidents was the 1992 riot in Los Angeles that occurred when white police officers accused of beating a black suspect (Rodney King) were acquitted by an all-white jury. Although framed in black-and-white terms, the altercation unleashed long-harbored grievances, and once the rioting began in the African American neighborhoods, the primary casualties were the Asian merchants and their businesses. Both were targeted almost immediately by their black renter neighbors.

To date, nothing on the scale of those riots has dramatized the conflict between African Americans and their Hispanic neighbors in American cities. But similar lines of battle can now be seen emerging in the Southwest and other areas between the Hispanic communities and urban blacks. Conflict thus far has essentially been restricted to wars of words and battles at the ballot box (involving the absence of bilingual ballots in heavily Hispanic areas, or overt efforts such as California's Proposition 187 aimed at denying public benefits to illegal immigrants). Still, the words have gotten ugly. At a Dallas school board meeting as early as 1997, for example, the rhetoric became so heated that a fight broke out between an Hispanic member of the board and a New Black Panther Party member. The fight turned into such a melee that it took four hours to restore order. Less often recorded are the daily incidents of verbal abuse—and sometimes physical violence—along the unofficial borders (cross streets, parks, railroad tracks, etc.) that separate the low-income African American, Asian, and Hispanic neighborhoods in San Diego, Los Angeles, Dallas, Houston, El Paso, San Antonio, Phoenix, and smaller towns throughout the Southwest. Each has within it the potential to escalate into highly volatile, perhaps even violent mass confrontations.

Symbols, Emotions, and the Prospect
for Political Violence

Exacerbating the conflict is the central role played by symbols. The presence of Mexican flags in immigrant demonstrations against the criminalization of an alien's illegal status set conservative teeth gnashing across the country. So too, in some quarters, did the idea of students reciting the Pledge of Allegiance in Spanish, and "The Star-Spangled Banner" being sung in a foreign tongue drew even President Bush's reprobation. Such issues have normally been stand-ins for the larger issue of whether bilingual education should be limited, states should adopt bilingual policies, and/or English should be made the country's official language—all in the name of promoting assimilation. And because of the culturally sensitive nature of language issues, these debates keep the temperature high on all sides.

The Border

Finally, if the southwestern sector of the United States is the region most likely to experience political turbulence as a result of the growing numbers of illegal immigrants entering it from Mexico, the Mexican border area is the single most likely flashpoint. Life there is as often surreal as it is dramatic. Approximately 10,000 U.S. Border Patrol agents (approximately 90 percent of the Border Patrol personnel), wearing uniforms made in Mexico, sometimes find themselves in a cat-and-mouse game with Mexican authorities monitoring their movements and assisting illegal entrants by steering them away from the more heavily patrolled areas of the border. The government of Mexico has even printed and distributed a comic book-style guide to the United States that U.S. officials argue, not without cause, amounts to a "how to" guide for illegal immigrants. In illustrated lessons, for example, immigrants are advised that heavy clothing makes it difficult to swim, and that they should avoid drawing attention to themselves after arriving in the United States.[42]

More serious are the periodic tensions between Mexican officials and troops who cross the border in hot pursuit of drug dealers and the U.S. Border Patrol, which occasionally stops them. There are serious foreign policy disagreements between the United States and Mexico over (1) Mexicans' access to the United States; (2) the summary deportation of illegal Mexican aliens from the United States; and (3) the proposal to extend the current wall the full length of the nearly 2,000-mile-long border.[43] By the 2006 congressional election year that plan had not only been debated in Congress but had reached the point where firms were offering bids for the work (Lockheed was reportedly the winner).

Meanwhile, there is the activity of such quasi-vigilante groups as the Minutemen Brigade, Range Rescue, and Civil Homeland Defense, whose members ostensibly serve as unarmed "volunteer spotters" and claim to be interested only in helping the U.S. Border Patrol and protecting ranchers in the area. They are usually present with U.S. government approval, but they are nonetheless inflammatory. Finally, there are the armed National Guard detachments sent to bolster the Border Patrol, the coyotes smuggling illegal immigrants into the United States, and the growing number of bandit gangs operating along the border strip. In short, the long border zone—whether walled or not—has become altogether one of the very worst places in the United States to have a picnic or take a solitary hike. Less facetiously, it is a grim and potentially deadly zone that daily brings together individual hotheads, patriotic organizations, soldiers, and criminal elements—all usually armed—and two national governments who do not usually agree on the issue. Accordingly, the border is certain to remain in the news for years to come as a potential site of violence at any time.

Timeline

1840–1914	United States establishes itself as an immigrant country, receiving 44 million immigrants from abroad (mostly Europe); first large wave (1840–50) is composed of German and Irish immigrants.
1865–66	Ku Klux Klan founded following Civil War; with arrival of Jewish and Catholic immigrants in southern United States it becomes a center of violence against both immigrants and emancipated slaves.
1899	"Yellow Peril" anti-immigrant campaign against Japanese begins in United States.
1912–13	Laws passed in western states forbidding Japanese immigrants from owning land.
1917	As World War I raises issue of loyalty of German Americans, United States closes gate to open immigration.
1931	California responds to unemployment during Great Depression with a mass deportation of its Mexican workers.
1941–45	World War II: United States opens detention camps for Japanese Americans (and briefly for Italian Americans).

Conditions of Mexican workers in Texas become so bad that Mexican government prohibits its citizens from working there in 1943; ban not lifted until 1957.

1950–70   With Japanese and Korean war brides, immigration to United States becomes increasingly multicultural.

1954–64   Civil rights movement in the United States revives the KKK; numerous violent acts against civil rights groups occur in the south.

1970s   Animal Liberation Front founded in Britain and its activities will gradually become increasingly extreme. In United States, Sovereign Citizen Movement, World Church of the Creation (now Creativity Movement), and Aryan Nations founded in mid-1970s, along with the white supremacist National Alliance.

1973   Supreme Court in *Roe v. Wade* recognizes a woman's right to terminate an unwanted pregnancy in first trimester, launching an antiabortion movement that over the next 30 years became the most violent U.S. single-interest group.

1982   Ruby Ridge standoff with federal authorities encourages state militias to form; Army of God antiabortion group emerges in United States; Earth Liberation Front (ELF) founded in England.

1986   Congress enacts immigration law designed to settle illegal immigrant issue; border security is strengthened and an estimated 3 million illegal immigrants offered amnesty or regularized status.

1990s   Illegal immigration grows in Southwest.

1993   Waco standoff between federal authorities and religious cult ends in tragedy; in aftermath, militia movements form across United States.

1994   North American Free Trade Agreement (NAFTA) has the unintended consequence of feeding illegal immigration by forcing Mexican farmers to compete with more efficient American agriculture. At least 2 million Mexican farmers leave the land between 1993 and 2002; California voters endorse Proposition 187, denying social

	welfare benefits to illegal immigrants and public schooling to their children.
1995	Stormfront.org founded as first white nationalist Website and destruction of federal building in April kills 165; backlash negatively affects recruiting of antigovernment activists.
1996	Standoff between federal agents and Montana Freemen sovereign citizens movement lasts 81 days. ELF's American branch surfaces in arson attack on U.S. Forest Service truck in Oregon.
1997–2000	People for the Ethical Treatment of Animals (PETA) makes repeated headlines as leaders openly advocate violent and illegal means of pursuing their struggle.
2001	With states already increasingly passing legislation aimed at illegal immigrants, 9/11 terrorist attack on United States injects security considerations into immigration debate, even as it has a dampening effect on groups advocating violence.
2005-06	President Bush's appointees to Supreme Court revive U.S. antiabortion movement; Congress authorizes construction of an additional 700 miles of wall along border with Mexico.
2007	More than 100 municipalities in twenty-seven states pass or consider laws prohibiting the renting to or employment of illegal aliens, and/or making English the official language of government.

Notes

1. "Rudolph Sentenced to Life for Birmingham Clinic Bombing," *The Baltimore Sun* (July 19, 2005).

2. MSNBC, "Abortion Clinic Violence" (http://www.msnbc.com/modules/clinic, accessed June 23, 2005).

3. Frederick Clarkson, "Anti-Abortion Violence: Two Decades of Arson, Bombs, and Murder," (http;//www.splcenter.org/intel/intelrport/article.jsp/aid=411, accessed January 31, 2006), an intelligence report of the Southern Poverty Law Center.

4. See the Committee's Website (www.nrlc.org). Abortions were first made illegal in mid-1890, when it became a felony to perform abortions even before fetal life could be felt (the quickening). For the history of abortion policy in the United States, see Abortionfacts.com (http://www.abortionfacts.com/history/history.asp, accessed June 20, 2005).

5. Ontario Consultants on Religious Tolerance, "Violence and Harassment at U.S. Abortion Clinics" (http://www.religioustolerance.org, accessed January 31, 2006).

6. Clarkson, op. cit. In addition to Eric Rudolph, whose notes contained repeated references to the organization, other extremists linked to the Army of God include James Kopp (alias Atomic Dog), the Army of God member convicted of the 1998 slaying of Dr. Barnett Slepian, a physician in Amherst, New York, and suspected in the shootings of others in Rochester, New York, Ontario, and Vancouver, and Shelley Shannon, a convicted arsonist and suspect in the murder of a clinic doctor.

7. See ADL, "Ecoterrorism: Extremism in the Animal Rights and Environmental Movements" (http://www.adl.org/learn/ext_us/Ecoterrorism, accessed January 31, 2006).

8. Gibson, op. cit.

9. See Lois Romano, "Cosmetic Extremist Groups Weaker but Still Worrisome," *The Washington Post* (April 19, 2005), and "11 are Indicted as Terrorists for Environment, Animals: U.S. Alleges Arson, Sabotage in 17 Incidents from 1996 to Late 2001," *The Baltimore Sun* (January 21, 2006).

10. Cited in Romano, op. cit.

11. Ibid.

12. Ibid.

13. Anti-Defamation League, "The Militia Movement" (http://www.adl.org/learn/ext_us/Militia_M.asp, accessed January 31, 2006).

14. The federal government's efforts to arrest Randy Weaver on a variety of charges in late 1992 ended in the death of Weaver's wife (by sniper fire) and one of his children, as well as the wounding of one of his friends and the death of a federal agent. In 1995 the government awarded Weaver and his surviving three children $3.1 million in damages. Militias continue to use the incident as an Internet recruiting story of government lawlessness. See, for example, the collection of materials relating to the incident posted under the title "Ruby Ridge: There are NO statute of Limitations on MURDER!" [*sic*] (http://www.apfn.org/apfn/rubyridge.html, accessed March 9, 2006).

15. For a succinct summary of the Waco incident, see Rick Webb, "The Waco Davidian Standoff," (Rick A. Rost Institute, September, 1999; (http://www.cult-education.com/waco.html, accessed March 9, 2006), under "The Changing Face of Cults."

16. "The Militia Movement," op. cit. Anti-Defamation League analysts also attribute the growth of anti-government militias in the early 1990s to such varied factors as the widespread aversion of the American Right to the presidency of Bill Clinton; the catalyzing effect of the race riot in Los Angeles following the initial acquittal of the police officers charged with the beating of Rodney King (especially the effect on the supremacists drawn to the militia movements); the opposition on the political right to federal gun control laws and the mistaken belief that militia members would be exempt from those laws; and the willingness of many militia members to accept the even more outrageous conspiracy theories then circulating about the federal government's plan to disarm American

citizens and suborn the United States government to the political whims of the United Nations.

17. There have been far fewer left-wing antigovernment terrorist organizations in United States history, given their usual sympathy with the concept of equality, the mainstream nature of the U.S. political culture, and the dampening effect on far-left-wing sympathies of the long Cold War with the communist Soviet Union and the Cold War revelations of the atrocities committed during Joseph Stalin's 1927–1953 reign. The most notable organizations emerged during the Vietnam War era, as much motivated by their antiwar orientations as their commitment to political change and the implementation of a communist-oriented social and economic order.

18. Gail Gibson, "War on Homegrown Terrorism: Proceeding with Quiet Urgency," *The Baltimore Sun* (April 17, 2005).

19. Anti-Defamation League, "The Ku Klux Klan" (http://www.adl.org/learn/ext_us/KKK, accessed January 31, 2006). The ADL concludes simply that "today there is no such thing as the Ku Klux Klan" in any semblance of its former self.

20. Kait Berry, "Internet Hate Groups" (Towson University (Maryland), August 7, 2005), an unpublished independent study project.

21. The Aryan Nations and National Alliance were also formed during the 1970s, the former in the mid-1970s by Richard Butler and the National Alliance by William Pierce. Pierce died in 2001 and Butler in 2004, only briefly outliving Robert Millar (deceased 2001), the leader of the northeastern Oklahoma white separatist organization Elohim City, which had once been linked to Oklahoma City bomber Timothy McVeigh. Meanwhile, the man responsible for reviving the Creativity Movement during the 1990s, Matthew Hale, has been incarcerated for threatening a Chicago judge.

22. See Anti-Defamation League, "Creativity Movement" (http://www.adl.org/learn/ext_us/WCOTC, accessed January 31, 2006).

23. "Most Support Abortion with Limits, Poll Shows," *The Baltimore Sun* (March 13, 2006). Another 27 percent in the poll indicated opposition to abortion in most cases. A slight majority, 51 percent, favored the legalization of abortion in all or most cases.

24. See Sonya Geis, "Aryan Brotherhood Racketeering Trials Begin: 40 Affiliated with Prison Gang Face Charges Including Murder and Drug Sales," *The Washington Post* (March 15, 2006). The quoted analysis was offered by Melissa Carr, an ADL special project director based in California.

25. See, for example, "Many Illegal Immigrants Shun Protest:, Non-Hispanics Fear Notice," *The Baltimore Sun* (April 17, 2006); Krissah Williams and Karen Brulliard, "Rift Could Diminish Boycott's Strength: Immigrant Groups Argue over Agenda," *The Washington Post* (May 1, 2006); David Montgomery, "At Immigrant Rally, Divided They Stand: Calls for Work Boycott Breed Disagreement," *The Washington Post* (May 2, 2006); and Clarence Page, "Not-So-Hidden Costs of Immigration Policy Hurt Black Americans," *The Baltimore Sun* (January 9, 2005). On the racial divide separating Hispanic immigrants, see also Kelly Brewington, "Latino racial outlook varies: Census: To some Hispanics

identifying with a certain race is paramount; Others emphasize national origin," *The* Baltimore *Sun* (January 9, 2005).

26. I am indebted to one of my undergraduate students, Alexa Siegel, for uncovering this fact in Eric Zolov and Robert H. Holden, eds. *Latin America and the United States: A Documentary History* (New York: Oxford University Press, 2000: 165–66).

27. See D'Vera Cohn, "Report Details Growth in Illegal Migration: Undocumented Immigrants Outnumbered Legal Ones from 2000 to 2006, Study Says," *The Washington Post* (September 28, 2005).

28. U.S. Bureau of the Census figures, reported in Sylvia Moreno, "Flow of Illegal Immigrants to U.S. Unabated: Mexicans Make Up Largest Group; D.C. Area Numbers Up 70 Percent Since 2000," *The Washington Post* (January 22, 2005). By some estimates, the number of illegal immigrants in the United States by 2005 was nearer to 20 million than 12 million.

29. U.S. Bureau of the Census figures, reported in D'Vera Cohn, "Hispanic Growth Surge Fueled by Births in U.S.," *The Washington Post* (June 9, 2005). By comparison, Hispanics accounted for approximately 40 percent of the U.S. population growth between the 1990 and 2000 censuses.

30. Nearly four out of ten (38 percent) of New York City's 8 million people today, for example, are foreign-born—a proportion common in the late nineteenth century, but subsequently unknown until recently, even in that most cosmopolitan of American cities.

31. See D'Vera Cohn, "Immigrants, Yes; Immigration, Maybe: Poll Finds No Consensus on What to Do About Those Who Are Here Illegally," *The Washington Post* (March 30, 2006), and Darryl Fears, "After Protests, Backlash Grows: Opponents of Illegal Immigration are Increasingly Vocal," *The Washington Post* (May 6, 2006). Immigrants as a group were viewed less favorably than Hispanics. On the question of immigration in general, the nonpartisan Pew Research Center and the Pew Hispanic Center found a 52 percent majority agreeing that immigration today burdens the United States by taking jobs from Americans and placing a strain on our health care system, but very large majorities also expressed the belief that Hispanics work very hard (80 percent) and have strong family values (80 percent). Only 37 percent believed that Hispanics often go on welfare. In all instances, Hispanics were seen more favorably than when a similar poll was conducted nearly a decade earlier, in 1997.

32. Milton Esman, *Ethnic Politics* (Ithaca, New York: Cornell University Press, 1994: 176). The lure of migrating to the United States is particularly obvious in the case of Mexican immigrants. Apart from the proximity of the border, more than one Mexican worker in four is either unemployed or underemployed, and the average gross domestic product per capita in Mexico is less than one-fourth that in the United States. See the United States Central Intelligence Agency online fact sheet on Mexico (http://www.cia.gov/cia/publications/factbook/geos/mx.html), and the Organization for Economic Co-operation and Development data for Mexico (http://www.stats.oecd.org).

33. See, for example, Hanah Cho, "Immigrants Taking U.S. Jobs, Report Says," *The Sun* (Baltimore), March 23, 2006, discussing a recent report by the Center for Immigration Studies, a pro-control immigration think tank.

34. See Mary Jordan, "Mexican Workers Pay for Success: With Labor Costs Rising, Factories Depart for Asia," *The Washington Post* (June 20, 2002).

35. See Robert Barnes, "Immigration Resonating With Voters, Candidates," *The Washington Post* (September 12, 2005). The article focuses on a fall 2005 poll that discovered an expanding number of Americans (42 percent, versus 36 percent in January of that year) in favor of deporting illegal foreign workers rather than offering them the chance to legalize their status.

36. See, for example, Karin Brulliard and Paul Dubban, "55 Illegal Immigrants Arrested at Dulles Site: Raid at Construction Area Is Part of National Effort to Deflect Terrorist Threats," *The Washington Post* (June 15, 2006). Ironically, in the immediate aftermath of 9/11 the effort to punish employers hiring illegal workers declined substantially, from 182 prosecutions in 1999 to only 4 in 2003, as the Immigration and Naturalization Service (INS, now a part of the Department of Homeland Security) diverted its resources to look for potential Arab terrorists. See Spencer S. Hsu and Kari Lyndersen, "Illegal Hiring Is Rarely Penalized: Politics, 9/11 Cited in Lax Enforcement," *The Washington Post* (June 19, 2006).

37. By 2005 that price had reportedly already risen from an estimated average of approximately $700 in 1999 to approximately $1,200 per passenger per crossing.

38. See, for example, Mary Jordan and Kevin Sullivan, "Border Police Chief Only Latest Casualty In Mexico Drug War: More Than 600 Killed This Year Despite Aggressive Crackdown," *The Washington Post* (June 16, 2005).

39. The United States has traditionally used the jus soli approach to defining citizenship (as opposed to basing it on the ethnicity or nationality of the parents). That principle provides that individuals born in the United States are automatically eligible for citizenship. One dimension of the gravity of the immigrant issue is that by 2005, several members of Congress were in favor of denying this right to children born of illegal immigrants. See Associated Press, "Renewed Debate Surrounds Right to Citizenship by Birth," *The Baltimore Sun* (December 27, 2005).

40. Mary Beth Sheridan and David Cho, "MS-13 Crackdown Arrests 35 in Region," *The Washington Post* (March 14, 2005). The organization began as an El Salvadoran association, but it has since accepted members from several Hispanic countries. Nationwide in structure, its members have been frequently accused of intimidating the voluntary Minuteman Project patrols monitoring the United States-Mexico border for illegal immigrants crossing into the US.

41. Prior to World War I, the question of "illegal aliens" scarcely presented itself. Passports were not required, and essentially anyone who managed to make it to the ports of entry with identification papers and without any obvious communicable diseases was admitted.

42. See Mary Jordan, "Guide for Mexican Migrants Draws Ire," *The Washington Post* (January 6, 2005).

43. The border between the United States and Mexico is 1,945 miles long. As of mid-2007, only the 20 miles of the border between San Diego and the slum just south of the border, near Tijuana, were fenced off—the result of a decision made during the Clinton presidency that has been effective in reducing substantially the number of aliens illegally crossing into southern California. Beyond this area, along the United States' busiest and most protected border, there are another forty miles (the total of the other official customs areas) along the border that are well staffed by the U.S. custom agents on duty at these official crossing points. The remaining 1,885 miles were still unfenced or otherwise blocked by manmade barriers in 2007, despite Congress's having authorized construction of additional walls for Arizona (to fence all of its border), New Mexico, and Texas.

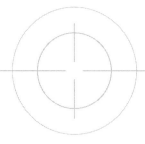

A BIBLIOGRAPHICAL NOTE

Thoughts on Conducting Research
on the Here and Now

Whether you are beginning to write a short essay, a term paper, a scholarly article, or a two-volume study, sources are always a concern. What primary resources are available? How much attention should be devoted to background materials? When do you stop chasing down footnotes? Are newspapers and news magazines appropriate? Is *Wikipedia* a gift from the heavens or a creation of hell bent on leading you astray? When should you stop researching an ongoing matter and finish the project?

These and similar questions haunt every researcher and writer, and they are particularly troublesome for those whose focus lies within the field of government and politics. It is axiomatic that all political systems—be they local governments, national political processes, alliances such as NATO, or supranational entities such as the European Union—are ever in the process of change. What differs across space (that is, from country to country, entity to entity) and time (from era to era) is the pace and direction of change. The political processes that have endured and that compose the consolidated democracies of the advanced Western World are those that have been able, by and large, to adapt to or evolve with their changing political environments. Some have even been able to read the tea leaves well enough to get ahead of the curve and mold the process of change to their needs, as when Britain's nineteenth-century leaders voluntarily introduced universal male suffrage before their citizens mobilized to demand it. Those systems that have not adapted to change have often been casualties of it, ending in revolutions or descending into long periods of prolonged political instability. That happened on the continent of Europe during the nineteenth century, when the resistance of those in power to the demands for a share of political authority by the upwardly mobile of their societies led to revolutions across much of Western Europe in 1830, 1848, and 1870.

What has been true in the past remains true today, and those examining the existing and potential hot spots in the contemporary world face especially difficult research challenges. The subject matter here often begins with already unstable political processes or simmering, potentially explosive issues awaiting a catalyst to set them off. Political hot spots can thus materialize overnight, and even as the result of geographically remote events. The success of the American civil rights movement, as noted in this volume, inspired the civil rights movement in Northern Ireland. When violently opposed by members of the majority community there, that movement culminated in tit-for-tat communal violence that did not end with London's rule and the suspension of its civilian government in that province for more than thirty-five years. Similarly, although the situation besetting Europe's Muslim underclass might have eventually produced political extremists, viewing European politics from the vantage point of 2000 it is difficult to imagine that homegrown terrorists would have conducted the lethal attacks committed on Madrid's and London's mass transit systems in mid-decade without the inspiration provided by the suicide bombers who attacked the United States on September 11, 2001.

Keeping pace with developments in areas where political instability is already boiling over and affecting adjacent states, or where simmering issues are apt to explode violently in even the most sedate of political systems, necessarily requires greater reliance on journalist sources than should normally be needed in serious research ventures, if only because of the time delay between the disruption of a tenuous peace and the publication of scholarly analyses of those developments. That has certainly been true in the writing of this volume; for example, homegrown Muslim terrorism in Europe and North America seemed unthinkable when the project was initially outlined. Moreover, during the last weeks before this text was turned over to the publisher, political events overtook the democratic peace in Georgia; an ominous arms race between Armenia and Azerbaijan developed, with serious implications for the "frozen" Nagorno-Karabakh conflict over which these two states had come to blows only fifteen years earlier; and Kosovo voters elected as their future premier a former Kosovo Liberation Army leader whose single-interest platform in campaigning was that he would unilaterally declare Kosovo's independence within a month of taking office.

Finally, the worlds treated in this volume may be especially challenging to research, because mixed among those areas that qualify as hot spots by any criteria are other zones and issues that are tottering on the brink between lapsing into the politics of tense normalcy and slipping over the edge, exploding, and threatening the peace of neighboring states. Bosnia, Kosovo, Transnistria, Nagorno-Karabakh, and Georgia all fit into this second category, as of this writing. Indeed, even in the established democracies of Western Europe—where traditional hot spots such as Basque Spain, Northern Ireland, and Cyprus seem to be in the process of cooling down for the long term—the pairing of racism with the foreigner issue in England, the French commitment to the secular state and the nonassimilating Muslim communities in France, and the underclass status of immigrant and foreign workers throughout the region create a highly volatile situation in the heart of democratic Europe.

Because it is impossible to keep absolutely current in a topical area where currency is primarily important, this work concludes with a half dozen general suggestions for conducting research on the present and developing hot spots of today and tomorrow, followed by an annotated bibliography of the sources that this author found to be the most helpful in writing this volume.

Scholarly Books and Articles Come First

Before exploring any topic lying within the domain of current events, some background reading is essential for context. The longer the study, the more time you should devote to research of this variety. The essays in this volume are intended to provide only a starting point for that research, and for that reason virtually every essay indicates in its endnotes highly recommended published and online sources for additional reading on the topic. In general, before straying too far beyond these sources and into the unguided realm of the Internet (see below), those just beginning research work are urged to stay within the area of published analyses, where there is greater quality control. Trust your library to have selected well-reviewed books on the subject matter. Trust the editors of the respected, refereed scholarly journals in the field to have screened out the unworthy. You will usually not be led astray. For similar reasons, if lost in a sea of books whose titles seem equally valuable to you, and if you do not know the reputation of the publishing house, choose books from university presses. Their editors are also good gatekeepers for quality publications.

More broadly, if you are into delving into professional journals, be certain to read the full article, not just the abstract or online summary. Remember, at this level of your research you are reading for the background and context necessary to understand rapidly unfolding current events. Abstracts will focus on the authors' theses, not on the broader scope within which the writers have developed their analyses.

Finally, even when researching very current topics, do not automatically exclude older studies simply because of their date of publication. No one has done better work on the problems of managing nationalism, for example, than Walker Connor, and the collection of essays edited by Douglas Greenberg and Stanley N. Katz on the problems of democratization in post-communist Europe—*Constitutionalism and Democracy: Transitions in the Contemporary World* (New York: Oxford University Press, 1993)—is still the basic starting point for background reading on this topic. Likewise, if you are studying France, Germany, or the area of foreign workers in Europe, any work by William Safran, David Conradt, and Anthony Messina, respectively—whatever its publication date—will provide a vast amount of useful background, and their studies are universally printed by trustworthy and widely respected presses.

Reports of Government Agencies and Respected International Study Groups Come Second

Also valuable as sources of background information and commentary on recent developments are the reports of governmental organizations such as the United States Congress, the United Nations, and (on domestic threats to the peace in the United States) the Federal Bureau of Investigation, as well as the studies of such international monitoring bodies as Transparency International (on levels of corruption abroad). In many instances, the reports and position papers of these sources can be found online—for example, those of the highly respected International Crisis Group, which is one of the preeminent sources of information on political developments in post-communist Europe, and whose reports have been often cited and recommended in this volume. In fact, anyone interested in doing research on hot spots in the contemporary world is well advised to bookmark its Website—www.crisisgroup.org—and register for its weekly list of new studies. Still, because government agencies and such groups as the ICG often have their own interests at stake, their work is best consulted second, not at the outset, by researchers in need of background material.

Demographic Data Are Important

Politics is always contextual, and a useful first step in moving from acquiring background information to examining the present is to get a sense of the broader economic and political environment in which events are unfolding. Is the economy healthy, or are poverty and high unemployment rates fueling discontent? Is the government open, or repressive? If the system is democratic, is it coherent or amorphous; that is, are there so many parties vying for influence that parliamentary governments dependent on majorities in the legislature may tend toward instability? Is society rife with ethnic, linguistic, and religious divisions, or is it relatively homogeneous? Such data may need interpreting some of the time and may be subject to manipulation just as often, but they can also paint a valuable profile of the economic, social, and political environment of the time. For up-to-date data, no source is more easily accessed and routinely kept current than the Central Intelligence Agency's *World Factbook* (*sic*), whose coverage of all countries is available online (www.cia.gov/library/publications/the-world-factbook/index.html).

Journalists and Weekly News Magazines Come Last

Studying hot spots necessarily means self-saturation in the news of the day. The journalists who trek to those zones and report daily or weekly are every scholar's eyes and ears until they can follow them into the field. Nor is reliance on their stories a necessary evil. Good journalists immerse themselves in the societies on which they report and ferret out as many details on the event(s) as they can. Those who win Pulitzer Prizes for such work are only the tip of the iceberg compared to the multitude of good journalists whose work is available daily. Still, their job is to report what is happening, usually only in the context of relatively recent developments. Moreover, reporters are often sent to where the story is because they are good at their job of *reporting*, and not because they are experts on the politics or societies of their assignments. Accordingly, their work is best digested only after having established a knowledgeable frame of reference for absorbing it, and that type of understanding—more often than not—comes only by relying on those with specialties in the areas to which the stories have come. With that important qualification, however, there is no substitute for consulting the work of good reporters in order to obtain immediately the details regarding breaking hot spots. Their news is immediate, whereas even journal articles on the same subject matter will take months to appear.

Know Your Source

In a world where "Google-ing" a word can result in thousands of hits, knowing your sources may be the most important admonition of all. The Internet can be like flypaper. It can catch everything from reliable studies to diatribes posing as reliable studies, to just plain (and sometimes willfully offered) misinformation. Internet encyclopedias can be particularly

treacherous, precisely because they are so easily penetrated by contribu-
tors with their own agendas. *Wikipedia* has probably received far more
bad press than it deserves as a result of such revelations as the fact that
Exxon employees were able to insert scaled-back numbers relating to the
amount of damage that the *Exxon Valdez* oil spill caused in Alaska, or
such show-and-tell demonstrations as Stephen Colbert removing whole
species from the endangered listings for the amusement of his "nation" on
his Comedy Channel show. But for the most part, it is a relatively useful
source of general information, and of specific Websites where additional
information can be found. Used with caution, skepticism, and selectively,
Wikipedia and its ilk still warrant visitation. But the bottom line remains
the same for all of the open information galleries on the Internet: a source
to which anyone can contribute is ultimately of *reliable* value to no one.

The good news is that the Internet also makes it easy for you to know
your sources. Before citing an unknown person or agency, no matter how
objective material may sound, take the time to find that person and/or
entity's name on Yahoo, Google, or (insert the search engine of your
choice), and learn about the person or entity.

Mix Your Sources

Properly forewarned, do not be afraid to take full advantage of the
information so easily accessible in the current age. In part, this means
going beyond the obvious—for example, the *New York Times* or the
BBC for daily news—and seeking out foreign newspapers in the areas
you are exploring. Many have their own English-language presses, and
many (such as the *Prague Post,* which was used for the essay on the
Romani in this volume) allow free access to their Website and their
archives. When used for what they are, even biased polemics can provide
a measure of the intensity of local feelings on the issues that produce hot
spots, and add color to any analysis.

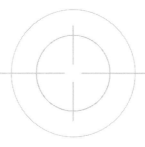

ANNOTATED BIBLIOGRAPHY

Akcaper, Burak. *Turkey's New European Era: Foreign Policy on the Road to EU Membership* (Lanham, MD: Rowman & Littlefield Publishers, 2007). A solid consideration of Turkey's candidacy for EU membership, with an extensive discussion of the official European Union reports concerning Turkey's candidacy and interesting reflections on the meaning of Europeanization in Turkey's case.

Aksin, Sina (trans. Dexter H. Mursaloglu). *Turkey from Empire to Revolutionary Republic: The Emergence of the Turkish Nation from 1789 to the Present* (New York: University Press, 2007). A major effort to chronicle Turkey's history from the time of the Ottoman Empire to the present. The concluding sections on post-World War II Turkey and Cyprus, and on the military as the defender of the Republic, are particularly valuable in understanding contemporary Turkish politics.

Arbetov, Alexei G. *The Kosovo Crisis: The End of the Post-Cold War Era* (Washington, DC: Atlantic Council Occasional Paper, 2002). A short but dense professional paper on United States intervention in Kosovo and a pragmatic consideration of the challenges faced by state-builders there in the early days of the twenty-first century.

Arikan, Harun. *Turkey and the EU: An Awkward Candidate for EU Membership?* (Aldershot, UK: Ashgate, 2006). An extremely good treatment of the basic issues involved in Turkey's application for EU membership and discussion of the efforts on both sides to address those issues. Turkey's policy with respect to Cyprus and the role of the military in Turkish politics are prominently considered.

Aslund, Anders and Michael McFaul, eds. *Revolution in Orange: The Origins of Ukraine's Democratic Breakthrough* (Washington, DC: Carnegie Endowment for International Peace, 2006). A good collection of reflections by authors who were present during the critical period leading up to the Ukraine's spontaneous effort to move in a more democratic direction.

Aydin, Mustafa. "Crypto-Optimism in Turkish-Greek Relations: What Is Next?" *Journal of Southern Europe and the Balkans,* Vol. 2 (August 2003: 223–40). The refugee issue still looms as the greatest obstacle to ending the conflict between the Greek and Turkish Cypriots, and this article highlights the many facets of that issue and the obstacles still complicating its resolution.

Bawer, Bruce. *While Europe Slept: How Radical Islam Is Destroying the West from Within.* (New York: Random House-Doubleday, 2006). Opinionated without becoming bombastic, Bawer's work indicts European liberalism for too long turning a blind eye to the danger of radical Islamic groups in Europe, and discusses the dangers both in terms of the threat that these groups pose to security on the Continent and to liberal values.

Biermann, Wolfgang, and Martin Vadset, eds. *UN Peacekeeping in Trouble: Lessons Learned from the Former Yugoslavia* (Brookfield, VT: Ashgate, 1998). Published just three years after the Dayton Peace Accords and the launching of the subsequent international peacekeeping and state-building operations in Bosnia, this edited volume remains relevant on the dangers of being overly optimistic and under-prepared for the frustrations and risks of peacekeeping and "peace-building" operations. It should have been read by policymakers before the West undertook the mission in Kosovo.

Bose, Sumantra. *Bosnia after Dayton: Nationalist Partition and International Intervention* (New York: Oxford University Press, 2002). An excellent critique of the problems involved with state-building and coercive diplomacy in a historically divided multinational country, drawing skillfully on the author's personal field experience.

Bowser, Benjamin P., ed. *Racism and Anti-Racism in World Perspective* (Thousand Oaks, CA: Sage Publications, 1995). Primarily useful as background reading on racism in Europe's past, the essays also provide a good backdrop for understanding the Muslim issue in contemporary European politics.

Broad, Robin. *Global Backlash: Citizen Initiatives for a Just World Economy* (Lanham, MD: Rowman & Littlefield, 2002). One of the better books to appear after antiglobalization protesters began to draw attention to their cause, Broad's work provides a good basic and intermediate discussion of the issues involved in both the globalization process and the resultant resistance to it.

Carment, David, John F. Stack, Jr., and Frank Harvey, eds. *The International Politics of Quebec Secession: State-Making and State-Breaking in North America* (Westport, CT: Praeger, 2001). A thoughtful series of essays on the "what if" question: what if Quebec votes "yes" in a future referendum proposing its departure from Canada? Very interesting reading on the type of future relationships that might emerge between Canada and Quebec, not all of which are attractive ones.

Chollet, Derek H. *The Road to the Dayton Accords: A Study of American Statecraft* (New York: Palgrave-Macmillan, 2005). The foreword by Richard Holbrooke, one of the architects of the Dayton Peace Accords, is a good indicator of the book's tone. Nevertheless, it is a useful guide to understanding what was achieved at Dayton, if not why more was not done earlier to end the suffering caused by the civil war in Bosnia.

Chorbajian, Levan, ed. *The Making of Nagorno-Karabakh: From Secession to Republic* (New York: Palgrave, 2001). At times the selections in this work descend into being a defense of the war from the Armenian side, and the book perhaps pays too little attention to the Azeri, who were also victims of the war and of the long conflict between Armenia and Azerbaijan over the region. However, the work also offers useful insight as to why outside negotiators have been unable to resolve the conflict.

Conversi, Daniele. *The Basques, the Catalans, and Spain: Alternative Routes to National Mobilization* (Reno: University of Nevada Press, 1997). Published by the Center for Basque Studies at the University of Nevada, Conversi's book is basic introductory reading for anyone interested in Catalan and Basque nationalism in Spain, and why Catalonia's nationalism took such different courses from Basque nationalism after Spain joined the European Community.

Cook, Steven A. *Ruling but Not Governing: The Military and Political Development in Egypt, Algeria, and Turkey* (Baltimore, MD: Johns Hopkins University Press, 2007). A significant, scholarly contribution to understanding the role of the military in Middle East politics. Framed in a comparative context, this book is primarily useful for further research in its detailed discussion of the role of the Turkish military as the protector of Kemal's Republic.

Crenshaw, Martha, ed. *Terrorism in Context* (University Park, PA: Pennsylvania State University Press, 1995). A solid set of essays on terrorism in the contemporary world. Particularly recommended in the context of our study of hot spots in Western Europe is its discussion of the often-violent struggle by Basque groups to achieve their political goals by employing terrorism in contemporary Spain.

Croissant, Michael P. *The Armenia-Azerbaijan Conflict: Causes and Implications* (Westport, CT: Praeger, 1998). More even-handed than the Chorbajian work, this volume offers a straightforward history of the evolution of the conflict, placing it into the framework of both the self-images of the protagonists and the impact of the changing geopolitical nature of the Caucasus in the 1990s. It is still highly useful for further reading on the origins of the Nagorno-Karabakh conflict and the war over that region.

Crowe, David M. *A History of the Gypsies of Eastern Europe and Russia* (New York: Saint Martin's Press, 1995). Recommended for advanced background reading on the migration that brought the Roma to Europe, their history there, and their struggle to survive and preserve their culture. Given its publication date, follow-up reading is necessary on the status of the Roma in contemporary Europe.

Curtis, Glenn E. *Yugoslavia: A Country Study* (Washington: Library of Congress, 1992). The last American Field Research study on Yugoslavia before its explosion in the 1990s. This work contains a wealth of information on the demographic, economic, and social conditions then prevailing in the country, including data from the last census conducted in Yugoslavia.

Danforth, Loring M. *The Macedonian Conflict: Ethnic Nationalism in a Transnational World* (Princeton, NJ: Princeton University Press, 1998). Well researched and equally well written, Danforth's study is the place to begin in researching the conditions prevailing in Macedonia on the eve of its mini-civil war in the early years of the twenty-first century.

Diller, Daniel C. *Russia and the Independent States* (Washington, DC: Congressional Quarterly, Inc., 1993). One of the early books to appear following the implosion of the Soviet Union, Diller's work is still very useful for additional background reading on the fallout states and the challenges initially facing them.

Douglass, William A., et al. *Basque Politics and Nationalism on the Eve of the Millennium* (Reno: Basque Studies Institute, 1999). A varied and useful set of essays for understanding Basque nationalism. The topics range from the efforts to formulate a Basque foreign policy, to the Basques in France and abroad, to the images of the ETA in the Spanish media and films.

Esman, Milton. *Ethnic Politics* (Ithaca, NY: Cornell University Press, 1994). A readily accessible work by one of the United States' foremost students of ethnic conflict. Readers will find both the chapter on Quebec nationalism and the more conceptual chapters on the nature of ethnic politics useful in understanding the durability of ethnic nationalism in the developed democratic world, as well as in post-communist Europe.

Fetzer, Joel S., and J. Christopher Soper. *Muslims and the State in Britain, France, and Germany* (Cambridge, UK: Cambridge University Press, 2004). The focus is on reconciling Muslim religious practices with politics in Western Europe, using the case studies of Britain, France, and Germany—countries with three different approaches and histories on the matter. The work covers a wider ground, however, including European attitudes toward accommodating Muslim religion in self-consciously secular states.

Fings, Karola, Herbert Heuss, and Frank Sparing (trans. Donald Kenrick). *The Gypsies During the Second World War* (Hatfield, Hertfordshire, UK: Gypsy Research Center, University of Hertfordshire Press, 1997). Useful for advanced research on the Romani in Nazi-occupied Europe, and on the successful survival of many who found safety in the remote areas of rural Central Europe, where the Roma now make their primary homes.

Gauvreau, Michael. *The Catholic Origins of Quebec's Quiet Revolution, 1931–1970* (Montreal, Canada: McGill-Queen's University Press, 2005). A source for advanced reading on the topic. Gauvreau treats both the role of the Catholic Church as a one-time defender of the old order prior to the Quiet Revolution in post-World War II Quebec, and its changing policies at the time of the Quiet Revolution.

George, Vic and Robert M. Page, eds. *Global Social Problems* (Malden, MA: Polity Press, 2004). This volume's essays are best referenced as intermediate and advanced readings on the globalization process and on the world in which it is unfolding, where social problems can no longer be confined to individual countries but represent challenges to international policy making.

Guerette, Rob T. *Migrant Death: Border Safety and Situational Crime Prevention on the U.S.-Mexico Divide* (New York: LFB Scholarly Publishing, 2007). The recent debate over Mexican immigration has produced a flurry of books on "the border." Guerette's is the best on the growing violence and crime surrounding the border zone, and on the risks that those crossing it run.

Headrick, Daniel R. *The Tools of Empire: Technology and European Imperialism in the Nineteenth Century* (New York: Oxford University Press, 1981). A classic in its field, Headrick's book links technological change to the development of the empires that redefined the globe. The book does not discuss it, but Europe's current foreign underclass has sprung from those empires, and this study explains how they reached so far.

Heisler, Martin O., and Barbara Schmitter Heisler, eds. "From Foreign Workers to Settlers? Transnational Migration and the Emergence of the New Minorities," *Annals of the American Academy of Political and Social Sciences,* 465 (Beverly Hills, CA: Sage, 1986). These essays collectively provide one of the first, and still one of the better comparative studies of Europe's immigrant and foreign worker communities. Published at the time when Europe's anti-immigrant parties were having an impact on public policy, the selections are highly recommended for further background research.

Helsi, Vicki I. *Government and Politics in Russia and the Post-Soviet Region* (Boston: Houghton Mifflin Company, 2007). Designed for classroom use, Helsi's book is one of the best recent studies of Russian politics, useful for introductory to advanced research on the contemporary Russian political scene.

Hughes, H. Stuart. *Sophisticated Rebels: The Political Culture of European Dissent, 1968–1987* (Cambridge, MA: Harvard University Press, 1988). Valuable in its own right, Stuart's work is an excellent complement to the previously cited volume by the Heislers. It explores the status of Europe's foreign communities, but it is chiefly interesting because it puts the politics involving them in the context of the time.

Hughes, James. *Chechnya: From Nationalism to Jihad* (Philadelphia: University of Pennsylvania Press, 2007). Must reading for anyone doing advanced research on the Chechen conflict. Hughes evenhandedly explores the causes of the conflict and the degree to which a fundamentally nationalist struggle for self-determination in Chechnya has been used by political leaders on all sides to serve their purposes.

Human Rights Watch. *Azerbaijan: Seven Years of Conflict in Nagorno-Karabakh.* (Helsinki, Finland: Human Rights Watch, 1991). Note the date on this early report on the Nagorno-Karabakh conflict and the evolving hostility between the Armenian and Azerbaijan union republics over the simmering issue. Highly interesting background reading for anyone researching this conflict.

Hunter, Shireen T. *The Transcaucasus in Transition: Nation Building and Conflict* (Washington, DC: Center for Strategic and International Studies, 1994). Another highly useful work for background research. The early years after the implosion of the Soviet system defined the ongoing conflicts in the Northern and Southern Caucasus. Too often more recent works give those years a too-compressed treatment, but Hunter covers the events of those years with a wealth of detail.

Inglehart, Ronald. *The Silent Revolution: Changing Values and Political Styles among Western Publics* (Princeton, NJ: Princeton University Press, 1977). A landmark study of the changing political attitudes in the countries of the advanced democratic world as they evolved into post-industrial societies. Like the Headrick work cited earlier, Inglehart's study is not about conflict in Western Europe or North America, but it helps the reader understand the nature of the environment in which conflict currently takes its shape.

Innes, Michael A., ed. *Bosnian Security after Dayton: New Perspectives* (New York: Routledge, 2006). Primarily useful as a study of state-making in Bosnia a decade after the signing of the Dayton Accord and the launching of the massive international effort to make Bosnia-Herzegovina a stable, functioning multinational democracy.

International Crisis Group. "Abkhazia Today" (ICG Europe Report No. 176, September 15, 2006; http://www.crisisgroup.org). Internationally recognized as one of the world's ten best think tanks, the International Crisis Group steadily issues studies of recent developments in hot spots around the globe that are indispensable for anyone researching ongoing conflicts. Each report provides background information, detailed analyses of current conditions and developments, and policy recommendations for easing and/or managing the conflict. All reports are freely available at the Group's Website, and all reports are characterized by very high quality control standards. This report is no exception. It offers a careful discussion of the growing tension between Abkhazia and Tbilisi following Georgia's July 2006 acquisition of the one part of that breakaway region that had not been controlled by its capital.

International Crisis Group. "Abkhazia: Ways Forward" (ICG Europe Report No. 179, January 18, 2007; http://www.crisisgroup.org). A follow-up to the previous report, this study reviews subsequent events and proposes a series of policy recommendations designed to ease the conflict.

International Crisis Group. "After Milosevic: A Practical Agenda for Lasting Balkans Peace" (ICG Europe Report No. 108, April 1, 2001; http://www.crisisgroup.org). Perhaps the best available short-overview analysis of the Balkans in the early days of the twenty-first century, this report stresses the opportunities that existed for headway on a variety of fronts, but also notes the broad obstacles to further progress in Bosnia, Kosovo, and Macedonia.

International Crisis Group. "Armenia: Internal Instability Ahead" (ICG Europe Report No. 158, October 18, 2004; http://www.crisisgroup.org). A candid assessment of the health of the Armenian government following the 2004 protests by Armenians about the direction of the state. The report notes that although the Armenian economy has had robust growth and the number of protesters is still small, stabilizing the state requires more "robust" attention to further democratization policies.

International Crisis Group. "Azerbaijan's 2005 Elections: Lost Opportunity" (ICG Europe Briefing No. 40, November 21, 2005; http://www.crisisgroup.org). Recapping the continuing conflict between Armenia and Azerbaijan, as well as some of the domestic challenges facing Baku, the report laments, as its title suggests, that those running for office did not use the opportunity to stake out a new road to progress on either front.

International Crisis Group. "Bosnia's Stalled Police Reform: No Progress, No EU" (ICG Europe Report No. 164, September 6, 2005; http://www.crisisgroup.org). One of the first tasks undertaken by the post-Dayton institution builders who descended on Bosnia was the creation of a "Bosnia-Herzegovina" police force, rather than separate police forces for the Serbian and Croat-Muslim states in the federation. This report discusses the reasons for their failure to achieve that goal a decade after the Dayton Accord.

International Crisis Group. "The Cyprus Stalemate: What Next?" (ICG Europe Report No. 171, March 8, 2006; http://www.crisisgroup.org). The defeat of the 2004 referendum on merging Cyprus's two halves left those trying to resolve the Cyprus conflict without a follow-up plan. This report surveys developments in Cyprus since that vote and proposes options for jump-starting the peace process again.

International Crisis Group. "Ensuring Bosnia's Future: A New International Engagement Strategy" (ICG Europe Report No. 180, February 5, 2007; http://www.crisisgroup.org). The report inventories the successes and failures that have characterized the international efforts to build a multi-ethnic civil society in Bosnia and the points where those efforts are currently stalled, and then proposes steps to address some of those bottlenecks.

International Crisis Group. "Georgia: Avoiding War in South Ossetia" (ICG Europe Report No. 159, November 25, 2004; http://www.crisisgroup.org). An up-to-date analysis of the deteriorating conditions in Georgia's South Ossetia region, released shortly after the resumption of hostilities in the cease-fire zone. The report also contains a concise summary of the events leading up to the war between Tbilisi and that breakaway republic in 1990–1992, and what has happened since.

International Crisis Group. "Georgia: Sliding toward Authoritarianism?" (ICG Europe Report No. 189, December 19, 2007; http://www.crisisgroup.org). An immediate and detailed discussion of the factors leading up to the November 2007 demonstrations against the post-Rose Revolution government in Tbilisi, and the government's response to them.

International Crisis Group. "Georgia: What Now?" (ICG Europe Report No. 151, December 3, 2003: http://www.crisisgroup.org). An outstanding, immediate analysis of Georgia's Rose Revolution, coupled with a careful discussion of why Georgia matters to Europe and the United States, as well as within its own backyard.

International Crisis Group. "Georgia-South Ossetia: Refugee Return the Path to Peace" (ICG Europe Briefing No. 38, April 19, 2005; http://www.crisisgroup.org). A detailed discussion of the refugee issue as an obstacle to a lasting peace between Tbilisi and South Ossetia, and of the status of the current refugees from the South Ossetia conflict in Georgia and elsewhere.

International Crisis Group. "Georgia's Armenian and Azeri Minorities" (ICG Europe Report No. 178, November 22, 2006; http://www.crisisgroup.org). A comprehensive discussion of the status of Georgia's Azeri and Armenian communities, of the recent political conflicts involving them, and of the policies that Tbilisi needs to pursue in order to prevent these regions from becoming additional hot spots in South Caucasus politics.

International Crisis Group. "Georgia's South Ossetia Conflict: Make Haste Slowly" (ICG Europe Report No. 183, June 7, 2007; http://www.crisisgroup. org). A thorough analysis of post-2004 events leading to the deteriorating situation involving Georgia's South Ossetia conflict, coupled with background details of proposals for alleviating tensions and the conditions producing those tensions.

International Crisis Group. "Kosovo after Haradinaj" (Europe Report No. 163, May 26, 2005; http://www.crisisgroup.org). Released one year after the violent rioting in Kosovo in 2004 and shortly after the province's prime minister had to resign after being indicted by an international tribunal for war crimes, this report offers an excellent snapshot of Kosovo in mid-decade, only two years before its international overseers would propose that the province ultimately be slated for independence.

International Crisis Group. "Kosovo: The Challenge of Transition" (ICG Europe Report No. 170, February 17, 2006; http://www.crisisgroup.org). A follow-up to the May 2005 report, this release focuses on the possible futures for Kosovo. The International Crisis Group eventually accepts independence for Kosovo as the least negative of the available options.

International Crisis Group. "Macedonia: Make or Break" (ICG Europe Briefing No. 33, August 2, 2004; http://www.crisisgroup.org). A succinct review of the situation in Macedonia following the civil war there several years earlier, this report takes the position that specific reforms can no longer be delayed if the country is to stabilize as a multi-ethnic state—in particular, the compromises to which its leaders agreed in the accord that marked the end of that war.

International Crisis Group. "Macedonia: No Time for Complacency" (ICG Europe Report No. 149, October 23, 2003; http://www.crisisgroup.org). Stressing the need to revise the conventional wisdom at the time that Macedonia had become a political success story in the region following the agreement ending the civil war there, the report points to the continuing crime and corruption in the state and the immediate need to address the problems undermining the integrity of the country's law and justice system.

International Crisis Group. "Macedonia: Toward Destabilization? The Kosovo Crisis Takes Its Toll on Macedonia" (ICS Europe Report No. 67, May 21, 1999; http://www.crisisgroup.org). Noting that the cost of hosting the approximately 200,000 Kosovar Albanians entering Macedonia during NATO's bombing campaign over Kosovo left "hardly any money . . . for unemployment benefits, pensions, and health care provisions," this report paints a prophetic image of Macedonia as a potential casualty of the conflict in Kosovo if the international community does not immediately assist it in meeting its economic needs.

International Crisis Group. "The Macedonian Question: Reform or Rebellion?" (ICG Europe Report No. 109, April 5, 2001; http://www.crisisgroup.org). Released at the time of the outbreak of violence in the Albanian sections of northwest Macedonia, the report focuses on the conditions of Albanians in the country and the tensions between its Albanian and Macedonian communities.

International Crisis Group. "Macedonia's Name: Why the Dispute Matters and How to Resolve It" (ICG Europe Report No. 122, December 10, 2001; http://www.crisisgroup.org). A good source for additional research on

Macedonia's dispute with Greece over the name of the country, and also the significance of its name from the standpoint of interethnic relations in Macedonia.

International Crisis Group. "Macedonia's Public Secret: How Government Corruption Drags the Country Down" (ICG Europe Report No. 113, August 14, 2002; http://www.crisisgroup.org). An early warning by the ICG of the dangers of the international community's continuing failure to stress the need for real reforms in the country and of the danger of mistaking policies on paper for progress in attacking the widespread problem of corruption in Macedonia.

International Crisis Group. "A Marriage of Inconvenience: Montenegro, 2003" (ICG Europe Report No. 142, April 15, 2003; http://www.crisisgroup.org). A discussion of an area that did not become a hot spot: Montenegro's relationship with Serbia, and its desire to sever that relationship. Montenegro would soon vote to split from its then federal relationship under Belgrade's rule, and would do so peacefully.

International Crisis Group. "Moldova: No Quick Fix" (ICG Europe Report No. 147, August 12, 2003; http://www.crisisgroup.org. The focus is on Moldova in the early years of the twenty-first century, but this report is chiefly recommended as a general, easily available account of post-Soviet Moldova, and for its extensive discussion of Moldova's "frozen" Transnistria problem. The report notes in particular the unwillingness of the elites involved on all sides to cooperate in settling the conflict.

International Crisis Group. "Moldova: Regional Tensions over Transdniestria" (ICG Europe Report No. 157, June 17, 2004; http://www.crisisgroup.org). The follow-up to the previous ICG report, *Moldova: No Quick Fix,* this analysis focuses on Russia as both an interested party in the conflict and as a peacekeeper, and on Russia's generally unsupportive actions in terms of resolving the long "frozen" conflict involving Transnistria.

International Crisis Group, "Moldova's Uncertain Future" (ICG Europe Report No. 175, August 17, 2006; http://www.crisisgroup.org). A discussion of the continuing stalemate in Moldova in the context of neighboring Romania's admission to the European Union and, hence, the EU's new border on an unstable state in Eastern Europe. Also discussed are the factors that earlier gave hope that the Transnistria matter might be resolved, and the reasons why that optimism proved to be false.

International Crisis Group. "Montenegro's Referendum" (ICG Europe Briefing No. 42, May 30, 2006; http://www.crisisgroup.org). A detailed analysis of the referendum in which Montenegro chose to withdraw from its federal relationship with Serbia, and of the significance of that vote in the context of regional affairs.

International Crisis Group. "Nagorno-Karabakh: Risking War" (ICG Europe Report No. 187, November 14, 2007; http://www.crisisgroup.org). A troubling report on the hot spot in the Caucasus that the ICG has perhaps most closely followed. Noting the arms buildup in the area and the reluctance of either side to engage in meaningful negotiations, the analysis suggests that this "frozen" conflict may not stay frozen much longer.

International Crisis Group. "Nagorno-Karabakh: Viewing the Conflict from the Ground" (ICG Europe Report No. 166, September 14, 2005; http://www: crisisgroup.org). Useful for advanced research on what has happened to the peoples involved in the conflict over Nagorno-Karabakh and what is going on in that zone and in the two countries at odds over its future. The general conclusion is that developments have made conflict resolution less, rather than more likely, and that this conflict continues to be, in ICG eyes, the most dangerous conflict in the region.

International Crisis Group. "Pan-Albanianism: How Big a Threat to Balkan Stability?" (ICG Europe Report No. 153, February 25, 2004; http://www.crisisgroup.org). The report generally answers its question with "not very much," noting that since 1999 Albania has been courting the West (clamping down on corruptions at home, for example, and supplying troops for Western military operations in Afghanistan), and that Albanian nationalism in Kosovo and Macedonia has focused on the conditions of the Albanians in those areas, not on visions of a Greater Albania.

International Crisis Group. "Return to Uncertainty: Kosovo's Internally Displaced and the Return Process" (ICG Europe Report No. 139, December 13, 2002; http://www.crisisgroup.org). The report focuses on the sluggishness of the process of returning Serbs and Romani to Kosovo and the dangers that they face in returning. It notes that the Romani, in particular, fit into an "enclavization" of minorities pattern in Kosovo that is typical of groups returning to insecure environments.

International Crisis Group. "Saakashvili's Ajara Success: Repeatable Elsewhere in Georgia?" (ICG Europe Briefing No. 34, August 18, 2004; http://www.crisisgroup.org). Another rhetorical question posed in an ICG report, and another negative answer. The analysis points to the unique conditions that made it possible for Tbilisi to resolve its longstanding difficulties with its Ajara area and the absence of those factors in its disputes with the breakaway regions of Abkhazia and South Ossetia.

International Crisis Group. "Serbia's New Government: Turning from Europe" (ICG Europe Briefing No. 46, May 31, 2007; http://www.crisisgroup.org). A general discussion of the degree to which the government in Belgrade has been moving away from a strong commitment to pluralistic democracy, but primarily a good analysis of the degree to which the Kosovo issue has become the dominant one in Serbian politics and the likelihood that Belgrade will never compromise on that province remaining in Serbia.

International Crisis Group. "Southern Serbia: In Kosovo's Shadow" (ICG Europe Briefing No. 43, June 6, 2006; http:// www.crisisgroup.org. The focus of this report and the following one is Serbia's Albanian majority in Presevo Valley, adjacent to Kosovo, and the uneasy truce there between its Albanian and Serbian citizens. This report suggests the growing vulnerability of that truce, in the sense that the discussions over Kosovo's future have emboldened the Albanian nationalists there to demand autonomy-to-independence for themselves.

International Crisis Group. "Southern Serbia's Fragile Peace" (ICG Europe Report No. 152, December 2003; http://www.crisisgroup.org). An earlier

ICG examination of interethnic relations in Serbia's Presevo Valley in the aftermath of the war over Kosovo and the international arrangements on behalf of that province, including its autonomy and the introduction of democratic machinery guaranteeing its 90-percent Albanian majority control over their affairs.

International Crisis Group. "Turkey and Europe: The Way Ahead" (ICG Europe Report No. 184, August 17, 2007; http://www.crisisgroup.org). A recent analysis of Turkey's candidacy for EU membership, the obstacles to it, and the very long timetable involving it, regardless of the disposition of the Cyprus matter or Turkey's conflict with its Kurdish minority.

Isaacs, Arnold R. "Post-Soviet Blues: Georgian Sketches" (Dart Center for Journalism and Trauma, Dart Center Special Report, 2005; http://www.dartcenter.org). A uniquely personal reflection on the declining fortunes of a former Soviet Union republic by a widely respected professional journalist and scholar. Isaacs's observations with respect to Georgia easily apply to life in many of the former union republics examined in this volume.

Joseph, Joseph S. *Cyprus: Ethnic Conflict and International Politics—From Independence to the Threshold of the European Union* (New York: St. Martin's Press, 1997). Suitable for advanced background reading, and highly recommended as such. No known earlier work better captures the importance of the ethnic factor in shaping and affecting the domestic and international politics of the island of Cyprus.

Judah, Tim. *The Serbs: History, Myth, and the Destruction of Yugoslavia* (New Haven, CT: Yale University Press, 1997). A well-researched examination of the factors woven into the Serbian sense of nationhood, the concept of a Greater Serbia, and the final days of the Yugoslav federation. For advanced research on the causes of the Yugoslav civil wars.

Kaufman, Stuart J. *Modern Hatreds: The Symbolic Politics of Ethnic War* (Ithaca, NY: Cornell University Press, 2001). An award-winning study of the causes of ethnic conflict. Though written broadly, Kaufman's case studies are heavily laden with hot spots whose origins were in the former Soviet Union.

Keating, Michael. *Nations against the State: The New Politics of Nationalism in Quebec, Catalonia, and Scotland* (New York: Palgrave, 2001). Written by a student of ethnoterritorial movements in Western Europe, Keating's book is comparative in nature but contains a useful discussion of Quebec nationalism for those seeking additional introductory information on the development of Canada's Quebec "problem."

Ker-Lindsay, James. *EU Accession and UN Peacekeeping in Cyprus* (New York: Palgrave-Macmillan, 2005). Cyprus's pending admission to the European Union and the latter's aggressive efforts to resolve the ethnic conflict on that island before admitting it awakened considerable academic interest, and produced several outstanding books on the efforts of the international community to resolve the conflict between the island's Turkish and Greek communities. This is one of those books.

Kostelancik, David J. "The Gypsies of Czechoslovakia: Political and Ideological Consideration in the Development of Policy," *Studies in Comparative*

Communism, XX.4 (1989: 307–21). The Roma of Eastern Europe did not attract much attention in the Western World during the communist era, and few case studies of their status on the eve of communism's collapse exist. This is one of those studies, and it is highly recommended as background reading for anyone researching the status of the Romani in contemporary, post-communist Europe.

Kronenwetter, Michael. *Northern Ireland* (New York: Franklin Watts, 1990). An older but widely available general work on the evolution of Britain's "Irish Problem" and on Northern Ireland during its first 20 years of direct rule by London.

Legrain, Philippe. *Open World: The Truth About Globalization* (Chicago: Ivan R. Dee, 2004). A proglobalization explanation of how the process is changing everyone's life and of the bountiful opportunities that lie ahead. Legrain, an economist, does not sweep all of the antiglobalization arguments under a convenient carpet, but if you desire a book to balance out the arguments of globalization's foes, this is a good one.

Llera Ramo, Francisco J. "Basque Polarization: Between Autonomy and Independence," *Nationalism and Ethnic Politics,* V (Autumn-Winter, 1999: 101–20. The Basque movement in Spain is increasingly split between die-hard separatists wanting independence and those willing to settle for autonomy, if not necessarily only the autonomy that the Basquelands currently have. Llera Ramo does a very good job of analyzing that split and its implications for the future of Basque nationalism, and therefore Spain.

Malashenko, A.V., et al. *Russia's Restless Frontier: The Chechnya Factor in Post-Soviet Russia* (Washington, DC: Carnegie Endowment for Peace, 2004). The starting point for advanced research on Chechnya today, this study treats the conflict as what it is—unfinished. The various essays offer insights into such aspects of the war as the role of Islam in it, its international ramifications, and—particularly interesting for anyone looking at the conflict from a human rights angle—"Chechnya and the Laws of War."

McFaul, Michael, Nikolai Petrov, and Andrei Ryabo. *Between Dictatorship and Democracy: Russian Post-Communist Political Reform* (Washington, DC: Carnegie Endowment for International Peace, 2004). Highly recommended for those doing work on Russia during the Putin era. A generally balanced analysis of the pros and cons of government under Putin, set against a discussion of democratization reforms in Russia since the Gorbachev era and written by highly respected experts on politics in contemporary Russia.

Mingst, Karen A., and Jack L. Snyder, eds. *Essential Readings in World Politics* (New York: W.W. Norton and Company, 2001). Designed as a supplement to be used in university classes on international politics, this book naturally contains essays on the phenomenon of globalization, including such basic reading as Thomas Friedman's early writings on the topic.

Palley, Claire. *An International Relations Debacle: The UN Secretary-General's Mission of Good Offices in Cyprus, 1999–2004* (Oxford, UK: Hart Publishing, 2005). The long title is itself a description of its content concerning the UN's concerted efforts to resolve the conflict on the island prior to its entry into the

European Union—only to have the majority on the island vote against merger with the Turkish Cypriot minority in the island's north.

Papadakis, Yiannis, Nicos Peristianis, and Gisela Welz. *Modernity, History, and an Island in Conflict* (Bloomington: Indiana University Press, 2006). This book is a set of multidisciplinary essays recommended for those seeking a better understanding of the general environment of politics on the island.

Podobnik, Bruce and Thomas Ehrlich Reifer. "The Globalization Protest Movement in Comparative Perspective," *Journal of World-Systems Research*, X.1 (Winter, 2004). A short but dense article on antiglobalization protest that is recommended for basic preliminary research on that topic.

Ramet, Sabrina P. *The Disintegration of Yugoslavia: From the Death of Tito to Ethnic War* (Boulder, CO: Westview Press/Harper Collins, 1996). A careful study of the key (approximately fifteen) years preceding and encompassing the disintegration of the Federal Republic of Yugoslavia, written by one of the most respected Balkans scholars.

Ramet, Sabrina P. *Nationalism and Federalism in Yugoslavia, 1962–1991* (Bloomington, IN: Indiana University Press, 1992). Recommended for general reading on the origins and turbulent history of Yugoslavia. This is Ramet's earlier work on Yugoslavia. Its focus is on the utility and limits of the federal structure in holding together the country's diverse national groups, most of whom long resented dominance by the country's Serbian majority.

Rapoport, David C. and Leonard Weinberg. *The Democratic Experience and Political Violence*. (London and Portland, OR: Frank Cass, 2001). An ambitious study of its topic, the book provides a useful framework for examining the prevalence of political violence, even in the countries of the developed democratic world. Good introductory reading of a general nature, especially when used as a supplement to the von der Mehden book listed below.

Ruane, Joseph and Jennifer Todd. *The Dynamics of Conflict in Northern Ireland* (Cambridge, UK: Cambridge University Press, 1996). A highly recommended work on the search for peace and stability in Northern Ireland, written at a time when the peace process was about to begin again. Excellent for further reading on Britain's "Ulster Problem."

Rudolph, Joseph R., ed. *Encyclopedia of Modern Ethnic Conflicts* (Westport, CT: Greenwood Press, 2003). Reference works rarely cite other reference works, but for additional information, the essays in this work on Basque Spain, Chechnya, Corsica, Georgia, Nagorno-Karabakh, and other hot spots in Europe and North America, all written by specialists on their topic, make excellent starting points.

Rudolph, Joseph. *Politics and Ethnicity: A Comparative Study* (New York: Palgrave, 2006). Although some consideration is given to the problem of ethnic conflict in the former Soviet Union, this book is primarily recommended for its section on the conflict surrounding Europe's large Muslim community, with particular attention to France and its Muslims, and its treatment of Central Europe's Romani minority.

Rudolph, Joseph R., Jr., and Robert J. Thompson, eds. *Ethnoterritorial Politics, Policy and the Western World* (Boulder, CO: Lynne Rienner, 1989). An older work on ethnoterritorial conflict in Western Europe, chiefly useful in this study for its chapter on Spain written by Robert Clark, which focuses on the efforts of Spain's post-Franco democratizing elites to accommodate the country's restive minority regions. Good companion reading for the Llera Ramo article on Basque and Catalan Spain listed earlier.

Russell, John. *Chechnya: Russia's "War on Terror"* (London: Routledge, 2007). An excellent and wide-ranging recent analysis of the conflict in and involving Chechnya, with attention not just to the origins of the conflict, but also to its evolution (and demonization of participants), lost opportunities, and the impact of 9/11 on it.

Shanklemer, Jill. *Oil Profit and Peace: Does Business Have a Role in Peacemaking?* (Washington, DC: United States Institute of Peace, 2007). A unique discussion of the obligations of international businesses to consider the consequences of their investments. The sections in this book on Azerbaijan's use of its oil money are recommended reading in regard to prospects for a peaceful settlement of the Nagorno-Karabakh conflict.

Shevtsova, Lilia (trans. Arch Tait). *Russia—Lost in Transition: The Yeltsin and Putin Legacies* (Washington, DC: Carnegie Endowment for International Peace, 2007). Another well-written analytical consideration of the gains and the slippages involved in Russia's democratization efforts, this one written by a Russian internationally respected for her body of work on political leadership and political change in Russia.

Silitski, Vitali. "Still Soviet? Why Dictatorship Persists in Belarus," *Harvard International Review*, XXVIII.1 (Spring, 2006). So little is being written on Belarus politics that, in lieu of any recent book, this article on Lukashenko's political adroitness and capacity for survival is recommended for additional research on not just the man, but also the nature of politics and life in Belarus under Lukashenko.

Smith, Graham, ed. *The Nationalities Question in the Post-Soviet States* (New York: Longman, 1996). This set of edited essays is recommended for further, intermediate-level research on the breakup of the Soviet Union, the establishment of the independent countries formed out of the former union republics, and their struggle to cope with the primary source of conflict confronting most of them.

Smith, Sebastian. *Allah's Mountains: The Battle for Chechnya* (New York: Tauris Parke, 2005). A journalist's-eye view of the second civil war in Chechnya, and of the multinational world of the Caucasus in which it is located. Very readable and generally sympathetic to the Chechens, but strictly for additional introductory reading—and only if supplemented with more scholarly analyses.

Spector, Bertram I., Svetlana Winbourne, Jerry O'Brien, and Eric Rudenshiold, report preparers. *Corruption Assessment: Ukraine, Final Report, February 10, 2006* (Washington, DC: USAID Management, 2006). A government study of corruption in the Ukraine that is detailed and authoritative, with a wealth of interesting findings on the topic—for example, that prior to the Orange Revolution the courts imposed sentences *below* the minimum prescribed penalties in almost half of the cases.

Steger, Manfred B., ed. *Rethinking Globalism* (Lanham, MD: Rowman & Littlefield, 2003). For those interested in follow-up readings on various topics related to globalization, the selection of essays in this work cover a wide area but do not go too deeply into any single topic.

Sullivan, Noel G., ed. *Terrorism, Ideology, and Revolution* (Boulder, CO: Westview Press, 1986). The essays in this book are all solid, but the work is primarily listed here because of Charles Townshend's essay, "The Process of Terror in Irish Politics." It represents a major study of the changing nature of terrorism in Ulster between 1969 and 1985, as "the Troubles" spilled out over decades of tit-for-tat violence in Northern Ireland.

Suny, Ronald Grigor. *The Making of the Georgian Nation* (Bloomington, IN: Indiana University Press, 1988). An earlier study highly useful for background reading on the history and birth of contemporary Georgia, written on the eve of the nationalist movement that would lead Georgia to independence, and two of its provinces to secede.

Tiersky, Ronald. *France in the New Europe: Changing Yet Steadfast* (Belmont, CA: Wadsworth, 1994). An older, but widely respected study of French politics, and one of the best at the time to capture the importance that the changing composition of the French population would have for the future of politics in France.

Trenin, Dmitri V., and Alexei V. Malashenko. *Russia's Restless Frontier: The Chechnya Factor in Post-Soviet Russia* (Washington, DC: Carnegie Endowment for International Peace, 2004). A good counterweight to Sebastian Smith's work, this more scholarly examination of the war in Chechnya provides useful insights into the impact of the war on Russia's domestic politics, as well as on its relations with the United States.

United Nations Office for the Coordination of Humanitarian Affairs (OCHA). *Humanitarian Risk Analysis No. 18—Humanitarian Situation, Protection and Assistance: Internally Displaced Persons in Serbia and Montenegro* (Belgrade: OCHA, 2002). A good study of a topic that continues to be an important sticking point in resolving the Kosovo conflict—the large displaced and refugee communities of Serbs and Romani who fled Kosovo when the war ended and the Albanian militants threatened their security, and who still have not returned to their former homes in any significant numbers.

von den Mehden, Fred. *Comparative Political Violence*. (Englewood Cliffs, NJ: Prentice Hall, 1993). One of the first books to examine comparatively the problem of political violence in politics around the world, this short book provides the basic foundation for further reading in that field. It explores the causes of political violence and its manifestations, both as a tool of control by the state and as a means of challenging a state's authority.

Yavuz, M. Hakan, ed. *The Emergence of a New Turkey: Democracy and the AK Party* (Salt Lake City: University of Utah Press, 2006). The essays in this book provide an excellent analysis of many of the more recent developments in Turkish society and politics, and in particular of the growing importance of a party with Islamic roots in the politics of this self-consciously secular Muslim state.

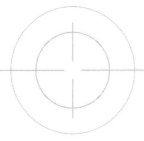

Index